RACE AND ETHNICITY

Broad-ranging and comprehensive, this completely revised and updated textbook is a critical guide to issues and theories of 'race' and ethnicity. These concepts are shown to be inextricably linked to colonial domination which legitimated forms of discrimination and disadvantage. This book provides students with a detailed understanding of colonial and post-colonial constructions, changes and challenges to race as a source of social division and inequality.

Drawing upon vivid international case studies from Australia, Guyana, Canada, Malaysia, the Caribbean, Mexico, Ireland and the UK, the book clearly explains the different strands of theory which have been used to explain the dynamics of race. These are critically scrutinised, from biologically based ideas to those of Critical Race Theory. This key text includes new material on changing multiculturalism, immigration and fears about terrorism, all of which are critically assessed.

Incorporating summaries, chapter-by-chapter questions, illustrations, exercises and a glossary of terms, this student-friendly text also puts forward suggestions for further project work. Broad in scope, interactive and accessible, this book is a key resource for undergraduate students of 'race' and ethnicity across the social sciences.

Stephen Spencer is a Senior Lecturer in Sociology at Sheffield Hallam University. His research interests include the exploration of 'race' and ethnicity, media representation and social identities, as well as the use of visual methods in the exploration of social issues. Other publications include: *Visual Research Methods in the Social Sciences: Awakening Visions* (2011) Routledge, and *A Dream Deferred: Guyanese Identity Under the Shadow of Colonialism* (2007) Hansib.

Stephen Spencer brilliantly combines theoretical analysis with case studies drawn from eight countries, to offer a compelling argument about the centrality of representation to an understanding of the issues of 'race' and ethnicity': an argument with 'real world' consequences for the oppression and exploitation of different communities globally. This thoroughly revised second edition of *Race and Ethnicity: Culture, Identity and Representation* is quite simply a classic text and nothing less than an essential read for students, teachers and scholars.

Bob Franklin, Professor of Journalism Studies, Cardiff University, UK

This is an engaging and textually rich exploration of the construction and significance of race and ethnicity. Case studies from across the world, as well as the migratory, diasporic flow of people, are examined with great insight and aptitude. This is a must-read for anyone trying to make sense of the complexity of identity, media representations and the realities of contemporary society.

Associate Professor Panizza Allmark, Edith Cowan University, Western Australia;
General Editor, Continuum: Journal of Media & Cultural Studies.

This is a great book, which can be recommended without any reservations. It is better written than most of its rival texts, more broad-ranging than any of them in its choice of examples and adopts an approach to theory that is at once accessible and even-handed. Nor does it shy away from policy or politics. Stephen Spencer is an important voice in the field, and his *Race and Ethnicity* should be high up everyone's reading lists.

Professor Richard Jenkins, Department of Sociology, University of Sheffield, UK

RACE AND ETHNICITY

Culture, identity and representation

Second edition

Stephen Spencer

Routledge
Taylor & Francis Group

LONDON AND NEW YORK

This edition published 2014
by Routledge
2 Park Square, Milton Park, Abingdon, Oxon OX14 4RN
and by Routledge
711 Third Avenue, New York, NY 10017

Routledge is an imprint of the Taylor & Francis Group, an informa business

© 2014 Stephen Spencer

British Library Cataloguing-in-Publication Data
A catalogue record for this book is available from the British Library

Library of Congress Cataloging in Publication Data
Spencer, Steve, 1956-
Race and ethnicity : culture, identity and representation / Stephen Spencer. – Second edition.
    pages cm
    Includes bibliographical references and index.
    1. Ethicity. 2. Race. 3. Ethnic relations–Political aspects. 4. Race awareness.
    5. Group identity. 6. Identity (Psychology). 7. Ethnospychology. I. Title.
    GN495.6.S69 2014
    305.8–dc23
    2013033855
ISBN: 978-0-415-81380-8 (hbk)
ISBN: 978-0-415-81381-5 (pbk)
ISBN: 978-0-203-51916-5 (ebk)

Typeset in Adobe Garamond
by Sunrise Setting Ltd, Paignton, UK

CONTENTS

List of illustrations   x
Preface to the second edition   xiii
Acknowledgements   xiv
Introduction   xv

1 Representation   1

And now the news ...   5
    Complex war   8
What is the 'other'?   10
Barthes and the reader's role in constructing meanings   16
Rhetorical images   19
Whiteness as myth   23
Scared?   26
The Matrix of Cultural Identity   28
    Production   29
    Consumption   30
    Identity   30
    Regulation   31
    Representation   32
    The Unfair Campaign   32
Chapter summary   36
Exercise 1.1 Ideology and mythologies   37
Exercise 1.2 'Scared?' and the Unfair Campaign   37
    Further reading   38

2 The Politics of Naming   40

Defining race and ethnicity   41
    'Race'   41

Shifting meanings of race 44
  Monogenism 44
  Polygenism 45
  Evolutionism 47
Race and class 52
Race as culture 55
Ethnicity 55
Race as ethnicity 58
Chapter summary 64
Exercise 2.1 64
  Further reading 66

3 Colonialism: Invisible histories 67

Construction of the colonial subject 69
Slavery 69
Enlightenment views 73
Rationalisation of colonial exploitation 75
Casta – representations of race and race making in New Spain 82
Effects of colonialism 85
Reparation movement 88
Neo-colonialism and auto-colonialism 91
Chapter summary 94
Exercise 3.1 Guyana: look what they done to the mother 94
Exercise 3.2 95
  Further reading 95

4 Theories of Race and Ethnicity 97

Primordial or instrumental ethnicity 97
  Primordialism 98
  Criticisms of primordialism 100
  Instrumentalism 100
  Criticisms of instrumentalism 101
Plural society theories 102
Marxist theories 104
Structuralist criticism of Marxism 111
Weberian/neo-Weberian theories 115
Symbolic interactionism 119
Foucault and discourse theory 121
Bourdieu 124

Gender, sexuality, race and ethnicity   129
Black feminism   132
Chapter summary   137
Exercise 4.1   138
    Further reading   139

5 Identity: Marginal voices and the politics of difference   140

Postmodernity: maps and terrain   141
Holocaust and relativity   141
Identity politics and traditional Left thought   144
Consequences of postmodern thought   145
Post-colonial identities   146
Theories of post-colonialism   148
Feminism and post-colonialism   150
Critical Race Theory   160
Chapter summary   162
Exercise 5.1   163
    Further reading   164

6 Case Study: Indigenous Australians   165

Land rights   166
Living conditions   167
Contested homelands: Darwin's 'itinerant problem'   171
    Framing the fringe dwellers   171
    The 'itinerant problem': community conditions   175
    Law and order   176
    Media manifestations   177
    Deconstructing the 'itinerant problem'   183
    Larrakia Nation   184
    Postscript   188
    Conclusion   191
Theoretical framing   193
    Plural society theory   193
    Marxist approaches   194
    Weberian notes   195
    Elite theory   197
    Symbolic interactionism   197
    Rational-choice theory   198
    Postmodernity   199

Bourdieusian analysis: habitus and symbolic violence 199
Critical Race Theory – a case of interest convergence? 201
Chapter summary 202
Exercise 6.1 202
Further reading 203

7 Conflict **204**

The struggle for symbolic dominance 210
The persistence of ethnic stereotypes 211
African-Guyanese stereotypes 212
The 'other' – theft of legitimate pleasures 213
Religion 220
Ethnic cleansing 221
'Race riots' or social and economic exclusion 223
Chapter summary 227
Exercise 7.1 Guyana 228
Exercise 7.2 Malaysia 228
Exercise 7.3 229
Exercise 7.4 229
Further reading 229

8 Living the Contradiction **232**

Diaspora and hybridity 232
Multiculturalism 248
History and the conception of the multicultural state 248
What is multiculturalism? 249
Promise and reality: life in a multicultural society 250
How multiculturalism stole Christmas! 254
Chapter summary 260
Exercise 8.1 Hybridity and multiculture 260
Exercise 8.2 Boundary crossing 261
Further reading 261

9 Futures **263**

Globalisation 266
Mixed race 270
Significance for theorising racialisation 274
Race in cyberspace 276
Cyber terrorism 277

A pair of brown eyes   278
Conclusions   283
Exercise 9.1   285
Exercise 9.2   285
    Further reading   286

Glossary   287
References   304
Index   330

LIST OF ILLUSTRATIONS

FIGURES

I.1	'Take the crown': poster of Jessica Ennis in Sheffield, 2012	xxvi
1.1	The process of signification	17
1.2	Stone Age people of the desert, from H. Wheeler, *Peoples of the World in Pictures* (1935)	21
1.3	Negro women tending young sugar canes, from J. Hammerton's *Peoples of All Nations* (1933)	22
1.4	Scared? Poster from the Commission for Racial Equality's controversial campaign in Sheffield, 1999	27
1.5	The Matrix of Cultural Identity adapted from the *Circuit of Culture*	29
1.6	Unfair Campaign image, Unfair Campaign, Duluth, Minnesota, 2012	33
2.1	Negroes: portraits by Thomas Landseer in Baron Cuvier's *Animal Kingdom*	49
2.2	Mongols: portraits by Thomas Landseer in Baron Cuvier's *Animal Kingdom*	50
3.1	Defaced statue of Queen Victoria, Georgetown, Guyana	67
3.2	Hierarchy of sixteen racial pairings. Las castas, Anonymous, eighteenth century, oil on canvas, 148cm × 104cm, on display at the Museo Nacional del Virreinato, Tepotzotlan, Mexico.	82
4.1	Dynamics of plural society	103
5.1	'Bejewelled Beauty of the Kabyle', from J. Hammerton's *Peoples of All Nations* (1933)	152
5.2	'Circe of the Sudanese Dancing World', from J. Hammerton's *Peoples of All Nations* (1933)	153
5.3	Arabia: 'Unveiled Charms of Beduin Women', from J. Hammerton's *Peoples of All Nations* (1933)	154

5.4 Egypt: 'Fleeting Glimpses of Feminine Charms', from
     J. Hammerton's *Peoples of All Nations* (1933)   155
5.5 'A Pleasing Contrast', from J. Hammerton's *Peoples of All
     Nations* (1933)   157
6.1 Australia, from *terra nullius*, 'empty', in 1788 to 'full' in 1988   167
6.2 'Breathing while Black'. 'Prior to their being "moved on" by
     NT Police, these people were peaceably assembled in Darwin's
     city centre, instead of their isolated and (according to ex-NT
     Chief Minister Shane Stone) "dysfunctional" communities.
     Don't you love the Aboriginal Art (for the tourists) in the
     background'   168
6.3 'Australian Aborigines': typical representations of Aboriginal
     culture   174
6.4 Front page of *Northern Territory News*, 15 April 2003   179
6.5 'Amongst the Queensland Blacks', *Queensland Figaro*,
     10 December 1888   180
6.6 'Nature – Civilization', *Queensland Figaro*, 6 August 1887   180
6.7 'England – Blackfellows at home: They are kindly received in
     fashionable circles – ladies play the piano to them etc.' *Sydney
     Punch*, 15 August 1868   181
6.8 'Purposeful drinking'. Beer can boat at the annual Beer Can
     Regatta, Darwin   182
6.9 Sign posted outside the One Mile Dam Community near
     Darwin in 2009   191
6.10 David Timber, Coordinator of the Kumbutjil Association at
     One Mile Dam Community near Darwin   192
7.1 'Only believe all things are possible': scene in the Stabroek
     Market, Georgetown, Guyana   208
8.1 Zapata sign for underground station in Mexico City   245
8.2 Beginning the struggle: Zapatistas in San Cristobal de Las
     Casas, 1991   247
8.3 Celebrating diversity: Commission for Racial Equality
     poster, 2004   252
9.1 'Life Savers': Metropolitan Police anti-terrorist poster   279

TABLES

1.1	Shifting faces of the 'other'	15
2.1	Evolving discourses of race	43
2.2	Ethnic categories used in the 1991 UK Census	59
2.3	Ethnic categories used in the 2001 UK Census	60
2.4	Ethnic categories used in the 2011 UK Census, showing changes and additions	60
2.5	Typical breakdown of ethnic categories in the US Census	63
6.1	Patterns of indigenous disadvantage	168

BOXES

1.1	They eat horses, don't they?	14
1.2	Response to the Unfair Campaign	34
3.1	Guyana: 'Look what they done to the mother'	67
3.2	Scene from a sugar estate in British Guiana, c 1938	80
3.3	Witness to a flogging on a sugar estate in Albion, British Guiana, c.1938	89
4.1	British-born Chinese	134
6.1	Aboriginal Australians	178
7.1	Interview with Martin Carter	205
7.2	Conversation with two African-Guyanese professionals	211
7.3	Conversation with Indian-Guyanese man	212
7.4	Chinese Malays, interviews recorded June 2004, Sheffield Hallam University	214
8.1	Buxton, Guyana 1991	232
8.2	British-born Chinese	237
8.3	Between two cultures	240
8.4	Contrasting norms between the UK and Mexico	243
8.5	Guyana: boundary crossing	258
9.1	Interview with Yvonne Howard-Bunt	271

PREFACE TO THE SECOND EDITION

Nearly eight years on, this second edition of *Race and Ethnicity: Culture, Identity and representation* comes with significant changes and additions. However, the perspective of the book remains constant, demonstrating that representation offers a powerful, if often neglected, window on the world through which the complex issues of race and ethnicity become comprehensible. Ethnographic and interpretative approaches to ethnicity are central to the discussions in these chapters. The key focus is on the role of collective signs and symbols; the semiotic resources of a culture. Our understanding of these concepts is always formed within the process of representation – as, indeed, are our identities. At one level this is a truism, in that all knowledge is filtered and interpreted through conventional codes, but even at the abstract level of theorising this is done through the developed paradigms and discourses of thought reflecting the genealogy of sciences in the western world. Furthermore, the intention of this text is not merely to skim over the surface of these representations, discursive formations and collective signs, but to examine their expedient and contingent uses in social contexts. Race is not some academic exercise; it has material consequences for the way society is organised and the ongoing exploitation and oppression of different groups.

There are several new inclusions as well as a careful revision of some of the existing material. The intention was always to use a variety of different 'windows on the world' to convey the pervasive nature of colonial/post-colonial thinking in everyday life. For this reason I have made the rather unusual decision to include examples from interviews. These soundings from different cultural sites of ethnic identity provide an immediacy and honesty that enhances academic discourse, showing the lived realities of division and complex identities in action. Further examples of theoretical approaches which might be used to critically examine race and ethnicity have also been added. This has the advantage of presenting theoretical paradigms as relative explanations, giving a sense of the development of ideas historically, and further suggests that there may be multiple and, in some cases, complementary approaches to understanding complex cases of race and ethnic division. The specific contexts described have been updated and there are now links to a range of definitive texts for further reading.

ACKNOWLEDGEMENTS

Many thanks to all of those who contributed their voices to this book. Special thanks go to Mark Quah for the interviews with British Chinese people and to Stuart, who added an articulate personal perspective on the British-born Chinese identity. Thanks to Dr Yvonne Howard-Bunt for providing some thoughts on mixed-race identity, to Diego Uribe for his insightful comments on the eve of his return to Mexico and to Chas Critcher for allowing me to use extracts from a filmed interview. I am indebted to David Timber and the Kumbutjil Community at One Mile Dam in Darwin for allowing me to use interview material and some stills from a film made there, and to Mick Lambe, for permission to use the Pariah website which he developed and hosts. Thank you also to the Malaysian students whose candid comments provided insight into the situation there.

Certain sections of this book draw on case-study material from Guyana which is part of a text titled *A Dream Deferred: Guyanese Identity Under the Shadow of Colonialism* (Hansib, 2007). For other Guyanese examples I would like to thank Balchand Basdeo for recounting vivid memories of life on a 1940s sugar estate. The case study in Chapter 6 (concerning an Aboriginal community in Darwin) is a modification of an article originally published in the *Pacific Journalism Review*, Auckland University, April 2005.

Thanks also to the Commission for Racial Equality for permission to use the *Scared?* poster from their 1998 campaign and also the poster *Britain: We All Make it Unique; Northern Territory News* for the use of its front page from 15 April 2003; Ross Woodrow, Newcastle University, NSW, Australia for his permission to include three illustrations: 'Amongst the Queensland Blacks', *Queensland Figaro*, 10 December 1888; 'Nature–Civilization', *Queensland Figaro*, 6 August 1887, and 'England – Blackfellows at home', *Sydney Punch*, 15 August 1868; and New Scotland Yard for permission to use the *Life Savers* anti-terrorist poster.

Every effort has been made to contact copyright holders for their permission to reprint material in this book. The publisher would be grateful to hear from any copyright holder who is not here acknowledged and will undertake to rectify any errors or omissions in future editions of the book.

INTRODUCTION

Images of others, images of ourselves

Consider the following image. Paul Sharrad describes a press photo from the 1991 Gulf War:

> In a camp of refugee workers from Kuwait containing amongst others, Indians, Pakistanis, Nepalis and Arabs of inconvenient nationality without the means of getting home, there huddled a group of Filipinos, triangulated like paintings of Custer's Last Stand or the Iwo Jima statue under a flag which pleaded 'Don't leave us among Asians'.
>
> (Sharrad 1993: 1)

This strange image is an example of the complex negotiated identities generated by global diasporas. It provides a graphic example of the urgency of striking a distinct identity and finding means to 'flag' this to others as well as the complex and ambiguous cosmopolitan relations in which identity and 'otherness' are defined. The Filipinos in this story came to recognise themselves as a distinct group, united by common characteristics which to them made their difference self-evident; their identity then was quite removed from the category 'Asian' within which any western observer would almost certainly pigeonhole them. Under conditions of extreme anxiety their common history as a people at once united them and separated them from others – now those attributes of their unique and complex colonial ancestry had to be urgently signalled.

How does this 'alienation of body and soul' (ibid.) come about? Diaspora is of increasing significance in a post-Fordist decentralised world, more than ever dependent upon flows of migrant labour, where outbreaks of conciliatory multiculturalism are punctuated with policies of regressive racism, moral panics, asylophobia and islamophobia; anxieties outside and inside the increasingly uncertain boundaries of the western world. The shared histories and transitory cultures are the breaking news of our globalising world. Without some recognition of the multi-layered history of Filipinos, their struggle and colonial history of connection to the USA, such scenes may appear surreal.

What can such examples tell us about the way we make sense of our identity and the way in which these meanings are constructed and communicated? Examples such as these make us recognise the reflexive and constantly negotiated nature of ethnicity. As Sharrad and others suggest, the growing emphasis on post-colonial identities reflected in courses of study and literature poses an important challenge to one-dimensional approaches to ethnic identity.

The long colonial era has left a legacy of deeply embedded divisions in many national cultures. Nations have been shaped by the exploitation and racism of a handful of European colonial empires. Today, contemporary literature bears witness to the same exploitation and racism: 'the doctrine of divide and conquer persists, the pattern of varying psychic upheavals continues to be registered in "diaspora literature"' (ibid.).

This book examines the complex representations, identities and relationships of groups differentiated by 'ethnicity' or 'race' through analyses of examples from around the world. I should stress that these samples are not drawn only from 'exotic' ethnographies but largely reflect, as Marcus suggests, ethnography that 'begins at home' (Marcus 2012). There are two significant studies from Australia and Guyana, but the others are based on reflections from the migratory, diasporic flows of people interviewed on the home front, here in Sheffield, South Yorkshire.

This is a book about the construction and consequences of race and ethnicity. I begin from the position that these are concepts which have a historical geneal-ogy: they are social constructions which often become identifiable where and when the boundaries between groups become noticeable, perhaps owing to competitive relationships or differences of cultural identity or practice. Sometimes there are real physical differences; at other times, these are culturally or linguistically ordered. The two concepts in this title are among the most complex and problematic in the social sciences. They are also inextricably linked: 'race is an allotrope of ethnicity' (Jenkins 1997: 167). Jenkins' use of this analogy from chemistry is very fitting – in other words, ethnicity is a different structural modification of a base element (i.e. the concept of race). While the social currencies of ethnicity are perhaps of the most vital importance in social affairs, race has been (and continues to be) 'an organising principle of domination without parallel' (ibid.).

To understand this difference it is important to examine the process by which categorisation and segregation came into operation, stemming, as they did, from racial schema in the service of exploitative colonialism. The long-term effects of slavery have left their taint on the world order and have persistent structural influence on social organisation to this day. Loic Wacquant argues that the racial ghettoisation of African Americans is of a different order to the class-based ghettos of Britain and France because the former is an ongoing result of the stain of enslavement. African American culture can be understood only in relation to its genesis: 'the historical crucible of two and a half centuries of slavery followed by another century of rigid racial separation subtended by various forms of state-sponsored discrimination and racial violence, many of which persist in attenuated forms' (Wacquant 2010: 185).

American cities are divided in a way which is extreme compared with the British experience. Nevertheless, slavery casts a shadow over the relative prosperity of western countries whose imperial power and wealth was based on the productivity and commodities gathered and exchanged through the stolen labour of slavery. Slaves were the ultimate commodity and the trade in human misery was enormously lucrative. The expedient construction of racial categories to permit such moral degradation is certainly one reason why race and racial categorisation has proved an enduring feature of global societies.

This book builds on the viewpoint, well accepted in the literature, that ethnicity is a matter of shared meanings and conventions. As several authors have pointed out, this view derives from the seminal work of Fredrik Barth (see e.g. Jenkins 2008; Malesevic 2004) and in turn Barth's view rested on older strands of sociology (Weber, Simmel and others). Hence the focus here will be on recognising the language of 'race' and ethnicity, a dialectical way of speaking simultaneously about 'others' as well as a means of affirming identification of self and community.

While the constructed nature of race and ethnicity is time-bound and expedient – a reflection of the zeitgeist, of the economic and social realities of the day – it is not sufficient to proclaim race and ethnic identity to be mythical constructs when experiences of racism are very much an everyday reality. The case studies and discussions in this book underline the inherent problems behind the question: Can we have an empirical approach to 'race' and ethnicity that is not reductionist and does not reify the dynamic, interrelated and situated meanings of lived experiences of 'race' and ethnicity?

The complex variables at play in these examples show the contingent and local forms in which 'race' and ethnicity are manifest. It is important not to reproduce an essentialist view of 'race' and ethnicity – where experiences are predetermined – as real-life experience is much more complicated, contingent and mercurial.

It is for these reasons that this text examines post-structuralist approaches: because they question the stability of categories of 'race', along with those of class, gender and sexuality, which help us to understand subtleties of identity and subjectivity. In addition, it is foolhardy for any research into ethnicity to neglect the fact that the researcher's own identity is always an aspect of the interplay of meaning and interpretation; hence, researchers must recognise their cultural baggage and strive for a more intersubjective approach. However, here too the nuanced constructed nature of ethnicity is problematic, as it may result in difficulties in demonstrating the experience of racism. Thus it can be seen that there is a pernicious quality to 'race': on the one hand it is a social construct (used expediently in different ways, evoked as a resource, as a positive source of identity, especially in times of repression, conflict or competition) which should be confined to the dustbin of useless terms, but on the other hand it has real-life consequences. Indeed, in some contexts avoiding 'race' and only using 'ethnicity' may seem like treacherously avoiding the issue.

WHY FOCUS ON REPRESENTATION?

The realm of representation is central to questions of identity and this book examines the crucial social processes which reaffirm and perpetuate or challenge and overturn our constructions of 'otherness'. This is, again, a legacy of the realisation that differences are contingent on cultural perception and arise when groups determine differences as significant to foreground.

Representation is the social process of making sense of the many signifying systems within a culture. It refers both to the active process as well as to the products of the process of representing. This process of interpreting signs is central to how we see other people and ourselves. More profoundly, by critically exploring those commonplace representations it is possible to demonstrate that the accepted order of things, often presented as 'natural', is really the product of culture.

The example of the alienated Filipino refugees in the war zone of Kuwait highlights this process in action. In this instance the meaning of 'Asians' is an alienated one which arises from the origins of contemporary Filipino culture and the complex Euro-American influences which have been formative of the cultural identity of these beleaguered guest workers. The Philippines were under Spanish colonial rule for over 300 years before becoming subject to American colonial rule after America defeated Spain during the Spanish–American War in 1898, a situation which ended only after the Second World War. This history makes Filipino identity unique among nations in South East Asia, with most Filipinos having some facility with spoken English and knowledge of American culture. Unlike other ethnic groups, when they arrive in the USA most Filipinos can easily adapt to the American way of life because of the absence of language and cultural barriers (de Torres 2002). This example highlights how ethnic identities and the way in which boundaries are drawn are complex consequences of historical processes.

Chapter 1 of this book focuses specifically on the way in which issues of race and ethnicity are represented, examining the process by which we make sense of the 'other'. The social world in which we live is saturated with signs, images and stories projected through every form of media, permeating our consumer culture and all levels of social relationships. It is argued that the media are powerful sources of – in McQuail's term – 'referent power' (2010: 470), presenting persuasive and authoritative messages from celebrities and 'experts', and that the media plays the role of a bard in our culture, functioning as 'a *mediator of language*' (Hartley 1998: 85–6). In other words, some of the complex negotiated views that form our self-identity are shaped by the media.

The collective images and representations which circulate in a culture can be considered a 'cultural imaginary';[1] that is, the available resources that are drawn upon to shape and mediate our cultural identities. It is important to examine and understand these interlinked discursive themes, images and stories circulating in the public arena because they exert influence, albeit perhaps less obviously because they are unspoken and mundane, and are woven into the fabric of everyday life. These cultural forms, mediated signs and images are a reflecting surface, mirroring underlying values which have condensed into everyday language and imagery. 'Whiteness', for example, is rarely spoken about; being largely an invisible 'given', it is no exaggeration to suggest that 'Whiteness has become the default race in our society' (Wang 2006: 12).

'Myth'[2] is a term that has been used to designate collective meanings within the broader cultural imaginary. In this sense myth denotes 'a systematic organisation of signifiers around a set of connotations and meanings' (Fiske *et al.* 1987: xi). Furthermore, myth is of particular interest when considering ethnicity, national identity and the concept of 'race' because it:

> has an important role within ideas of nation, where it is an essential part of cultural meaning and maintenance. Foundations of national ideas and values are established through myth and highlight what is considered natural and accepted or alien and excluded within a culture. These continuous narratives are embedded with various rituals and symbols leading to a collective discourse.
>
> (Price 2010: 453)

In relation to these accepted collective meanings, this chapter discusses Roland Barthes's use of myth to denote banal commonplace signs of colonial paternalism. A Barthesian interpretation of 'myth' suggests that the habitual portrayal of certain issues disguises this human process of construction and makes the portrait appear to be the thing itself. Other recent examples are presented that will allow the reader to recognise the signifying practices employed in constructing (and deconstructing) images and other popular representations of 'otherness'. This is an abiding theme; like the flickering shadows in Plato's cave, representations of the world around us are always at a distance, prone to distortion, open to multiple interpretations and sources of symbolic power. Cultural uses of difference are malleable and can be utilised as a resource, reinvoked in times of conflict and competition or expediently played down and ignored. Representation is, as Stuart Hall points out, the sphere in which identity is always constructed; representational forms are the available resources through which we express our subjective sense of self and, by the same token, 'the pole of the other' (Bagnoli 2004) provides the collective lexicon for the attributes of difference which in turn define our ideas of shared identity. A dialectical process permits us to draw on this multiplicity of voices and signs, which could be role models or fictional or imaginary characters.

'Present within one's individual consciousness in the form of representations of significant others, this 'other' can be thought of as pertaining to the world of everyday experience, as well as to the world of one's imaginary' (ibid.: 3). The forms of expression may be uniquely individual but they often reflect broadly shared cultural and ethnic values interpreted though our own experiential framework. This chapter gives more detailed consideration of the apparent 'givens' in western culture, and the difficulties of exposing and challenging these.

Chapter 2 addresses the problem of naming, permitting analysis of the history of race, ethnicity and racism. The 'problem of definition' highlights the fact that race is a 'floating signifier' (Hall 1996b); the meanings of both race and ethnicity are never static. Making assumptions based on well-worn definitions and attempting to fix identities misses the point that how 'they' can be defined at any one time and place is dependent on the unique coordinates in operation; it depends on the 'us' as well as the 'them' axes. The meaning of 'otherness' changes with social context over time, shaped by political ideologies and shifting regimes of social and scientific thought. A notable shift is the change from more essentialist views of race based on biological determinants to a politics of identity based upon cultural differences. Nevertheless, the focus on culture may merely provide a disguise which masks a more intractable unreconstructed racism. For example in the way that the more acceptably cultural term 'ethnicity' is regularly drawn back towards more primordial biological origins as another synonym for race.

'Who are you?' 'How would you describe yourself?' Answers to these questions are politically charged and to address them means considering the 'givens' of identity. Concepts of 'race' and ethnicity, gender, sexuality, citizenship and nation are discussed along with the attendant problems and sensitivities surrounding the categorisation of identity that arise when the state attempts to record these details. Are these rational, essential differences or 'socially imagined'? The evolving social sciences have been far from neutral in this process of categorisation, and their role will be highlighted here. A brief history of the development of terms and conceptions of the 'other' will be included, drawing on the work of Brackette Williams, Stuart Hall, Theo Goldberg and others. The UK and US censuses are a case in point – recent changes reflect progress made and the more fine-grained recognition of categories. One example in the UK is the use of terms such as 'Arab' that are not merely linked to linguistic communities; many groups of people who speak Arabic may dis-identify with the term and its legacy of ethnic connotations. Similarly, for the first time in 2011 a category has been included for Travellers and Irish Travellers. Research into this change suggested that people felt gratified that the category was recognised.

Imagery is used to demonstrate the accumulation of values that constitute the spectacle of race on which western nations were founded. Drawing from popular nineteenth-century natural histories such as *Goldsmith's Animated Nature* and Baron Cuvier's *The Animal Kingdom*, and twentieth-century works such as Hammerton's *People of All Nations* (1933), the first two chapters discuss the construction of the 'other'. By examining the discourses that have constituted such images it is possible to open a window onto the jingoism, racism and fascination with diversity reflected in these popular ethnographies.

Chapter 3 provides some illustrative examples from the history of colonialism, the legacy of which has so moulded contemporary ethnic relations. Through the re-examination of histories of colonialism comparisons are drawn between several nations and their construction of the colonial subject. Also considered here is the infra-human treatment of the colonial subject and the need to come to terms with histories that have been disguised, revised or simply ignored. Several examples of colonialism in action are recalled and the long-term consequences of regimes which sometimes treated local people ruthlessly are examined; such aspects witness the complex interplay of race and class in the founding of hierarchical systems. Among other narratives, eyewitness accounts, including descriptions relating to 1940s British Guiana,[3] are included here because they reveal the harsh outcomes possible under colonial systems of rule that rely on racial and class-related beliefs to maintain their dominance. The colonial impact is not just on the bodies of its subjects but on their minds, through the divisive internalisation of colonial values (as Du Bois and Fanon have eloquently explained). Finally, the chapter considers forms of neo-colonialism which operate today through the perpetuation of the relations of exploitation and domination by global economic structures.

Chapter 4 reviews a number of theories that have sought to give explanations for ethnic divisions, including various Marxist-inspired viewpoints, neo-Weberian and feminist strands of theory and post-structuralist ideas. It becomes increasingly clear that 'race' and racism are the result of social and political discourses that change between times and places. Theories, when they compete for a universal explanation of 'race' and the dynamics of racism, show their weaknesses all too quickly. Perhaps it is more realistic, as John Rex stated, to consider that:

> The study of race relations, in common with a number of other politically charged areas in social sciences, seems beset by feuds and conflicts of a quite theological intensity. Thus such approaches as plural society theory, socio- biology, Marxism, Weberianism, the anthropological theory of ethnicity and psychological theories of identity all seem to be making imperialist demands to command the whole field to the exclusion of all other theories. ... Closer investigation of these theories, however, reveals that they are in large measure complementary.
>
> (Rex 1986: 64)

While a synthetic approach that merely cuts together disparate explanations may not necessarily give greater insight, Rex's willingness to remain open to the value of different theories may be valuable in assessing their relative adequacy as explanations of unique expressions of ethnic identity and racism.

Racism, and its forms, causes and consequences, is discussed here as a phenomenon occurring at all levels of society, from the undermining experience of many visibly different minorities characterised by infrequent but regular verbal assaults using derogatory terms and stereotypes but often defended as jokes or off-hand remarks, to violent and organised abuses and incidents of institutional racism that have been identified in education, health care, the legal system, media reporting, employment practices and policing. However, apart from these institutional forms of discrimination, it can be argued that racism is implicit in our conceptions and structures of difference. Miles argues that 'race' and 'race relations' are invalid terms that merely perpetuate the hegemony of racist culture (Miles 1989). One of the concerns here is how far race or ethnicity could constitute a primary site of social division and a genuine category for critical social analyses. Is race a strictly instrumental category derived from the economic base and relations of production? Or is it instead a category with semi- or complete autonomy from other determinants of inequality, such as class?

This chapter also looks at the 'dual burden' of oppression experienced by women within ethnic groups. Black feminism has drawn attention to the intersection of gender and race and to quite different forms of oppression and resistance experienced by black women to those emphasised by white middle-class feminists. Implicit in this fragmentary vision of the self as competing voices of difference is a recognition of the complex intersectional construction of identity, and of what has been termed identity politics.

Chapter 4 goes on to consider the social-constructionist viewpoint that discourses or discursive practices play a significant role in constructing race and ethnicity. This is achieved through a variety of disciplinary and institutional structures that define the borders of social consensus and difference. The term 'discourse' has come to mean a broad disciplinary field and its uses of language. For example, anthropology, psychiatry and economics constitute regimes of thought, make claims to truth and impose their schemes of classification upon the social world. This approach has been heavily influenced by the so-called 'linguistic turn' in philosophy and social theory. Especially influential in this discussion is the work of Foucault, Pecheux and others. However, the chapter focuses on the work of theorists who have effectively applied the approach to studies of racial and ethnic 'others'. Stephen Muecke, for example, has shown how entire ethnic groups of Aboriginal Australians have been positioned by restricted categories of discourse.

The chapter finishes with a discussion of Bourdieu's contribution to the empirical understanding of social relations of difference. By examining the homogenous conditions through which habitus is formed, and the use of forms of capital in specific fields a complex understanding of the individual emerges, suggesting that race and ethnicity influence the manner and power of class effects.

While Chapter 4 introduces the increasing fragmentation and syntheticism of theories of race and ethnicity, Chapter 5 specifically addresses postmodern and post-colonial readings of ethnicity that highlight how avoiding essentialist and universalising views of the 'other' in favour of specific localised subjects can have the uneasy consequence of developing an uncritical acceptance of relativism at any price. However, the complexity and fragmentation of these postmodern analyses more closely mirrors the complex and hybrid forms of ethnic identities. It is in just this way, perhaps, that the diasporic identities of Filipino guest workers in Arab states seem a case in point. There are not so much clear roots and genealogies as fractured experiences of different homes and the gradual emergence of new hybrid identities which might still retain memories of 'home', albeit the home territory has meanwhile changed at a pace that has no mercy for stranded expatriots.

Following on from the previous chapter, post-colonial feminist critiques are discussed in Chapter 5. Portrayals of Asian women are, as Yegenoglu (1998) suggests, instrumental, if not pivotal, in the maintenance of western cultural hegemony. Asian women are portrayed as passive and exploited, subject to a culture presented as backward, while, in contrast, women in the west enjoy a growing independence – a situation, Yegenoglu argues, that merely helps to reinforce the myth of Orientalism. The chapter also examines traditional leftist criticisms of identity politics, which are seen as an obstacle to socialist ideals. The chapter ends with a brief discussion of Critical Race Theory, suggesting that despite the abiding problems shared by postcolonial theorising of relativism, subjectivism, and reduction to processes of signification, CRT has some salutary qualities, reminding us that changes which appear to be progressive and empowering often have more to do with maintaining the power of white elites while giving displays of liberal-mindedness.

Chapter 6 focuses on the situation of indigenous ethnicity with one multi-faceted case study. Based on research in Darwin in northern Australia, the chapter highlights the realities of life in an urban Aboriginal community on the fringes of white Australia's monocultural affluence; it considers the consequences of the historical exclusionary treatment of Aborigines and modern-day discourses that show the persistence and function of white Australian attitudes. At the end of the chapter the case is further analysed through the prism of several theoretical approaches. This is intended to provide the student with a case to consider from a variety of different theoretical positions. Aside from direct ethnographic research (with all its attendant problems) and the theoretical paradigms that can be used to examine and explain the situation in Australia, the representation of indigenous Australians provides a sort of 'indirect ethnography' (Harper 2005: 748; Spencer 2011) revealing the popular views manifest in different cultural forms. This approach, broadly semiotic and discursive, is at the heart of the approach pursued in this book. The point is not merely to look at the semiotic terrain in a distant and aridly formalist manner, but to ground this analysis in social realities and combine the poetics of meaning with the politics of experience and dynamic change.

Building on the theoretical discussions of the previous chapters, Chapter 7 explores conflict in ethnically divided societies. One intention is to show that imagery, stereotypes and other popular representations embody ingrained political differences and are employed situationally. Some examples are given of tensions within multicultural societies, changes and threats to the orthodoxy of social meanings and the struggle for symbolic dominance between groupings in ethnically divided post-colonial nations. The chapter will draw upon research into cases of bipolar ethnic relations in Guyana as well as similar rivalries in Malaysia.

In reference again to the Filipinos described at the head of this Introduction, at the time of writing the Philippine government had reached a framework peace agreement with the largest Muslim rebel group, the Moro Islamic Liberation Front (MILF), which has been fighting for an Islamic state in the southern Philippines region of Mindanao for several decades. The settlement is likely to grant this Islamic faction a separate status and territory (BBC News, 7 October 2012; Philippines profile www.bbc.co.uk/news/world-asia-15581450). Thus, the Filipinos in the opening vignette represent just one entangled story of identification and division. Many nations experience complex ethnic divisions and conflicts, struggles to break away from or claw back majority perceptions relating to religion, language, region, politics and history; societies are stratified economically and socially along lines of class and caste that are often linked intersectionally with ethnicity.

Certainly, ethnicity does generally describe groups with a shared identity and shared origins, interests and codes, but, just as with class, where there is a tension between the concepts of a 'class in itself' and a 'class for itself' (where the latter represents class consciousness), ethnicity has both internal and external definitions. Individuals belonging to the dominant culture may find it unnecessary and peculiar to consider *themselves* an ethnic group, yet officialdom readily monitors and catalogues ethnic distinctiveness within 'ethnic minorities'. This is an example of the process of delineating ethnicity as an external phenomenon. (The example of the exnominated[3] nature of 'whiteness' is used as a case in point here.) Conversely, the internal definition of a group as united by common culture, language, beliefs and aspirations may draw boundaries in quite a different fashion. The chapter explores the way that internal and external ethnic boundaries are drawn and reviews key areas of theory used to explain the dynamics of ethnic divisions. The examination of boundaries and their constant drawing and redrawing is of fundamental importance to issues of 'race' and 'ethnicity'. These should be considered as terms indicative of change and fluidity rather than of fixed or static identities. Racial or ethnic boundaries are subject to periodic softening or hardening, blurring or sharpening of emphasis. These boundaries are not only structures of state power and legislation or geographical or political lines drawn on a map to delineate territorial rights: they are part of the internal landscape of people living on either side of ethnic boundaries. 'Boundaries define the borders of nations and territories as well as the imaginations of minds and communities' (Cottle 2000: 2).

One primary intention of this text is to demonstrate in several unique global contexts these processes of racialisation and boundary-drawing and the cultural content (those shared meanings of ethnic identities) as well as the interactive contexts from which such collective identities are constantly developing and changing. The cases of Guyana, Australia, Malaysia and Mexico are given special attention.

Chapter 8 is concerned with issues of diasporic and hybrid responses to ethnic diversity. In some societies adaptation is apparent through a process of creolisation; in other circumstances there is less 'middle ground' and 'ethnic enclaves' develop or assimilation policies are implemented with the purpose of extinguishing cultural difference.

The problems encountered in a multi-ethnic society are highlighted by interviews. Examples (from Mexico and Guyana) of the crossing of ethnic boundaries further indicate the permeability of ethnic boundaries and emphasise the contingency of ethnic identity.

Chapter 9 draws together several strands and considers the impact of emerging cultural forms. What trends are observable in our globalising world? Multiculturalism has always been a highly contentious term. Here it is examined from both sides of the political divide. Three forms of emergent cultural forms and the social meanings through which they are represented are briefly discussed: 'mixed race' relations, cyberspace and terrorism. Across Europe there is a considerable upward trend in mixed marriages. A 2012 Eurostat study shows that for the period 2008–10 an average of one in twelve married persons was in a mixed marriage. This can inevitably be linked to changes in the socio-cultural character of the host population, as it represents a gradual melding of boundaries that in turn may imply more knowledge about and between cultures and undermining of stereotypes that might have persisted before (Lanzieri 2012: 3).

In the popular iconography of Britain (a country with a mixed-race population reaching over a million) mixed-race Olympic heptathlon star Jessica Ennis, who was lauded for her gold medal-winning performances in the 2012 Olympics (pictured in Figure I.1 when she returned as a hero to her home town of Sheffield) has been embraced as a signifier of a successful, buoyant and optimistic Britishness in the midst of a seriously divided and recession-blighted country.

But what do such images really foretell? Are they signs of a new acceptance and disregard for visible difference? Or do such celebrities belong to a different realm, where the grinding injustice of an 'ethnic penalty' has no place? It is tempting to be lulled by the multicultural balm which suggests that such events are signs of a new tolerance and maturity, when at the same time a constant rhetoric about Muslims, gang-related violence or xenophobic and racist fears about migrants is kept up in a steady flow.

The fragile global situation and fears, real and imagined, of global terror, neo-imperialism and homogenising global forces have led to new struggles for cultural hegemony and widespread resistance in response to anticipated global risks and very real consequences of the economic chaos that has divided society. The future significance of terms such as 'race' and 'ethnicity' cannot be divorced from wider societal (or global) dynamics.

Figure I.1 'Take the crown': poster of Jessica Ennis in Sheffield, 2012.

USING THIS TEXT

It is important that the central importance of race and ethnicity is understood not as an academic exercise in which exotic cultures are studied in far-flung outposts or under benighted colonial regimes in another era, but instead as one of the defining aspects of social identity today. Along with class, gender and sexuality, ethnicity (within which the uneasy concept of 'race' is often implicit) is one of the central problematics of social existence, yet one that is elusive and a source of anxiety and confusion.

The world around us is an inescapable mirror held up for us in which we see an image of what we are supposed to be. The social meanings gleaned are produced from the selective words and images of the mass media, whether 'news' or what passes for entertainment (which is increasingly hard to differentiate), documentary or fiction, or from the political system – its rhetoric, policies and debates – and, of course, from peers and family and their attitudes, values and beliefs. Even everyday objects such as stamps, coins, flags and consumer products are imbued with values and understandings of nationalism, citizenship and what makes 'us' different from 'them'. This book asks students of race and ethnicity to look into the mirror and reflect on aspects of identity rendered invisible by convention. Identity, culture and representation are intimately interlinked through social interactions and in our constant monitoring of the social world and our ideas about ourselves.

This book provides a series of contemporary contexts from which key questions are drawn. It sets out to illustrate the complex processes through which race and ethnicity are socially constructed and disseminated. The realities of life in post-colonial contexts are illustrated through images, anecdotes and popular representations as well as through interview material.

Each chapter has a summary and poses a number of questions for further consideration. For those wishing to gain an understanding of contemporary issues, this book provides some critical markers in the contested theoretical landscape of race and ethnicity.

NOTES

1 See Glossary.
2 See Glossary.
3 This is a term that refers to concepts which are not culturally foregrounded but are taken for granted, assumed as natural or normal – hence, not named.

CHAPTER 1

Representation

What, then, is truth? A mobile army of metaphors, metonyms, and anthropo-morphisms – in short, a sum of human relations, which have been enhanced, transposed, and embellished poetically and rhetorically, and which after long use seem firm, canonical, and obligatory to a people: truths are illusions about which one has forgotten that this is what they are; metaphors which are worn out and without sensuous power; coins which have lost their pictures and now matter only as metal, no longer as coins.

(Nietzsche 1954: 46–7)

Against that positivism which stops before phenomena, saying 'there are only facts', I should say: no, it is precisely facts that do not exist, only interpretations...

(Nietzsche 1954: 458)

'Race' and 'ethnicity' are terms which appear confusingly unstable: hedged about with sensitivities and mirroring the shifting social and cultural contexts in which they are encountered. This book began life as a series of images, with the notion that images convey immediacy about the complex issues of race and ethnicity in ways that written texts cannot always deliver. However, while images may seem to communicate in a direct and less abstracted way, their interpretation is often more problematic. As the above quotes by Nietzsche convey, the expressive resources of a culture can become well worn, a hackneyed currency, not fully capable of capturing the complex fluidity of changing identities. Meaning is not implicit in signs, images, words and other cultural codes; rather, it is based on shared conventions, and these vary between and within cultures. Some meanings are recorded in dictionaries; others, such as subtle non-verbal signs or pictorial forms, are more ambiguous and difficult to pin down.

Two key aspects of race and ethnicity need to be highlighted here: first, neither 'race' nor 'ethnicity' have simple referents 'out there'; they are not stable definitions of some static social reality – rather, as central concepts of identity, they are constantly changing and being adapted to fluid social contexts. Second, following from this, race and ethnicity are constructs defined through the circulation of social meanings. The vast array of popular representations, advertising, films, news from television and newspapers, tweets and blogs, policy documents, organisational culture, everyday conversations – indeed, every social act of communication – operates to implicitly or explicitly reaffirm these meanings in context. These representations are not fixed and eternal but the mediated products of social and historical circumstances.

How can images, words and media representations of 'others' assist in the task of unravelling the construction of race? This process inevitably depends on the social, cultural and political contexts in which such representations are employed. Relevant here is the concept of the 'cultural imaginary', which suggests that a collective sense of how the culture is defined emerges from representations: interlinked stories, portrayals of people, issues and events. Lykke suggests that such an imaginary 'refers to the intersection of fantasy images and discursive forms in which cultural communities mirror and articulate themselves and which act as points of reference for their collective identity formations' (Lykke 2000).

Portrayals of difference are clearly one important aspect of the imaginary, presenting the reader with cultural narratives about identity and often denoting the norms of belonging and exclusion. One clear example involves the representation of colour. Several authors have demonstrated the significance of whiteness to our understanding of race. Stuart Hall (1997) has been especially influential in illustrating how race and ethnicity are interlinked with ideas about sexuality and gender identity. In addition to illustrating the process of 'racialising the other' through the popular imagery of colonial domination, Hall suggested counter-strategies through which representation could contest, parody, reverse or confront the 'dominant gendered and sexual definitions of racial difference by *working on* black sexuality' (ibid.: 274, emphasis in the original).

Dyer's seminal text *White* recognised the naturalised invisibility of 'whiteness': 'Whites must be seen to be white, yet whiteness as race resides in invisible properties and whiteness as power is maintained by being unseen' (Dyer 1997: 45). Dyer's emphasis exposes the march of white iconography from classical painting to films such as *Alien* and *Falling Down*, imagery that serves to legitimise and maintain white dominance as the 'default race' in western culture (Wang 2006). Knowles (2004: 188) criticised Dyer's claims to have exposed the 'mechanisms of race making' through a lexicon of images as flawed and unsustained. Furthermore, she refutes the claim made by Dyer and others that racist discourses and imagery of the past are still active and influential. Instead she suggests that 'If the past lives on in the present – it most certainly does so in *new* social forms' (ibid.: 189). However, while Knowles quite correctly points out the dangers of conflating the complexities of 'race making' with images of white domination and the domestication of empire, it is by re-evaluating the historical imagery of racial superiority that the deeply embedded and tacit acceptance of whiteness might be exposed. It also seems clear that stereotypes of race can endure over long periods of time and that, while their articulation in each era may be nuanced rather differently, the core values may remain starkly preserved.

In addition, there has been a trend to make whiteness an academic field of study with, perhaps, the attractive though misguided aim of attempting 'to displace the normativity of the white position by seeing it as a strategy of authority rather than an authentic or essential "identity"' (Bhabha 1998: 21). Roediger argues:

> to the extent that those studying whiteness see themselves as involved in a distinct and novel enterprise … the charge that new work recentres whiteness and takes the edge off oppression has considerable force. Indeed even when those are not the intentions, the risk that scholarship on whiteness will be read in such a way is real. The lamentable terms 'White Studies' and 'Whiteness Studies' lend themselves to such readings.
>
> (Roediger 2001: 78)

Undoubtedly, simply enumerating images of colonialism and whiteness (or blackness) will not reveal the construction of race. A model known as the 'circuit of culture' (Du Gay *et al.* 1997) offers a fluid and holistic view of the practices involved in the production of culture. In this model 'representation' is one position in a matrix alongside processes of identity, production, consumption and regulation. This focus on the circulation of shared meanings shows that meanings and ideas have material consequences. For example, the racial thinking that led to ideas about eugenics and racial purity, and to paternalistic views on the part of whites towards indigenous peoples, had consequences for millions of people under colonial rule in Australia. For instance, up to the 1970s, 'half-caste' children were removed from their Aboriginal families and adopted out to white families in a clear attempt to 'breed out' mixed individuals. Similarly, images and notions of whiteness or blackness are also converted into items for consumption, television programmes, hair products, toys and so on. Products are often purchased because we feel some affinity to their style or to the brand image and identity being communicated much more than for their utility or material value. It appears that the underlying values and beliefs in a society are bound up with forms of representation that mediate our experience of the social world and constitute elements with which the individual identifies.

This internal process could be considered to be the effect of ideologies. The traditional Marxist understanding of ideology was a form of false consciousness: the individual experiences social reality through a distorting mirror, disguising the exploitation implicit in class-based societies. For example, we might suppress the knowledge that purchasing a discounted product is possible because of the exploitation of workers. By contrast, for Althusser, 'ideology does not "reflect" the real world but "represents" the "imaginary relationship of individuals" to the real world; the thing ideology (mis)represents is itself already at one remove from the real' (Felluga 2011).

Furthermore, ideology always has a material existence: 'an ideology always exists in an apparatus, and its practice, or practices' (Althusser 2001: 112) and always manifests itself through actions, which are 'inserted into practices' (ibid: 114): for example, rituals, conventional behaviour and so on. Indeed, Althusser goes so far as to adopt Pascal's formula for belief: 'Pascal says more or less: "Kneel down, move your lips in prayer, and you will believe"' (ibid.). It is our performance of our relation to others and to social institutions that continually instantiates us as subjects (Felluga 2011).

This system underpins our social and cultural life and mediates between people and their relationship to society as well as their social identities. These representations operate at the level of unconscious desires as well as through an individual's rationality. For Althusser, the material objective of ideology is in '"constituting" concrete individuals as subjects' (Althusser 2001: 116). This is achieved through 'interpellation', a process by which people are hailed as a particular subject. Althusser uses the example of a policeman, teacher or priest calling to a person on the street: 'Hey you!' As the person turns around, they have become the subject. This hailing takes place in reality at many levels (conscious as well as unconscious callings) and aligning with specific identities or cultural roles. Consider the invitation to be constituted as a particular (perhaps aspirational) identity in advertising or in the pointing finger of a recruitment poster – 'Your country needs you!' Ideology in this way constitutes the person's 'lived' relation to the real. One constant and authoritative source for ideologies which could be said to perform this interpellation individually and culturally is the national news. Take one particular day –

AND NOW THE NEWS ...

Headlining stories on Saturday 31 March 2012 (*The Guardian*)

- 'Police face racism scandal after black man records abuse'

   Scotland Yard is facing a racism scandal after a black man used his mobile phone to record police officers subjecting him to a tirade of abuse in which he was told: 'The problem with you is you will always be a nigger.'

   The recording, obtained by *The Guardian*, was made by the 21-year-old after he was stopped in his car, arrested and placed in a police van the day after last summer's riots.

   The man, from Beckton, east London, said he was made to feel 'like an animal' by police. He has also accused one officer of kneeling on his chest and strangling him.

   In the recording, a police officer can be heard admitting he strangled the man because he was 'a cunt'. Moments later, another officer – identified by investigators as PC Alex MacFarlane – subjects the man to a succession of racist insults and adds: 'You'll always have black skin. Don't hide behind your colour' (Lewis 2012).

- 'George Galloway hails Bradford spring as Labour licks its wounds'

- 'Anger over plan to X-ray young asylum seekers to check age'

- 'Tombstone on grave of Adolf Hitler's parents removed'

- Tibetan grief – A Tibetan exile weeps as the body of Jamphel Yoshi who burned himself to death on Monday is cremated in the Northern Indian town of Dharmsala (image p. 26)

- Afghanistan – Policeman kills 9 officers at command post

- 'Trayvon Martin and how racism is still destroying lives in the US' (by Jesse Jackson)

- Protest at death of Trayvon in Washington. The youth was shot dead in Florida by a neighbourhood watch captain after an altercation (image p. 26)

- French police arrest 19 in anti-terrorism crackdown on radical Islamists in areas of France; suggestion that this crackdown provides collateral for Marie Le Pen of Front National in the midst of the French election

It is quite apparent that these headlining stories 'hail' us as particular types of subject and embody the pre-existing ideological values implicit in our society. There are implicit 'others' here: asylum seekers, Tibetan exiles, Afghan police, black youth in London and Florida, radical Islamists, Hitler's parents, racist police; *they* are not being addressed by this liberal news channel while *we* are implicitly embodied in the narrative point of these stories and their reporting. This news demonstrates the way that race, racism and difference permeate society, being accepted and central to the way social and cultural boundaries are drawn and events are expressed. Sometimes the story is especially shocking (and hence newsworthy), perhaps because it presents a stark reminder of the continued material existence of apparatus and practices which are not supposed to be recorded. The headlining story came to media attention only because the victim was able to record the incident on his mobile phone. The IPC had dismissed the case initially, suggesting that there was no case for the officers to answer. Since the 1993 murder of Stephen Lawrence, (murdered in a racist attack 22 April 1993) ninety-six Black Minority Ethnic (BME) people have been killed, a fact that is not very often publicised 'other' than through the efforts of groups such as the Institute for Racial Relations (Institute for Racial Relations (IRR) (2012)), which has reported these race-related killings (about five a year). This is a stark reminder that, although on the surface British society has turned away from a culture of overt racism in which racist epithets were commonplace in public or in the media, racism and racist violence are still everyday experiences, with the overall number of racist incidents recorded by the police standing at 47,678 in 2011/12 (Home Office 2012).[1]

The notion of George Galloway's by-election victory in Bradford for the Respect Party as a 'Bradford Spring' refers to the 'Arab Spring', the series of revolutions against the old dictatorships in the Middle East from 2010 which affected Egypt, Libya, Tunisia, Yemen, Bahrain and Syria (the last of which has slipped into a protracted and bloody civil war).

Respect ran an 'Islamicised' campaign, appealing to the area's many Muslim voters on the basis of divisive and insular communal politics. This included a remarkable leaflet, signed in Galloway's name, which assured them 'God KNOWS who is a Muslim. And he KNOWS who is not … I, George Galloway, do not drink alcohol and never have … I, George Galloway, have fought for the Muslims at home and abroad all my life … And with your support, and if God wills it, I want to give my remaining days in service of all the people – Muslims, Pakistanis, and everyone in Bradford West' and much more in a similarly 'socialist' vein.

(Hume 2012: 1–2)

Should this be read as cynical opportunism or heartfelt support for a beleaguered community? What is interesting, nonetheless, is the use of carefully tailored rhetoric.

These headlines give a sense of local and global relations of power, narratives about the manner in which the western nations divide the world and the divided consciousness of those people in it. An immense chasm, that some scholars have referred to as the 'representation gap', exists between the world as it is represented and the world in actuality. Jen Webb states that 'there is always a gap between the thing and its articulation' (Webb 2009: 139). Representation is not the thing, the event, the phenomenon itself: it is an encoded interpretation of the thing, event, phenomenon. While representation connects us to the real world and allows us to experience, if by proxy, real events, it is always 'an artefact of human practice' (ibid.: 143). There is no final 'real' beneath the culturally ascribed practices, however, so the idea of a 'gap' is problematic because it cannot be closed: each alternative reading is still not the thing itself. Nevertheless, the danger is abundantly clear; it is demonstrable how easily one viewpoint can be foregrounded as *the* 'truth' or the only available perspective. As I write this, further news is unfolding about another Israeli attack on Gaza. The media begins to generate images and packaged sound bites of the effects of the bombardment on the people in the walled area of Gaza. Thus Webb comments on the prevalence of certain types of construction of Palestinians available to us in the western media:

> the Western networks tend to show Palestinians in one of two ways. The first is images of exhausted old men, grieving women and shattered children, living in dire circumstances in refugee camps; the second is furious young men, hurling stones at Israeli soldiers, or heading off to become the next wave of suicide bombers. Both are empirically true: certainly these images are not invented. But they are limited and interested images – *limited* in that the entire Palestinian community is framed only as loss or violence, *interested* in that it reinforces the general Western perspective of Arabic people being marked by lack and otherness.
>
> (ibid.: 142)

Our knowledge of other aspects of life in the occupied territory is thus severely limited. Representation is always partial and fragmentary and like, for example, British acquiescence to US foreign policy, most certainly reflects dominant interests. The spotlight of the dominant media focuses on stories that are easily represented, while other aspects of global conflicts or the everyday details of people's lives are often never presented or are deemed 'un-newsworthy'. In addition, the stories, and their presentation to us as audience, are turned toward us, hail us as particular kinds of subjects taking our roles in a particular kind of system.

Complex war

Another case in point here is the war which devastated the Congo from 1998 to 2002. However, the official cessation of the war did not prevent thousands more dying from infectious diseases in the aftermath, as a direct result of the conflict, at one stage at a rate of 54,000 a month (McGreal 2008). This deadly conflict directly involved eight African nations and as many as twenty-five armed groups. By 2008, the war and its aftermath had accounted for the deaths of 5.4 million people, mostly as a result of disease and starvation. In terms of loss of life the Second Congo War counts as the most deadly conflict since the Second World War.

Yet this is also one of the least reported wars in recent times. Why, then, did the western media not focus on this war? Bob Franklin (professor of journalism at Cardiff University) made a very salient point in an interview I conducted on media practices: 'Philip Knightley's famous book about the media coverage of war suggested that the truth is the first victim. Well, the first victim isn't truth, it's complexity' (Spencer 2004a). Galtung and Ruge, in their examination of the 'news values' that underpin the selection of viable news stories (1973), put forward the criterion of 'unambiguity', suggesting that the less complicated a story is, the more likely it is to be reported. Primary colours are preferable to shades of grey and 'elite' people or nations often provide this clarity: they are known and recognisable and can come to personify a story:

> Personality becomes a metonym for the story and its theme, and the characteristics of both become interchangeable. There seems to be the need for somebody to blame, to shoulder responsibility, to be answerable: after all, you can't take a picture of an issue.
>
> (Watson 2005: 121–2)

This is likely to be one of the main reasons why complex situations do not come under scrutiny: reporting during warfare is notoriously confusing but the situation in the Congo seemed more tangled than most. At least eight African countries were involved, within which were complex divisions and factions; in addition, the countries taking part did not fit into the easily recognisable, culturally consonant mould that many western news consumers would recognise. There is frequently a spotlight on the involvement of celebrities and other VIPs in these arenas, however: recently the practice of mass rape as a weapon of war in Congo was highlighted by the presence there of the actress Angelina Jolie and, the UK Foreign Secretary at the time, William Hague.

However, another reason for the comparative media silence could be that there is less interest in the relatively remote areas of southern Africa and western interests are notably not involved (nor is there any question of the war involving oil, which is an apparent issue in the Sudanese ethnic cleansing). There is a journalistic convention known as 'McLurg's Law'[2] a version of which I remember having seen posted on the wall next to a journalist's desk, one dead Briton is worth five dead Frenchmen, twenty dead Egyptians, five hundred dead Indians and a thousand dead Chinese' (e.g. cited from Chandler 1994). Stories with higher potential for dramatic conflict are also more likely to appear; many 'news stories' are interpreted in terms of conflict, as this is more dramatically interesting. There is thus a bias in favour of 'bad news', many perhaps the majority of news stories feature negative aspects, crimes or natural disasters for example. (The Glasgow University Media Group made this point long ago with their famous series 'Bad News' (1976) and 'More Bad News' (1980).) Like drama, the news does tell a story. On landing in the (Belgian) Congo during its evacuation, an American journalist rushed over to a group of white women and asked, 'Has anyone here been raped, and speaks English?' As Fiske comments, 'His story had been "written" before landing, all he needed was a few local details' (Fiske 1987: 283).

An extension of this journalistic convention that narrows the focus to appeal to the home market has been put forward by Herman and Chomsky and is explained here by Glasgow Media Group scholar David Miller:

> So you tend to have a serious double standard, you have what Herman and Chomsky called 'worthy' and 'unworthy' victims. So, for example, in the bombing of Istanbul – clearly a terrible attack which claimed a number of civilian lives, you had wall-to-wall coverage of that, but you don't have wall-to-wall coverage of things happening at the same time with greater consequences for human lives – such as the dropping by the US of one-ton bombs on Northern Iraq, which had virtually no coverage in the mainstream media – partly because it's not being put out by their authorised sources – sources of the government and the political elite.
>
> (Spencer 2003)

Perhaps the cynical journalistic convention in which relative cultural and geographic distances determine news values is well known, but to these internal production criteria for manufacturing the news we must add, as Miller suggests, the fact that political motives dictate what news is made available in the first place. In addition, the media are controlled mostly by corporate interests and hence, as Herman and Chomsky (1988) have argued, are tied to the interests of the marketplace and have very little independence. Furthermore, the media are increasingly dependent on government sources for their stories. In times of 'national crisis' – wars, strikes, civil unrest – the state seeks to maintain control of audience perceptions through a variety of means, from direct censorship through a whole spectrum of more subtle techniques, to ensure that a certain perspective dominates. The value of human lives is thus dependent not only on their perceived significance as news stories but also on the political agenda. Mark Curtis, in *Web of Deceit* (2001), gives a long list of the chillingly titled 'unpeople' whose fates are to be, as Salleh writes,

> the victims of this global order ... Curtis [2001] [notes] the million or so Indonesians who were slaughtered during General Suharto's bloody seizure of power in 1965. Declassified documents show British complicity in the killings – the then Labour government supplied Suharto with warships, logistics and intelligence, as well as secret messages of support.
>
> (Salleh 2003)

This brief foray into the media mechanisms, the realpolitik behind the news, illustrates the need to cast a critical eye on everyday cultural production that presents us with an apparently natural surface of cultural events which may disguise the ethnocentric values which have produced them.

The circulation of cultural meanings in the mass media is a pervasive means by which the separation of differences is affirmed. Boundaries between ethnicities are not only physical and geographical but also social, economic and cultural. How 'otherness' is recognised can turn on visible differences or clusters of these: skin colour, clothing, location and cultural practices are at times used as an 'Identikit' to exclude, single out, scapegoat, even to murder and ethnically 'cleanse' or, conversely, to find allegiance with and to celebrate common identity. Boundaries are socially drawn and may be redrawn, heightened or lowered and, in some instances, crossed. In the following section some of the contradictions, stereotypes and political determinants of 'otherness' are highlighted.

WHAT IS THE 'OTHER'?

The simple answer is 'not self'; in other words, an alien subjectivity, a being who exhibits characteristics notably different from our own, whether gender, race, class, custom or behaviour. To an extent we are each born into a social system that, while constantly evolving, is a pre-existing influence on our behaviour and outlook and on our understanding of difference. The 'other' exists as a metaphysical concept rather than as a genuine entity. It represents an area of consensus, a way of delineating self and the shared values of our culture or subculture. We create ideals and typifications and the 'other' presents us with tests and measures for these ideals. In this way the 'other' is inextricably linked to the self and is part of the cultural imaginary. The process of forging an identity at the individual as well as at the group level is dependent on interaction with others. This 'pole of the other'

> significantly contributes to the shaping of identities [and] can thus be broadly understood as a multiplicity of voices, arising from both within and without the subject. Present within one's individual consciousness in the form of representations of significant others, this other can be thought of as pertaining to the world of everyday experience, as well as to the world of one's imaginary.
>
> (Bagnoli 2004: 2–3)

So the existence of an out-group – a 'them' rather than an 'us' – can be seen to be important in human society, as it affirms qualities and characteristics that the majority group sees as normal as the rules by which they live. In the most obvious cases these affirmations gain official and legal status and those breaking the rules are portrayed as 'criminals', 'insane', 'deviants' or 'anti-social'. They may live and work on the fringes of 'respectable' society and make up a marginalised group or underclass, but they are also frequently associated with racial or ethnic groups. Such boundaries are, by their very nature, implicitly political and strike at the heart of personal and social identity.

The role of the media as a 'mediator' in this process of identity formation is a continuous and pre-eminent one. Media representations of race mediate meaning between complex networks of people and political ideologies, but 'Is it the reflector or the director?' as the song goes.[3] The social world in which we live is awash with signs, images, stories and complex symbols projected through every form of media, permeating our consumer culture and all levels of social relationships. It is argued that the media is a powerful source of – in McQuail's term – 'referent power' and the influence of attractive and powerful celebrities or authority figures in the media is frequently acknowledged. Fiske and Hartley used the term 'bardic function' to explain the process by which the media broadcasts 'a series of consciously structured messages which serve to communicate to the members of that culture a confirming, reinforcing version of themselves' (Fiske and Hartley 1978: 85–6). In other words, some of the complex negotiated views that form our self-identity derive from the media's images of 'others' as well as images of ourselves as we would aspire to be. Our language itself mirrors and reproduces social divisions: at times it may serve to fix definitions or bound the debate, at others to challenge them.

The media can be seen as 'the most generalised of generalised others' (King 2004: 185), but inevitably we build views of our own identity from these disparate communications. One way in which we do this is by interpreting signs presented to us that contain embedded views and values of national, cultural or common subcultural identities and, conversely, the identities of others with whom the communicative opportunities are few. As Hartley suggests, 'The only real contact with others is, paradoxically, symbolic, and rendered in the form of stories, both factual and fictional' (1992: 207). On the outer boundaries of this unknowable 'imagined community' is what Hartley calls 'Theydom' (as opposed to our own, or 'Wedom'). The rules of representation for these two kingdoms are quite different.

> People from Theydom, such as Aboriginals in news stories ... are exempted from the established systems of balance which apply to Wedom's own adversarial politics; there are not 'two sides' to an Aboriginal story – not two *Aboriginal* sides, that is, only an Aboriginal side and a 'balance' supplied by, for instance, police, welfare, legal or governmental authorities.
>
> (Hartley 1992: 207; emphasis in the original)

While we are not aware on a daily basis of the manner in which our subjectivity is constructed, we are constantly monitoring our environment and establishing reference points, alignments with shared values and beliefs and contradistinctions with others with whom we have less in common – or who are portrayed as enemies of our society. These relations of inclusion and exclusion are far from simple and tend to be organised around different identities at different times in our history. For example, at the time of writing there is a heightened fear of terrorist activity and in some quarters this is also equated with asylum seekers, refugees or – as these displaced people may not always be so visibly apparent – anyone who has a different ethnic appearance.

As Fredrik Barth, in his seminal study *Ethnic Groups and Boundaries* (1969), persuasively argues, the existence of ethnic groups depends less on the intrinsically shared common culture of an ethnic group than on the maintenance of social boundaries. 'For social boundaries to be actively maintained, they need to be continually validated, and this requires regular interaction with members of out-groups' (ibid.: 32–3). While the media may play a key role in this validation, it should not be conceived of as a mere conduit for racist propaganda. Several studies in the 1970s and 1980s reflected a view of black youth as demonised in the British media. This was particularly the case with the moral panic over 'mugging' (Hall *et al.* 1978). This emphasis on African Caribbean communities as deviant and threatening mirrored the Conservative government's agenda of the time. The divisive Thatcherite rhetoric about law and order and street crime could be seen as a form of reactionary common sense that helped to affirm and popularise increasingly authoritarian policies. In fact, the media cannot be seen as operating in a vacuum. Media interests and advertising revenues often imply an agenda constrained by political and economic forces (see Herman and Chomsky 1995).

A number of recent studies indicate that the portrayal of race in the media reflects ideologies of multiculturalism and has moved away from crude stereotypes in favour of a representation of more subtle cultural differences. Cottle warns that 'the dynamic nature and subtleties of media discourse and representation, ... cannot always be captured through simplistic and static applications of the concept of "stereotype"' (Cottle 2000: 124). However, a glance at our popular press may tell a different story. While media discourses are inevitably parasitic on social and political formations in the wider society, the perennial invective against asylum seekers and 'others' might suggest an implicit xenophobia; indeed, in some cases where the media power is focused and highly monopolistic the treatment of certain issues goes well beyond merely reflecting the prevalent value system. Thus Pilger points out that the Murdoch news machine in Australia has presented a consistently negative and distorted treatment of Australia's indigenous peoples.

> In railing against what it called the 'black armband view' of Australia's past, the conservative government of John Howard encouraged and absorbed the views of white supremacists – that there was no genocide, no Stolen Generation, no racism; indeed, white people are the victims of 'liberal racism'. A collection of far-right journalists, minor academics and hangers-on became the Antipodean equivalent of David Irving Holocaust deniers. Their platform has been the Murdoch press.
>
> (Pilger 2011: 2)

At certain times the media reaffirms crude popular stereotypes (see Box 1.1). While we know that these are probably stereotypes we still recognise them and they may have the appearance of 'home truths' reinforced by habitual usage and familiarity. Such stereotypes abound; they can be gender based or relate to generalised national characteristics such as those of the French, Chinese, Australian, English or African-Caribbean cultures. Perennial stereotypes are invoked in times of crisis. For example, attitudes about the French that are dormant for much of the time were reactivated in the European Community 'apple war' of 1980 (Box 1.1), while in 2003 the French refusal to join the alliance with the USA and UK reignited old grievances, with the French being reviled variously by different American media:

> The 'petulant prima donna of realpolitik' is leading the 'axis of weasels', in 'a chorus of cowards'. It is an unholy alliance of 'wimps' and ingrates which includes one country that is little more than a 'mini-me minion', another that is in league with Cuba and Libya, with a bunch of 'cheese-eating surrender monkeys' at the helm.
>
> (Younge and Henley 2003)

BOX 1.1 THEY EAT HORSES, DON'T THEY?

A world survey by a French magazine says that the best friends of France are the English, which will surprise a great many Englishmen who think we hate each other. Noel Coward summarised the Anglo attitude to the French when he said; 'There's always something fishy about them.' *The fact is that we don't know them very well and what we don't know we don't trust.*

It is true we have often fought in the same wars. But the only time we came close to losing was when they were on our side. Maybe they do have the best wine, the most glamorous women, the cleverest cuisine and the most elegant style. But do they deserve any of them? It is said that they cook while the British only open tins. But what do they cook? Snails (disgusting). Frogs' legs (distasteful). And horses (barbaric).

They grow an apple called Golden Delicious which is green, not gold, and about as delicious as a ball of wool marinated in castor oil. What's more, it's putting our growers out of business.

And now we are told we are their best friends. It's ridiculous. The only thing we've got in common is the Channel. The English Channel.

(*Daily Mirror*, 10 September 1980, p. 2)

The rhetoric exhibited in the media about the French was not only a result of France's refusal to be drawn into the Iraq war, however, but was also indicative of Britain's ambivalent role in Europe and its unwillingness to relinquish ties with the USA or to abandon its relative separatism within Europe. Nonetheless, the characterisation of the ritually reviled group(s), often led by the tabloid press, employs a ready-made stock of stereotypical traits and insults derived from a historical lexicon of economic, political and military rivalry.

The groups that constitute an 'other', however, are not constant. The aspects of difference that are perceived as threatening change over time and between nations. The construction of a group as 'other' depends on the social and historical character of a nation and is parasitic on developments in science, social theory and belief systems that function to create a sense of national identity. Table 1.1 shows the shift from the primacy of religious belief (social solidarity based upon collective worship, a belief in a battle between supernatural forces) through the beginnings of race science and the ranking of colonial and imperial subjects within an order based variously upon civilisation and evolutionary (Darwinist) notions of development to more pragmatic criteria such as geographical and economic notions of development and modernisation.

Table 1.1 Shifting faces of the 'other'

TIME	BOUNDARIES	EXTERNAL DIFFERENCES	INTERNAL DIFFERENCES
CE–present	Religion	Pagans, non-believers, Christianity v. Islam	Heathens, heretics, witchcraft, Roman v. Orthodox
1790–1950	Race	Race, language	Class, status, nation, ranking among European countries
1800–1970	Imperialism, colonialism, neo-colonialism, internal colonialism	Civilisation & savagery Darwinism Orientalism	'Backward areas' within Europe (e.g. Celtic fringe, 'urban jungle')
1950–present	Developing North/South divide	Developed/advanced Industrial/post-industrial Information age Core/periphery	Uneven patterns of development
1900–present	Europe	European civilisation, identity, boundaries	'Multi-speed' Europe.* Tension between deepening and widening of EU
1960–present	Cultural difference	Cultural difference, identity politics, Foucauldian discourses	Multiculturalism, sub-cultural differences in lifestyle, sexual preference, age
1980–present	Citizenship, legal status	'Fortress Europe'. Illegal immigrants, asylum seekers, 'financial migrants', guest workers, terrorists, etc.	Citizens, denizens, terrorism

* Describes the idea that different member states of the EU will need to integrate at a different pace and level depending on their relative political and economic situation. (Adapted from J.N. Pieterese ('Europe and Its Others Over Time') in Goldberg and Solomos 2002: 18.)

Pieterese (2002) identifies the changing face of 'otherness' within Europe. These shifts in discursive structures generated by economic and cultural globalisation seem to encourage more porous national boundaries and yet also – perhaps as a result of these lowered frontiers and cultural homogeneity – generate heightened anxieties: for example, disputes around the expansion of the EU frequently relate to the concern that the future inclusion of Turkey – a predominantly Muslim nation – may threaten the core values of European identity.

The displacement of millions of people throughout the world, often as a result of wars and global poverty (but increasingly also because of global environmental changes), has resulted in fears that a mass migration of the worlds poor is occurring as they seek asylum and refuge in wealthier European countries, and this has led to the development of a 'fortress Europe' mentality. Given this, it is ironic that Britain, for example, is often reliant on migrant workers from Eastern Europe and elsewhere for basic services, just as parts of America are dependent on Hispanic workers.

Finally, there is the current trend to define groups by an emphasis upon cultural differences, an ethos at the heart of western forms of multiculturalism, often characterised by superficial celebrations of difference. However, as discussed in Chapter 9, some critics see multiculturalism as racism behind a mask of political correctness. Under the indelible sign of the dominant culture (Britishness, for example) groups that have been been born and bred in the country and consider themselves British continue to find themselves classified as BME on the basis of their visible difference, or, in case of Eastern Europeans, because of their accents.

Pieterese has shown that the creation of 'others' plays a role in cementing social relations and defining the boundaries of the nation state. These boundaries create a moral consensus that unites people around the core values of society. Therefore, 'race' and ethnicity are markers of difference that reflect the social construction at a particular time. As Hall (1996b) suggests, race is a 'floating signifier'; where and how it is used to draw boundaries and determine rules of inclusion and exclusion will depend upon historically specific conditions. These trends in defining the 'other' are certainly tied to global and national shifts and boundary drawing. The 'other' may be physically (i.e. geographically) distant, or 'othered' owing to cultural labelling, seen as deviant, beyond the pale.[4]

BARTHES AND THE READER'S ROLE IN CONSTRUCTING MEANINGS

Meaning in some schools of thought is very much dependent on the intentions of the sender, but in semiotics 'the message is a construction of signs which, through interacting with the receivers, produce meanings. The sender, defined as transmitter of the message, declines in importance. The emphasis shifts to the text and how it is "read"' (Fiske 1990: 3). Meanings from our social world are not so much 'out there' but reside within the reader and are actively decoded by knowledge of conventional codes. Hence the intended nuances in a word, a photograph, a dance or a piece of film are recognised only if our cultural understanding of these meanings allows us to decode the intended meaning. For example, cultural knowledge is required to recognise that the red rose is a symbol adopted by New Labour or a traditional sign for romance and chivalry. The truth in the famous line 'A rose by any other name would smell as sweet' (Shakespeare, *Romeo and Juliet*) lies in the sense that the word 'rose' is an agreed convention and has nothing intrinsic to do with the scented flower: language is an arbitrary conventional code. This is an important point as it indicates that we are actively making meanings and that, while people might show general agreement on some signs, there is a range of interpretations possible that depends on our own subjective identity, ethnicity, class, gender, generation, education, experience and state of mind.

Roland Barthes, using the structuralist linguistic principles of Saussure and others, mapped out the process of signification, as shown in Figure 1.1. The reader interprets the surface meanings (signifier) and from the word or image recognises the implied social and cultural meanings (signified). First we perceive the signifier (this could be a written, spoken or graphic element) and we interpret this conventional code based on our cultural knowledge. In this example, 'the rose' refers to a flower (among other things). These aspects make up the first level of signification, that of denotation. However, the denotative sign is also a signifier at the deeper level of connotation. The connotative sign, in turn, can be seen as another layer of meaning, which again becomes the signifier at a third level – the level of myth.

For example, the word or image of a rose carries the connotation of romance, part of the lexicon of courtly love; it can also, more narrowly, be a political emblem developed as part of the reinvention of the UK Labour Party under Tony Blair along centrist lines to increase its appeal to the electorate, while keeping the socialist iconography of the red rose. The way in which we interpret these signs and the

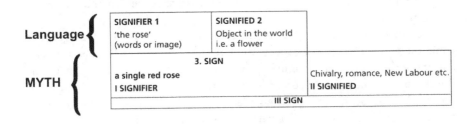

Figure 1.1 The process of signification.

process by which we make meaning is largely dependent on the context in which we are 'reading' the signs.

Images of race can be analysed in this way, recognising the layering of socio-cultural meanings and paying attention to the manner in which the image is chosen and framed to contextualise and foreground a 'preferred reading'[5] while maintaining the myth of the image as 'natural'. These deeply embedded conventional values are illustrated in Barthes's ground-breaking 1957 article 'Myth Today' (Barthes 1972: 109–37). Consider Barthes's deconstruction of a specific image of 'otherness':

> And here is now another example: I am at the barber's, and a copy of *Paris-Match* is offered to me. On the cover, a young Negro in a French uniform is saluting, with his eyes uplifted, probably fixed on a fold of the tricolour. All this is the meaning of the picture. But, whether naively or not, I see very well what it signifies to me: that France is a great Empire, that all her sons, without any colour discrimination, faithfully serve under her flag, and that there is no better answer to the detractors of an alleged colonialism than the zeal shown by this Negro in serving his so-called oppressors. I am therefore again faced with a greater semiological system: there is a signifier, itself already formed with a previous system (a black soldier is giving the French salute); there is a signified (it is here a purposeful mixture of Frenchness and militariness); finally, there is a presence of the signified through the signifier.
>
> (Barthes 1972: 116)

Barthes is suggesting that images such as this are elements in a myth – superficially benign and obvious (at the denotative level) while, underlying this surface, there are connotations of colonialism and deference to French paternalism by her subjects. It was also obviously important to maintain a sense of order and control during struggles against French colonial rule in North Africa and very harsh and repressive actions were taken by the French in defence of their colonies, especially in Algeria.

Such imagery could be viewed as elements within a reified language of common sense, a statement of fact, the bourgeois efforts (as Barthes saw it) to continuously disguise the complex process of historical change. In this process the struggle of the colonial subject or the proletariat is obscured behind reified objects that can be measured and hoarded. We talk of *the* stock exchange and *the* balance of payments. These alienated objects obscure conflict and manipulation by the elite. Such nominalised terms disguise the reality of human toil.

This is how myth in Barthes's sense operates: the second level of signification becomes the signifier for a third level that is disguised and naturalised by association with the simply denotative (and 'innocent') objects in the world:

Just as the cuttlefish squirts ink in order to protect itself, it cannot rest until it has obscured the ceaseless making of the world, fixated this world into an object which can be forever possessed, catalogued its riches, embalmed it, and injected into reality some purifying essence which will stop its transformation, its flight towards other forms of existence.

(ibid.: 155)

Every day we are inundated with images, words, non-verbal signs, advertising, television and posters that communicate to us, in a similar way to Barthes's encounter with *Paris-Match*, information about the society we are in and affirm and reinforce or question and oppose this mythical common-sense view of the world. Yet such meanings are dependent on the codes and practices we bring to their interpretation. We are intimately bound to the codes that are presented to us and our cultural knowledge allows us to make sense of these messages. However, some social meanings are taken as a self-evident part of an unquestionable social order: for example, the ownership of the wealth of the nation is in the hands of a privileged elite; and the status 'white' is not nominated as an ethnic status but, rather, as seen as 'natural' in our common-sense reality. There is a sense of closure, a myth of naturalness, about the operations of capitalism.

These are the invisible yet dominant codes that underpin our experience of social reality, so familiar and habitual that they are effectively unspoken conventions. Many of our everyday assumptions are based on these myths and subject to a process of ex-nomination. As Barthes remarks: 'the bourgeoisie is defined as *the social class which does not want to be named*. "Bourgeoisie", "petit-bourgeoisie", "capitalism", "proletariat" are the locus of an unceasing haemorrhage: meaning flows out of them until their very name becomes unnecessary' (ibid.: 138, italics in original). In a very similar way, whiteness is constructed as natural, innocent and omnipresent, attributes of 'depoliticised speech' – of myth.

RHETORICAL IMAGES

The implication of language as a conventional and arbitrary code became central to the culturalist analyses of texts which exposed the embedded values presented as natural in society. Raymond Williams, Stuart Hall, John Fiske and John Hartley, among many others, have applied these structuralist understandings to their interpretations of popular culture.

Barthes's essay 'The Rhetoric of the Image' (in Barthes 1977) was an important contribution to the study of the process of signification in photographic images, especially in popular cultural forms such as advertising. Barthes focused upon the internal process of signification played out in our 'reading' of images – the dialogue between the denotative level and the symbolic connotative level. The manner in which this denotative, literal level is coded 'prepares and facilitates' (ibid.: 43) our reading of the connotative level. Hence, slight changes in the mode of portrayal will inevitably change the relationship to consciousness and the manner of interpretation the viewer employs. Barthes highlights the contrast between the interpretation of photographic images as opposed to film: 'the photograph must be related to a pure spectatorial consciousness and not to the more projective, more "magical" fictional consciousness on which film by and large exists' (ibid.: 45). He talks about a process of 'eviction' that takes place when we perceive an image, a conscious suspension of the faculty through which the connotative potential becomes associated with the denotative sign. This is necessary when coping with the clutter of mundane subjects (e.g. advertising images). Deeper meanings are necessarily 'mentally deleted'. Yet the naturalistic codes through which photographs are encoded are not experienced as manipulations of reality, as illusions; rather, they indicate the actuality of 'having been there'. Photographs appear to be objective evidence of existence. This complex cognitive process that occurs as we perceive operates so that, in Barthes's words: 'the denoted image naturalizes the symbolic message, it innocents the semantic artifice of connotation' (ibid.: 45). This implies that photographs underwrite the objectivity of an event. Stuart Hall argues (in his 1973 analysis; see Hall 1980) that news photographs neutralise the ideological function of the newspaper (ibid.: 188). The authority and supposed objectivity of news photographs seems to counter the political bias that we know the paper possess.

Ethnographic images of the type employed in many early twentieth-century volumes gave the reader a neat summation of 'peoples of the world': banal, ethnocentric and trivialising, they present a filtered cultural collation of stereotypes of places and people, their traits and livelihoods. Egypt is the Nile, camel trains, the pyramids, veiled women; the Arctic is Eskimos fishing through ice holes and building igloos, dogs pulling sleds; Argentina is gauchos on the Pampas drinking maté from a gourd; Australia is Aborigines holding spears or boomerangs, roustabouts in the shearing sheds; Malaysia is sarong-wearing Malays tapping rubber trees; and so on. These lantern-show slides reduce the world to maps showing characteristic ethnic types, symbols of produce and industry. The world effectively reduced seems manageable, apolitical. Figures 1.2 and 1.3 are two of this ilk: published before the Second World War, they present the world pictorially as a pageant that parades before our eyes, to be consumed. For your pleasure the diverse typifications of the world's peoples are assembled, the images that seem to embody the essence of each nation sought out.

> If it were possible for a pageant of the world's peoples to be shown on the silver screen of your nearest cinema, and each individual took no more than a second to play his part, the performance would go on night and day without cessation for over sixty years. Of the 2,000,000,000 men, women and children in the grand march past, the majority would be of the white race, followed by members of the yellow, brown, black and red races in decreasing but amazing numbers.
>
> (Wheeler 1935: 7)

Figure 1.2 exemplifies the manner in which a whole people may be reduced to an icon. Racism is deeply embedded in the project of these trivialising taxonomies. Such images show elements of anthropological and romantic discourses that Muecke (1982) argues are among the narrow lexicon available when talking about indigenous Australians. The anthropological discourse, with its focus on kinship, ceremony, totemism and mythology, creates the 'other' as totally removed from the viewer, remote, fixed in time. Significantly, they are portrayed as an evolutionary 'cul-de-sac' and doubts are expressed about their survival. Such images are instructive not only for what they reveal about the people in question but also for what is revealed about how white European culture sees itself through the objectification of others. How 'they' are catalogued, the iconic postures and cultural artefacts shown, the use of the landscape and the positioning of the family groups, as well as the continuity with imagery used today, suggests that this view of indigenous Australians as members of a timeless 'primitive' culture serves a marked social function that helps to define and legitimate white Australian culture.

Figure 1.3 is surprising in some respects. Compared with the stereotypical images that I have just described, it seems to have an authenticity, a lack of posing that is unusual. The text describes this as 'a pleasant rural scene'. However, the

Figure 1.2 Stone Age people of the desert, from H. Wheeler, *Peoples of the World in Pictures* (1935).

Figure 1.3 Negro women tending young sugar canes, from J. Hammerton's *Peoples of All Nations* (1933).

women's clothing – at once puritanical and ragged – encumbers their exhausted bodies, giving an oppressive sense of back-breaking physical labour in stifling heat that makes the scene anything but 'pleasant'. It is a reminder of colonialism and slavery, despite the fact that the description makes attempts to draw a clear distinction between slavery and this 'pleasant' scene, informing us that

> For many years Jamaica was one of the world's greatest slave marts; the emancipation of the slaves took place in 1834. The negro peasant population is chiefly employed on the sugar plantation, and here we have a typical group of women busily working among the young canes.
>
> (Hammerton 1933: 203)

Yet in pictures such as this, which objectify the colonial subject, there are no attempts to consider them as people oppressed, although they are burdened by transgressionary signs that undermine the superficial voyeurism employed in the text. The face of the woman in the centre of the picture, half turned and regarding the photographer narrowly, with suspicion and resentment, forms in Barthes's terminology the punctum of this image and transforms it from the artifice of the popular trivial ethnography by opening up other readings to this intended apolitical diorama, in which separate subjects are entirely removed from the perception of Hammerton's ideal reader. In this way, a small sign, a look, a gesture, the set of a body (a feature unintended by the photographer who composed the image) transforms and denies the dominant reading's implied closure.

WHITENESS AS MYTH

'Whiteness' is an example of a dominant yet naturalised and mythologised cultural form. Michael Pickering exposes the underlying truth about the discourse of race as a marker of difference from a position of invisible white domination:

> In contemporary discourse, 'race' refers to people who are non-white, and denotes cultural 'difference'. 'Race' is used as a way of designating certain categories within our culture, and it does this from an invisible, undesignated position. This is the position of whiteness. As a normative position, whiteness is taken to be a natural fact, existing beyond the bounds of consideration. It is not racially marked *as* white in the way that black is so marked.
>
> (Pickering 2004: 91)

This is easy to illustrate in everyday language: to specify that something is 'white' may seem nonsensical or transgressive, while using the labels 'black' or 'Asian' may seem quite justifiable. The song 'White Riot', by The Clash (1977), challenges our assumptions of what a riot can or should be. The development of 'White' Studies is an interesting phenomenon in that it recognises and scrutinises 'whiteness' in an attempt to reveal what is typically rendered invisible and normative. The unearned privilege accorded to 'white' people in our societies operates in a comparable way to other markers of power in society. Similarly, young, male, able-bodied, heterosexual, middle-class people may reap the benefits of special privileges simply by accident of birth.

Writer Kimberly Hohman (2000) comments on several aspects of white privilege that are taken for granted by white mainstream culture, but which, she suggests, are a constant source of unease for others:

- being able to turn on the television and see people of their race widely represented;
- never being asked to speak on behalf of their entire race;
- being able to succeed without being called a credit to their race;
- being able to have a bad day without wondering what their race had to do with specific negative incidents.

Hohman thus demonstrates the pernicious everyday effects of being marked out as different. However, the consequences can be much more serious. It is well evidenced that BME people in the UK suffer inordinately high rates of 'stop and search' by the police, rates which even seem to have increased in recent years: 'Per 1,000 of the population, Black persons were Stopped and Searched 7.0 times more than White people in 2009/10 compared to 6.0 times more in 2006/07' (Ministry of Justice 2011).

Frantz Fanon was one of the first to articulate the seamless dominance of white ideology, a recognition that whiteness permeated every aspect of the context in which black people found themselves. As a psychiatric worker in Algeria during the war against the French, he explored the traumatic effects of colonial domination in the scarring and distorting of the psyche of the post-colonial subject. Such insights were of profound importance to the civil rights movement of the 1960s and to the politics of resistance to colonialism around the world. Fanon's insight into the experience of metropolitan and colonial racism helped to forge a critical consciousness, exposing the links between racialism and white western culture that present whiteness as a platform of unspoken, invisible superiority. The effects of white colonialism are not just on the outer, material shell of the colonised but also on their insides, through the psychological damage caused by this inescapable whiteness. Fanon captured the sense that the entire world of discourse is permeated and possessed by whiteness: 'All around me the white man, ... and there is a white song, a white song. All that whiteness that burns me' (Fanon 1959).

Here are the poetics of alienation, but Fanon also gives a lucid account of the hegemony by which such effects become naturalised:

> To speak a language is to take on a world, a culture. The Antilles Negro who wants to be white will be the whiter as he gains greater mastery of the cultural tool that language is. Rather more than a year ago in Lyon, I remember, in a lecture I had drawn a parallel between the Negro and European poetry, and a French acquaintance told me enthusiastically, 'At the bottom you are a white man.' The fact that I had been able to investigate so interesting a problem through the white man's language gave me honorary citizenship.
>
> (Fanon 1967a: 38)

It is clear that Fanon had a deep insight into the struggle for symbolic dominance and the way in which signs (linguistic or otherwise) were the tokens by which post-colonial power operated. Newly arrived in Paris from Martinique, he describes the devastating experience of racism. Brought up in a colonial society, the son of a white French father and a black mother, Fanon had no experience of the hostile forms of metropolitan racism; in a sense, he had not been confronted by the interpellation of his own blackness as a form of 'otherness':

> I came into the world imbued with the will to find a meaning in things, my spirit filled with the desire to attain to the source of the world, and then I found

that I was an object in the midst of other objects. Sealed into that crushing objecthood.

(Fanon 1967a: 109)

He describes the experience as shattering: his self-image was shattered into pieces as a small French boy called out to his mother in alarm:

"Look, a Negro!" It was an external stimulus that flicked over me as I passed by. I made a tight smile.
"Look, a Negro!" It was true. It amused me.
"Look, a Negro!" The circle was a drawing a bit tighter. I made no secret of my amusement.
"Mama, see the Negro! I'm frightened!" Frightened! Frightened! Now they were beginning to be afraid of me. I made up my mind to laugh myself to tears, but laughter had become impossible.'

(ibid.)

Reducing people to mere clusters of physical features and invented signs of difference – a Jewish nose, Asian eyes, African pigmentation – denies individuality. Richard Dyer's *White* (1997) examines whiteness, a state that on the surface seems mundane and unexceptional. However, when whiteness comes under scrutiny the profound depths of racialist ideologies and their links to culture are exposed. By contrast, non-whiteness is always marked as different, out of the ordinary. A focus on the naturalised form is an important moment of recognition that race and racism are not just adjuncts, afterthoughts to the cultural practices of a group; rather, they are discourses that are intrinsic to white cultural superiority. Dyer illustrates the all-pervasive whiteness of western culture through paintings of classical antiquity and modern filmic portrayal of white heroes such as Hercules, Tarzan and Rambo. These popular icons are forms of excessive whiteness and function as idealised signs aspired to by commonplace whiteness. In a similar way, in relation to gender, Connell (1987) posits several kinds of masculinity, including a 'hegemonic masculinity' that portrays the extreme position of maleness, in relation to which other forms are either complicit or subordinated. Whiteness (like patriarchy) attains invisibility, and bodies of the 'other', black or female, can be rendered unproblematically as objects. Ware and Back (1992: 2) highlight the cultural imaginary of whiteness in Melville's *Moby Dick*, as a metaphor for the 'leviathan of white supremacism'.

This iconography is pervasive in western culture. One striking evocation of the reality of 'otherness' was the bold experiment into embodied participation conducted by John Howard Griffin. Griffin took the idea of empathy (walking around in the other's shoes) to an ontological extreme by dyeing his skin black and experiencing at first hand the segregation and hatred of the Deep South in 1959. The telling examination of racial hatred came with Griffin's reflection on the deep-seated sense of 'otherness' and how he could rid himself of 'those old racist poisons' (Griffin in Ware and Back 1992: 281). He suggests that a profound recognition of racism at both an intellectual and emotional level (closing the gap between the personal and the political) was needed, and, significantly, the white vision of 'otherness' would only dissolve when the individual understood that: 'there is no "other" – that the "other" is simply oneself in all the important essentials' (ibid.: 282). In the next section the ontology of whiteness/blackness is evoked by the examination of two well-meaning but flawed equality campaigns.

SCARED?

Travelling through the once-thriving industrial hinterland of a city in northern England, I was confronted by this disconcerting and incomprehensible image: a huge black face, brooding and threateningly lit, and the word 'SCARED?' in blood red (Figure 1.4). In what way does this text anchor the image – is it addressed to us or to the face itself? We are, I suppose, far from innocent observers of advertising – a cultural form that has learnt to derive maximum benefit from manipulating our expectations and the intertextual nature of our visual knowledge. Behind a poster such as this there lies a lexicon of well-worn cultural expressions: the style of under-lighting, the passive trance-like facial expression, the size and form of the lettering. This is a face emerging from the gloom like Brando's in *Apocalypse Now*. Our understanding of this image is dependent on a matrix of cultural knowledge, and to construct meaning we refer back through images associated with film, TV, poster art and archive imagery. Is this a 'teaser ad' for a forthcoming movie or a public-safety ad? We might look at it with a certain cynicism, or with humour or irony, as we are frequently confronted by advertising campaigns that make abstract metaphoric allusions to branded products. Is this simply the signifier for a product or brand that we have missed the television ad for? Or a sinisterly lit face of another TV celebrity we have not paid attention to?

Depending on the currency of popular concerns at the time we view such an image, we might well consider it to be about the threat of terrorism or even about the popular anxieties exacerbated by tabloid newspapers over asylum seekers. Yet the starkness of the poster does suggest another meaning, somehow subversive and less likely: that the poster is suggesting an implicit fear of 'blackness', a primordial myth bolstered and reaffirmed by hundreds of images of drug-related black street crime, tabloid stories of mugging and violence, lurid Hollywood images of gangsters in films such as *Boyz n the Hood* (1991) and *Adulthood* (2008). Indeed, a whole genre of film from the 'blaxploitation' era of the 1970s onwards portrays black culture in the USA in gross physical terms of sexual and

Figure 1.4 Scared? Poster from the Commission for Racial Equality's controversial campaign in Sheffield, 1999.

aggressive action. These are the very attributes that were perpetuated as stereo-types throughout the colonial period (see Spencer 2007). Constructing the black body as physically powerful, menacing and with enormous sexual energy can be seen to persist in these genres of popular culture.

Aside from the possible intertextual links we might make to interpret such an image, it could be argued that the only reason this campaign could be seriously considered is that an underlying given exists that white observers, consumers and motorists passing this billboard see black faces as deviant. As Dyer suggests, 'the assumption that the normal face is a white face runs through most published advice given on photo- and cinematography' (Dyer 1997: 94). Such implicit values indicates the operation of a deep and unspoken cultural system: 'The secret of whiteness ... is that it is empty, defined only negatively by what it is not, a rule or norm established only after the phenomena that it came to define as inadequate or abnormal' (Montag 1997: 291).

On driving past the billboard it was possible to make out another line of print in smaller white type: 'YOU SHOULD BE. HE'S A DENTIST'. This denouement serves to both explode and expose the unspoken cultural meaning: blackness, without a biography, is a signifier connoting an alien 'other'. Our culture has marked out blackness as 'other', as deviant, and whiteness as ex-nominated and inherently privileged. So, by juxtaposing a deviant assumption with a white professional category 'it' becomes 'he'; it is this shocking transformation that so exposes the racist expectations popularly harboured. This is the message – the rhetoric of the image. The campaign had intended to address complicit racism by allowing the viewer to expose, through readers' practices of signification, their own implicit cultural bias. We recognise the gross stereotypes, disturbing and distasteful as they may be, and at some level they may influence judgement, may become naturalised, despite their banality.

Another poster, ostensibly an advert for a recruitment agency with the slogan 'Dominate the Race', pictured a besuited white executive climbing a ladder and treading on the hands of a similar dressed black candidate, who was grasping the lower rungs. This poster, and the one described above, may have left people gasping in amazement at the extraordinary breaches in political correctness, but by all accounts few complaints were registered. The 'SCARED?' poster (a Commission for Racial Equality (CRE) administrator informed me) had more complaints from dentists who felt that it was scornful of their profession than from individuals concerned about racism. The Director of the Commission for Racial Equality at the time, Sir Herman Ouseley, had decided to use shock tactics in the form of overtly racist billboards that were planted in hope of a reaction. One, masquerading as an advertisement for the 'TDX-5 rape alarm', showed a white woman sitting on a bus anxiously eyeing a young black man. The poster's text read: 'Because it's a jungle out there'. This poster clearly alluded to the pernicious myth of threatening black sexuality. This campaign was alarming, distasteful and arguably in danger of reaffirming popular stereotypes rather than shaming people for recognising them. However, the entrenched nature and invisibility of white prejudices is clearly the obstacle to which the CRE was trying to hold up a mirror.

THE MATRIX OF CULTURAL IDENTITY

Figure 1.5 shows a Matrix of Cultural Identity (adapted from du Gay *et al.* 1997). The matrix contains five interrelated processes in the circulation of social meanings within culture: production, consumption, regulation, representation and identity. Looking at each of these in turn sheds light on the importance of how meaning is produced, affirmed or challenged and the central place of culture in defining personal identity. The poster image in Figure 1.4 will be considered here as an example of the way in which the five interlinked processes may operate. Although the emphasis here is on the construction of identity as the centre point of these processes, identity itself is simply another domain in the construction of social meaning. Any point in the matrix could be considered first.

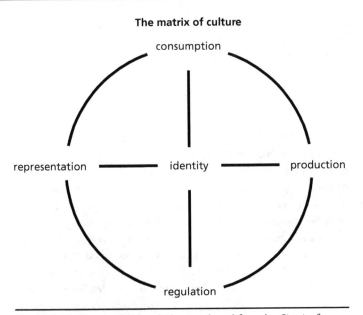

Figure 1.5 The Matrix of Cultural Identity adapted from the *Circuit of Culture* (du Gay *et al.* 1997).

Production

The poster (Figure 1.4) is a result of cultural meanings and cultural economies. It was the product of a poster campaign by the Commission for Racial Equality, a non-departmental public body in the UK set up under the 1976 Race Relations Act to promote racial equality, tackle discrimination and disseminate positive portrayals of diversity. The mission statement of the Commission was: 'We work for a just and integrated society, where diversity is valued. We use persuasion and our powers under the law to give everyone an equal chance to live free from fear of discrimination, prejudice and racism.'[6]

No doubt this poster, along with others in the same campaign, was a serious attempt to question entrenched racist beliefs, but, like other mass media forms, the campaign reflected beliefs about the audience(s) who would decode these images. The image itself was a product of the genealogy of ideas of representation about blackness and its popular meanings. Yet, in terms of encoded rhetoric, it might appear that this was an attempt to choose imagery that epitomised the lowest common denominator of racism. Hence there is a hyperreal grossness, an obviousness in these posters that may be akin to the recognition of artifice that Barthes suggested in his writing about the 'obtuse meaning' that 'declares its artifice but without in so doing abandoning the "good faith" of its referent' (Barthes 1977: 58). Here the referent is determined by each reader's recognition of the larger domain of cultural assumptions about generic blackness, a face without a biography.

Consumption

Consumption practices are an intrinsic expression of the individual's relationship to the forces of production and to their social and economic class position and, hence, such practices highlight social status and cultural capital. In terms of the consumption of meanings, such as those implicit in this poster, culture divides us into different types of consumer. Hence, it is a fair assumption that there will be a range of possible meanings and interpretations to open images such as this one. Consumption, and the choices we make within it, is central to the ways in which our identity is constructed. Cultural capital, as Bourdieu suggests (1989a), is linked to class-related differences in consumption. So the codes and aesthetic sensibilities we have, or believe we have, shape our sense of identity and difference. Thus, an image such as this is a cultural product that can be consumed in various ways depending on our social and cultural location. Status and social class can be reproduced through patterns of consumption. Ideas of high culture, aesthetics and popular cultural forms divide readers sharply, as they highlight class distinctions of taste made about cultural products: identity is certainly linked to consumption in many ways. Consumption is, therefore, not just about commercial and economic activity: it is an intrinsically cultural process and one which is increasingly central to definitions of identity (Bourdieu 1989a).

Identity

The way in which individual and shared identity is constructed will determine how an individual relates to this image. Ethnicity, gender, nationality, social class, sexuality and community are aspects of the self that may lead to complex and conflicted interpretations of this image and its meaning as a public message, part of an organised campaign. Indeed, the interplay of all such images and ideas of self create a constant dialectic within the individual's identity.

Identity is a work in progress, a negotiated space between ourselves and others; constantly being re-appraised and very much linked to the circulation of cultural meanings in a society. Furthermore identity is intensely political. There are constant efforts to escape, fix or perpetuate images and meanings of others. These transformations are apparent in every domain, and the relationships between these constructions reflect and reinforce power relations.

(Taylor and Spencer 2004: 4)

Hence, the ways in which different groups identify with the image are not fixed either. A black man's face is enormously meaningful in our culture, but for very varying reasons. The accumulation of imagery of metaphors of blackness and whiteness raises questions for the construction of identity. It is only because of identities' potential for exclusion that they can serve as points of commonality and identification, 'every identity naming as its necessary, even if silenced and unspoken "other", that which it "lacks"' (Hall and du Gay 1996: 5). This has psycho-social consequences for those identities that are marginalised. Cornel West asks: 'How does one come to accept and affirm a body despised by one's fellow citizens?' He considers that the 'demythologizing' of black sexuality is crucial for black America because much of black self-hatred and self-contempt has to do with the refusal of many black Americans to love their own black bodies (West 1995).

Regulation

Like other economies, the cultural economy is subject to regulation and sanctions. Some of the posters generated by this poster campaign were covered up by the police for fear that they might incite racial hatred. Yet, while regulation and production depend on formal policies and decision-making, the CRE had a mandate to address the issues of societal racism and to attempt to intervene. Therefore, they employed 'creatives' to design a campaign that would confront public complacency and convey the concerns about embedded racism. Individuals, as they observe the poster, may assess whether it affirms or contradicts their values. Indeed, it later became apparent that the CRE was anticipating mass complaints against the posters, which they felt would show robust public outrage against the implicit assumptions being made by the campaign. A follow-up campaign was planned, with posters that would carry smaller versions of the original 'Shock' posters framed with the words, 'What was worse? This advert or your failure to complain?' However, this never eventuated, as official regulation was imposed – as this *Telegraph* online journalist explains:

> The CRE has not had a chance to put up the second set of ads. The police of Avon and Somerset have threatened to prosecute the CRE under the Race Relations Act – the very law that established the CRE, and forbids 'racism'. In some areas, the original ads were ordered covered with white paper. The CRE stands by its campaign. It says there were only 82 complaints about the posters, adding that thousands of Britons saw them and did nothing – proof that the campaign is badly needed.
>
> (Tweedie 1998)

Representation

Every culture uses signs and symbols to represent concepts, ideas, values and feelings. The face shown in the poster could act as a cultural icon – that is, a multi-layered image that reflects dominant values and beliefs, as well as conflicts and contradictions of the time. It begs the question, 'What is the meaning of blackness?' In semiotics of the image, it is recognised that words anchor images and their significance. Here, the word 'SCARED?' contains a rhetoric that suggests that certain features of blackness are being highlighted. We might see within the image other contemporary portraits. This image of a generic black male is interpreted through our ability to make intertextual reference to a limited western lexicon of similar images.

Interestingly, the image in the 'SCARED?' poster is reminiscent of a demonised popular icon, O. J. Simpson, whose public trial gave media channels opportunities to dwell on his impassive features and reinvoke notions of primordial racial evil. Apparently some media channels went further and actually darkened his features to emphasise his blackness, with *Time* magazine suggesting that the darkening of the image was for '"aesthetic" reasons' (Dickinson and Anderson 2004: 271).

The Unfair Campaign

Figure 1.6 is an example of the Unfair Campaign anti-racist posters which were displayed in Duluth, Minnesota, in 2012, again with the avowed intention to 'raise awareness about white privilege in our community, provide resources for understanding and action, and facilitate dialogue and partnership that result in fundamental, systemic change towards racial justice' (http://unfaircampaign.org/about-us/background/).

This series of posters featured white faces or parts of faces and hand-written messages, in some cases superimposed on the skin. The messages address the sort of inherent and taken-for-granted aspects of whiteness; for example, superimposed on a white woman's face are the texts:

> 'lucky that people see us, not a color'
> 'we're lucky that car doors don't get LOCKED when we walk by'
> 'we're lucky we don't get followed by security when we go to the store'
>   (UnfairCampaign.org 2012)

In another example, over the face of a young white man, are the words:

> 'I AM A WHITE MAN. And you don't see my color before you see my face. You don't judge me before you know me. You DON'T FEAR me and you don't secretly hope I'll stay out of your neighbourhood. What you do is worse. You give me

Figure 1.6 Unfair Campaign image, Unfair Campaign, Duluth, Minnesota, 2012.

BETTER jobs, better pay, better treatment, and a better chance – all because of the color of my skin – and you don't even know you're doing it. THAT'S UNFAIR.

(UnfairCampaign.org 2012)

There is also a campaign video that shows several people talking with writing on their faces giving similar messages. Perhaps not surprisingly, the posters and video have attracted angry responses. That white faces were used was seen as provocative, alienating, 'anti-white' and even racist by some critics. According to one oppositional site, in July 2012 an Unfair Campaign billboard was defaced with a Confederate flag and a racial slur (Stop Unfair Campaign 2012).

Why should this exposure of white privilege attract such anger? It has to be remembered that Duluth is a very white area (around 90 per cent). The Stop campaign, clearly incensed by the message being conveyed, suggested on its site that the Unfair Campaign is a front for a liberal/progressive push by the Democrats in the area; these white faces proclaiming selfless liberal values are really propaganda, part of a malign conspiracy. Again, it is hard to see why there is such a sense of threat and guilt; if those so opposed to the campaign are so unassailably right in their views, why is there such apparent insecurity and sensitivity? As the allegations of divisiveness and racism grew by July 2012, the University of Duluth withdrew its support for the campaign.

In many ways the representational codes for both the CRE and the Unfair Campaign posters are the same: the silence about racism and privilege is deafening, and the posters and videos, in their different ways, attempt to spell this out. The manner in which they tried to achieve this was, arguably, problematic in the CRE case and all too effective in the Unfair Campaign case. The sheer amount of aggressive rhetoric, which was inherently 'racist and proud', that the latter attracted is perhaps also an indicator that it accurately targeted the issue and hit a nerve within the white community. Predictably, the responses include the usual 'political correctness gone mad' arguments. So bitter are the feelings that this campaign seems to have aroused that their simple video (still visible on YouTube) has now been defaced with pop-up messages (with dubious attributions to websites), including the following:

- The President of the United States has recently issued an executive order that whites should not be hired for government jobs.
- Universities routinely add points to the SATs scores of minorities based solely on racial issues.

These, however, are the relatively rational end of the responses; there are also plenty of out-and-out racist rants directed towards the campaign and its initiatives in Duluth – a ready vanguard of hateful and self-congratulatory responses. The flak which such campaigns are likely to attract is not surprising; indeed, it would be surprising if such responses were not forthcoming. However, there was also a video response from an alliance which appeared to be united against the message in the Unfair material as patronising and wrong. The video features several people of non-white origins mimicking the same approach, with close-up faces and handwritten messages, but, in this instance, the video forms a sharp (and clearly non-racist) critique arguing that the white faces and sentiments were suggesting that others must be 'unlucky' and helpless and that their campaign was merely affirming stereotypes ('Only white people can save minorities'). The exchange of comments, made between four different people, is transcribed below:

BOX 1.2 RESPONSE TO THE UNFAIR CAMPAIGN

What do you mean I'm unlucky to be black?
I'm not unlucky, I'm good at Math.
I'll do the jobs white people won't do.
I'm an amazing basketball player.
I can play the violin.
I'd make a really great nanny.
Oh and I can dance.
These are things you see when all you see is colour.
Are you the one who's following me when I'm shopping?
These stereotypes are ridiculous –
dividing people by race does not help me.
I'm a part of society and I get to decide my own life.
Don't feel sorry for me, I'm doing fine.

(Unfair Campaign Response – www.youtube.com/
watch?v=RfnMovEhLWc), accessed 4 March 2013

'Othering' can take many forms and may arise from what are apparently laudable motives. Yet such campaigns, perhaps owing to their style and presentation, seems likely to harden attitudes. To suggest that there is an inbuilt advantage to whiteness is contrasted with the outraged assumption that minorities are 'playing the race card' and earning unwarranted privileges through quotas and discourses of political correctness. Some of the outspoken responses on YouTube mirror this anger at solemn white middle-class people talking about fairness. The spectrum of opinions visible shows the complexity of intersectional identities operating in the reading of this video. In the US, as in the UK, Australia and elsewhere, an aggressive conservative ideology is ready to remind us that a liberal bias reduces the white minority to powerlessness and poverty, while the 'minorities' themselves see the tone of the video as disempowering and patronising. There is often a sense that much of the liberal concern around multiculturalism is a lukewarm guilt-invoking discourse which only further undermines the robust agency of minority individuals. Bonnett makes the point that 'To continue to cast "whites" as antiracism's "other", as the eternally guilty and/or altruistic observers of "race" equality work, is to maintain "white" privilege and undermine the movement's intellectual and practical reach and utility' (1996: 107).

The discourse in this and other campaigns may achieve little, as it plays to both guilt and altruism simultaneously. The dilemma of whiteness is a further demonstration of the overarching problems of reification. These campaigns, while beginning from an ostensibly wholesome equality agenda intent on making the implicit advantage and privilege of whiteness conscious and visible, are a double-edged sword.

Interpreting signs, pictures, words or voices relies on complex intertextual knowledge because such representations are artefacts which are decoded from the cultural position of the observer. The meaning of whiteness, for example, has become established, as Wang comments: 'People are presumed to be white unless otherwise stated. Thus the standard judge, teacher, student or customer – the standard person – is imagined to be White' (Wang 2006: 12). The two campaigns above address this issue of the invisibility of whiteness and the general negativity readily triggered by blackness at the heart of metropolitan US and UK culture. But while both attempt to expose and shame the unspoken secrets of this default whiteness, neither succeeds because intertextually they cannot escape from the ambit of the dominant representational codes. In its attempt to confront racism the CRE campaign falls back on exaggerated stereotypes which merely appear confused or, worse, complicit. Where the Unfair Campaign tried for transparency, the message resonated with the guilt at the core of the liberal white. The minority response to the campaign understandably strives for autonomy and rejects white liberal advocacy as paternalism, yet real structural disadvantage caused by racism and invisible white privilege *is* the cultural DNA in US society.

This discussion has presented an array of examples of the way in which representation is fundamentally constitutive of our understanding and sense of identity, and, being a construct, can be part of the active making of culture – the struggle of ideas and counter-ideas which is a ceaseless aspect of social life: 'What we have, by and large, is a dynamic environment that consists of interactions between the abstract, ephemeral logic of representation, and the lived, felt world of experience' (Webb 2009: 143). These examples have shown the problems implicit in representation; the problem of exposing racism, ingrained prejudice and the invisible sense of white supremacy is compounded by the fact that, like DNA, a deep structure of the culture is implicit in the language and other codes that we have available. Intersectional identities of race, ethnicity, class and gender are operating in the impact that such image-based campaigns have: thus the association of the Unfair Campaign with a university led to some negative responses about white intellectuals, while the tone and language used infuriated some viewers, leading to some very aggressive responses. The irony is that there is plenty of evidence to support the key points the campaign tried to make – the anger comes from the implicit class coding, the tone of white liberal concern, which some viewers found repugnant.

CHAPTER SUMMARY

This chapter has presented the reader with some of the theories and concepts used in cultural studies and sociology. Messages in the media and in everyday circulation can usefully be analysed in terms of their surface and deeper structures. It is important to recognise that the manner in which the understanding of 'others' has been constructed is contingent on the implicit values of whiteness, which are ex-nominated and therefore so often not recognised. Race is not about whiteness or blackness per se, but rather about difference from a platform of unnamed dominance. The inclusion of Barthes's ideas about myth is important for two reasons: first, Saussure's notion that all elements in a linguistic system are meaningless without their relation to other elements is the foundation of the understanding taken up by Barthes that our most central cultural precepts are nothing other than artefacts, totems of our belief; and, second, this recognition allows us to expose them for what they are. It has been demonstrated that images can be understood as cultural products and meanings which social agents produce and consume, and that such meanings and values are an inevitable part of our identity, regulating our behaviours and drawing boundaries around our perceptions. Two campaigns were discussed to highlight the intrinsic inequality in society; the examples demonstrate ingrained stigma or normality and unspoken privilege, depending on colour. However, the process of making this visible is clearly threatening and gives rise to strong reactions, but the anger thus generated is also about recognising complex intersectional identities which cut across the trenchant colour divide, further complicating and dividing responses. There are some responses from white viewers of the Unfair Campaign that are not primarily racist but signal opposition to what appears patronising and presumptuous. In other words, the type of white middle-class person speaking to us is a reminder of class advantage, and the example demonstrates the importance of recognising the intersection of race with class.

EXERCISE 1.1 IDEOLOGY AND MYTHOLOGIES

1   Choose an example from the day's news and examine how it positions the reader ideologically.
2   Consider what Barthes means by 'myth'. Can you think of contemporary examples?
3   Advertising typically uses these given, conventional meanings (myths) to persuade us that a product's attributes are important. Choose one or two examples from advertising and explain how the myths operate.
4   Give examples of myths of masculinity and whiteness in our society. (These can be seen to operate in literature, television and film or popular anecdotes, urban myths or jokes.)
5   Apart from those listed by Kimberly Hohman, what other aspects of white privilege can you think of that are taken for granted in western societies?
6   Choose a photograph from a book or an advertisement from a magazine and show how the interplay of signs works:
    (a)   within the Matrix of Cultural Identity;
    (b)   to disguise or mythologise ideas as natural that are in fact socially constructed;
    (c)   in relation to Althusser's conception of ideology and interpellation.

EXERCISE 1.2 'SCARED?' AND THE UNFAIR CAMPAIGN

1   On first glancing at this image (Figure 1.4), what is your initial response? Write down your impressions. What is the context of this image? Who is it aimed at?
2   How did you arrive at this interpretation of the poster? What cultural sources informed your view?
3   Consider the cultural aesthetics that come into play when we interpret such images. Which of the following oppositions (or points in between) are useful in considering your response or ability to interpret this poster (or another image you have seen)?

easy	↔	difficult
realism	↔	abstraction
proximity	↔	distance
polemical	↔	neutral
function	↔	form
necessity	↔	luxury

4   How do you locate this image in a cultural genealogy? Can you give examples of other similar images that are known to you from other media such as film, television and news stories?

5   What is the effect of the word 'SCARED'? How does it function in relation to the image? Compare other pictures, advertisements or posters, and the effect of any wording (or absence of wording).

6   Compare your interpretation with that of two or three others. List their responses.

(a)   Was there a consensus or was the diversity of views a sign of the openness of the poster?

(b)   What does the difference or similarity of the readings say about your backgrounds?

7   Imagine that the face on the poster was white instead of black. What codes might we use to make sense of it?

8   View the posters and videos of the Unfair Campaign – what is the purpose of this campaign? How effective is it? Why might it have received unfavourable reactions (a) from white communities? (b) from minorities?

9   In what way might the posters and videos in these campaigns have been improved to make them more effective?

Further reading

For an accessible book that covers various aspects of socio-cultural representations and ideas of difference, Kath Woodward's *Identity and Difference* (Sage, 1997) highlights the materialist matrix of the 'circuit of culture' referred to in this chapter. Also in this series is *Representation: Cultural Representations and Signifying Practices* (Sage, 1997), edited by Stuart Hall, the godfather of cultural studies. A recent addition is the short introductory text *Understanding Representation*, by Jen Webb (Sage, 2009), from which I have drawn several examples in this chapter. J. H. Griffin's 1961 book *Black Like Me* (New American Library) is a vivid account of racism in the southern USA in the late 1950s. Griffin used chemicals to change his skin colour and travelled through the segregated South seeing cities he knew well in the guise of a black man. The account is very revealing, not only about unreasoning racism but also about Griffin's sense of his identity. See also

Sarfraz Manzoor's account of rereading the book (Manzoor 2011). In addition, bell hooks' 1992 book *Black Looks: Race and Representation* (South End Press) offers another culturally nuanced US analysis.

Notes

1 A significant decrease on the previous year. But at the same time the number of racist incidents in UK schools was recorded at 88,000 (BBC 23 May 2012).
2 Named after a duty editor who assessed events in terms of their diminishing importance in proportion to distance from the capital.
3 The Disposable Heroes of Hiphoprisy: 'Television, the drug of a nation'.
4 The phrase 'beyond the pale' derives from the Norman attempts to conquer Ireland in the thirteenth century. The 'pale' (meaning boundary) was an area that fluctuated widely over the centuries and represented the territory around Dublin held by the English monarchy. 'Beyond the pale' became established in English as meaning 'uncivilised' and 'socially unacceptable' (Curtis 1984: 12).
5 Texts are potentially open to multiple readings, but in practice one is 'preferred'. The analysis of the text often exposes this preference.
6 Its work has been merged into the new Equality and Human Rights Commission.

CHAPTER 2

The Politics of Naming

A single English word can effectively, in an instant, disembowel the vast 100,000 year histories and culture of about five hundred different peoples in Australia by naming us 'Aborigines'. That language was used by the colonisers as a weapon can be seen in the experience of numerous colonised peoples (here and in other countries) who were forced to use the coloniser's language.

(Foley 1997: 1–2)

In this chapter the importance of classifications and naming inherent in language and other codes is explored. We have shown that the connotations of cultural codes are actively interpreted from different 'reading positions' that reflect inherently different social attributes: class, gender, ethnicity and so on. Language can be a source of intense ethnic rivalry; in some instances it can be used to belittle, abuse or, as in the opening quote, almost to deny the separate existence of unique and complex cultures.

It is exactly because language is so intrinsic to culture, identity and meaning that colonisers were at pains to control its use, and also why it may become a flashpoint in ethnic struggles of resistance, as with, for example, the unique Basque language and the desire for Basque autonomy within Spain. There are many other such struggles, including movements in support of Welsh and Catalan. These are examples of what Hechter (1975) has termed 'internal colonialism', in which ethnic enclaves struggle for autonomy within the boundaries of the nation state. The means by which regional languages were discouraged has been a source of long-standing enmity to those who felt the power of the state at school and elsewhere.[1]

One of the indications that race and ethnicity do not have fixed referents but rather belong to the domain of shifting social and cultural meanings in which boundaries are constantly negotiated is the fact that conventions of naming are a constantly changing and sensitive area. More generally, as Kohn notes, 'we' harbour anxieties about 'race': 'We feel that the subject is covered by a taboo, but we don't know exactly what the rules of the taboo are. It seems important, if not obligatory, to discuss cultural differences, but dangerous even to mention physical differences' (Kohn 1996: 1).

How a group is denoted is not merely an arbitrary label but a meaningful and often challenging semantic field. The naming and categorising of individuals is highly political. The way in which these boundaries are established at times admits individual choice and self-determination but at other times is enforced by the dominant culture, colonial power or government. At the level of popular understandings, there is frequent uncertainty about the correct (and politically correct) terms to describe ethnic groups. It is significant that students are often concerned to ensure they have the right terminology; at times the misrecognition of others by the use of outdated terms such as 'coloured people' ('people of colour' is accepted in the USA) reflects the lack of communication between mainstream culture and 'minority' groups. Terms which are permissible are uncertain and changeable: 'ethnic minority' might be tolerable in some textbooks but suggests marginal identity; 'black' is fraught with a legacy of connotations, at once negative and racist, but also relating to political essentialism and ethnic pride. Whichever title is chosen, it may be accompanied by an aura of anxiousness and uncertainty.

DEFINING RACE AND ETHNICITY

It is important to recognise that the complex meanings of these terms are a consequence of the fact that they refer to socially constructed concepts. At times they have been used interchangeably (in Europe); at others they are strongly differentiated. 'The modernist connotation of "race" and "ethnicity" sees "race" either subsumed in "ethnicity", or referred to euphemistically through "ethnicity"' (Popeau 1998: 177). In fact, the term 'ethnicity' is typically used as a 'polite and less controversial term for "race"' (ibid.: 166).

'Race'

'Race' is an extraordinarily problematic term. It is debated, reviled and contested so fiercely, yet still employed because it is so intrinsically woven into the fabric of western cultural history. Indeed, the use of inverted commas so often seen around the term indicates that the term is, at best, part of a dubious fossil record of an inglorious history. It is certainly a candidate for being placed 'under erasure' (Derrida's convention 'sous rature'), a principle by which such terms are scored through when used in print, to indicate their problematic or spurious nature. However, despite this, many nations continue to use the term. For example, Malaysia and the USA both employ the term in contexts where Europeans would prefer the term 'ethnicity'. This use of the term 'race' as a marker of difference derives from differing social histories, stark divisions and, in the case of Malaysia, a long period of colonial rule. Furthermore, the term is woven into understandings about definitions of citizenship and lineage. Ideas of blood quantum are still used to determine identities and rights of membership to cultural and national groups. For example, membership of an ethnic grouping can be determined by lineage or blood or by fact of birth within a country or by self-determination. The official status of people with different 'blood quantums' could equate to material reward being different for full blood, half-caste, quadroon, octoroon. Among the indigenous peoples of Australia and America it has been a means of determining a person's right to belong or their exclusion. In the former country it was the basis on which decisions were made about taking certain mixed-race children from their Aboriginal parents (a practice that was carried on into the 1970s):

> Quadroons and octoroons, under 10 or 12 years of age, should, where such can be done without inflicting cruelty on the half-caste mother, be placed in an European institution, where they can be given a reasonable chance of absorption into the white community to which they rightly belong.
>
> (Bleakley 1929: 17)

Not only were many thousands of Aboriginal families devastated by these forced removals, based on ideas of actively 'breeding out' aboriginality, but Aboriginal people of mixed ancestry encountered the dilemma of being caught in the middle of a system in which exclusive markers shifted and where an individual with ambiguous skin pigmentation might experience rejection from both sides:

> In 1935 a fair-skinned Australian of part-indigenous descent was ejected from a hotel for being an Aboriginal. He returned to his home on the mission station to find himself refused entry because he was not an Aboriginal. He tried to remove his children but was told he could not because they were Aboriginal. He walked to the next town where he was arrested for being an Aboriginal vagrant and placed on the local reserve. During the Second World War he tried to enlist but was told he could not because he was Aboriginal. He went interstate and joined up as a non-Aboriginal. After the war he could not acquire a passport without permission because he was Aboriginal. He

received exemption from the Aborigines Protection Act – and was told that he could no longer visit his relations on the reserve because he was not an Aboriginal. He was denied permission to enter the Returned Servicemen's Club because he was.

(Read 1998: 196)

Race is central to ideas of culture which evolved during the Enlightenment. The concept emerged in European languages in the late fourteenth and early fifteenth centuries and the term 'race' was first used in English in the sixteenth century. In *Keywords* (1983) Raymond Williams cites its earliest uses as meaning 'offspring in the sense of line of descent'. Yet, from the Spanish origins of the term (*raza*), as Sollors (2002: 102) points out, 'race' was used to designate not only Moors and Jews but also heretics and their descendants. Young (1995) and Malik (1996) show that divergent views about race and racial categories stem from the Enlightenment: while divisive categorisation based upon pseudo-scientific views of racial difference emerged at this time, it was met with resistance from some philosophers, who held fast to ideas of universal humanity united by given capacity for reasoning and civil life. Among such philosophers differences were, in fact, due to climatic or agricultural variations. As a discourse, the concept has a long and complex history of shifting meanings 'parasitic on theoretical and social discourses for the meaning it assumes at given historical moments' (Goldberg 1992: 553). This suggests that different uses of the term can be traced within historically specific discourses. The interpretation of race as a 'floating signifier' (see Hall 1996b) is anchored to the prevailing social realities of the time. Table 2.1 is based on the discourse of race as expressed by Theo Goldberg (ibid.) and charts some of the strands that have composed the socially interwoven ideas about the construction of race. These will be given some consideration in turn.

Table 2.1 Evolving discourses of race

DISCOURSE	DESCRIPTION	CONSEQUENCES
Monogenism (fourteenth–eighteenth century)	focus on origin, breed, stock; descent from Adam and Eve	commitment to race as lineage, pedigree
Polygenism (eighteenth–nineteenth century)	biological inheritance and hierarchy	species; population; rigid categories

Continued.

Table 2.1 Continued.

DISCOURSE	DESCRIPTION	CONSEQUENCES
Evolutionism (late nineteenth century)	more fluid taxonomies; race as sub-species genetically interpreted	breeding populations are species; races are sub-species.
Race as class (nineteenth century on)	socio-economic status or relation to mode of production, or status	race as determined by class; reductionist – ignores cultural dimension
Race as culture (nineteenth century on)	identification with language, religion, customs, mores, encultured characteristics	group-bound dictum 'manners (or language) maketh man'
Race as ethnicity (twentieth century on)	use of term 'race' inherently; ethnocentric 'ethnicity' used interchangeably with race; social choice to identify by natural rather than social criteria	reflects reification of concepts over time; ethnicity shifts back to objectified category: 'them' rather than 'us'
Race as nation (late nineteenth century on)	race as nation; similar to early concept of lineage, rallying force behind nationalist movements	for example, White Australia Policy; also current concerns about immigration and asylum seekers, etc.

SHIFTING MEANINGS OF RACE

Monogenism

This term refers to the belief that the human race has descended from a single pair of ancestors: for example, in the literal reading of Genesis, Adam and Eve were the progenitors of all people. With regard to questions of origin, Christian orthodoxy maintained a strong and constant influence on thought. The Bible and its explanation of the process of creation were accepted as incontrovertibly true: the world was 5,500 years old and humankind sprang from Adam and Eve. Moreover, from the Middle Ages to the Enlightenment, the Great Chain of Being provided a fixed and immutable order for creation. God's creations were set out in layers, from the infernal regions below the Earth through the lowliest terrestrial life to animals, birds, humanity and, above them, celestial beings, culminating in God the Father, all linked by a chain. However, there were anomalous gaps between the realms that were not easily accounted for. As non-Europeans were more frequently encountered and as the slave trade progressed, other biblical explanations were needed to safeguard Christian morality. The notion arose that black-skinned people were the descendants of Ham, the son that Noah cursed and banished to the land of Nod – east of Eden. Other explanations included the idea that pre-Adamic beings existed that were outside of orthodox Christian belief and not supported in the Bible, but nevertheless influential.

The voyages of discovery that began in earnest in the fifteenth and sixteenth centuries and the consequent acts of colonialism and empire-building began to broaden ideas about the world and its inhabitants. Initially shrouded in mystery and prone to mythological invention, 'other' peoples became the object of increased interest and study and even collection and exhibition. McCaskell (1994) describes how a chimpanzee was brought back to Britain in 1699 and efforts were made to over-represent certain of its features to make it appear more human, as it was considered a potential candidate for a 'missing link' between monkeys and humankind. There was a desire to eradicate the anomalous areas and gaps on the Great Chain.

Polygenism

In contrast to monogenism, polygenism refers to the theoretical argument that species derive from more than one ancestor; in its biological form it asserts that different races correspond to different species. Although monogenism was promulgated by many thinkers throughout the Enlightenment it gradually gave way to notions of hierarchical ordering and the separate generation of races as species. As early as 1677 William Petty proposed that 'savages were a permanently distinct and inferior species of humanity located between (white) men and animals on the Great Chain' (Fredrickson 1981: 11). Fifty years later the far-ranging consequences of Petty's classifications were realised by Swedish biologist Linnaeus, whose *General System of Nature* (1806; first published in 1735) established four basic colour types in descending order:

- White Europeans
- Red Americans
- Yellow Asians
- Black Africans.

By the tenth edition Linnaeus had also linked the colour categories to attributes of character, showing the influence of the idea that the stamp of character was innate and implicitly linked to physical differences. This naturally led to the belief that such traits were fixed and inviolable, and further emphasised the hierarchical and mutually exclusive natures of the 'races'. A century later, these categories and the stereotypical traits associated with them were apparently accepted and commonplace.

Later works such as Oliver Goldsmith's *Animated Nature* (1876) portray the races as separate. Well into the twentieth century the influence of such stereotypes and an acceptance of a polygenic divide were being reproduced in popular 'every-man' publications. Take, for example, the morally superior tone of *Savage Survivals* (Moore 1933), in which it was stated that:

> Savages cry easily and are afraid of the dark; they are fond of pets and toys; they have weak wills and feeble reasoning powers; they are notoriously fickle and unreliable and exceedingly given to exaggeration of their own importance – in all of these particulars being much like the children of the higher races.
>
> (ibid.1933: 73)

These frequently apocryphal and stereotyped traits seem to have remained impervious to change (partly owing to remoteness and lack of contact in some cases). Take the entry on Laplanders in Goldsmith's book:

> These nations not only resemble each other in their deformity, their dwarfishness, the colour of their hair and eyes, but they have in a great measure, the same inclinations, and the same manners, being all equally rude, superstitious, and stupid. The Danish Laplanders have a large black cat, to which they communicate their secrets, and consult in all their affairs. Among the Swedish Laplanders there is in every family a drum for consulting the devil; and although these nations are robust and nimble, yet they are so cowardly that they never can be brought into the field.
>
> (Goldsmith 1876: 209)

Little attempt was made to understand indigenous practices and belief systems other than in terms of such details from folklore and myth. The consequences of these classifications were far ranging. Human differences, once classified, seemed more fixed, and once terms are habitually used they become naturalised and embedded in the culture and the discursive categories used. The linking of physical and behavioural characteristics fitted with long-standing, common-sense values – that differences in physical appearance betoken differences in habit and temperament. These crude typologies of human types, however, tended to ignore the geographically gradual nature of biological differences and examples which didn't fit. Gross differences are readily seen, but subtle variations are not recognised as easily. In addition, it could be argued that powerful Christian metaphors such as the 'Great Chain of Being' had already predisposed European culture to a view which legitimised as a God-given 'natural' order of things the inferiority of non-Europeans. The views of scientists such as Blumenbach and Linnaeus, who were widely renowned, lent the aura of scientific authority to such beliefs. For all of these reasons a value-laden hierarchical view of different peoples tended to be reinforced; and a major consequence of this hierarchical thinking was that the human species was divided into subgroups – in fact, sub-species – and that these species represented separate races.

Historically, perhaps as a result of this perception of species/race differentiation and hierarchical categorisation, there seemed to be a gradual hardening of racialisation in the USA and in Europe, further narrowing the racial frame of reference. Black thinkers, writers, scientists, philosophers were discredited and their works censured and removed from records and histories, their considerable achievements negated.

Evolutionism

Ideas about processes of evolution did not begin with Darwin, and many were far from rational and based on little more than speculation and prejudice. Hierarchical schemes of varying sophistication were developed from the seventeenth and eighteenth centuries onwards. Comte Arthur de Gobineau's pessimism about the outcome of the French Revolution of 1789 stemmed from a belief that inequality was a natural state and that the democratic views that stripped the aristocracy of their elevated positions were the outcome of racial miscegenation that would lead to a degraded racial stock, inevitably levelling a naturally uneven playing field. Again, this early conception linked race with social strata as well as racial types. This view was highly influential into the nineteenth and twentieth centuries. Various conceptualisations of 'evolution' preceded and framed Darwin's radical views on biology. In the early nineteenth century Jean-Baptiste Lamarck had suggested that acquired traits of the parents could be inherited by their offspring. His ideas were appealing at the time, as the suggestion that learned social traits could be inherited biologically was looked at favourably by social reformers. At the same time, Lamarck maintained that there was a grand design towards greater perfection and elaboration: 'Nature, in producing in succession every species of animal, and beginning with the least perfect or simplest to end her work with the most perfect, has gradually complicated their structure' (Lamarck 1809: 16). This did not send out the same shock waves to devout religious believers as Darwin's suggestion that the process of natural selection was apparently random. The Lamarckian view, by contrast, may have appeared more aligned to the hierarchical value system which imagined a grand design, unlike the disconcerting Darwinian view that change was based on chance.

Darwin's *On the Origin of Species* had, as intimated above, a major impact on nineteenth-century thought and ran contrary to racial theory, which 'required the fixity of characteristics – race only had meaning if characters which defined a racial group remained constant over time' (Malik 1996: 90). However, the theory of natural selection argued that biological types or species do not have a fixed, static existence but exist in a permanent state of change and flux. This startling theory, which was supported by Darwin's empirical work, presented all living organisms in a struggle for survival, a struggle to produce offspring, of which only those best adapted to prevailing conditions would survive. One of the catalysts for Darwin's ground-breaking vision of change was the work of Charles Lyell (e.g. *Principles of*

Geology (1830)), which showed the Earth to be in a continuous process of geo-logical change and also indicated, by reference to fossil records, that mankind was much older than calculations based on biblical accounts would admit (a mere few thousand years). The immense periods of time that Darwin suggested implied that change was more random and accidental than pre-ordained.

The effect of all this work was to move human beings away from the centre of creation and imply that they were not necessarily its crowning glory. Some writers and cataloguers of humanity seemed to take note of this greater fluidity and, while they used racial categories, illustrated the extraordinary diversity within these groups. Thus the plates from Baron Cuvier's *Animal Kingdom* (1890) that portray the human race are divided into four categories (American Indian, Caucasian, Mongol and Negro – corresponding to Linnaeus's red, white, yellow and black) but show also the variety within these groups (see Figures 2.1 and 2.2). Each plate purports to show details of human types, the inclusion of the skull indicating the preoccupation with materialist anthropology and physiognomy at the time. The studies, from drawings by Thomas Landseer, are sensitive and sympathetic to the dignity and character of their subjects, and a long way removed from the crude stereotypes that can be seen in other works of the period. The accompanying text explains that these categories of humankind are not considered separate species, as interbreeding between species is not possible, whereas between human groups it clearly is. However, the physical boundaries of race are affirmed by the presence of 'hereditary peculiarities':

> Although the human species would appear to be single, since the union of any of its members produces individuals capable of propagation, there are neverthe-less certain hereditary peculiarities of conformation observable, which consti-tute what are termed *races*. *Three of these* in particular appear eminently distinct: the *Caucasian*, or white, the *Mongolian*, or yellow, and the *Ethiopian*, or negro.
>
> (ibid.: 37, italics in original)

Yet there are hierarchical connotations in the text that are seemingly at odds with the sensitive *individual* portraits of Landseer. Each Mongolian or Negro type is based on a specific portrait and is presented as a member of a diverse, sentient and complex culture. The illustrations, which show the wide physical differences *within* a category, further contradict rigid ascriptions of race. However, Cuvier's text falls back on crude racist stereotypes, describing his subjects as debased and irrevocably primitive:

> The Negro race is confined to the southward of the Atlas chain of mountains: its colour is black. Its hair crisped, the cranium compressed, the nose flattened. The projecting muzzle and thick lips evidently approximate it to the Apes: the hordes of which it is composed have always continued barbarous.
>
> (ibid.: 38)

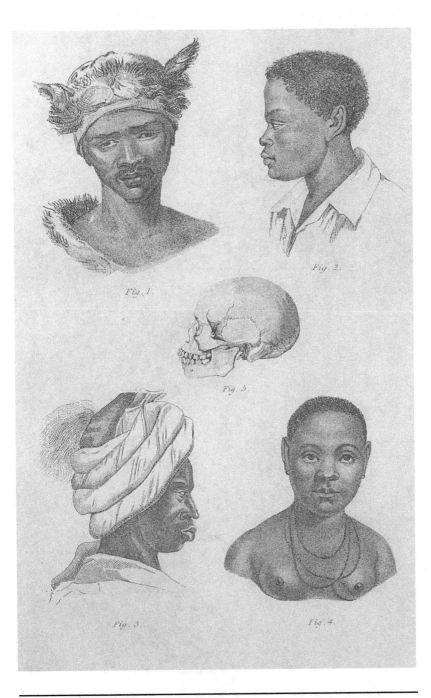

Figure 2.1 Negroes: portraits by Thomas Landseer in Baron Cuvier's *Animal Kingdom.*

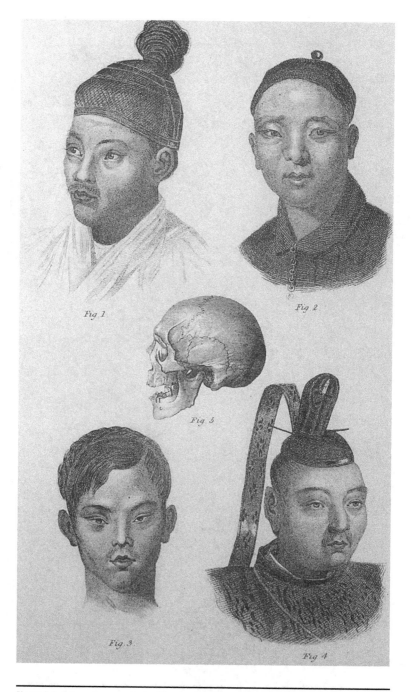

Figure 2.2 Mongols: portraits by Thomas Landseer in Baron Cuvier's *Animal Kingdom*.

Social critics of the time were scornful of these attempts to caricature attributes of the world's human varieties. It is not difficult to imagine how weaknesses and negative values observed in one's own society were projected onto the individuals of groups that the race scientists had never encountered. In the 1890 edition of Cuvier's work an additional note by W. B. Carpenter and J. O. Westwood reads: 'With all deference, I would suggest that naturalists are much too prone to confound resemblance with identity' (ibid.: 39). This very revealing comment reflects a growing dissent about crude claims of links between appearance and character. However, while *On the Origin of Species* led to recognition of the non-uniqueness of the human race, it also

> gave the rationale for a racially stratified view of evolution based on an ethnocentric colonial view of the subjugated nations who, with reference to their relative lack of western technology, were deemed more lowly. Europeans represented the highest point of evolution, diverse Asians and Indians fell in somewhere behind, and Africans brought up the rear, with Aboriginal and Papuan peoples allocated the very bottom.
>
> (Young 1976: 50)

The radical nature of Darwin's vision of humanity attracted a spectrum of thinkers wishing to call upon his work to imbue their own projects with evolutionary power:

> Imperialists, calling upon Darwin in defense of the subjugation of weaker races, could point to the 'Origin of Species', which had referred in its subtitle to 'The Preservation of Favoured Races in the Struggle for Life'. Darwin had been talking about pigeons, but the imperialists saw no reason why his theories should not apply to men.
>
> (Hofstadter 1955: 171)

Use of the discourse of Social Darwinist thought accords with a popular view of the inherent morality and civilised virtue of the 'white race'. There was a proliferation of popular pseudo-scientific treatises on the evolution of human types that had foundations in the physical analogies made to identity, character, intelligence, criminality and so on by phrenology, physiognomy and craniology. Shape and size of skull or other features, such as the Jewish nose (which was 'discovered' in 1711 (Mosse 1978)), came to be seen as measurable means of assessing an individual's position on an imagined genetic ladder.

Darwin developed his theory of natural selection to explain the evolving differences between species, but some of his contemporaries, including Herbert Spencer (1820–1903), an English philosopher who had recognised the selectivity and adaption of evolution before Darwin's *On the Origin of Species*, and Darwin's own cousin Francis Galton, used his ideas to promote philosophies such as Social Darwinism and eugenics. Spencer developed the principle of 'survival of the fittest' to explain changes in social organisation, arguing that societies grow from an initial militant phase into large organised social units, from 'an indefinite incoherent homogeneity, to a definite coherent heterogeneity' (Spencer 1860). Social Darwinism, similarly, was the theory that the principle of 'survival of the fittest' was at work in societies and classes as well as between species; leading to the elimination of weaker persons and groups through natural selection. Most Social Darwinists were, therefore, against improving the conditions of the poor. To let nature run its course was considered best, as a natural equilibrium would eventually result. The theory, in effect, justified poverty and social stratification by combining Darwinism with individualistic and liberal values. Social Darwinists maintained that certain groups of people were poorer than others and more likely to be exploited because they were 'less evolved' and therefore inferior.

In this period laissez-faire economics and the Industrial Revolution produced a large underpaid and exploited wage-earning class. Capitalists grew rich and the poor stayed poor. Industrial nations grew into large empires and exploited colonies to further fund industrial expansion and the growing desire for consumer products through the plunder of booty, or adventurer capitalism. In such a context, the concepts of 'struggle' and 'survival of the fittest' were convenient justifications for exploitation. Ideas of 'progress', which underpinned the drive towards greater industrialisation and scientific rationalisation, seemed analogous to 'progress' in evolution. However, the meanings embraced by the term were quite different. Industrialists and social reformers saw progress as the expansion of capitalism and the nation's productive capacity; Social Darwinists saw the improvement of the race; and biologists the selective adaptation of living things to their ecological environment.

However, the initial principle of eugenics, defined by Galton (1996), can be detected more directly in the work of Darwin, himself very influenced by the work of Thomas Malthus. According to Darwin, the mechanisms of natural selection are thwarted by human civilisation, which entails the desire to help the underprivileged, and hence civilisation would seem to be opposed to natural selection, which is responsible for the extinction of the weakest. According to eugenicists, this intervention could affect the natural balance, leading to an increase in individuals who were weaker genetically and who would have normally been eliminated through the process of evolution.

RACE AND CLASS

In the nineteenth century racial differences, which effectively drew species divides between people, were perceived among those of different social classes as well. Charles Tilly (1998) illustrates how the physical differences between members of the different classes were very significant and reinforced the belief widely held among the Victorians that race denoted social distinctions as well as differences of colour. As Malik observes: 'What we would now consider to be class or social distinctions were seen as racial ones' (1996: 81). It could be argued that the use of racial divisions emerged as a way of resolving the conflict between, on the one hand, the ideology of equality for all and universal reason and, on the other hand, facts of social inequality. We might think of Orwell's *Animal Farm* and the pig Napoleon's dictum: 'All animals are equal but some animals are more equal than others' (Orwell 1945). The development of a contradictory concept of 'race' stems from just this style of reasoning. Indeed, without such a concept, inequality might have been a much more bitter pill to swallow: 'Racial ideology was the inevitable product of the persistence of differences of rank, class and peoples in a society that had accepted the concept of equality' (Malik 2002: 5).

So it appears that race was readily associated with and used to legitimate social inequalities: where one lives, one's occupation, one's language, one's style of dress and so on. A Marxist interpretation challenges this, suggesting that there is no intrinsic or biological origin for these aspects of being. Race is meaningless unless it is turned to capital advantage in relationship to the means of production:

> A Negro is a Negro. Only under certain conditions does he become a slave. A cotton-spinning machine is a machine for spinning cotton. Only under certain conditions does it become capital. Torn away from these conditions, it is as little capital as gold is itself money, or sugar is the price of sugar.
>
> (Marx 1849)

In this view, race is seen to be a mask for other forms of social inequality and is reducible to socio-economic conditions (see also Chapter 4).

Class and race are intrinsically linked, and, as already shown, racial differences have been linked to status in a hierarchical system. However, class is not simply indexed to race in an objective way; colour is partly a question of performance rather than an irreducible and tangible marker of difference. As Goldberg (1992: 547) points out, there is the sense that if one behaves 'white', one is seen as white. So, race is composed of conventional discourses and if performers 'play white' then they are likely to be considered white. Furthermore, perceptions of class status seem to alter perceptions of colour. Gans suggests that in America darker skin has long been associated with lower socio-economic class (2005: 19). He goes on to argue that

> because skin color is socially constructed, it can also be reconstructed. Thus, when the descendants of the European immigrants began to move up economically and socially, their skins apparently began to look lighter to the whites who had come to America before them.
>
> (Gans 2005: 26)

However, this is not true of how white Americans perceive African Americans. African Americans are often prevented from the sort of mobility which allows them to become middle class, but if they break through the glass ceiling they are not perceived as more white. As to why this should be the case, Gans rejects ideas of racism and primordial fear of blackness, as other equally dark-skinned groups are not treated in the same way. Instead he argues that class-based explanations may hold the key. He suggests the possibility that African Americans are particularly stigmatised owing to the prevalence of their involvement in street crime and their much higher rates of arrest without cause. In addition he argues that, following the abolition of slavery, black mobility has been successively blocked:

> white exceptionalist treatment of African Americans is a continuing effect of slavery: They are still perceived as ex-slaves. Many hateful stereotypes with which today's African Americans are demonized have changed little from those used to dehumanize the slaves. (Black Hispanics seem to be equally demonized, but then they were also slaves, if not on the North American continent.)
>
> (Gans 2005: 26)

In the same vein Wacquant has argued forcefully that not only has mobility been blocked but there is a rationale for this which stems from the economic, symbolic and social subjugation of African Americans. Beginning with the institution of slavery, Wacquant argues that continuity of oppression is maintained by a 'historical sequence of "peculiar institutions" that have shouldered the task of defining and confining African Americans, alongside slavery, the Jim Crow regime, and the ghetto' (Wacquant 2001: 95) up to the present day this task is continued by hyper-ghettoisation and incarceration. In this way African Americans remain virtual slaves and are treated quite differently to other ethnicities in America.

It seems clear that the relationship between socio-economic status and race derives from unique historical and cultural conditions, and the situation for African Americans in the US is quite distinct from that of Pakistanis and Bangladeshis in the UK and North Africans in France. The British, it has been observed,

> may have indeed seen the peoples of their empire as alien, as 'other', as beneath them – to be lorded over and condescended to. But from another perspective, they also saw them as similar, as analogous, as equal and sometimes even as *better* than they were themselves.
>
> (Cannadine, quoted in Malik 2008: 142)

While rank had to be respected abroad, in the latter half of the nineteenth century those seen as members of an underclass in Britain – including poor whites – were increasingly recognised as racial inferiors, members of an alien caste (see Malik 2008: 142–3).

RACE AS CULTURE

Whether 'culture' is taken to mean a whole way of life or as signifying discursive practices through which hegemony is produced, it is integral both to the lived realities of race and the construction of boundaries, making it an intensely political concept. Race, from a culturalist viewpoint (such as that espoused by Stuart Hall), is a series of shifting and unfinished points of identification. While these may have some biological referents, they are quite removed from inheritable biological concepts of race. As Goldberg explains, 'In its non-biological interpretation, then, race stands for historically specific forms of cultural connectedness and solidarity' (Goldberg 1992: 551). It is here that the concept of ethnicity seems to overlap with this discourse of race. Culture has taken a central place in many areas of social science. There has been a marked 'cultural turn' away from structuralist paradigms, with their focus on macro-level forces of social change that obscure the more individual experiences of social actors. The cultural stuff that is contained within the lived experience of ethnic boundaries becomes the focus for a differentialist approach. However, culture is also prone to reification and correlates, at times, closely to more physical attributes. As Frederickson states, it is 'difficult in specific historical cases to say whether appearance or "culture" is the source of the salient differences because culture can be reified and essentialised to the point where it has the same deterministic effect as skin colour' (Frederickson 2002: 169).

ETHNICITY

According to the OED, 'ethnicity' derives from late Middle English (denoting a person not of the Christian or Jewish faith) via Latin *ethnicus*, Greek *ethnikos* 'heathen', from *ethnos* 'nation'. 'It was widely used in the senses of heathen, pagan or Gentile, until C19, when this sense was generally superseded by the sense of a racial characteristic' (Williams 1983: 119). However, in the modern era, ethnicity has come to be generally used as a term for collective cultural identity (while race categorises 'them' from outside, ethnicity is used for shared values and beliefs, the self definition of a group, 'us'). Van den Berghe drew the influential distinction between ethnicity as 'socially defined but on the basis of cultural criteria' whereas race is 'socially defined but on the basis of physical criteria' (Van den Berghe 1967: 9).

In western multicultural societies ethnicity has become the preferred term, used to avoid 'race' and its implications of a discredited 'scientific' racism. Ethnicity is generally taken to be a more inclusive and less objectifying concept indicating the constantly negotiated nature of boundaries between ethnic groups rather than the essentialism implicit in divisions of 'race'. The crossing of ethnic borders and encounters with those of different ethnic backgrounds is one of the most significant experiences in the formation of our identities. In the same vein Stuart Hall writes that:

To be English is to be your self in relation to the French and the hot-blooded Mediterranean, and the passionate, traumatized Russian soul. You go round the entire globe: when you know what everybody else is, then you are what they are not. Identity is always, in that sense, a structured representation which only achieves its positive through the narrow eye of the negative.

(Hall 1991: 21)

The way in which ethnic boundaries reflect often heartfelt values and ideas of maintaining national integrity is frequently portrayed through the use of every-day discourse often involving hackneyed images. There are racist veins running through jokes, urban legends and popular media. However, there is also evidence that ethnicity can be an instrumental category that is activated during times of external threat. It is a functional aspect of groups that allows them to compete, often using predetermined values and beliefs (self-affirming stereotypes and nega-tive stereotypes of the 'other' – the stoical 'Dunkirk spirit' of the Brits, as opposed to the supposed insouciance of the French) to strengthen their case.

Guyanese academic and author Brackette Williams points out that it is impor-tant to consider the way groups produce meaning and which signs and symbols they attach meaning to. Perhaps there is no final, definitive 'ethnicity', only specific readings of ethnic identity at specific times and places:

What is the use of these categories in studying the production of meaning and its relationship to power? For me, these terms and concepts are simply working tools. I'm not especially concerned with the ultimate meaning of 'ethnicity,' but rather with the reasons it keeps intervening as a category through which people shift kaleidoscopic kinds of meanings in relation to economic regimes and shifts in those regimes.

(Williams 1995: 1)

Charles Taylor highlighted the dangers of classification becoming a practice that has distorting and belittling consequences:

our identity is partly shaped by recognition or its absence, often by the misrec-ognition of others, and so a person or group of people can suffer real damage, real distortion, if the people or society around them mirror back to them a confining or demeaning or contemptible picture of themselves. Nonrecognition or misrecognition can inflict harm, can be a form of oppression, imprisoning someone in a false, distorted, and reduced mode of being.

(Taylor 1994: 25)

The way in which ethnic identity is ascribed is important to consider. Is it a shared characteristic, an attribute which is a defining feature to the 'group' itself, implying shared goals, or is it merely a feature seen as significant by an outsider? The implication of being a member of an ethnic group is that at some level one has an awareness of shared values and interests which could motivate collective action; that there is common purpose built around ethnic identity as an organising principle. What makes an ethnic category an ethnic group is the sense of 'we-feeling' and common interests in advancing the group's position in society through collective actions. In Guyana, for instance, the creolese term 'ahwe people' is a uniting term that designates a Guyanese identity, ostensibly across ethnic boundaries,[2] as in the following exhortation on the Guyanese Land of Six Peoples website – a plea to bring back the old practices before the ethnic unrest of the late 1960s:

> Is wha it gon tek fu bring back some a dem ting wha we talk bout – leh we tink, what about forming groups to plant up de land either in we backyard or in de back dam, forming a steel band, youth group(s), drama group(s), and so on.
>
> My people yu interested? Alright, afta dis village day leh we organse ahwe self and show dem big people dat ahwe can du ting like dem and even betta – Right! Leh we try.
>
> (Robinson 2004: 6–7)

The strong sense of communal identity in Robinson's statement shows the intentionality of ethnic identity. Here, a strong memory forms a potent exhortation for collective action across ethnic boundaries united by shared creolised language and culture. It shows how an 'imagined community' can perhaps mobilise a sense of identity and, possibly, action. In a similar vein, Jenkins (1996: 23) relates the Marxist concepts of 'class in itself' and 'class for itself' to this character of group identity. In other words, class can be a passive term that simply describes apparently common features, but when the class recognises its true nature in relation to the means of production then the identity is activated and class consciousness occurs. Similarly, ethnicity, like race, can be an imposed category or, conversely, it can become central to a revolutionary sense of identity in a struggle for independence or political power, or simply a recognition of shared experiences or attributes. This tension between externally prescribed and internally held identities is extremely political and may lead to conflicts, civil war and persecution or, conversely, it may be the catalyst to restore a sense of positive community.

Ethnicity, then, can be considered as a transient concept. It is not necessarily useful to try to pin down a final meaning. Rather, the different possible dimensions reflect the shifting terrain of social theories about difference. As we shall see, attempts to fix or reify terms such as 'ethnicity' are problematic as they reduce a complex, ever-changing phenomenon: to a static identity marker. Loomba highlights the fluidity of the concept:

The term 'ethnicity' has dominantly been used to indicate biologically and culturally stable identities, but Hall asks us to decouple it from its imperial, racist or nationalist deployment and to appropriate it to designate identity as a constructed process rather than a given essence. For Hall, the new black ethnicities visible in contemporary Britain are results of the 'cut-and-mix' processes of 'cultural *diaspora-ization*'.

(Loomba 1998: 176)

RACE AS ETHNICITY

In the concept of 'ethnorace', as suggested by Goldberg (1992), phenomena that are ostensibly separated by the terms 'ethnicity' and 'race' are liable at times to overlap. For example, 'Jews, Blacks, Hispanics, and Japanese in the United States may now be referred to as either race or ethnic group' (Goldberg 1992: 554). These categories may have different connotations, and ethnicity tends to be seen as less tendentious. Furthermore, more recent US data (2000 Census) defines ethnicity as the broader term, cutting across possible divisions of race:

In general, the Census Bureau defines ethnicity or origin as the heritage, nationality group, lineage, or country of birth of the person or the person's parents or ancestors before their arrival in the United States. People who identify their origin as Spanish, Hispanic, or Latino may be of any race. According to the revised Office of Management and Budget standards noted above, race is considered a separate concept from Hispanic origin (ethnicity) and, wherever possible, separate questions should be asked on each concept.

(US Census Bureau 2000)

The association of 'race' with scientific racism and Nazism and the lack of any evidence for basic biological differences in the genetic composition of 'races' have led to the cautionary use of inverted commas and the preference for the term 'ethnicity', which has become the acceptable term used for 'otherness' in multicultural societies such as Britain, Canada and Australia; and yet the term has different and sometimes contradictory meanings. As a means of categorisation, the term 'ethnicity' can be another manifestation of the dominant culture marginalising minority groups in its midst. In Australia, for example, over recent years the term 'ethnic' has become a generic noun for anyone of other than Anglo-Celtic origin (and is especially associated with Greeks and Italians, as the term 'wog'[3] becomes recognised as racist and unacceptable) – as in, 'He (or she) is ethnic'. This reification of terms is exactly why Hall (1996a) is concerned to reclaim the process of construction in the term 'ethnicity' and to avoid ready-made labels, indicating

that ethnic identity is a process of becoming, a question of intersubjective negotiation, not a final state. However, in popular culture as well as in 'official' documents ethnicity is conflated with race.

A prime example of this semantic confusion is demonstrated by the census
categories used in the UK and the USA, where there is often uncertainty about
the correct term to use to describe people. The term 'background' (as suggested by
Soysal 2000) could be argued to indicate the subject's loss of continuity, perhaps as
a member of one of many diasporic communities (see Chapter 8). A 'background'
might be an expression of an 'imagined community', a constant reminder that one
has been separated from one's past – or that the past is constantly being reshaped
by the present. Appropriate titles and forms of address change rapidly and, as can
be seen in the tables below, demonstrate that the politics of naming, the process of
determining ethnic identity, can be fraught with problems. There is a noticeable
lag between official forms used for the census and the social reality of people's self-
identifications.

The categories included in the 1991 UK Census (Table 2.2) gave an indication
of the difficulties inherent in categorising people. Forms like this telegraph certain
imagined identities, but they do not appear to actually be considering 'ethnicity'
– or at least, if they are, they do so in a most contradictory fashion. As Ratcliffe
points out, '"White" is clearly a pseudo-"racial" term based on phenotype, "Black-
Caribbean" also prioritizes phenotype and conflates a variety of island origins and
language groups … "Indian", for example, brings together under one label those
of many different religious, linguistic and regional backgrounds' (Ratcliffe 2004:
37–8). In short, there is little suggestion of the collective cultural identifiers that we
might consider to be included in ethnicity.

The changes between Tables 2.2, 2.3 and 2.4 illustrate the constant process of
reinventing and reshaping past identities and forming new, hybrid identities more

Table 2.2 Ethnic categories used in the 1991 UK Census

White	0	
Black Caribbean	0	
Black African	0	
Black other	0	(please specify)
Bangladeshi	0	
Chinese	0	
Indian	0	
Pakistani	0	
Asian other	0	(please specify)
Other	0	(please specify)

Table 2.3 Ethnic categories used in the 2001 UK Census

White	British
	Irish
	Other
Mixed	White/Black Caribbean
	White/Black African
	White/Asian
	Other
Black/Black British	Caribbean
	African
	Other
Asian/Asian British	Indian
	Pakistani
	Bangladeshi
	Other Asian
Chinese	
Other ethnic group	

Source: Office of National Statistics 2001

Table 2.4 Ethnic categories used in the 2001 UK Census, showing changes and additions

White	English/Welsh/Scottish/Northern Irish/British
	Irish
	Gypsy or Irish Traveller
	Other White
Mixed	White & Black Caribbean
	White & Asian
	White & Black African
	Other Mixed
Asian/Asian British	Indian
	Pakistani
	Bangladeshi
	Chinese
	Other Asian
Black/African/Caribbean/Black British	African
	Black Caribbean
	Other Black
Other ethnic group	Arab
	Any other ethnic group

Source: Office of National Statistics 2011

realistically aligned with current social experiences. However, the categories used are, again, problematic. Origins, allegiances to cultural heritage, questions of citizenship and belonging as well as the marked inter-ethnic relationships in the UK are all issues that underpin the decisions taken in constructing the changing census categories.

In the 2001 Census a range of more detailed categories was included. Although this marks an attempt to recognise the changing perceptions and dynamism within and between communities, there are still fundamental problems. The 'white' category was extended, breaking down the hegemonic and monolithic nature of whiteness into several categories. However, the ascriptive choices offered give little recognition of ethnic identity. These labels are by themselves unable to address questions of the multifaceted forms of cultural identification that cut across the borders of such broad categories. The category of 'black' also takes on a different meaning as a master category, arguably asserted as more inviolable. And 'Asian', too, is now recognised as a unifying category (but 'Chinese' was offered as a separate status/identity).

These decisions are, of course, intensely political. The self-identity of an 'Asian' within this bracket, for example, is extraordinarily complex, and is further defined by regional, ethnic and religious cleavages. One of the most significant shifts between the 1999 and 2001 Censuses is the inclusion of 'mixed' as a category. This raises the question of how a significant percentage of people chose to designate themselves in 1991, in the absence of such a category. The term 'mixed' could also be considered problematic as it implies that there are pure ethnicities. The preferred term today is 'dual heritage' (or 'multiple heritage').

In the 2011 Census further changes were made in the categories (see Table 2.4), again reflecting consultation with communities and showing the growth of several groups, with mixed-race households recorded at 12 per cent. Notable changes were the inclusion of a category for 'Gypsy or Irish Traveller' under the 'White' heading – an important change, as it recognises a group which have been marginalised in the past. In addition, the isolation of the category 'Chinese' ended, as this category was now moved to the 'Asian/Asian British' section. Similar fine-tuning was seen in the relabelling of 'Black or Black British' to 'Black/African/Caribbean/Black British'. A new category, 'Arab', was added under 'other ethnic group'. The 'British' category was relabelled as 'English/ Welsh/Scottish/Northern Irish/British'. The latter is important, and helps to negate the increasingly problematic presumption of Britishness as a distinct and unified ethnic category, particularly since the devolution of Scotland, Northern Ireland and Wales away from immediate Westminster control.[4] In addition, the complex hybrid identities that comprise the mix of Asian, Caribbean and African groups, which make up nearly 9 per cent of the UK's population, are gradually being recognised.

In the USA similar semantic struggles are being conducted. Brackette Williams (1995) discussed the consequences of the detailed semiotic process of naming. For members of the majority white culture who have, perhaps, had less cause to feel marginal, such concerns might seem surprising, but in the USA, as in many multi-ethnic nations, citizenship and identity are often struggles for equality and recognition in the face of political and economic marginalisation.

In the United States, when you look at categories like Asian American, African American, Hispanic American and then look at the category *black*, you notice that it remains one of the few uncapitalized categories. Part of the reason for people wanting to change this label is precisely to acquire that capitalization. That may seem trivial, but to have that capital, as opposed to being lowercased, is a way of speaking semiotically about status positioning. It does not create the position. It does not really alter status. But what one attempts to do is to reorient one's position in this struggle to attain that status one doesn't yet have. By capitalizing everybody, perhaps one puts everyone on the same terrain of struggle.

So you look at things like that and you think, how have categories changed? We now talk about Native Americans instead of Indians, but we don't hyphenate Native and American. What does acquiring a hyphen, acquiring a capitalization, altering it from a color category to a so-called cultural or transcontinental category, mean for the political positioning of that group? Does it alter that positioning? Is it archaeological? That is, is it a trace of what has already been accomplished? Or is it a signal for what will happen, for what one expects to happen in the future? If you want to be hyphenated in an environment where everyone else is not hyphenated, what is the motivation?

(Williams 1995)

This semiotic struggle indicates the power relationships that play out in the official naming of groups. It could reflect shifts between ideas of race (colour-based) and the ascendancy of ethnicity. However, the US Census has fewer racial categories than the UK version, and the typical breakdown of results are distinct in certain interesting ways from the British model, as shown in Table 2.5.

The striking fact about the categories shown in the table is that they are based on race and, in fact, are not far removed from some of the oldest forms of racial categorising (based on colour and other phenotypical attributes). Therefore, because Hispanics (who are a significant population in the USA, currently at 16.7 per cent) are not seen as a race they have previously not been effectively recorded in the Census, as it is assumed that 'ethnic' is the wider category and race is subsumed under this broader term. So it is possible for black people or Asians to also be Hispanic. This could be interpreted as a positive practice in the sense that it actively resists

Table 2.5 Typical breakdown of ethnic categories in the US Census

Population Counts for City X

Total population	500,000
One race – total	450,000
White	400,000
Black or African American	10,000
American Indian or Alaska Native	5,000
Asian	500
Native Hawaiian or Other Pacific Islander	100
Some other race	34,400
Two or more races – total	50,000

Source: US Census Bureau, Public Information Office, 2001

the conflation of race with ethnicity. Yet the legacy of meanings associated with restrictive racial categories meant that the second largest category after 'White' was 'Some other race' and 95 per cent of those who ticked this box were Hispanic.

Interestingly, there appears to be an intention to change the US Census to give Hispanics their own category: the 2010 Census included an experimental alternative questionnaire to gather information about the preferences among the Hispanic population for expressing their identity. Whether gaining a separate racial identity will be perceived as a positive affirmation is difficult to gauge, however. Hispanics are the fastest-growing population in America, but there is uncertainty about this move to race and some are uneasy: 'There is no unanimity on what any of this stuff means,' according to Angelo Falcon, director of the National Institute for Latino Policy and co-chair of a coalition of Latino advocacy groups that recently met with Census officials. 'Right now, we're very comfortable with having the Hispanic (origin) question. ... Hispanic as a race category? I don't think there's any consensus on that' (El Nasser 2013).

However, while selection on the basis of race for Hispanics may be perceived as giving recognition to the struggle for parity with other groups, it also maintains the power and credence of what are arguably anachronistic and divisive terms. The history of such categorisation in the USA has a darker past. Kertzer and Arel remind us that under the 'one-drop rule', which persisted in the southern states until the 1960s, even one black ancestor determined one's identity as black: such a recording of race in one's birth certificate 'could be used to discriminate against blacks and Indians' and was 'often used in Southern states to bar individuals of racially-mixed ancestry from marrying Whites' (Davis 1991: 57 in Kertzer and Arel 2002: 4). Kenneth Prewitt, scholar and census researcher, suggests that 'We ought to get rid of the race question and go to national origin ... That's what the country needs – not these 18th-century old race groups' (Prewitt 2013, quoted in El Nasser 2013).

Another contentious issue which has been discussed extensively in the USA is the lack of recognition of 'mixed' categories, although in reality the USA has very significant mixed (or dual heritage) populations:

> Between 1970 and 1990, the number of multiracial children under age 18 has quadrupled to 2 million according to the U.S. Census Bureau. That number will grow as interracial marriages continue to soar. There were 1.4 million inter-racial couples in 1995, a 114% increase since 1980, the Census Bureau said.
>
> (El Nasser 1997: 1)

The unwillingness to utilise a category that would affirm people's mixed or dual identities is puzzling (in 2000 the US Census Bureau gave some ground on this issue by permitting individuals to mark several boxes to indicate their mix of eth-nicities), although by all accounts the decision may be motivated by political resist-ance on the part of African Americans, who may see a significant 'mixed' category as diminishing the resources which they as a group might receive.

CHAPTER SUMMARY

Race and ethnicity, like other cultural terms that are central to social identity, are especially complex and difficult to define. Some scholars and census takers might insist on separating the terms and seeing race as a very different category based on physical and objective differences, hinting at a nature–culture divide between the two terms. Pieterese has shown the changing and expedient manner in which boundaries have been drawn over time to include and exclude different groups in Europe, and Goldberg's work has traced discursive changes that reflect social and political realities in different historical periods. While race-makers categorised human types and sug-gested sharply demarked physical differences, there was always dispute about where and how to draw boundaries. Forms of categorisation are linked to implicit ideas about hierarchy, status and power and hence the use of language to denote difference is intrinsically political.

EXERCISE 2.1

1   When you look at the census forms (Tables 2.2–2.4), do you feel confident that your identity is adequately captured? Why? Why not?
2   Which category allowed you the most approximate identification? Why?

3 What are the implications of the category 'white' and 'black other'?

4 Prior to the inclusion of 'mixed race' as a census category, how might a mixed-race individual have designated themselves?

5 What do the forms suggest about the manner in which such categories have come into being?

6 What is your regional identity? How defined is it? Are you aware of a distinct cultural history, regional dialect or accent? Do you choose to identify or dis-identify with these? Why?

7 What role does class play in regional identities?

8 Discuss images of regional identities (e.g. of Geordies) in magazines (such as *Viz*'s Basher Bacon, etc. and in cartoons like 'Andy Capp'). Do such caricatures capture anything enduring?

9 Consider the speculative comments made by Brackette Williams. What differences do you think would occur between the USA and the UK in terms of the drawing of ethnic boundaries and the sense of identity experienced in each country?

10 Compare the categories in the UK Census with those in the US Census.

11 What might be the reasoning in the USA for not using a 'mixed' category on a national basis? (Several states have instituted this, but it has been resisted nationally.)

12 Consider other semiotic forms of expression of citizenship and nation. How do the following reflect identity?
(a) flags
(b) coins/notes

13 Consider words that we commonly use to designate other peoples, such as Asian, Arab, Caribbean, European. These terms generalise and obscure differences. When does it become necessary to use more specific terms and why? What is the possible impact on your identity to be subsumed under an umbrella term?

14 What signs are there today that there is still some belief and support for eugenics or eugenic-type policies? Are such policies always wrong?

15 The strand of evolutionist biology that was applied to Social Darwinism has survived today in certain theoretical ideas and principles. What are they, and do they have any credence?

16 There is, as Goldberg points out, the sense that race is composed of conventional discourses and if the performer 'plays white' then he/she is likely to be considered white. Discuss this observation and relate it to situations of adaptation to the dominant culture. Are visible differences partly or wholly negated by impression management? (You might relate this to Indians who take on the 'dreadfully English' stereotypes or to other ethnic minority groups. Such behaviours are frequently parodied on TV – consider *Goodness Gracious Me*, *The Kumars at Number 42* and, more recently, *Citizen Khan*.)

Further reading

For a discussion of the political consequences of naming from the point of view of Asians in Britain, Tariq Modood's 1994 article 'Political Blackness and British Asians' (*Sociology* 28(4): 859–76) captures some of the dynamics around Asian identities and their resistance to being subsumed under the political banner of 'black' – what Stuart Hall has dubbed 'strategic essentialism'.

The dilemma of US Asians' naming was reflected interestingly in Jhumpa Lahiri's novel *The Namesake* (London: Perennial, 2004), in which the second-generation protagonist Gogol Ganguli seeks the story behind his father's choice of his name. This was also an engaging 2002 film.

Kenan Malik's work has been referred to several times in this chapter and his 2009 text *Strange Fruit* (Oxford: Oneworld Books) is a source of fascinating social historical and scientific discussions about how we understand race.

Two interesting and critical texts which examine the role of census in the arena of ethnic identification are David I. Kertzer and Dominique Arel Kertzer (eds) (2002) *Census and Identity: The Politics of Race, Ethnicity, and Language in National Censuses* (Cambridge and New York: Cambridge University Press) and K. Prewitt (2013) *What Is Your Race? The Census and our Flawed Efforts to Classify Americans* (Princeton, NJ: Princeton University Press).

One of the great sociological texts with detailed substantive work is Charles Tilly's 1998 *Durable Inequality* (Berkeley, CA: University of California Press).

Richard Jenkins' *Rethinking Ethnicity* (2nd edn, 2008) has a great deal of relevance here and Jenkins' analysis of the nominal and the virtual is intrinsic to this work.

Notes

1 Consider the example of the treacherous 'Welsh Not', a piece of wood that had to be carried by a child at school if caught using the Welsh language. They could, though, pass it on to children who were heard to speak Welsh, so it encouraged betrayal as the last child carrying the hated object at the end of the day was the one to be punished.

2 However, while many Guyanese have elements of creolese it is doubtful that this would be genuinely perceived as a plea for unity; it could equally be interpreted as a rallying call to beleaguered African-Guyanese.

3 A term used to denote Greek/Italian Australians. An interesting phenomenon is the re-claiming of this derogatory term by the Greek/Italian communities; this has been seen in several popular TV and stage comedies, such as *Wog Boy* and *Wogs Out of Work*.

4 Of course, censuses do not recognise the defined regionalism in many nations. It has been argued that 'more people can define themselves as Londoners, Brummies, Mancunians or Geordies first, and English second. Scots often divide on east–west lines in terms of instinctive local identities' (from a speech by MP Barbara Roche, 2002).

CHAPTER 3

Colonialism

Invisible histories

The settler makes history and is conscious of making it. And because he constantly refers to the history of his mother country, he clearly indicates that he himself is the extension of that mother-country. Thus the history which he writes is not the history of the country which he plunders but the history of his own nation in regard to all that she skims off, all that she violates and starves.

(Fanon 1967: 40)

How can you measure progress if you don't know what it costs and who has paid for it? How can the 'market' put a price on things – food, clothes, electricity, running water – when it doesn't take into account the REAL cost of production?

(Arundhati 2002: 40)

BOX 3.1 GUYANA: 'LOOK WHAT THEY DONE TO THE MOTHER'

Indian–Guyanese bus driver commenting on the defaced statue of Queen Victoria in Georgetown (conversation on a minibus, Georgetown, recorded 15 April 1991).

Figure 3.1 Defaced statue of Queen Victoria, Georgetown, Guyana

Continued.

BOX 3.1 GUYANA: 'LOOK WHAT THEY DONE TO THE MOTHER' (CONTINUED)

BUS DRIVER (EAST INDIAN): See see, thas how this country run like. Queen Victoria they pushed her to the back of the Promenade Gardens.
SS: They chucked her out?
DRIVER: Queen Victoria ... the mother.
SS: Yeah I heard.
DRIVER: Queen Victoria who gave us this country ... its independence ... put her at the back.
SS: Desmond Hoyte[1] pulled her out again?
DRIVER: *Not Desmond Hoyte!* No. Not Desmond Hoyte ... the people. is the people. When they elect a new mayor for this town, the people call on the Mayor, 'Why have you got the Queen, the statue at the back of ... Burnham[2] used to go shit on her. This government just trying to squeeze this nation, they trying to see this nation wasting ... they just going over the world and just asking for aid and help and all them ting. What are they doing with our own resource?
SS: They've got their export market haven't they?
DRIVER: We main crop is sugar and rice ... and it more expensive than the stuff they bring in. They exporting sugar ... tha fair?
SS: No it's crazy.
DRIVER: The rice ... long brown rice, the polished rice ... they exporting It and they giving we to eat the white rice ... and the low grade of rice ... low grade.
SS: Yeah.
DRIVER: You know like rice umm we use to feed umm pigs. Yes pig, this the food we eating, majority food we eat is fertilizer, fertilizer!

---

[1] Desmond Hoyte was the African-Guyanese President at the time of the recording (1991).
[2] Forbes Burnham was the African-Guyanese President from 1965–85.

This brief excerpt from an interview invokes some of the dynamics of a country that was facing an economic crisis and was divided along ethnic lines. It seemed surprising that the broken, stony face of an old statue could so quickly call up political mismanagement and profligate trade policies, or that the treatment of a statue could evoke, not colonial exploitation, but from the bitter inter-ethnic struggles which preceded independence. But in the divisive post-colonial context of countries like Guyana daily life is fraught with such tensions. The

Indian-Guyanese had economic power largely through holdings in agriculture, whereas the African-Guyanese (at the time of recording) held political power and dominated the public sector. The reference to the damaged statue is a story, almost a social and political allegory, that I heard from several Indians: when the African-Guyanese leader Forbes Burnham finally achieved office, one of his first acts was the near-ritual desecration of this colonial icon.

Calling the statue 'the mother' surprised me, as it certainly didn't mark an especially benevolent period of British colonial rule. But it must be remembered that the early 1990s were a politically tense period in Guyana. Since independence the country had become increasingly polarised along ethnic lines and the economy was facing desperate levels of inflation, making it one of the poorest in the western hemisphere. The Indian-Guyanese had been denied access to the political system and an African-Guyanese regime hung on to power, despite suspicions of repeated electoral fraud. Therefore the resurrection of the battered statue held all sorts of complex meanings for the speaker about a sense of origins and the fractured, diasporic identities of a post-colonial setting. Interestingly, the stage-managed calm that could be witnessed in public places when both groups were together quickly dispersed when the spatial boundaries were redrawn (as in this case, in which an Indian conductor and driver were alone with me in a minibus).

CONSTRUCTION OF THE COLONIAL SUBJECT

The division of the world between a handful of European empires, which began to unravel only after the Second World War, has had the most profound impact on human groups the world over. The advantage this pillage provided the western nations was a springboard for their relatively superior economic and commercial power right up to the present day. Yet the records of what really took place and the way each generation has been taught about colonialism have rendered it part of an invisible history, an exercise in collective amnesia on a monumental scale.

SLAVERY

When I visited Liverpool in 1984, it was a defiant Militant-led Labour stronghold. Derek Hatton was making a stand against the rate-capping imposed by Thatcher's government. The streets were covered in litter; basic services were breaking down; the dockers, the miners and other heavy industries were against the wall or had already succumbed. In a charity shop I found a late-nineteenth-century encyclopaedia, and under 'Liverpool' it mentioned that by the mid 1800s this western seaboard port was one of the wealthiest cities in the world. I did not quite believe what I had read, but Liverpool's imposing waterfront buildings told a different story. This prosperity, at its pinnacle (around 1900), meant that the city was regarded as the 'second city' of the British Empire (Belchem 2006), a status that resulted from the city's central role in the Atlantic slave trade.

On the eve of the millennium, the Mayor of Liverpool made a public and unreserved apology for the city's role in the Atlantic slave trade.

'This was the proudest moment of my political life,' says Lord Mayor Joseph A Devaney. The resolution stated that while the city had been bequeathed a rich diversity of people and cultures, learning, architecture and financial wealth, the human suffering had been obscured. 'The untold misery which was caused has left a legacy which affects Black people in Liverpool today.' The Council expressed its shame and remorse for the city's role in 'this trade in human misery'.

(Henderson 2000: 1)

Indeed, at the height of the slave trade, Liverpool, along with Bristol and London, was the main British port involved with the slave trade. As many as 500 ships sailed from Liverpool in the years 1785–1787, collecting African slaves to trade in the Americas and bringing back produce from the plantations. This so-called triangular trade was one of the reasons for Liverpool's immense growth. When walking through the city today it is hard to believe that many of the grand, monumental buildings were built on the proceeds of the slave trade. On 23 August, for the last thirteen years since the mayor's apology, Liverpool has marked Slavery Remembrance Day, organised by the Museum of Slavery (McSweeney 2012).

The transportation of thousands of people packed into specially layered ships' holds, in conditions that beggar belief, resulted in countless deaths. There are not many accounts of the conditions from the point of view of the slaves themselves, but one famous account has survived, that of Olaudah Equiano, who wrote in 1789:

The white people looked and acted, as I thought, in so savage a manner; for I had never seen among my people such instances of brutal cruelty. The closeness of the place, and the heat of the climate, added to the number in the ship, which was so crowded that each had scarcely room to turn himself, almost suffocated us. [...] The air soon became unfit for respiration, from a variety of loathsome smells, and brought on a sickness among the slaves, of which many died. The wretched situation was again aggravated by the chains, now unsupportable, and the filth of the necessary tubs, into which the children often fell, and were almost suffocated. The shrieks of the women, and the groans of the dying, rendered the whole a scene of horror almost inconceivable.

(Equiano 2005: 58)

Slavery existed centuries before the concept of race was invented, back more than 4,000 years into antiquity. Drescher agrees that people of all physical variations have been enslaved at different times, and yet there is no evidence that 'before the last four centuries ... any society invented race ideology as a reason for enslaving others' (Drescher and Engerman 1998: 322). More than thirteen centuries before Aristotle, the Hammurabi Code in Babylonia[1] defined a concept of chattel slavery that served as a way of classifying the lowliest and most dependent workers in society: 'slaves could be sold or inherited; the same features would reappear through the ages in scores of cultures' (ibid.: ix).

Slavery has always been problematic: the attempts to reduce human beings to the state of beasts of burden have never been easily achieved. Aristotle believed it possible to distinguish 'the natural slave' as being similar to other domestic animals for the service of their human masters. The very fact of their subservience – he believed – was evidence of their natural role. The slave trade was barbaric and treated people as mere objects that could be used and disposed of without any danger of moral outrage. The African trade vied for by European powers (the Portuguese, Dutch and French, followed by dominance by Britain) led to the systematic pillage of much of Africa and, as argued by many scholars (see e.g. Rodney 1972), to the underdevelopment of the continent.

By the seventeenth century the foundations were being laid for a racial ideology in New World colonies: 'as the English were institutionalising a form of slavery for which they had no precedents, they were also constructing the ideological components of race' (Drescher and Engerman 1998: 322). The linkage of these two historical occurrences gave rise to a new form of servitude known as racial slavery. However, both slavery and race were incompatible with the Christian principles and social values espoused by the English colonists. The result was that slavery and the idea of race functioned to reinforce each other in complex ways. These colonists were driven by an insatiable desire for land and the labour to work it – both primary sources of wealth. Enormous profits could be turned and fortunes were made across the Caribbean.

The use of indigenous peoples as slaves was largely unsuccessful. They had no immunity to Old World diseases, often escaped as they had intimate knowledge of the land, or died from overwork. Therefore,

[t]he decision to restrict chattel slavery to those of African ancestry was a pragmatic one. Africans were visibly different; they were on alien soil with no familiar places to go even if they escaped; and they had no powerful political supporters or allies in the international Christian community to object to their enslavement.

(ibid.: 323)

This practical set of differences was expanded and overwritten as the realities of colonial life evolved. 'Laws forbidding intermarriage between "racial" groups, laws increasingly restricted the freedom of slaves, and practices prohibiting the education and training of slaves exacerbated the cultural differences between slaves and free whites' (ibid.). There were laws against interracial marriage (see McCaskell 1994: 11). Any white person who married a 'negro, mulatto or Indian' was liable to permanent banishment from the colony. The Carolina Law of 1741 sought to prevent an 'abominable Mixture and spurious issue' by levying a prohibitive fine against any white person who married 'an Indian, Negro Mustee or Mulatto Man or woman, or any Person of Mix Blood, to the Third Generation' (Vaughan 1982: 995).

Black slaves had no human rights. Casual killings of black people became legal by the mid-seventeenth century, interracial marriage became punishable by law in 1705 and, six years earlier, 'white' became a recognised racial category in law: 'by 1705 Africans were legally removed from the family of man and relegated to the status of property. Africans came to be known as black (or Negro), black and slave became synonymous, and whiteness was born' (Santas 1998).

Slavery allowed ruthless treatment of those under its yoke, colonial regimes dealt with slaves and other subjugated people with unrelenting barbarity: the conditions in the slave houses were infrahuman. Casual murder, rape and executions were commonplace. Further into Equiano's account he relates the conditions on the Southern States plantations, in which cruel, dispiriting conditions prevailed:

> I have often asked many of the men slaves (who used to go several miles to their wives, and late in the night, after having been wearied with a hard day's labour) why they went so far for wives, and why they did not take them of their own master's negro women, and particularly those who lived together as household slaves? Their answers have ever been – 'Because when the master or mistress choose to punish the women, they made the husbands flog their own wives, and that they could not bear to do.' Is it surprising that usage like this should drive the poor creatures to despair, and make them seek a refuge in death from those evils which render their lives intolerable – while
> With shudd'ring horror pale, and eyes aghast
> They view their lamentable lot, and find
> No rest.
>
> (Equiano 2005: 107)

As Drescher and Engerman point out (1998: xiv) 'the basic "problem of slavery" [...] arises from the irreducible humanness of the slave'. Drescher gives examples of behaviour on the part of slaves that is contrary to the typical notions of them as broken and subservient to the end: 'throughout history slaves have run away, outwitted their masters, rebelled, murdered, raped, stolen, divulged plots for insurrection, and helped protect the state from external danger' (ibid.). Perhaps the most famous rebellion was that of the black Jacobins and the formation of the first free black state in Haiti (then San Domingo) in 1791. The troops of Toussaint l'Ouverture defeated first the Spanish and the British, overcame internal insurrection and finally held off the Napoleonic French army of 20,000 by brilliant military strategy before Toussaint was finally captured (see Beard 1970; James 1963). It is this extraordinary act of resistance which is commemorated every year in Liverpool, being chosen by UNESCO as a reminder that enslaved Africans played a major part in their own liberation (UK Government 2012).

ENLIGHTENMENT VIEWS

As discussed in the previous chapter, the Enlightenment was an era in which profound consideration was given to understanding human difference. Released in part from the dogmas of Christianity and the rigid world order, speculation grew about origins, ideas of reason, ethics and morality. Some of the themes that emerged had certainly been visited before. Was society natural? The Ancient Greeks, in the fourth century BC, had already considered this question but in the Enlightenment more questions arose about the nature of human societies and their various forms and cultural practices and about whether universals of human nature existed that dictated human relations and the structure of society. Did societies evolve naturally and organically or were they the result of human agency?

Several historical encounters had already been influential in these debates. Columbus characterised natives from some islands that he visited, who were receptive to Christianity, as 'simple children of nature', while other natives, who had met them with hostility and resistance, were seen as 'cannibals' who should be subdued or exterminated. This early nature/culture dichotomy is perhaps the beginning of that Manichean divide that was further elaborated during the Enlightenment. Rousseau's idealised conception of the 'noble savage' was an intermediate position between the dehumanising effects of culture and the rawness of nature. On the other hand, the growth of interest in cataloguing human types, along with species of plants and animals, eventually led to suggestions that certain human types were more evolved than others and had more claims to full human status than others.

Two hundred years earlier, in 1550, another landmark debate took place in the city of Valladolid between the Spanish jurist Sepulveda and the Dominican friar Bartolome de Las Casas, who had witnessed the killing and enslaving of native people in South America under Pizarro earlier that century and who had been arguing for the freeing of indigenous people since 1519. Sepulveda argued, using Aristotle's conception of 'natural slavery', that all Indians were 'non-rational beings' and hence should be forcibly enslaved. They were, he said, 'barbarous and inhuman peoples abhorring all civil life, customs and virtue' (Fredrickson 1981: 36–7). On the contrary, argued Las Casas, they 'possessed reason and a capacity for civil life' (Frederickson 2002: 36–7). Although Las Casas won the debate, the support of Pope Paul III and the eventual agreement from Emperor Charles to abolish Indian slavery in 1542, the ruthlessness of colonialism, which brought hundreds of tons of gold and silver to Europe, had enabled the development of a new source of labour in Africa.

Most European societies were involved in African slavery in one way or another. And, in general, the image that most Europeans had of Africans was that of slaves, of subordinate and powerless peoples. Similarly, their knowledge and understanding of Native Americans was distorted by the facts of their conquest and apparent demise. By then it was widely accepted that the indigenous peoples of the Americas were weak savages who had to be conquered to make way for a superior civilisation. The scholars and scientists of Europe could hardly have attitudes towards these peoples or make judgements about them that were uninfluenced by these social and political realities.

Some Enlightenment philosophers were staunchly opposed to the exploitation of other nations, but even those, such as Baron de Montesquieu (1689–1755) an early opponent of slavery, showed signs of ambivalence: 'It is impossible for us to suppose these creatures to be men, because, allowing them to be men, a suspicion would follow, that we ourselves are not Christian' (Montesquieu 1748: XV Ch. 5). Montesquieu, an ardent opponent of the evils of despotism, highlights here the thinking of the age; and this type of sophistry stems from guilt at not having opposed such a pernicious trade. Despite this example of expedient reasoning, he launched bitter attacks against slavery in his writings. However, to permit those subjugated as slaves to live as fully human presented a threat, an anomaly that undermined the progressive reasoning of the time. Despite the high ideals of reason and liberty, the Atlantic slave trade was in full swing at the time of the Enlightenment and some philosophers and thinkers were slave-owners or profited from slavery (John Locke, for example, was Secretary of the Board of Trade and Plantations). Certainly the scholars associated with Enlightenment thought were working in the eighteenth century, a time when the African Atlantic slave trade was reaching its peak, and hence the perception many had of Africans was as valuable commodities from which enterprising colonists could realise enormous profits in a very short time.

However, the introduction of plantation slavery did not originate, as Hall (1980: 58) reminds us, in notions of racial superiority. Rather, it is more useful to consider

how slavery (the product of specific problems of labor shortage and the organization of plantation agriculture – supplied, in the first instance, by nonblack, indigenous labor, and then by white indentured labor) produced those forms of juridical racism which distinguish the epoch of plantation slavery.

(Hall 1980: 58)

To their credit, many Enlightenment thinkers accepted the principle of the unity of the human species, if for no other reason than adherence to scriptures. Most also expressed a belief in the potential improvement of so-called 'savage' peoples in accord with Enlightenment ideas about environmentally induced change and human progress. Differences were explained as the result of environmental factors that had led to the degeneration into savagery. However, this state could be risen above, as is clear from one of the first novels, Daniel Defoe's *Robinson Crusoe* (1719), which examines the trials of the castaway Crusoe, who is restored to a state of nature yet retains his cultural training and the tools of civilised endeavour salvaged from the ship wreck. Despite being stripped of the external trappings of culture he is able to construct a microcosm of western culture based on his reasoning. His meeting with the 'savage' whom he names Friday is a confrontation between the bearer of western culture and one living in 'a state of nature'. However, Crusoe acknowledges that God 'has bestow'd upon them the same Powers, the same Reason, the same Affections […] and all the Capacities of doing Good […] that he has given to us' (Defoe 2001: 165). Indeed, the thrust of Enlightenment thinking embraced the universality of reason and sociability and the existence of a common human nature. There was a notion that, owing to local conditions, these finer sensibilities had 'degenerated'. Yet, at the same time, *Robinson Crusoe* is a blueprint for the colonial spirit as Crusoe recreates the island as his own personal fiefdom and a working economic system (see Said 1993).

Despite the vehement resistance to slavery that existed in some quarters, the collusion of many with it ensured that it became one of the largest and most significant movements of people ever experienced, in which it is estimated between 12 and 20 million people were transported to the New World colonies (there is an ongoing debate about the actual numbers see e.g. Sherwood 2007: 3) and many of these died during the journey there. What is perhaps less well known, however, is the effect that the wealth thereby generated had on the economic prosperity of western countries, making the Industrial Revolution possible.

RATIONALISATION OF COLONIAL EXPLOITATION

One of the most striking events in the recent history of mankind is the expansion throughout the entire world of most European peoples. It has brought about the subjugation and, in some instances, the disappearance of virtually every people regarded as backward, archaic, or primitive. The colonial movement of the nineteenth century was the most important in magnitude, the most fraught with consequences, resulting from this European expansion. It overturned in a brutal manner the history of the peoples it subjugated.

(Balandier 1974: 34)

Yet this brutal exploitation was by no means the only example of empire building. Wallerstein's world-systems theory suggested that there have certainly been capitalist-type colonial powers from the earliest period of human civilisation, of which examples include the ancient empires of Egypt, Rome, China, Mughal India, feudal Russia and Ottoman Turkey. The difference may be one of global scale and scope. The scale of upheaval that occurred between 1500 and 1850, however, was unprecedented. The scale of colonisation reached its apogee in the nineteenth century, when the 'Great Migration' took place in which over 40 million people moved to the new colonies.

The so-called 'New Imperialism', from c.1870 to 1918, was brought about by the Industrial Revolution, which created large surpluses of European capital and high demand for raw materials. Nationalism and Social Darwinist thought provided a powerful rationale for this expansionist movement. The scientific evidence for the concept of natural selection appeared to give credence to the earlier and less empirically based notion of 'survival of the fittest'. There was an emphasis placed on the moral superiority of the exploiters and the obligations of the 'white man's burden', as popularised by Kipling. These fuelled the spirit of nationalism. It was also politically prestigious to have colonies. England, France, Germany, Belgium, Portugal and the Netherlands made the largest additions to their colonial domains during this period. Chineweizu makes the point forcefully that the success of the western nations, however, came at a very high price for the rest of the world:

In the case of the West, the human price of western industrial prosperity was paid by other peoples over several centuries. Among these other peoples must be reckoned the aboriginal peoples of the Americas, Australia, and New Zealand, who were exterminated to make room for European immigrants; the millions of black Africans who slaved for over three centuries in the Americas, furnishing forced labour for the capital formation that powered the rise of British, French and United States industrialism; and the millions of peasant immigrants from Eastern Europe whose cheap labour paid for American industrialization after her civil war.

(Chinweizu 1987: 425)

As argued earlier the change from more inclusive Enlightenment thinking which embraced ideas of universal human kind was at least in part prompted by the need to explain the growing inequalities in rapidly expanding European cities. Even today many of the stories of ethnic divisions that confront us around the world are the consequences of historical events in which a few European countries took forcible possession of nine-tenths of the globe and ruled and exploited countries of Africa, Asia, the Americas and Australia for around 500 years. Yet today it is a history that is dimly remembered in the west or actively resisted and contended when it seems likely to paint an inglorious picture of a nation's history. Colonisation has meant the erasure of histories and cultures, and the forced removal of indigenous people from their lands, and the introduction of mass labour force to power the empire's industrial age (through slavery, and later indentureship) to generate wealth for European elites.

The colonising of America and Australia was achieved partly through the use of convict labour to build the infrastructure of the new colonies: railway systems in America, timber and agriculture in Australia. The powerful impetus to colonise new lands and passivise the indigenous peoples was rationalised through several dominant discourses. The influential writings of John Knox, Comte Arthur de Gobineau and Thomas Arnold claimed to prove the inherent superiority of the 'white races'. This superiority was the reason for European technological advances and colonial domination. Such views pre-dated but helped set the agenda for later Social Darwinist thought, reinforcing a popular view of the inherent morality and civilised virtue of the 'white race' attained through evolutionary struggle. There was a proliferation of popular pseudo-scientific treatises on the evolution of human types, with a variety of uses being made of biological evolution. Some simplified the idea to the 'survival of the fittest'. Others believed that what occurred among species in the animal kingdom was identical to the process which took place in humans, considering that white Protestant Europeans had evolved much further and faster than other 'races'.

Herbert Spencer (whose notion of 'survival of the fittest' was discussed in Chapter 2) had suggested that human society was engaged in constant evolutionary struggle in which the fittest – who happened to be the most successful and affluent – were able to dominate. It was a vision which blamed the victims of illness and poverty, seeing them as inherently unequipped to prosper and hence an enlightened society ought to weed out its unfit members, permitting them to die off so as not to weaken the racial stock. This idea eventually led to a variety of practices and beliefs. For example, 'Nordic racism', based on eugenic principles, became very influential in the USA as well as in Europe. The American Breeders Association, a lobbying organisation, published an influential journal that was sent to thousands of homes. It 'contained a mixture of short, readable articles and reviews on a variety of topics, from plant and animal breeding to calls for sterilization of delinquents and racist immigration laws' (McCaskell 1994: 14). Largely owing to pressure from this association US immigration policy was changed in 1924 to allow in only northern Europeans, or so-called 'Nordics'. American eugenic ideas, based upon ideas of the Nordic type, were widely influential and there is evidence that Hitler himself held the US programme in high esteem. Eugenics promulgated the belief that the unfit transmit their undesirable characteristics; however, through a controlled breeding programme, the racial stock could be protected from the degeneration that resulted from the transmission of these 'undesirable' characteristics.

As a consequence of these myths the early settlers frequently discounted the indigenous populations as less than human, as part of nature to be vanquished. On the early maps of the Antipodes Australia was labelled '*terra nullius*', meaning 'the empty land', indicating that Aboriginal people were seen as having no prior claim over the land. Where indigenous groups were not systematically slaughtered, they were removed from their lands and taken into the custody of missionaries (these regimes often had the same effects as active genocide). A mixture of paternalism and evangelism has meant that, up until the 1960s, Aboriginal people were denied the right to vote; they have been granted recognition as being the prior inhabitants of Australia only since the 1990s. In 1992 a landmark court case, the Mabo Ruling, overturned centuries of legal refusal to grant this recognition. After a protracted legal struggle lasting nearly ten years, Eddie Mabo and four other Torres Strait Islanders were able to establish ownership of their land prior to annexation by the state of Queensland. The implications of this ruling shattered the legal fiction of *terra nullius* – the idea that Australia had been an empty land before white colonists arrived.

Despite this affirmation, recent legal constraints have placed a heavy onus on Aboriginal people to give exhaustive evidence in court of their prior ownership of land. As Geoff Clark (2002) said, reflecting on another land-ownership case that had been lost:

> the test of a continuous connection to land since occupation is onerous and unjust. The effects of the forced removal of our people from traditional country make it impossible for us to have their rights recognised. The mere closing of a pastoralist's gate can sever the connection with traditional lands.
>
> (Clark 2002)

There is also a very prevalent romanticism regarding native peoples: in particular, the notion of their closeness to nature and their mythical status as being untainted by the artifices of civilisation. The 'romantic' has the same paternalistic, passivising effect as the directly racist, but under the guise of extolling their innocence as child-like or closer to nature. Romanticism, from Rousseau and through the Romantic literature of the nineteenth century, has exerted an influence that is still prevalent today in beliefs about romantic and primordial ethnic stereotypes. It is a small step to argue for genetic inferiority if one believes in a primordial theory of ethnicity or race.

Anthropology seems to present an objective account of people, yet frequently functions, unwittingly perhaps, to reinforce attitudes of romantic or directly racist discourses. Early anthropology served merely to catalogue the 'primitive' rituals and to collect artefacts and could be seen as another link in the chain of colonial domination. The discourse of the popular television documentary about these 'others' serves as a kind of armchair museum of exotic, primitive and colourful (*National Geographic* style) imagery in a manner not dissimilar to the genre of nature programmes. In the 1970s and 1980s such programmes included *Face Values*, *Millennium* and *Strangers Abroad*, among others. More recently, the BBC 2 series *Tribe*, in which ex-marine Bruce Parry visited and lived in some of the world's most remote communities for a month at a time, received mixed views from anthropologists, who found it largely superficial and lacking in any social and cultural context (see Caplan 2005). This vision of tribal societies typically focused on their most exotic and obviously extreme aspects: cannibalism, shamanic drug experiences, bodily adornment, use of lip plates, the piercing of the septum with thorns and penis inversion. Parry's taking part in these practices (with the exception of cannibalism) imparted a reality-TV feel to the programme, and the series commanded high viewing figures.

Religious missions to the colonies probably helped to convince the colonists that they had God and virtue on their side, further rationalising a paternalistic, aggressive and vengeful approach to indigenous peoples. There was (and still is) a scramble for the Earth's resources, which were needed as raw materials for the growing industrialisation; particularly important in this period were plantation crops such as rubber, sugar, coffee, cotton, tobacco and cassava, as well as, of course, the labour to produce these crops: slaves. When slavery was abolished in the British Empire in 1838 (not until 1865 in America), the era of the indentured labourer began. Colonial masters required cheap labour so they sought migrant workers from India and other colonies. The situation in the Caribbean and Malaysia and on Pacific islands such as Fiji reflects this pattern of employment, which in practice was not unlike slavery. Colonial overseers were still known to have flogged workers in the Caribbean up until the 1940s. I recently interviewed a Guyanese man who, growing up on a sugar estate, regularly witnessed this ritualised brutality.

One of the features associated with colonial rule was a tendency to play on divisions between subject groups within the colony to seed internal dissent as a means of weakening unified resistance to the colonial regime. 'After all, it is now widely accepted that colonial regimes and their successor states invented, promoted, and exploited "tribal" differences and traditions' (Comaroff 1995: 246). The internalised divisions that are part of the impact of colonialism create an active divestment of original culture and emulation of the colonial values. The divisions were not just external, through segregation and divisions of labour, but were part of the mind of the colonial subject.

The realities of colonial life, however, were that, despite such protestations of purity and moral superiority, there was a great deal of intermixing between Europeans and different indigenous groups. However, the prevailing bourgeoisie value system meant that this behaviour was looked upon as a threat to the colonial order and was to be resisted at all costs. Thus, once more, class, sexuality and race and ethnicity collide in practices and codes. Chludzinski's study of travelogues in the late nineteenth and early twentieth centuries highlighted this injunction against miscegenation and noted the fears 'that interracial marriage blurred the lines of the racial hierarchy that the British had established' (Chludzinski 2009: 57). Evidence suggests that such values persisted later into the twentieth century.

BOX 3.2 SCENE FROM A SUGAR ESTATE IN BRITISH GUIANA, C 1938.

My Guyanese interviewee (mentioned above), now in his 80s, gave a vivid description of an Englishman who was employed as an overseer on a sugar estate in Albion. This man was described as poorly educated and trying to disguise his illiteracy by bandaging his hand when in public so that he was apparently unable to write. This suggested that he was from a relatively lower socio-economic background but was seeking nevertheless to make a living in the colonial world of 1940s British Guiana. However, he had been carrying on an affair with a local girl and she fell pregnant. The memorable narrative point of the story concerned his disgrace and expulsion from the sugar plantation at the hands of the English woman who was a self-appointed moral guardian on the plantation. My interviewee described it thus:

BB: We used to call her M— ... She was evil, she was a racist, not to coloured people but to all the English men.

SS: And did she arrive later in Guyana?

BB: She probably went in the 30s. An Englishman named P— he was friendly with a local girl and she had a son by this Englishman ... And this racist M— heard about it and she had this fellow marched out of his house ...

SS: What was his job?

BB: He was an overseer.

SS: Oh, overseer ...

BB: He was an overseer ... and he was marched out of his house ... and before he leave the premises they brought his bed and all the furniture and made a big bonfire and burnt it in front of him. So that no other Englishman will sleep or use this filthy furniture ... So the fellow was fired. He wasn't even given a lift to the road, he had to walk out with a little leather suitcase with his belongings ... A little suitcase.

Yes yes ... Mrs M— was a cruel, cruel lady, a cruel lady. ... had this fellow fired [shaking his head] no notice no ... on the spot fired. And before he leave they brought all his furniture, bedding, mattress, and burnt it before he leave. And lovely things ... but no other Englishman will use it.

These are manifestations of a colonial system underpinned by an implicit belief in hierarchy. Transgression could not be tolerated, as it would threaten the fragile regime of thought by which exploitation was legitimated. Stuart Hall suggests that at a certain historical point (before the end of the Second World War and the decades which followed in which the colonial project unravelled) the English projected an imperious gaze of superiority on the rest of the world, feeling that they could command: 'within their own discourses, the discourses of almost everybody else' (Hall 1997: 173). 'Certainly the colonized "other" was constituted within regimes of representation of such a metropolitan center. Those colonized persons were placed in their otherness, in their marginality, by the nature of the "English eye", the all encompassing "English eye"' (ibid.).

This surveillance under the discourses of Englishness – its imported hierarchical values, its ingrained class habits and vaunted (though often transgressed) moral codes of propriety and decency – is borne out by stories such as the one of the disgraced overseer, above. Such estates were microcosms of the colonial relationship, total institutions in which such transgressions, especially on the part of an employee, could not be tolerated.

The manner in which colonial systems exploited the colonised lands varied in some respects, however, and different cultural discourses show some distinct differences. For instance, Chludzinski cites evidence that the British were critical of Spanish and Portuguese miscegenation (in her example from South East Asia):

> In one American travelogue from the Philippines, the writer compared the way that the British and the Spanish treated the natives. He commented that the British ridiculed the Portuguese and the Spanish for allowing interracial marriage. The British felt that miscegenation would result in the decline of the colonial government and even the decline of home government of the colonizing power, even though they did not explain how.
>
> (Chludzinski 2009: 57)

The results of miscegenation were too difficult to contemplate and the British tended to use derogatory terms for such progeny. The 'British believed that interracial marriage produced "mongrel," "inferior and "renegade" Eurasian children' (ibid.: 58). However, the Sistema de Castas (or Caste System) instituted in New Spain (Mexico) shows a very developed cultural imaginary of Hispanicisation.

The images in the following section are taken from the study of 'casta' paintings in New Spain and their overt promotion of hierarchies of race. However, these paintings, perhaps more than anything else, reflect the anxiety of the 'Spanish elite' about the breakdown of a clear socio-racial hierarchy in colonial society – the sistema de castas or caste system – that privileged a white, Spanish elite' (Deans-Smith 2011).

CASTA – REPRESENTATIONS OF RACE AND RACE MAKING IN NEW SPAIN

The painting in Figure 3.2 demonstrates typical features of the genre of 'casta', a form which was produced for a period in the mid to late eighteenth century in Mexico (New Spain) and other Latin American countries. These visually arresting works, unlike any other genre of painting in western art, deal directly and concretely with the visualisation of racial categories within the Spanish colonial context. As such, casta paintings provide a unique glimpse into the formation of ideas about mixed-race identity and resonate in various ways with modern sensibilities about race.

Figure 3.2 shows the typical hierarchy of sixteen racial combinations. Each pairing of different racial types and their progeny, all of which are based on the notion of '*limpieza de sangre*' (purity of blood) and the superiority of the Spanish, provides a detailed and rigidly ascribed taxonomy of descent and ascent. These paintings have been considered to demonstrate the orderliness of inter-ethnic life in the colonies and to suggest that ethnic/racial differences are not inviolable but could be eventually 'bred out'. In addition, casta are also seen to celebrate and promote the new realities of Latin America, and are at times lavishly detailed. In quite a number of

Figure 3.2 Hierarchy of sixteen racial pairings. Las castas, Anonymous, eighteenth century, oil on canvas, 148cm × 104cm, on display at the Museo Nacional del Virreinato, Tepotzotlan, Mexico. Photo credit: Alejandro Linares Garcia/Wikipedia; http://en.wikipedia.org/wiki/File:CastaSystemVirreinato.JPG

casta paintings (the works of Miguel Cabrera (1695–1768) are a prime example) there are exquisite details: exotic foods, flora and fauna and courtly flourishes of fine fabrics, embroidery and jewellery, presenting a richly detailed world of textures and fruitfulness. It has been argued (Deans-Smith 2011) that part of the demand for these paintings was due to the burgeoning desire for natural history and exotica in Europe. Carrera urges that casta should not be seen as the pre-eminent colonial art but that, because they were not scrutinised, artists were able to exercise more licence than perhaps was possible in other works: 'The casta genre was not under the same orthodoxy prescriptions and Inquisition oversight as were the religious and portraiture genres; as a result, artists may have been more able to innovate and experiment with the iconography of the casta images' (Carrera 2003: 49).

Nevertheless, exquisite details do not mask the fact that in this schematised form racial lineage is all-important, and the colonial society prevailing at the time of these paintings was clearly obsessed with the recording of difference. There are also moral tones to these portrayals: the imagery and use of terms depicts an ever more baffling series of mixes and the names they are given reflect a sense of a descent to a degraded, bestial identity. From *Mulato* (mule) (Español and Negro) the images range through *Chino* (pig – porchino), *Salta atrás* ('a jump backward') and *Lobo* (wolf) to the sense of a total loss of genetic order with *Tente en el aire* ('hold-yourself-in-midair') and *No te entiendo* ('I don't understand who you are').

Cummins (2006) comments that while hierarchy 'has infinite possibilities' in terms of the potential combinations or mixtures, this is denied by the rigidly ascriptive, predetermined sequence, usually from one to sixteen, which effectively forms 'a closed series':

> The paintings visually order the interracial marriages of New Spain, beginning with a marriage between a Spaniard (Espanol) and an Indian (Indios); a Spaniard and a Negro (Negros); a Negro and an Indian. These marriages are compounded in racial diversity by the marriages of their children (mestizos, mulattoes, and so on). The progression has infinite possibilities in terms of the degree of mixture. However, casta paintings are organized in a predetermined sequence, often numbered from one to sixteen, so that the order cannot be altered. It therefore composes a closed series in which is found a bewildering and ultimately fictitious set of categories for the descending categories of racial mixing.
>
> (Cummins 2006: abstract)

As a means of containing difference and performing a sort of guarantee of order and gradual hereditary breeding out, casta paintings presented a rigid racial hierarchy, a form of ordering and naming imposed on a complex spectrum of identities. The hierarchy is heavily value-laden and the race terms used for the offspring of groups at the lower end of the scale reflect a sense of there being a gradual descent into chaotic and wild nature the further they move from the civilizing influence of the Español. And yet, far from presenting intermixing in a derogatory light, the paintings tend to portray a very orderly domestic existence far removed from the poverty and dissolution which travellers in New Spain reported. Reading the images suggests, however, subtle differences between the pairings and a gradual devolution to rougher and more anarchic bearing and behaviours. It appears that there are a wealth of signs secreted in these paintings about the popular meanings of race and miscegenation of the time. These perhaps send contradictory messages, for in the detailed cameo images produced by Cabrera there is a focus on the specific details of family scenes (e.g. *De Espanol y Negra – Mulato* and *De Mulata y Espanol – Morisca*[2]). These are sensitively detailed and nuanced paintings showing family groups in their domestic sanctum.

Cummins suggests that 'One might say then that these Mexican artists, through the act of painting, performed the habitus of colonial values assigned to racial relationships' (Cummins 2006: 3). Indeed, the image of the bodies of the different classes of people bear little relation to the labels, which are by turns nonsensical, animalistic and perhaps a reflection of the popular argot of the times and the nonsense of trying to fix people of mixed background into a rigid nomenclature. This obsession with lineage and provenance, and the taint represented by 'bad blood', is reflected in an example cited in Carrera's opening passage (2003). It concerns the efforts of a criollo (a Spaniard resident of the Americas) to prove his wife has been registered in the wrong baptismal book (the so-called *libro de color quebrado*, which translates as 'book of broken colour': in other words, the book in which those of mixed race are entered). Having won the case by producing documentation which persuaded the hearing that his wife was of '*limpieza sangre*' and untainted by African, Moorish, Indian or Jewish blood, her name was entered into the *libro de Espanoles*.

Mexico is a country with a long history of complex hybrid ethnic and racial identities. Nutini and Barry (2009) identifies four imprecise categories 'There are basically four operational categories that may be termed ethnic or even racial in Mexico today: (1) güero (which, due to genealogy, sometimes are born into the darkest families), denoting European and Near East extraction; (2) criollo (creole), meaning light mestizo in this context but actually of varying complexion; (3) mestizo, an imprecise category that includes many phenotypic variations; and (4) indio, also an imprecise category' (Nutini and Barry 2009: 55). It is the case that, despite proud and resistant indigenous traditions which overthrew the external colonialism of Spain, Spanish heritage still has a privileged status, and ethnic identity in Mexico is a touchy subject, it appears; and the suggestion that Mexico has a strand of Africanness in its complex hybrid mix is often ignored (the discussion in Chapter 8 reflects this perception).

The paintings themselves reflect a colonial desire to regulate the disorderliness of racial identities and breed out what were presented as increasingly wild and uncultivated elements. The Spanish, perhaps owing to their longer experience in colonial outposts, had more flexible attitudes to miscegenation than the British. Cooper and Stoler (1989) suggest that miscegenation was a problem which Europeans were unprepared to properly address. In particular, the fact of hybridity seemed to blur the boundaries which were supposed to clearly demark white supremacy. These paintings and their hierarchical depiction are ambivalent. On the one hand they show a local Eden, with their focus on produce and rich details of life in the colonial setting, and they are relatively orderly and sympathetic to the individual family groups. At a deeper level the paintings hint at two potentially different routes to meaning: one which seems to devolve into chaotic hybrid identities which are irrevocably lost to their 'pure' origins; and another in which, through judicious parenting, 'otherness' can be extinguished.

EFFECTS OF COLONIALISM

In some case the fragile ecosystems of colonised lands were changed irrevocably. Indigenous peoples had little resistance to diseases brought in by Europeans and, in some cases, died in their thousands. There were numerous cases of systematic ethnic cleansing in many areas of the world (e.g., in Namibia, Australia and in North America, see, e.g., Madley 2004) particularly during the peak of European colonial activity during the nineteenth century. The Tasmanian Aborigines were almost wiped out or relocated to the remote Flinders Island by 1835, just thirty-two years after the arrival of the first British settlers. Some textbooks simply list the Tasmanians as being extinct or as having died out, with no explanation given. There are scarce records of the full horror of the process of hunting down and killing these people, which was perpetrated with extreme brutality. John Pilger, in his book *Heroes*, reproduces one surviving account from an Aborigine known as Old Mr Birt of a story told to him by his mother:

> The buried our babies with only their heads above the ground. All in a row they were. Then they had a test to see who could kick the babies' heads off the furthest. One man clubbed a baby's head off from horseback. They then spent the day raping the women; most of them [the women] were then tortured to death by sticking sharp things like spears up their vaginas until they died. They tied the men's hands behind their backs, then cut off their penises and testicles and watched them run around screaming until they died. I lived because I was young and pretty and one of the men kept me for himself, but I was always tied up until I escaped into another land to the west.
>
> (Pilger 1986: 580)

Recently the historian Keith Windschuttle (2004a) claimed that the figures generally given for the numbers murdered were inaccurate and that most died from natural causes – that, in fact, the colonial experience in Tasmania was one of the most benign, and that full-blood Aborigines in Tasmania died out owing to their isolation and vulnerability to diseases such as pneumonia and tuberculosis. Colonisation can itself be seen as a form of genocide and while there are disputes about the scale of destruction, it is clear that this genocidal pattern has been repeated across Africa, Asia, North and South America and Australia.

These stories of inhumanity are guilty secrets which haunt the conscience, and tarnish the international image of the nation, so it was little wonder that Australian Prime Minister John Howard, welcomed Windschuttle's more benign analysis of the events in Tasmania. Howard refused to accept the negative historical readings of Australia's past, which he dubbed the 'black armband view' of history (see Chapter 6). However, these revisionist claims have been fiercely disputed, and Robert Manne of La Trobe University responded to Windschuttle by commissioning eighteen historians to address and firmly refute his claims (Manne 2003).

Such genocidal colonialism was not restricted to the British in Australia. The Belgian Congo was one of the most extreme cases, with possibly 10 million people being slaughtered. Rom, a minor official who became a commissioner, is said to have used Africans' heads for his garden borders and may be the inspiration for the shadowy figure of Mr Kurtz, the ruthless colonial administrator in Conrad's *Heart of Darkness*. America's genocidal destruction of indigenous peoples at home and the brutal repressive war waged in the Philippines, in which at least 20,000 were slaughtered, are hardly ever cited. The scale of these atrocities and the lack of remorse expressed for them reflect the perception of the colonial 'other' as not fully human. These are bodies without rights, 'unpeople' (a term Curtis (2004) uses to describe the civilian deaths in Iraq). As Gilroy suggests,

> [t]he countless tales of colonial brutality are too important to be lightly or prematurely disposed of. They cannot capture the whole complexity of imperial affairs, but these days they tend to get overlooked because a sanitized history of the imperial project is required by those who wish to bring it back to life.
>
> (Gilroy 2004: 52)

It is important, therefore, that such revisionism does not succeed.

The colonial subject experiences not just physical oppression but also forms of self contempt, a consciousness of self as inferior is socialised through an all pervasive white value system.

Through his psychoanalytic insights into the depersonalisation of the dispossessed, Frantz Fanon captured the plight of the black colonial subject as one of a shattered self-image. The colonial 'look' creates the mirror, and in it the black person sees himself as nothing human, as a mere object.

The black man has two dimensions. One with his fellows, the other with the white man. A Negro behaves differently with a white man and with another Negro. That this self-division is a direct result of colonialist subjugation is beyond question.

(Fanon 1967a: 17)

This contemptuous self image was identified by W.E. B Du Bois over a century ago when he wrote about the duality resulting from this internalised divide:

It is a peculiar sensation, this double-consciousness, this sense of always looking at one's self through the eyes of others, of measuring one's soul by the tape of a world that looks on in amused contempt and pity. One ever feels his two-ness – an American, a Negro; two souls, two thoughts, two unreconciled strivings; two warring ideals in one dark body, whose dogged strength alone keeps it from being torn asunder. The history of the American Negro is the history of this strife – this longing to attain self-conscious manhood, to merge his double self into a better and truer self. In this merging he wishes neither of the older selves to be lost.

(Du Bois 1897: 194–8)

It is important to comprehend these aspects of colonialism. The distortion that has relegated black and Asian cultures to the periphery of world events has shaped our modern/postmodern societies. However, it is unrealistic to portray colonialism as a one-way process imposed on passive victims. There were also profound affects on the lives and identities of the colonialists and furthermore their actions in far flung territories had a marked impact on how domestic 'others' were understood. The ripples of colonialism transformed the home front too:

the nether reaches of urban society were directly linked to colonies, to undo-mesticated primitive lands. Cultural colonialism, in short, was also a reflexive process whereby 'others' abroad, the objects of the civilizing mission, were put to the purposes of reconstructing the 'other' back home.

(Comaroff and Comaroff 1992: 293)

Colonialism has had a major impact on the structure of our contemporary socie-ties. It is a particularly significant factor in the historical roots of diaspora and the fractured and hybrid identities which are so much a part of our cities today.

The story of colonialism is also one of diaspora (see Glossary): the push and pull of people migrating around the world for labour or fleeing persecution; people taken by force from their homelands as slaves or as indentured labourers or imported in the modern post-war era as cheap labour; people transported to the New World or Australasia as convicts. These diasporas are the basis for multicultural or multi-ethnic nations such as Brazil, Australia, the USA, France, the UK and Canada, reflecting the social history of colonialism. For example, in the UK and France are nationals from colonial countries such as India, Pakistan, the West Indies or north African countries. Multiculturalism, as we will see in later chapters, can be seen as a progressive force for world unity or as a form of tokenism that really means assimilation and integration.

REPARATION MOVEMENT

A point made by the reparation movement is that transatlantic slavery constitutes the most significant crime against humanity from which the colonial nations were able – owing to their plunder at the expense of Africa – to attain the high ground of economic development while Africa remains impoverished and peripheral (and, indeed, still prey to the descendant forms of colonialism). In 1997, Lord Gifford made the following comment in a speech before the House of Lords:

> My Lords, the Question raises an issue which is being debated with increasing vigour and intensity by African people around the world; and by African people mean people of African descent, wherever they live, whether in Africa itself, in the United States, in Great Britain or in the Caribbean, where I now live and practise law.
>
> The issue is this. The underdevelopment and poverty which affect the majority of countries in Africa and in the Caribbean, as well as the ghetto conditions in which many black people live in the United States and elsewhere, are not, speaking in general terms, the result of laziness, incompetence or corruption of African people or their governments. They are in a very large measure the consequences the legacy – of one of the most massive and terrible criminal enterprises in recorded human history; that is, the transatlantic slave trade and the institution of slavery.

> (Gifford 1996)

The scale of the depopulation in Africa was enormous. Some black scholars estimate a holocaust of between 50 and 100 million people, rather more than the c.10 million suggested by conservative white researchers. What is certain is that five centuries of exploitation left Africa weakened, and it could be argued that its frequent geopolitical problems – droughts, famines, civil wars and so on – are part of the west's legacy to Africa, as well as to Asia and South America.

The scarring of colonialism has left its imprint on peoples across the world. Gilroy, in his examination of post-empire melancholia, makes the point that for colonising nations to shake off the lingering effects of colonialism they need to come to terms with some culpability at a national level:

before the British people can adjust to the horrors of their own modern history, and start to build a new national identity from the debris of their broken narcissism, they will have to learn to appreciate the brutalities of colonial rule enacted in their name and to their benefit, to understand the damage it did to their political culture at home and abroad, and to consider the extent of their country's complex investments in ethnic absolutism that has sustained it.

(Gilroy 2004: 108)

BOX 3.3 WITNESS TO A FLOGGING ON A SUGAR ESTATE IN ALBION, BRITISH GUIANA, C.1938

The notion that colonial excesses were only prevalent in the earlier days of colonial power and had largely abated in the twentieth century is, unfortunately, a myth. The Guyanese case is further illustrated by the story recounted below, an interesting and rare commentary, recently recorded, on the treatment of Indian–Guyanese workers in the early 1940s.

The interview below was with an Indian–Guyanese man, now in his 80s (see above), who spent his early life on the sugar estates at Albion. The account demonstrates how the colonial treatment of indentured workers, mostly Indian, was little better than the treatment meted out under slavery. Indeed, the rude loggies, or slave houses, were still the main housing for sugar workers and floggings for minor misdemeanours were apparently commonplace.

It seems that these floggings were held every Sunday outside the sugar estate factory, where the cane was crushed to make sugar and molasses. The barrel referred to in the interview had cuffs for ankles and hands and victims were thrashed so severely that they had to be physically lifted from it:

BB. I used to go to Sunday school – and it started at 7 o'clock in the morning and finish at 8 o'clock. Then used to go home and have breakfast … and thing like that …

SS. You were just a young boy then … about 9 or 10?

BB. About that.

SS. And after Sunday school you used to go to …?

BB. (Nodding) Change my clothes.

SS. Uh huh …

BB. Because you used to have to wear your Sunday best.

SS. Yeah.

BB. And people who didn't go to work on time or who commit silly little, little crime …

SS. Yeah …?

BOX 3.3 WITNESS TO A FLOGGING ON A SUGAR ESTATE IN ALBION, BRITISH GUIANA, C.1938 (CONTINUED)

BB. They had a special barrel ... a big barrel (gestures with both arms to indicate the size)

SS. ... So if they were late for work ...

BB. Yes ... or if they were rude to ... the supervisor ...

SS. Really?

BB. Yes ... it was like a prison ... an open door prison, life on a sugar estate.

SS. Yes?

BB. They were extra strict ... and people were flogged if they were rude to anybody.

SS. With a cane or ...?

BB. A cat of nine tails!

SS. Cat of nine tails?!

BB. Yes, it had plenty of leather strap, 7, 8, 9, 10, leather strap and all woven into a handle, a solid handle ... and then they used to rip the shirt, they used to put you over a barrel and then they'll rip the shirt off your back and pull your trousers down nearly to your bottom, and they used to flog them. And when they flog they have to be sleep on your tummy for a week or two, you were a ... cripple.

SS. That's awful ... and was this just on Sundays?

BB. Yes ... that's (laughing) right.

SS. Extraordinary.

BB. A fellow called Anthony Ayube Edun – you must have got that in your study of Guyana – he came to England and he saw how the English were living, some of them couldn't read or write – but when they went to the colonies they became superior and they were bosses, and he wrote the book, was it Jagan or him, 'The White Slave Trafficker' or something like that?

SS. Could have been him, yeah ...

BB. Anthony Ayube Edun.

SS. So you think that the sugar plantation wasn't far removed from slavery?

BB. No, it wasn't.

SS. Not far removed – even in the 30s and 40s – in the 30s?

BB. Semi slavery existed in the 30s, 40s, up to the 50s. I think up to 44 ... by 50 Dr Cheddi Jagan and Anthony Ayube Edun (Anthony Ayube Edun first) started the rebellion – not Dr Jagan – he came later in the scene ... and people who didn't say good morning or didn't take their hat off were flogged.

SS. Really?

BB. It was slavery ...

(An interview with Mr Balchand Basdeo, 6 April 2012)

The events recounted here provide a description of the colonial form of slavery which many believe to have been a thing long extinguished in the Caribbean at this period. But in fact in every area of the world where capital investment carried on under surviving colonial forms of administration such occurrences were not unusual (one well-documented example was the institutional removal and systematic abuse of Australian Aboriginal children and teenagers (Australian Human Rights Commission 1997).

NEO-COLONIALISM AND AUTO-COLONIALISM

At the end of the Second World War, a time when the type of ritual flogging of workers described above was still going on away from public scrutiny in places such as British Guiana, a landmark meeting of UNESCO brought together prominent scientists from around the world to make a definitive statement about 'race'. The Florence Declaration of 1950 states unequivocally that, based on the latest findings of scientific research at the time, they

> rejected the idea that there were fundamental differences due to race in the human species and unequivocally condemned the theories based on the superiority of one or more races. Those two statements were chiefly concerned with the biological and anthropological aspects of the problem.
>
> (UN Economic and Social Council 1999: 7–8)

Despite this, however, the hierarchical forms of racism have proved a powerful tool of domination which is endemic in many societies. Even as these tenets of a world free from systematic racism were being laid down, apparently drawing a line under the evils of colonialism and the Nazi holocaust, the spurious reasoning that gave them legitimacy was being promulgated elsewhere in the western world. Indeed, there is evidence that the US eugenics movement, as it began to wane and come under more critical scrutiny its thin veneer of science was stripped away and shown to be inaccurate and based on deep-seated prejudices, had been something of an inspiration to the Third Reich (see Kuhl 1994). Forced sterilisation was still being carried out in Puerto Rico (estimates of up to 35 per cent of working-class women). Sweden, up until the 1950s, pursued the largest per-capita eugenic programme targeting 'deviant' groups for sterilisation. Asian countries, too, have made clear attempts at ethnic cleansing, notably in Tibet under the Chinese (but also in East Timor and Irian Jaya under Indonesia). In addition, immigration policies and the treatment of refugees have frequently been viewed as either directly racist or else inspired by labour movements to protect the nation from an influx of labour that might undercut domestic work rates (for example, the White Australia Policy).[3]

Ostensibly, 'white' rule was at an end, in now independent African countries, but Kwame Nkrumah demonstrated the existence of neo-colonialism in his 1965 study of neo-colonialism (another landmark text), *Neo-colonialism: The Last Stage of Capitalism*, which gave this definition of neo-colonialism:

> The essence of neo-colonialism is that the state which is subject to it is, in theory, independent and has all the outward trappings of international sovereignty. In reality its economic system and thus its political policy is directed from outside [...] The neo-colonialism of today represents imperialism in its final and perhaps its most dangerous state.
>
> (Nkrumah 1965: 1)

Forms of colonialism then, seem still to be prevalent today – although the forms of exploitation are now linked to the dramatic changes wrought by political, economic and cultural globalisation. Evidence from the UN Human Development Index shows that the gap between the wealthy western countries and the poorest areas (Africa, Asia, South America) has increased steeply in the past forty years.

> [T]he richest 20% of people have seen the differential between themselves and the poorest 20% double: where in the 1950s the richest one-fifth of humanity received 30 times as much as the poorest fifth, this has now increased to 60 times as much. And this outcome occurred even while a potential alternative – however malign – still to some degree inhibited a capitalism as yet unsure of its ultimate triumph.
>
> (Seabrook 1996: 1)

The 'winners' and the 'losers' in this accelerating process are quite clear. Transnational corporations originating in the west have sales figures that are greater than the gross domestic product (GDP) of many countries combined.

> According to the latest published data on a group of 2000 global companies, just the top ten non-financial transnational corporations ranked by total sales realized 2.533 trillion dollars in sales in 2007, which is more than the aggregate BDP of 161 countries according to IMF data for 2008. At the same time, the assets of the 30 largest financial transnational corporations (from the same group of 2000 global companies from 2008) amount to 48.883 trillion dollars, or more than the world's 2007 GDP.
>
> (Petković and Rakić 2010: 292)

All this suggests a picture of the world in which power has followed the development of enormously powerful global trading blocs with vast resources in the hands of a small elite. The governance of poorer nations, often in massive debt to global corporations, has ceased to rest with their nominal leaders and has increasingly been passed over to western financial institutions and those transnational entities for which the preservation of western dominance is axiomatic.

> Their talk of poverty abatement, structural adjustment, their touting of economic success stories – once Brazil, now New Zealand, once even Nigeria, now Thailand – are calculated to conceal the real purpose of the integrated world economy, which is the supranational management of worsening inequality.
>
> (Seabrook 1996: 1)

Without wishing to present any overly polemic case, two events can be compared here, one virtually forgotten, the other still ringing in our ears: First, the tragedy at Bhopal in 1984, where 'toxic gas from a Union Carbide plant may have killed 20,000 people, with the toll still growing, a legacy of cancers, and genetic defects, and the fight for compensation not yet over' (Ramesh 2004); and, second, the attack on the World Trade Center in New York, in which 2,996 people died in the buildings and in the aircraft that crashed into them.

These are obviously not comparable cases: 9/11 was not an industrial accident, it was an intentional attack calculated to cause maximum impact and hurt. However, the lack of social justice in the first case, where many times more people were affected and continue to be so (Union Carbide, it was reported, have not cleaned up the area in which lethal chemicals are still a danger to people) arguably indicates the prevalence of core and peripheral values ('Wedom' and 'Theydom' writ large). Similarly, the number of Iraqi civilians who have died in the military invasion number, at best estimates, about 24,865 people killed up to 19 March 2005 and 45,000 wounded (see Steele and Norton-Taylor 2005). Attempts were made by the UK and US governments to persuade the public that Iraq was involved in 9/11, but there is no evidence that this was true.

What relevance do these cases have to issues of race and ethnicity? Quite clearly, the clash of belief systems is central to such actions, as is the impact of neo-colonialism. Decentralised industrial operations in developing countries have become the normal pattern. There are also firm precedents for invading oil-rich countries, and it is apparent that the overt invasion and colonial domination of Iraq and many other countries in the Middle East by several European countries in the early twentieth century (which left in their wake despots and dictators) is rarely remembered; it is an invisible history. It seems that, for some, the Twin Towers were a symbol of western affluence and neo-colonial domination: 'Religious fundamentalists do not single out the United States for any other reason than its hegemonic power' (Ali 2002: 282).

CHAPTER SUMMARY

The western world has been defined through its colonialist enterprises (and continues to be so). The expedient use of concepts of 'race' in the seventeenth century became a defining divide in the project of modernity. Slavery is an ancient institution stretching from pre-history to the present day, yet *racial* slavery was a unique and relatively recent movement associated with colonialism. The consequences of slavery and other forms of 'booty capitalism' have been two centuries of relative affluence and dominance for western countries alongside simultaneous underdevelopment in countries in Asia, Africa and South America. Ritual brutality and the maintenance of white supremacy in plantation settings perpetuated an exploitative system long after the formal abolition of slavery. Racial class and caste schemes were prevalent and constructed hierarchical categories for individuals in the colonial system that were obsessively recorded in terms of the measure of racial purity. Such a system left scars on the psyche as well as the bodies of colonial subjects, who internalised distorted self-contemptuous values. However, into the late twentieth century the scale of disadvantage and division has reached unprecedented levels as neo-colonialism and auto-colonialism have widened the gap (at the time of writing, there are an estimated 27 million slaves in the world, the scale of human trafficking today outstrips the numbers of slaves at the height of the Atlantic trade). Structural economic plans brokered by the World Bank and the International Monetary Fund (IMF) have enabled the west to exploit the lack of infrastructure of the world's poorest nations. Apart from the material effects of colonialism, Du Bois and Fanon have expressed the troubling duality of the post-colonial psyche but, although it is less apparent, the effects of colonialism are also manifest in the lingering post-empire melancholia of the white populations.

EXERCISE 3.1 GUYANA: LOOK WHAT THEY DONE TO THE MOTHER

1   How might we account for the apparent reverence that the Guyanese speaker has for the 'mother', Queen Victoria?
2   Do any elements of the exchange reflect an inaccurate or overly nostalgic view of colonial history?
3   What signs of a persistent hegemony of colonial values could you detect from the exchange?
4   What are the signs of ethnic tension in the exchange?
5   Why do you think rice could be such a grievously felt issue?
6   How might Goffman's dramaturgical theory be applied to this interview extract?
7   Discuss the defacement of the statue and its resurrection and the meaning of such cultural icons in post-colonial societies. You might consider other fallen statues and their meanings, such as that of Saddam Hussein in Iraq or those of Stalin and Lenin in Eastern Europe.

1   The scale of depopulation in Africa was enormous. What are the implications and consequences of this history of exploitation?

2   Colonialism and slavery are more about capitalism than racism. Discuss.

3   The colonial exploitation of people as slaves, as mere commodities in the production process, did become inextricably linked to skin colour. What arguments were used in the defence of slavery?

4   How much credence was given to 'race sciences' that attempted to justify slavery as the natural domination of inferior races?

5   How persuasive were arguments about the protection of private property and the livelihoods of colonists and slave-owners?

6   Colonialism has left its imprint on vast areas of the world: South America, Africa and much of Asia. What are the consequences for the post-colonial subject in these areas?

7   Should reparations be made to the countries and peoples who were subjected to such treatment, or to indigenous peoples such as the Maoris and Australian Aborigines who claim their countries were stolen by colonists?

8   Consider the world events mentioned in the last section. How are global trade and terrorism involved in the construction of ethnic/religious 'otherness'?

9   Look at the examples of casta – consider the degree of fluidity and constraint a caste system such as this would have permitted compared with the rigid autocracy and moral superiority of the British.

Further reading

Literature can evoke the profound impact of colonialism in a vivid way that many textbooks cannot. Among the most important are: Joseph Conrad's *Heart of Darkness* (1899); Frantz Fanon's *The Wretched of the Earth* (1961); Rudyard Kipling's *The White Man's Burden* (1899); Bartolomé de Las Casas's *A Short Account of the Destruction of the Indies* (1542, published in 1552); Chinua Achebe's *Things Fall Apart* (1958), which captures the clash of cultures in Nigeria; Albert Camus' *L'Etranger* (1942), which deals with the alienation of French Algeria; Salman Rushdie's *Midnight's Children* (1980), which engages with Indian independence and the meaning of 'nation' to millions of diasporic voices; and J. M. Coetze's *Life and Times of Michael K* (1983) and *Waiting for the Barbarians* (1980), which depict brutal colonialism in South Africa.

Of academic textbooks, Frederick Cooper's *Colonialism in Question: Theory, Knowledge, History* (Berkeley, CA: University of California Press, 2005) is a collection which questions our reading of history. Casta paintings are discussed eloquently in Ilona Katzew's *Casta Painting: Images of Race in Eighteenth-century*

Mexico (New Haven, CT: Yale University Press, 2004) and also in Magali Carrera's *Imagining Identity in New Spain: Race, Lineage, and the Colonial Body in Portraiture and Casta Paintings* (Austin, TX: University of Texas Press, 2003).

It goes without saying that films also provide a powerful vision of colonialism and the continuation of Eurocentric and paternalistic attitudes; an excellent example is *Cannibal Tours*, a 1988 documentary by Australian film maker Dennis O'Rourke.

Notes

1 Laws compiled during the reign of Hammurabi (1792–1750 BC), king of Babylon, include regulations governing slavery. These are among the oldest known civic regulations.
2 Some of Cabrera's paintings can be seen online at http://commons.wikimedia.org/wiki/File:Cabrera_Pintura_de_Castas.jpg.
3 From the time of federation in 1901 until the 1970s Australia actively discouraged the migration of people considered undesirable. This policy is widely known as the White Australia Policy. Undesirable people included 'coloured' people as well as prostitutes, criminals, the insane and any person suffering from a contagious disease.

Theories of Race and Ethnicity

This section provides a discussion of some of the important theoretical explanations which have emerged around racial and ethnic divisions and the way in which relations of shared identity and difference can be understood. Theory can be justly considered a form of representation: not just at the level of mental models of phenomena but also as the reasoned underpinnings beneath the manifest codes of representation. In some ways the mental maps that theoretical structures suggest are similarly prone to the representation gap. Like the shadows in Plato's cave, theoretical models are not the thing itself but a reflection we construct, an abstract approximation which is necessary when we begin to try to explain complex phenomena. It it clear from the previous chapters that, impossible as it might be to determine the referent of 'race' or 'ethnicity' in social life (the terms being mired in mythical and spurious ideas about human categories), there are severe material consequences and experiences which stem from race and racism. These are terms which go to the heart of the human condition, revealing the tensions between nature and culture, structure and agency; the form of boundaries between human groups and also the 'cultural stuff' inside the boundaries.

PRIMORDIAL OR INSTRUMENTAL ETHNICITY

Are 'race' and ethnicity part of our 'natural' make-up or are they features which can be exploited for social and economic advantage? Can they be both? This is the thrust of these two influential trends in theory. Can ethnic groups and the wide-spread experience of ethnocentrism be understood as primordial or instrumental phenomena?

Primordialism

Definitions of primordialism can range from simply the force and strength of traditions and cultural ties to ideas of genetically inherited features and characteristics. At the most biologically determined end of the spectrum, sociobiologists have argued that there is a biological aspect to the formation of ethnic bonds. They believe that social behaviour is guided by evolutionary strategies and motivated towards securing long-term survival of the group; theories such as 'inclusive fitness' (Hamilton 1964) and 'kin selection', which operate among animals, are suggested to be relevant also to human behaviour. 'A person's inclusive fitness is his or her personal fitness plus the increased fitness of relatives that he or she has in some way caused by his or her actions' (Reynolds *et al.* 1987: xvii). These concepts operate together; inclusive fitness is achieved through kin selection. These biological imperatives (which posit an invisible guiding force of biology) are considered by sociobiologists to explain altruism. The individual is a vehicle for the genes that must be passed on – however, in examples of self-sacrifice to save or defend a kinship group, the argument is that the gene stock will still survive even if the individual dies. Such explanations are reasonable when applied to the animal world – bees, ants or birds, for example – but sociobiologists extrapolate these ideas of the 'selfish gene' (Dawkins 1989) and inclusive fitness to human society. To consider a person as little more than a gene's 'survival machine' (ibid.: 132) entirely ignores the enormous evidence for social and cultural forces that shape behaviour. Furthermore, to conjecture that ethnic identification and acts of loyalty and sacrifice can be reduced to genetic determinism seems extreme. Sociobiology has met with resistance in the past thirty years, which is not surprising, as it has certain features in common with Social Darwinism – in particular, the notion of biological predestination. The successor to sociobiology, evolutionary psychology, seems also to depend on similar reductionist and adaptionist[1] arguments.

More reasonable forms of primordial explanation exist, however. Traditional ties are passed along to members of a defined group. These attachments of kinship and heritage are clearly part of many if not most people's upbringing. However, the concept may be extended further to include a harder primordial boundary in which ties of blood, religion, custom and belief become ineffable and have a deeper psychological effect on members of the group. Notions of primordial ethnicity such as those developed by Clifford Geertz (1973) suggest that ethnic identity developed from certain 'givens' of social existence, including blood and kin connections, religion, language (even dialect), region and custom.

Geertz suggests that these form 'ineffable', 'affective' and '*a priori*' bonds. Similarly, it is apparent that these bonds are also considered to be (via more irrational criteria of blood inheritance) the basis of character and the cause of long-standing ethnic rivalries and even hatreds. Primordialism (in its most extreme form) suggests that cultures are fixed and unchanging – almost genetic blueprints – indeed, sociobiology would suggest that there is a biological imperative to preserve the genetic stock. Such viewpoints may be ideologically employed when complex situations occur that require a careful analysis of social histories. Attributing such situations (e.g. inter-ethnic violence) to some irrational primordial core may fit with the dominant prejudices of the public. For example, during media coverage of the conflict in Rwanda explanations tended to centre on descriptions of primordial tribalism leading to some sort of blood lust. The true complexity of the situation became lost in the incessant media coverage of brutal atrocities. The underlying causes were typically not sought; rather, journalists merely focused on stereotypes of irrational tribalism.

The background to these conflicts can often be seen to be a history of invasion and reprisal over many decades or even centuries, as well as, frequently, the influence of colonialism. Tutsis massacred Hutus in 1972 (see Kuper 1996); the ongoing ethnic conflict between Russia and Chechnya can be traced back at least 400 years; the conflict in Northern Ireland can be traced back to the twelfth century (see Curtis 1984). As has already been discussed, the colonial practice of seeding derogatory stereotypes and manipulating group boundaries between the colonial subjects has a long history and can be shown in some cases to have led to factionalism that has occasionally led to genocidal conflicts. Kuper comments that:

> Where there were two tiers of domination in the colonial structure, decolonization was particularly charged with genocidal potential. Plural societies preceded colonial imperialism, and in some cases capitalist colonization of a plural society resulted in the superimposition of an additional layer of domination on an earlier domination. In a number of these societies, decolonization detonated explosive genocidal conflicts, as the earlier rulers and their one-time subjects engaged in violent struggle under the impetus of electoral contests in a democratic idiom, introduced by the colonial powers in the movement to independence.
>
> (Kuper 1996: 266)

This demonstrates the bitterness seeded in colonial administrations, whereby groups internalised a sense of self within the imposed hierarchy.

Criticisms of primordialism

The concept of apriority is problematic when it is considered that most ethnic identities seem to undergo renewal, modification and remaking in each generation. Second, the notion of ineffability can be easily criticised because in practice such supposedly primordial attachments are tied to circumstances. Affectivity is a concept that implies a mystification of emotion or belief in sociobiological worldviews; this is a very weak argument and a genetic dead end for analysis. While a moderate form of primordialism seems realistic, the extension of such notions allows the conventional racist views of the materiality of difference to intercede. Such hard-line definitions are unable to adequately account for ethnic change and dissolution or for the effects of immigration or intermarriage. But, furthermore, the tendency to invoke primordial roots of ethnicity may rightly be challenged as indicative, as Hall has suggested, of the societal need for some guarantee of the fact of 'otherness', of realising not just cultural differences and adaptations but something deeper:

> The biological referent is ... Never wholly absent from discourses of ethnicity ... The more 'ethnicity' matters the more its characteristics are represented as relatively fixed, inherent within a group, transmitted from generation to generation not just by culture and education but by biological inheritance, stabilized above all by kinship and endogamous marriage rules that ensure the ethnic group remains genetically and therefore culturally 'pure'
>
> (Hall 2000: 223)

Hall is suggesting that indelible ownership of ethnic origins has power: the power of certainty of difference, enabling hard-edged boundaries to be drawn around 'us' and against 'them'. Hence the tendency to essentialise even when such arguments can be rationally refuted.

Instrumentalism

This other broad axis of explanation is presented in various forms, which indicates that there are some intentional or conscious strategies behind the foregrounding of ethnic identity. In this perspective, ethnic groups and ties are strategically employed for attaining individual or collective goals. One form of this is the rational-choice approach advocated by Hechter (1995) and Banton (1987), in which any action can be seen as determined by a rational motive as the basis for the pursuit of scarce resources, usually in the form of public goods such as housing, benefits, political power or competition for employment. In contradistinction to primordial theories, here the basis for ethnicity is superficial and strategically employed. The model is that of an essentially individualistic and somewhat aggressive actor, self-interested, rational, pragmatic and, perhaps, with a maximising orientation as well. What actors do, it is assumed, is rationally to go after what they want, and what they want is what is materially and politically useful for them within the context of their cultural and historical situations (Ortner 1984: 151).

Perhaps the most significant words here are 'rational' and 'rationality'. Theories of rational choice seek to predict the conditions under which collective action emerges. How is social conformity and cohesion maintained in society? The Durkheimian–Parsonian answer is that people obey because they share certain common values and beliefs. In sociological terms, people internalise certain values and norms that induce them to participate in, accept and reproduce relations of production. However, rational-choice theories seem to derive from the materialistic premises alluded to by Ortner, in which a pragmatic behaviouristic view of human nature, to maximise gains and avoid losses, governs action.

Criticisms of instrumentalism

The criticisms of instrumentalist views of ethnicity are, first, that such views are unable to cope with ethnic 'durability'; second, they ignore mass passions evoked by ethnic ties and cultural symbols; and, third, they assume the ethnic nature of organisations. Ethnic identity and aspects of belief and cultural practice are relatively long-lived in many cultures.

> Ethnic identity undoubtedly is formed around real shared social space, commonalities of socialization, and communities of language and culture. Simultaneously these identities have a public presence; they are socially defined in a series of presentations (public statements, assertions, images) by ethnic group members and non-members alike.
>
> (Fenton 2003: 194)

So, can ethnicity be understood as a primordial or an instrumental phenomenon? Neither primordialists nor instrumentalists seem able to account for the long-term changes and movements of ethnic communities. It would appear that there are elements of both to be recognised in practice. However, to reduce complex human behaviour to mere biology, on the one hand, or mere pragmatism, at the other extreme, ignores the human capacity to operate at the level of the symbolic and denies the importance of culture in its broadest sense, allowing for expressions which break with traditions or compulsions to conform to the group. Individuals are neither 'cultural dopes', reproducing dominant cultural forms, nor merely at the mercy of 'hard-wired' biological systems.

In the next section we examine 'plural societies' and the theoretical models associated with this conception of ethnic dynamics, in which the tension between durable ethnicity and expressions of shared identity and desires for political and economic power are very significant. When colonial regimes have operated, the struggles between the post-colonial subjects can be intense.

PLURAL SOCIETY THEORIES

Theories that seek to explain the ways in which race and ethnicity operate as loci of power within society are relatively recent, as, indeed, the phenomena associated with plural societies themselves are fairly recent. The concept of a 'plural society' first emerged through anthropological analyses of colonial societies at the turn of the twentieth century. The anthropologist J. S. Furnivall, who studied Indonesia and Burma, wrote that 'the first thing that strikes the visitor is the medley of peoples – European, Chinese, Indian and native' (Furnivall 1948: 304) that constitute the society. The different groups, Furnivall wrote, 'mix but do not combine'. Each group 'holds by its own religion, its own culture and language, its ideas and ways' (ibid.). The result was a 'plural society, with different sections of the society living side by side but separately within the same political unit' (Malik 1998).

Furnivall's belief that plural societies are composed of essentially antagonistic ethnic groups prevented from all-out conflict by the coercive force wielded by colonial powers could certainly be interpreted as offering support to paternalistic colonialism. M. G. Smith elaborated theoretically on Furnivall's view of structurally segmented enclaves. The extension he proposed defined pluralism in terms of differences in compulsory institutions (for example, kinship, education, property, economy, recreation) and minority control of intersectional relations in most examples of colonial government. Such plural societies can be characterised, in Smith's view, as 'defined by dissensus and pregnant with conflict' (Smith 1974: xiii).

The situation in Guyana seems to fit with this dormant sense of ethnic antagonism. During an interview, Guyanese academic Berkeley Stewart suggested a diagram of a 'progressive' model of race relations (see Figure 4.1). In Figure 4.1a, 'A' would be the colonial force that governs the country: this group has obvious political and economic motives for exploiting any racial divisions and would often seed dissent in the form of slurs and scares about each of the enclaves (evidence of this can be found in diverse texts: for example, Gonzalez Casanova comments that 'racism and racial segregation are essential in the colonial exploitation of some peoples by others. They influence all configurations of development in colonial cultures' (quoted in Manley 1979: 85)). So the subject groups are divided. However, with time and the fluctuating influence over and support for the colony, the subjugated groups will begin to unite beneath the banner of resistance against a common oppressor (Figure 4.1b) and there will be increasing mobility between the groups as the pressure increases and the position of 'A' becomes more uneasy. 'B' could equate to the African-Guyanese and 'C' to the Indian-Guyanese: between them, certain

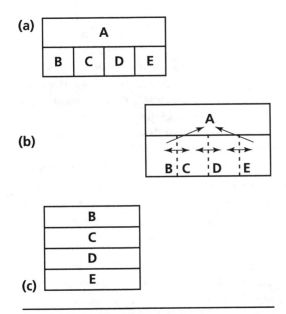

Figure 4.1 Dynamics of plural society

cultural/ethnic dimensions will operate to allow or delay this ascent to higher levels of administration and responsibility. In Guyana the Africans had the advantage of being more acculturated than the Indians: their original culture had been largely destroyed or lost and they therefore embraced the language and social mores of the dominant group. The Indian-Guyanese, having stronger cultural/language bonds to their origins, would be held back by religious considerations from participating in the education system. Stewart was, however, optimistic that the eventual outcome would be a levelling of boundaries and a thorough acculturation, which he believed was actively in process at the time. Figure 4.1c suggests that hierarchy is re-established. However, in the case of Guyana, it seems that the ordering of groups swung back and forth: the Indian-Guyanese won the popular vote in 1953 but the African-Guyanese assumed political power from 1964 and held it into the 1990s, after which the Indian-Guyanese regained power, which they have retained up to the present day. Hence, the process is clearly more cyclical than linear.

This model has several useful descriptive aspects and does account for the shifting identities within colonial and post-colonial plural societies. It places the traditionally conservative anthropology of Furnivall into a more dynamic model of change and ultimately of competition and ethnic rivalry. However, Stewart seemed to pursue a Durkheimian optimism about the ultimate levelling and acculturation in Guyanese society, which was, and continues to be, polarised ethnically. There is an inherent ambivalence in pluralist arguments: while underlining the negative aspects of colonialism they at the same time can be seen as presenting a defence of colonial leadership in its maintenance of order and stability within society. Plural-society theorists such as Furnivall (studies of Indonesia) and M. G. Smith (studies of the Caribbean) attempt to account for the manner in which separate ethnic groups or cultural enclaves are related to each other.

For Furnivall, the central agency that holds groups together is 'the market-place', emphasising economic and commercial relations albeit as a metaphor for the society as a whole. Smith, however, focuses upon political institutions. Both would consider their perspective to include relationships of production, yet do not spell out these distinctions. The recognition of the complex interplay of ethnic enclaves under colonial regimes may benefit from a closer examination of varieties of Marxist and Weberian theory which offer analyses of race and ethnicity and their interweaving with class, status and power.

MARXIST THEORIES

Although Marx made little mention of 'race', the legacy of his conception of society as a struggle between the exploited and the exploiters has remained an influential discourse and one that many social commentators see as increasingly relevant as the global forces of capitalism expand, consolidating their grip on resources, and as divisions between economic classes expand to unprecedented levels. Class is significant for all major social divisions, as social standing and status, centrality or marginality, have demonstrable economic consequences. Material conditions determine social being. This is true when the social meanings or subjective identity of difference are taken into account, whether division based on gender, sexuality, race/ethnicity or disability. For this reason the issue with assessing Marxist thought and its influence is not whether it is important but how complex social and economic factors interrelate with complex aspects of ethnic identity, citizenship and historical dialectical factors.

In the traditional Marxist approach 'race' was (and frequently still is) seen as illusionary, a mere element to be exploited by capitalism. Traditional Marxist thinkers see colonialism as a vital stage in the ultimate structural change that societies must undergo to evolve towards socialism. 'Marx himself recognised colonialism as a brutal precondition for the liberation of these societies' (Loomba 1998: 21). The historical dialectical process ground on from the primitive communism of small tribal communities through the barbarity of slavery to other forms (only marginally less barbaric, such as indentureship) of colonialism, subsequently to industrial capitalism (where the formally free labour force begins to gain consciousness of the vulnerability of the oppressor) and ultimately, through the collective action of the proletariat, to socialism. So each stage in this inevitable historical evolution was a necessary precursor of the next.

Race/ethnicity are seen as a part of the superstructure and hence are considered secondary or epiphenomenal to the economic base and relations of production.

The organisation of production creates class differences in each society. Traditional Marxist views such as those of R. T. Smith are typical of this viewpoint. Actively playing down ethnic differences, Smith calls them 'the residue of cultural peculiarities' (Smith 1962: 198). Moreover, he stresses that, should the source of inequality be removed and equality of opportunity be restored, any ethnic differences would dissolve. So, traditional Marxists still maintain that race and ethnicity are a mask that serves to obscure true relations of power in a society, which are, in fact, class-based:

> In British Guiana [...] there are forces tending to create different groupings, different occupations and different social classes, and there are forces tending to bind the members of these differentiated groups into some kind of unity and interdependence. Race, cultural differences, and even slight differences of colour are used to some extent as the basis for differentiation and the conflicts which could arise within a frustrated and dissatisfied society could easily crystallise around these factors.
>
> (Smith 1962: 143)

Certainly, differences in ethnicity are frequently channelled, amplified and strengthened through political allegiances. The ideological shaping of ethnic identities has been well documented in situations such as this. Premdas, focusing on links between voluntary associations and political campaigns in Guyana (Premdas 1972), has shown the way in which political and economic imperatives have led to mutually opposed ethnic enclaves.

However, the suggestion that ethnicity simply lies dormant, to be utilised as the most visible rationale or expression of deeper divisions inherent in economic structures and the state, is not wholly convincing. There are class distinctions, but these do not correspond simply with those of ethnic background. Why should ethnic boundaries persist when such boundaries do not correspond to the boundaries defining class interest groups? It is unnecessary for class and ethnicity to be seen as discrete independent variables in a competition for primacy. Rather, it may be possible for both to be viewed as interacting elements in a systematic theory of boundary formation in a society. As Rex has suggested, 'it is not necessary to exclude from consideration the possibility of a situation in which either ethnicity or class, or both together, operate as the main means of boundary marking' (Rex and Mason 1986: 6). Generally, however, the role of racism is seen to have its origins 'in the ideologies and racial typologies that were often invoked to justify the open exploitation of colonial times' (Cashmore 1988: 127). Examples of this tactical racism are plentiful. Walter Rodney writes of the divisive use of stereotypes on the plantations of British Guiana to maintain control and exploit labourers even after slavery had ended:

Early in the history of indentureship, planters recognised the value of having a working population segmented racially; and they never lost sight of the opportunity of playing off the two principal races – by using one to put down any overt resistance by the other.

(Rodney 1981: 188)

Rodney also quotes evidence given at the West Indian Royal Commission that shows that this manipulative attitude was commonplace in the colony:

The two people do not mix. That is, of course, one of our great safeties in the colony when there has been any rioting. If the negroes were troublesome every coolie on the estate would stand by one. If the coolies attacked me, I could with confidence trust my negro friends for keeping me from injury.

(ibid.: 188)

Marx's materialist vision of evolving eras of historical struggle – while it may regard other issues of identity to be part of the illusion of false consciousness, a veil that would be lifted after radical consciousness is achieved – does, nevertheless, clearly recognise the importance of abolishing slavery. Marx and Engels recognised the pivotal importance of the struggle for emancipation and organised workers in textile mills in the north of England to block purchases of Confederacy cotton. After 1790, as Steven Marcus reports, 'it was the slave states of the American South that became the major suppliers for Lancashire mills' (Marcus 1974: 8).

Writing about slavery just after the Civil War, Marx (1976: 414) made the following comment, which clearly shows that he recognised that racial divisions were crucial to the success of the exploiters: 'In the United States of North America every independent movement of the workers was paralyzed so long as slavery disfigured a part of the republic. Labour cannot emancipate itself in the white skin where in the black it is branded' (Marx 1990: 329). Furthermore, he realised that the conditions among the industrial working class in Britain were not dissimilar to the racist divisions between black and white people in the USA. The following passage comes from a letter that Marx wrote from London to Sigfrid Meyer and August Vogt in New York on 9 April 1870:

Every industrial and commercial centre in England now possesses a working class divided into two hostile camps, English proletarians and Irish proletarians. The ordinary English worker hates the Irish worker as a competitor who lowers his standard of life. In relation to the Irish worker he regards himself as a member of the ruling nation and consequently he becomes a tool of the English aristocrats and capitalists against Ireland, thus strengthening their domination over himself. He cherishes religious, social, and national prejudices against the Irish worker. His attitude towards him is much the same as that of the 'poor whites' to the Negroes in the former slave states of the U.S.A. The Irishman pays him back with interest in his own money. He sees in the English worker both the accomplice and the stupid tool of the English rulers in Ireland. This antagonism is artificially kept alive and intensified by the press, the pulpit, the comic papers, in short, by all the means at the disposal of the ruling classes. This antagonism is the secret of the impotence of the English working class, despite its organization. It is the secret by which the capitalist class maintains its power. And the latter is quite aware of this.

(Marx and Engels 1982: 222)

The contention contained in Marx's letter is certainly a valid assessment of the instrumental use of race as a strategic tool to enable the divide and rule of workers by the elite, whether the latter consists of factory and mill owners, colonists in the New World or, perhaps, recent government rhetoric about immigration and threats from terrorism, such as that surrounding Bush and Blair's invasion of Iraq in 2003, with its concurrent concerns about 'asylum seekers' and refugees. Critics of Marxist views might do well to consider the enduring relevance of the view that race is not an inherent identity based on biological or cultural characteristics but is used expediently as a fluid set of rationalisations, continuously shifting in response to considerations related to the demands of industry, military needs in times of war and calls for national unity in the face of economic global threat.

Racism is not a universal and transcendental phenomenon but rather socially constructed, manifest in historically specific policies shaped by the labour market, ideology, government intervention and political resistance. Efforts to create ethnic antagonism have been well documented during the period of European imperial power (see the case study of Guyana in Chapter 7) through the use of derogatory stereotypes and divisive policies that pitch different groups into competitive relationships, thus effectively dividing workers and creating obstacles for collective resistance to colonialism. In the post-war era there is evidence that more subtle ideological forces are employed in addition to the coercive apparatus of the state. More progressive Marxist forms recognise the influence of the media and cultural reproduction through the agency of education. (The case study in Chapter 6 illustrates the way in which the media can crystallise public concerns and channel the flow of collective anxiety.)

Marxism suggests that racism serves the ruling class in several ways. First, its legitimises domination and exploitation. If racial hierarchies are accepted as they become habitual and normal, the inequity is neutralised it has become ideological. For example, colonial attitudes expressed colonial relations as a 'natural' hierarchy:

Nature has made a race of workers, the Chinese race, who have wonderful manual dexterity and almost no sense of humour; ... a race of tillers of the soil, the Negro ...; a race of masters and soldiers, the European race. Reduce this noble race to working ... like Negros or Chinese and they rebel.

(quoted in Loomba 1998: 126)

Second, as also illustrated by the above quote (and Marx's own example of racism against Irish workers in the textile mills), racism provides a method of dividing and ruling the workforce. Not only does this prevent a collective working-class consciousness from emerging but it also develops functional divisions of labour. Third, racism is employed to distract attention away from the divisive actions of the elite by effectively scapegoating a vulnerable group. Within the Third Reich the argument that the Jews had been the reason for Germany's defeat in the First World War was used to rally collective support and a wave of revulsion that made the Final Solution possible.

The roots of racism could be argued to always have been grounded in labour relations. Race was a constructed concept which, as we have seen, enabled colonialists to justify an expendable workforce of slaves. In contemporary society it could equally be argued that the focus on difference (ethnicisation or racialisation) between workers is still maintained and serves a similar function. In recent years there has been considerable work around the dynamic intersection of race and class in specific contemporary situations especially post-war Britain. Race is fundamental to the formation of the working classes in general and to the experience of black labour in particular. It has been suggested that class relations within communities of black working-class people 'function as race-relations. The two are inseparable. Race is the modality in which class is lived' (Hall *et al.* 1978: 394). Similarly, race provides the lived reality of class relations. Hence, race has consequences for all within that class: it moulds and shapes their conditions of existence and it has transformative power, bringing about changes in opportunities and the relative open or closed conditions between those marked out as visibly different and their economic relationships with the greater society.

In assessing the connection between race/ethnicity and class the starting point is often the relative economic positions of ethnic groups, extrapolating from economic processes to class. The view that immigrants or migrants are part of an underclass is frequently put forward. Marxist theorising argues that migration provides a 'reserve army of labour' which functions to keep wages low and maximise profits (see Castles and Kossack 1985). However, the post-Fordist restructure of the labour force and the recognition that other forms of social division such as ethnicity and gender are not merely the result of class structures render any simple views of race as class highly problematic.

While notions of race and racism have been shown to have complex origins associated with the beginnings of capitalism in the USA and Europe, can racism be shown to have grown out of capitalism (as Oliver Cox, the black Marxist writer, claims (1976)), or does the structuration of racial boundaries have an influence on the formation of class (a view supported by John Rex (1980) and Stuart Hall (1980))? Some, such as Anthias, suggest that Marxist theories are not fully adequate, arguing that ethnicity has much more to say about the ways people live, communicate and interact with one another and that, historically, racial divisions pre-date capitalism and indeed have had a powerful influence on the formation of capitalism: 'Since the three hundred years of slave labour are central to the development of capitalism, the Marxist interpretation of history in terms of the dialectic of capitalist class struggle is inadequate' (Anthias and Yuval-Davis 1992: 134).

Sivanandan's view, based on UK studies (1986), gives support to the position that racism is fundamental to capitalism. Colonialism formalised racism as a means of rationalisation or economic justification that sowed the seeds for racist ideologies. Wallerstein (Balibar and Wallerstein 1991: 33) observes that racial hierarchies operate as a 'magic formula' for capitalism, allowing very low wages for some sections of the workforce and stifling protest through a process of 'ethnicisation' of the workforce.

Miles's (1982; 1986) critique of the sociology of race focused on racism, which he perceived 'as integral to the process of capital accumulation' (Solomos and Back 1996: 8). In this view, race and the process of racialisation are masks that disguise the real economic relations: 'racism is mostly conceived as ideological, a set of rationalizations for sustaining exploitative economic practices and exclusionary political relations' (Goldberg 1993: 93).

The migrant-labour model developed by Robert Miles and Annie Phizacklea (1980) prioritises the political economy of migrant labour and avoids any reference to 'race relations', a terms that they feel adds status to a divisive social and political construct. In other words, by attributing meaning to the term 'race' the term is reified, leading 'to a commonsense acceptance that "race" is an objective determinant of the behaviour of black workers or other racially defined social categories' (Rex and Mason 1986: 99).

To Miles race is only a political category, but the process of racialisation is 'a dialectical process of signification' (1989: 75) that goes hand in hand with the exploitation of 'migrant labour'. Racialisation can be used, Miles says, in 'those instances where social relations between people have been structured by the signification of human biological characteristics in such a way as to define and construct differentiated social collectivities' (ibid.). He gives an illustration of this process at work in 1920s colonial Kenya. As in many colonial outposts, the African population was prevented from planting coffee – not because they would pose a threat to the colonists but rather because the relative independence and contentment that this might bring to Africans who were forced to live on reserves was seen as likely to reduce their perception of the necessity of working for the colonial landowners. In addition, the imposition of a number of taxes forced Africans to work to afford to pay them (ibid.: 109–10).

The reification of 'race' and the use of terms such as 'race relations' and 'racism' run a significant danger, Miles warns, of giving reality to a spurious and ideological term: 'Race is an idea which should be explicitly and consistently confined to the dustbin of analytically useless terms' (ibid.: 42). Certainly this was a timely warning that some of the most prominent analyses, by implicitly accepting the term 'race' in sociological studies and by losing sight of the political meanings of such a dubious term, had inadvertently lent the concept some theoretical credence: '[Miles's] work constitutes an attempt to reclaim the study of racism from an apoliticised socio-logical framework and locate it squarely in a Marxist theorisation of social conflict' (Solomos and Back 1996: 10).

In post-colonial societies such as Britain and many countries in Western Europe and America, the exploitation of 'asylum seekers' and 'guest workers' – workers who are living in often desperately poor conditions and under the threat of exposure to the immigration authorities – seems to bear out Miles's migrant labour thesis. Governments are not averse to exacerbating public fears and xenophobia and routinely take a strong platform on immigration before elections, while the media often employs the most lurid stories about the threat from 'scroungers', 'skivers' or 'economic migrants'. However, many basic services in inner cities are staffed largely by migrant workers of one sort or another. A recent US survey of America's full-time farm workers suggests that 53 per cent of crop workers are 'unauthorized' (Martin 2007). Similarly, despite fluctuations, the overall picture of migrant contribution in the UK is a positive one. Against a backdrop of accusations that migrants travel to Britain solely to exploit the National Health System and welfare system, the Refugee Council highlighted a very different picture:

- Immigrants, including refugees, pay more into the public purse compared to their UK-born counterparts (Sriskandarajah *et al.* 2005)
- An estimated 30,000 jobs have been created in Leicester by Ugandan Asian refugees since 1972 (Harris 2002)
- About 1,200 medically qualified refugees are recorded on the British Medical Association's database (Refugee Council 2008)
- It is estimated that it costs around £25,000 to support a refugee doctor to practise in the UK. Training a new doctor is estimated to cost between £200,000 and £250,000 (NHS Employers 2009)

(Refugee Council online 2013)

At the same time these higher rates of participation in the labour market are not matched by the access of migrants to state benefits: Dustmann *et al.* (2010) found that even if A8[2] migrants had the same characteristics as UK-born individuals they would still be less likely to receive government benefits and social housing (Vargas-Silva 2013).

It has become clear, however, that these attempts to exclude migrants have the ironic consequence of constituting them as an ideal labour force that can be exploited, coerced and paid the very minimum (and in some cases not paid at all). In fact, the situation for many refugees who wish to leave their countries has been recognised as not much better than slavery.

> The economic position of black people is often a starting point when examining the connection between race and class. There can be said to be two strata within the working class: indigenous workers forming the upper, more privileged group and, beneath that, the immigrants who are (even in times of relative prosperity) the most exploited and underprivileged group in society.
>
> (Anthias and Yuval-Davis 1992: 62)

The black Marxist writer Oliver Cox perceived racism as developing out of capitalism 'and provid[ing] a means for furthering the use of labour as a commodity, pure and simple, resulting in ... greater exploitation' (Anthias and Yuval-Davis 1992: 63). Miles argues that 'The influence of racism and exclusionary practices is always a component of a wider structure of class disadvantage and exclusion' (Miles 1989: 9).

Certainly Marxist perspectives offer powerful insights into the use of racism as a means to an end. However, the weakness of traditional Marxist analyses for issues of race and gender was an over-emphasis on economic bases as primary and a blind spot where other instrumental intersections with the institutions of capitalism were concerned. The role of the family, culture, sexuality and ethnic identity were not given serious analysis. Marxist theory, through which the relations of the means of production are operationalised through human subjects caught up in the struggle for survival, has been criticised as economistic and reductionist, allowing very little recognition for human agency. Yet Marx's beliefs in social change through conscious and collective action suggest this may be an unfair conclusion.

STRUCTURALIST CRITICISM OF MARXISM

Stuart Hall and other scholars at the Centre for Contemporary Cultural Studies have been influential in the work of many post-colonial critics. Hall has made interesting use of concepts developed by the Italian Marxist Antonio Gramsci to allow a more sophisticated Marxism to be brought to bear on the discourses that compose racism. Gramsci's concept of 'hegemony', based on the suggestion by Machiavelli that political domination of the masses is achieved by a combination of force and fraud, led Gramsci to consider the manner in which elites were able to create willing submission to rule. This view was quite different to the notion of direct repression and coercion, but does not deny the existence of brutal repressive force as well. However, 'hegemony is achieved not only by direct manipulation or indoctrination, but by playing upon the commonsense of people, upon what Raymond Williams calls their "lived system of meaning and values"' (Williams 1977: 110). A similar argument has been advanced by Herman and Chomsky in their thesis on the propaganda model (1995). They argue that there is a subtle and covert process of control that is achieved through the logic of market forces and the complacency of consumer society. These operations are much less visible than the aggressive censorship exercised by more dictatorial governments.

Hall perceptively draws out the importance of these ideas for thinking about the relationship between race, ethnicity and colonialism on the one hand and capital and class on the other hand (see Hall 1996b). Gramsci's work in the ideological field has proved very fruitful when applied to the complex interrelation between capitalism and racism. Hall comments that:

> he altogether refuses any idea of a pre-given ideological subject – for example, the proletarian with its 'correct' revolutionary thoughts or blacks with their already guaranteed current anti-racist consciousness. He recognises the 'plurality' of the selves or identities of which the so called 'subject' is composed. He argues that this multi-faceted nature of consciousness is not an individual but a collective phenomenon, a consequence of the relationship between 'the self' and the ideological discourses which compose the cultural terrain of a society.
>
> (Hall 1996a: 433)

Like Gramsci, Althusser (1971) argued against any ultimate reduction to the economic base and, further, that ideology has a material existence, as it can always be found to be implicit in the apparatus of social control. Ideological apparatus could therefore exert influence on the economic base. He proposed the terms 'repressive state apparatuses' (RSAs) and 'ideological state apparatuses' (ISAs) to explain the dual nature of control articulated by Gramsci. The coercive effects achieved by RSAs are less noticeable in advanced capitalism, but when direct dissent and threat to the state occurs they will be used, as, for example, in the UK during the miners' strike or the poll-tax demonstrations of 1990. In this view, when policies and the state's hegemony are under threat RSAs in the form of the army and the police are typically employed. ISAs include church, family, media and schools; these both achieve consent more effectively and ensure that the state is not exposed as coercive (maintaining the aura of what Mark Curtis calls 'basic benevolence'). The media is especially influential in undermining opposition (Herman and Chomsky 1995). Media representation of black and Asian people is a case in point. The moral panic surrounding asylum seekers and refugees can be shown as a distorted view on an issue that is high on the political agenda, partly, perhaps, as a result of steady pressure from popular media sources. Media Lens recently reported that there is a high degree of uniformity in the 'quality' press in the UK when it comes to covering issues of asylum seekers. These papers

(*The Daily Telegraph*, *The Independent* and *The Guardian*) showed a 'consistent unity of themes' that focused on 'bogus' asylum applicants, crime/terrorism perpetrated by asylum seekers and accommodation/detention issues. Matthew Randall (2003) argues that, to qualify as a truly independent and honest 'quality' press, other 'macro-stories' should be given coverage, such as:

- The fact that the NHS would cease to function without overseas nurses. The Royal College of Nursing reported in February 2003 that a quarter of all nurses working in the NHS in London (42,000) come from overseas. In 2013 about a quarter of UK NHS trusts are recruiting from overseas and over 20,000 post in UK nursing are unfilled (BBC News Health Report, Dreaper 2013).
- The declining UK population, which is a cause for concern. A UN report recommended 'replacement migration' as a solution. This recommendation was rejected by the European Commission on the grounds that the impact of immigration on population was insignificant.
- The intriguing correlation between the countries in which Britain has a lucrative arms trade and those that top the list of asylum seekers' countries of origin.
- The conditions in countries of origin, which are generally ignored: many asylum seekers are escaping poverty, human-rights abuses, conflict and torture.
- US and UK involvement in Iraq, Afghanistan, the Balkans and Somalia, which has led to increased violence and uncertainty for millions of the citizens of these nations, who make up the largest percentage of the world's refugees.

The manner in which these and other issues are covered in the press illustrates the potential that we are exposed to a very narrow selection of possible news while being inoculated to this fact by the belief that our press has a liberal bias and covers a broad spectrum of political viewpoints.

It has been argued that, as the media is market driven and conforms to the will of political elites, a hidden agenda operates by which other stories are filtered out and papers with very different readerships and ideological biases in practice operate within a very narrow field, tending to fall into line with the dominant political agendas of the time. This could be seen as a vindication of a central theme in Althusser's work: the manner in which human subjectivity is shaped by external forces. 'In fact subjectivity, or personhood, Althusser suggested, is itself formed in and through ideology' (Loomba 1998: 32). This formative impact of ideology is particularly noticeable in the colonial situation, where ethnically distinct occupational boundaries, residential patterns and other social divisions were often encouraged and maintained by colonial administrators. This occurred either as a result of the pragmatic circumstances in which different groups were brought to the colony – for example, indentured labourers to replace slaves – or through intentional planning intended to foster separate and easily manipulated enclaves.

In addition, Althusser attempted to explain the internal process by which the subject was influenced by ideological means. He describes interpellation (discussed in Chapter 1) as a process of identification by which a subject (mis) recognises him or herself in an 'identity' or role which is offered to him/her in society. Althusser hopes to show how ideologies either 'recruit' people to particular, acceptable subject positions in society or else transform individuals into subjects who learn to identify with certain representations. Thus, the interpellation effect can be achieved by an actual person addressing me or by a representation in a media text. Books, advertisements, TV programmes and films all contain representations of characters and situations with which we might identify; and bound up with such representations are certain societal norms, gender roles, attitudes towards certain groups and so on which may be disseminated and normalised or satirised. Ethnic identification is in this view a process of interpellation. Events and the manner in which they are broadcast can serve as powerful interpellators. The recent brutal killing in Woolwich, London of a soldier by a man of Nigerian origins who was very much part of the East London community is a powerful example. The mass media's image of the murderer with bloody hands holding a meat cleaver and talking to those who witnessed the killing sent an immediate message, encouraging the closing of ranks and short-circuiting rational reflection and interpretation. Reports (Harding 2013) show the hardening of attitudes about immigration and the failure of security services, rising sympathy for far-right political groups such as the English Defence League (EDL) and British National Party (BNP) and concurrent increases in abuse and assaults of people who are visibly different. 'Muslim' is a label which is quickly interpreted as 'alien aggressor', although the actions and beliefs that lead to such atrocious acts are, of course, held by only a tiny radicalised minority.

These heterogeneous Marxist approaches indicate that racism and race identities are not merely determined by class but represent a social construction that is a complex interrelation of social, political, economic and cultural structures within capitalism. The cultural-studies approach, which recognises the material effects of the production and circulation of cultural meanings, has drawn on both Althusser and Gramsci, allowing subtle studies of the production and dissemination of ideas about race. Each context has a unique interplay of ideological forces which serve to form the identity of ethnic groups both in relation to one another as potential rivals and to the dominant group (which may not always be the majority culture, but which holds the position of dominant elite). Hence there appears much to recommend a nuanced approach to understanding the processes of race-making and the intersectional combining of identity positions. Varieties of Marxist theorising enable an understanding of power relations strengthened by the analysis of capitalism, which arguably underpins and is the rationale for racism (see, for example, Lemert).

WEBERIAN/NEO-WEBERIAN THEORIES

Weber's work has been viewed as an extension and refinement of Marx's. Indeed, some feel that Weber 'spent his life having a posthumous dialogue with the ghost of Karl Marx' (Cuff *et al.* 1990: 97). This is a view which has some credibility, and differences between the two should not be overstated. However, for many Marxists, Weber's idealism and specificity of approach (methodological individualism) illustrates the tendency of sociological analysis to avoid the broad political question (the overt realpolitik of inequality and exploitation) and shows acquiescence to the power of the marketplace. Weber was passionate in defence not of the underprivileged and exploited but of the individual's right to self-determination and freedom from being pigeon-holed. His bleakest vision was the ascendancy of bureaucracy and rationalisation, either in the interests of global capitalism or of communism, whereby the individual is trapped in a dehumanising 'iron cage'. Perhaps in relation to ethnocentrism and racism the Nazi holocaust is the paradigm case of this process, which Weber saw as inexorably reducing individual integrity. Only a cold and calculating bureaucratic machine could manage the slaughter of millions of people in death camps with the efficiency with which this was achieved, by the use of numerical codes converting people into mere numbers. A cataloguing system provided by IBM tabulating machines is alleged to have had a hand in expediting the Final Solution (see Black 2001).

John Rex and David Mason (1986) brought a Weberian emphasis to their studies of ethnic relations, broadening the scope of sociological analysis of this neglected field to allow other aspects of the individual psyche, which traditional Marxism would see as a distraction, to be taken into account in the study of race. For Weber, who had given more thought to ethnic relations, ethnic boundary-making could be seen as a method of closing ranks against outsiders, of creating monopolistic social closure. For traditional Marxists, social divisions other than those based on relations and forces of production are nothing other than false consciousness that allows the persistence of an elite that will encourage such divisions and profit from them (whether they are delusory or not). According to Weber:

> An ethnic group is based, in this view, on the belief shared by its members that, however distantly, they are of common descent. [...] race creates a 'group' only when it is subjectively perceived as a common trait: this happens only when a neighbourhood or the mere proximity of racially different persons is the basis of joint (mostly political) action, or conversely, when some common experiences of members of the same race are linked to some antagonism against members of an obviously different group.
>
> (Weber 1978: 35)

Furthermore, he suggests that:

> ethnic membership does not constitute a group; it only facilitates group formation of any kind, particularly in the political sphere. On the other hand, it is primarily the political community, no matter how artificially organized, that inspires the belief in common ethnicity.

(ibid.: 35)

Weber therefore considers that the belief in common ancestry is a consequence of collective political activity rather than its cause. So, far from some primordial view of ethnic roots, people begin to see themselves as belonging together as a consequence of this collective action. Therefore, the pursuit of collective interests can be seen to encourage ethnic identification.

John Rex's unique contribution has been to offer an analysis which takes account of the interwoven nature of class, race and ethnicity. Rex describes the dynamic relationship between ethnicity and class in terms of the structures of dominance operating in society:

> Those structures are classes and groups in conflict, which define themselves and are defined in ethnic and racial terms, but which also engage in a kind of class struggle resulting from their immediate relation to the means of production and its supporting political apparatus.

(Rex in Rex and Mason 1986: 77)

Furthermore, Rex sees different theoretical frameworks as useful contributions to the understanding of ethnic identities and relations. He argues that a more useful approach would be to look specifically 'at the point at which conflict most usually arises, namely in the business of employment relations and production' (Rex 1986a: 70). This shows the important unifying significance of Rex's approach.

Guyana provides a good example of the way in which employment relations and ethnicity have created a division which corresponds to class relations. The East Indians were brought in as indentured labourers and the African-Guyanese are the descendants of freed slaves. It can be argued that the two groups have, since their first encounters, been in a frequently antagonistic relationship that is attributable to the competition for labour and the resentment of one for the other, which was also exploited actively by colonists.

Rex (1980) suggests that in South Africa capitalism was installed through the enforced labour of the Bantu peoples. Thus race relations were crucial in making available a labour force. In *Capital* Marx had suggested that capitalism depends upon 'the free labourer selling his labour power' to the owners of the means of production (Marx 1961: 170). But in South Africa, as in a variety of other colonial situations, the labour of colonised peoples was commissioned through a variety of coercive measures. It was not free labour at all. Rex quotes an East African settler to make his point: 'We have stolen his country now we must steal his limbs ... Compulsory labour is the corollary of our occupation of the country' (Rex 1980: 129).

Rex refers to Weber's dual concept of capitalism, which involves a form of capitalism peacefully orientated to market opportunity (free labour markets) and 'adventurer' or 'booty' capitalism, which was characteristic of imperialism (for example, South Africa under Apartheid).

> I find these notions useful in that what seems to me to be involved in South Africa is not so much a society which articulates two modes of production as one in which a modern capitalist state is marked by strong elements of surviving booty capitalism. As far as the status of relatively unfree black labour is concerned I believe that it is best understood in terms of a typology of labour which can be derived from Weber's *General Economic History* (1961) and from his writings on agrarian institutions in the ancient world.
>
> (Rex 1986a: 68)

This is at odds with classical Marxism, which attributes capitalism's efficiency to having replaced the oppressive forms of coercion and slavery with the idea of the 'free' labour market. Capitalism then – contrary to traditional Marxism – does not always mark an end to coercive use of racial hierarchies, but uses them fully and intensifies them to produce the most efficient labour to power its enterprises. Indeed, as Miles reports on Kenya and Rex comments about South Africa, the capitalist systems there have exploited their resources very much following the principles of rationalisation. 'The South African labour system is the most efficient system of labour exploitation yet devised, resting as it does on the three institutions of the rural reserve, the mining compound and the controlled urban "location"' (Rex 1980: 129). Rex and others suggest that racism helps to structure capitalist expansion. It is especially important

> in maintaining certain hierarchies when the state and legal systems can no longer be blatantly partisan. [...] When the social order could no longer be buttressed by legal sanctions it had to depend upon the inculcation in the minds of both exploiters and exploited of a belief in the superiority of the exploiters and inferiority of the exploited. Thus it can be argued that the doctrine of equality of economic opportunity and that of racial superiority and inferiority are complements of one another. Racism serves to bridge the gap between theory and practice.
>
> (ibid.: 131)

Interpretative approaches to social phenomena place much more emphasis upon analyses of individual behaviours and the motives behind these, in contrast to Marxian methods, which are structuralist approaches to society that seek underlying laws of mass social change. Belief systems underpin much of our behaviour and thus Rex makes the point that

> the sociology of race relations must take account of subjective definitions, stereotypes, typifications and belief systems in the business of defining its field. And we would emphasize that patterns of social relations may be considerably changed through the causal agency of such belief systems.
>
> (Rex 1970: 9)

Belief systems are associated with a restricted range of structures and Rex therefore believes the task is to uncover these.

Some sociologists have tried to develop a more theoretical approach to explaining the position of ethnic minorities in the labour market and in society as a whole. From one point of view, ethnic minorities form an 'underclass', a concept based upon a Weberian analysis of stratification. The concept of a racialised underclass has been put forward by several researchers. Rex and Tomlinson (1979) argue that the position of many black people in the UK can be better understood in terms of a systematically disadvantaged underclass that appears in stark contrast to the majority of the white working class. Recent (UK) figures suggest that members of ethnic minorities are consistently discriminated against in terms of job opportunities and are three or four times less likely to be employed regardless of prevailing economic circumstances than members of the white community. So it is hardly surprising that

> instead of associating with working-class culture, community and politics, they formed their own organisations and became in effect a separate underprivileged class. In short they formed an underclass which was perpetuated by the predominance of ethnic minorities in the secondary labour market.
>
> (ibid.: 390)

However, such an approach fails to envision the interplay of social/cultural and political forces within a capitalist system and accepts the long-standing and self-fulfilling academic doxa of the underclass as composed of those morally defective or culturally deprived and of the social space of the city as a criminal and corrupting influence (see Wacquant 2009). 'Inner city culture conjures up the very real political economy of racialized space that the concept of the Underclass is assumed to be theorizing' (Goldberg in Back and Solomos 2000: 167).

In the American context Loïc Wacquant (2002) argues that the ghetto is the successor of chattel slavery and the segregation enacted by the Jim Crow laws. Each system is a means of controlling and exploiting the black population. The recent phase of the hyperghetto, in Wacquant's analysis, enhances the exploitation of ghettos with the disproportionate rates of incarceration which became the norm for the black population after 1988. These interlocking systems, he argues, are America's peculiar race-making engines, resulting from the collision of slavery with democracy.

Ethnic identity, then, is a construct which is at times negotiable and unfixed, but at other times has relatively firm boundaries set (especially where political movements reflect ethnic identity); but it can also be maintained and exploited as a resource by the interplay of cultural, social, political and material forces.

It is unnecessary for class and ethnicity to be seen as discrete independent variables in a competition for primacy. Rather, it is clearly possible for both to be viewed as interacting elements in a systematic theory of boundary formation in a society. As Rex has suggested, 'it is not necessary to exclude from consideration the possibility of a situation in which either ethnicity or class, or both together operate as the main means of boundary marking' (Rex 1986b: 6).

It can be seen from this discussion that Weber's methodology and his emphases on meaning and *verstehen* have added depth and complexity to conceptions of race and ethnicity. Weber used the term *verstehen* in reference to the sociologist's attempt to understand both the motives and the context of human action. It becomes apparent that human cultures are complex structures that we simultaneously create and are created by, or, as Clifford Geertz writes,

> Believing, with Max Weber, that man is an animal suspended in webs of significance he himself has spun, I take culture to be those webs, and the analysis of it to be therefore not an experimental science in search of law but an interpretive one in search of meaning.
>
> (Geertz 1973: 5)

SYMBOLIC INTERACTIONISM

One such interpretative science in search of meaning is symbolic interactionism, a field that stems from American social psychology, the work of the Chicago School of Sociology and the philosophical thought of George Herbert Mead. The term, which was first used by Herbert Blumer in 1937, was founded on the basic tenet that human beings construct and transmit culture through complex symbols. The key concern is with the way in which meanings are expressed about the self, human relations, feelings and bodies. There is a focus upon the way in which meaning is constructed which relates to the structuralist and semiotic project (explained in Chapter 1) whereby people encode and decode conventional codes by which they mediate their existence. In addition, the interactionist approach seems well suited to the study of dynamic situations such as ethnic relations, where there are constant changes and negotiations of identity.

One advocate of this approach is Richard Jenkins (2003). Drawing on anthropological approaches to ethnicity by Barth (1969) and Geertz (1973), Jenkins highlights the key areas of a consensual anthropology of ethnicity: ethnicity is primarily 'about collective identification based in perceived cultural differentiation' (2008: 78) and shared cultural meanings, but is produced by communication and interaction across boundaries. Further, in his works *Social Identity* (1996) and *Rethinking Ethnicity* (2008), Jenkins suggests that ethnicity is relatively flexible and that, although anthropologists have focused on boundary formation and maintenance, the content within the boundaries is equally important. The individual (and collective) sense of identity is constituted by a process of identification through constant interaction between others and self. Jenkins has called this 'the internal-external dialectic of identification' (1996: 20), noting that: 'ethnic identity is always a dialectic between similarity and difference' (2008: 169).

For interactionists, social contexts are always encounters that have shifting and unstable outcomes – a view similar to Stuart Hall's description of ethnic identity as always incomplete, always in the process of becoming. This approach, which certainly appears theoretically strong in interpreting the local dynamics of ethnic identities, has been criticised for emphasising the agent 'at the expense of the social structure' (Malesevic 2004: 72–3). It is hence less likely to recognise the impact of macro-structural and material factors, as the focus is on the social actor's negotiated response to social contexts encountered.

Erving Goffman's dramaturgical theory of social relations (see Goffman 1984) has some useful features too, such as the suggestion that ethnicity (like gender and sexuality) can be performative, obeying certain rituals and rules. The analogy to social interactions occurring in the public arena, like actors on a stage, is a useful one, allowing some recognition of how cross-cultural encounters may be rehearsed as people engage in 'impression management' and differentiate between 'backstage' and 'frontstage' zones. Examples of this abound in ethnically divided nations. In Malaysia I witnessed a manifestation of ethnic conflict in the east-coast Malaysian town of Mersing. A Chinese Malay entrepreneur entered a Chinese café where many western travellers typically assembled and was signing up tourists as passengers for a catamaran crossing to a nearby island. Conflict occurred when a Malay with an old fishing boat also tried to sign up passengers. Unable to compete with the faster, more luxurious catamaran, he suddenly exploded with rage, violently cursing and throwing chairs at the Chinese Malay. This certainly was not a context in which 'healthy competition' was acceptable. The Chinese Malay backed off quickly before the police (who are almost all Malay) had a chance to intervene. The apparent speedy acquiescence of Chinese Malays in this sort of confrontation is a reflection of the political and economic regulations within the country, which are designed to benefit Malay Malays through affirmative action (reflecting the Malay dominance of the political system, army and police and the Chinese power as business people in the country).[3] However, after this incident, when the Chinese café closed for the night, the Chinese owners of the café invited me in for a meal and, as the steel shutters were closed on the street, their previous silence and show of 'business as usual' and gave way to angry invective that had obviously been bottled up for most of the day.

In *Interaction Ritual* (1972), Goffman gives the example of 'face work'. 'Face' for Goffman means 'the positive social value a person effectively claims for himself by the line others assume he has taken during a particular contact' (Goffman 1972: 5). One basic type of face work is avoidance. In other words, the actor will avoid social contexts that present the possibility of 'losing face'. Goffman gives the example of the 'middle- and upper-class Negro who avoids certain face-to-face contacts with whites in order to protect the self-evaluation projected by his clothes and manner' (ibid.: 15).

Goffman's focus on everyday social exchanges adds another level of analysis to the internal landscape of racism, this constant negotiation of internalised self-identity negotiated between one's own community and the negative public image generalised by the wider society. It may also be used to show the phenomenon of self-contempt, where the stigmatised identity is internalised or projected onto others in whom the hated features are perceived. A consequence of structural injustice, it could be suggested, is a dehumanising self-contempt formed as the socially stigmatised identity is internalised. This self-contempt indicates the hegemonic power of racialised divisions.

FOUCAULT AND DISCOURSE THEORY

Michel Foucault's major contribution to critical thinking within the social sciences has been his analysis of a particular form of power that had been relatively overlooked in sociology, where there has been a tendency to talk about power being vested in the state, or about the power of the bourgeoisie or the ruling class, and to present a picture of society as containing good and bad, the power holders and those without power.

Foucault's analyses are effective in showing that those centralised forms of power do not exhaust what we have to say about power. Power also has other qualities and, even if we take the formal position, we have to try to explain how it might come about that power can be centralised in the form of the state. The work of Poulantzas (1973) makes reference to the importance of force and coercion and ultimately insists that this force is vested in the state. While it is clear that most, if not all, centralised states do have 'might', force and the power of coercion at their disposal, more often than not power is being exercised without any recourse to force and, furthermore, this is the most effective type of power. Foucault's notion of 'biopower' indicates how these discursive forms of power vested in scientific and medical practices can have material effects on certain populations. Foucault makes the point that a primordial discourse of blood could be invoked to validate ideas of race and sexuality. The supposed purity of a bloodline was the basis of a number of definitions of nationality, as, for example, in Germany and Japan:

> Beginning in the second half of the nineteenth century, the thematics of blood was sometimes called upon to lend their entire historical weight towards revitalising the political power that was exercised through the devices of sexuality. Racism took shape at this point (racism in its modern, 'biologising' statist form). It was then that the whole politics of settlement (peuplement), family, marriage, education, social hierarchisation and property, accompanied by a long series of permanent interventions at the level of the body, conduct, health and everyday life, received their colour and their justification from the mythical concern with protecting the purity of the blood and ensuring the triumph of the race.
>
> (Foucault 1984: 149)

Foucault is indicating that we should not envisage power as emanating from a single source. Power flows have real impacts but may originate from diverse disciplinary areas, shaping and modulating societal action to identify certain groups as deviant and threatening by constituting individual subjectivity. The relationship between language, thought and social action has long been recognised. Foucault's study of discourse has had a marked impact on social sciences as it recognises that our social institutions, policies and structures are organised through 'regimes of truth', dominant disciplinary domains that focus and filter concerns about the 'other'. Indeed, discourse creates 'otherness'. Discourse, as defined by Foucault, refers to:

> ways of constituting knowledge, together with the social practices, forms of subjectivity and power relations which inhere in such knowledges and relations between them. Discourses are more than ways of thinking and producing meaning. They constitute the 'nature' of the body, unconscious and conscious mind and emotional life of the subjects they seek to govern.
>
> (Weedon 1987: 108)

Discourse is the constituent of power, the conduit through which power flows. In Foucault's conception of power it is not possessed but rather it is created by interrelations of knowledge that construct positions for those who are subject to certain practices. For example, the shifting discursive practices of law, psychiatry, anthropology and social Darwinism 'produce' certain members of society as marginal, criminal, insane, immoral or racially inferior. The effect is never simply the elite imposing ideologically on the masses. In Chapters 2 and 3 we saw the gradual drift from universal ideas of united humanity through the complex development of views of the 'other' as inherently different, affirmed and challenged, never static, despite the attempts to impose laws that dictate new definitions of being (take the 1741 Carolina Law, for example). There is always resistance, never a unitary crushing power (although at times this is hard to accept, as the consequences of discourses can be crushing and genocidal).

> Truth is not outside of power nor itself lacking in power [...] the truth [is] not those true things waiting to be discovered but rather the ensemble of rules according to which we distinguish the true from the false, and attach special effects of power to 'the truth'
>
> (Foucault 1980: 131)

Foucault's conception of power is a diffuse one; power is everywhere and it is exercised at innumerable points. One can never be outside of the operation of power. Foucault argues that all discourses produce a discourse of resistance, but this omnipresence of power seems to make it hard to imagine resistance being practically or successfully utilised. Foucault did not focus on ethnicity, but it seems clear that this conception of the fluid movement of power and resistance could be applied to regimes of colonialism and anti-colonial struggles. His work allows the local intellectual to rally support to various micro-causes. Much of Foucault's work is aimed at giving individuals trapped within a particular discourse a 'voice'; universal ideas of human nature or humanity are meaningless. For him, the wider structures that control and create individuals are more important. Foucauldian genealogy has certainly been influential in providing theoretical tools to deconstruct regimes of power and disciplines or regimes of thought, although his denial of ideology and focus on micro-sites of power is seen by some (particularly Marxist thinkers) to come at the expense of neglecting the power of the state.

However, Foucault's unique contribution is to ask how disciplines have imposed their own needs on how we look at the world (for example, the disciplines of sociology or psychology). Foucault deconstructs (takes apart and examines) the origins of systems of thought and the historical development of institutions, which are argued to be formative of individual subjectivity and complex relations of power. He shows the complex institutional and historical relationships between knowledge and power, theorising that stable notions of identity are untenable as individual identity is never immanent but always contingent on social and political discourses which the person both consumes and contributes to.

Discourses that emanate from social, political, historical and cultural sources construct the social world and our identity in negotiation with this world. Discourse is much more than just language. It is also the institutional practices that follow from the partiality of naming and categorisation. For example, the dominant discourses of ethnicity, gender and sexuality entail political and legal definitions of the status of individual subjects. 'Discourses are the practices that systematically form the objects of which they speak' (Foucault 1972: 49). Muecke notes that 'One of the slogans of discourse theory is that "discourses create their own object", language itself becomes the material knowledge, since "advances" in knowledge involve reshuffling the classifications made available in discourse' (Muecke 1982: 100).

Discourse theory is important because it permits the recognition that social groups are often narrowly constructed in different disciplines, as in anthropological, criminal justice, medical or literary discourses. Such discursive construction was rarely questioned. Terms such as 'insane', 'disabled', 'Aborigine' and 'delinquent' are now recognised as part of a process of institutional categorisation, which often had severe consequences for people's human rights. Stephen Muecke points out the often narrowly ascribed ways of defining and speaking about the 'other'. The construction of the discourse of race is relatively new and socially imagined – reflecting not essential differences but regimes of thought that are subject to periodic shifts and transformations. Table 1.1 illustrates the social and historical nature of these broad transformations in our recognition of the 'other'. Muecke's seminal (1982) article 'Available Discourses on Aborigines' uses the post-structuralist linguistics of Michel Pecheux to show how Australians marginalise the Aboriginal peoples by a restrictive lexicon of 'otherness'. The case of Aboriginal Australians is not unique, however: we all use language that embodies categories and cases that can exclude or include and carry a legacy of positive or negative connotations. Muecke suggests that a restricted number of discourses (romantic, anthropological, literary and racist) provide the only means open to white Australians to speak of or construct ideas of aboriginality.

Hall makes the point that while Marxist ideology, Althusserian interpellation and semi-autonomy and Foucauldian discourse have each developed our conception of the forces that operate in producing human subjectivity 'of how individuals are summoned into place in the discursive structures' (Hall and du Gay 1996: 13), they fall short in addressing how the subject is constituted (although Foucault marks the furthest stage in developing this by the description of 'historically specific discursive practices, normative self-regulation and technologies of the self' (ibid.: 13).

BOURDIEU

Marx conceived of the relationship between human subjectivity and outside forces in the following way:

Circumstances create people in the same degree as people create circumstances. Both social servitude and the movement towards its abolition have as their condition certain subjective factors. material subjugation; the ideas of the dominant class are dominant ideas; the class which commands material force also commands the means of intellectual coercion, as it produces and propagates the ideas that express its own supremacy.

(Kolakowski 1985: 158)

This quote shows that Marxian thought is not crude reductionism. Statements such as this suggest a more equivocal understanding of the social processes through which power relations operate – not merely through structural means but also through internalised value systems. Later theorists, as we have seen, have begun the process of examining how the individual's internal value system is constructed. Pierre Bourdieu's contribution has been to offer a synthesis between the macro-structural processes of the materialist positions and the micro-interactionist and internalised processes of the interpretivists.

Bourdieu has presented a view of power relationships that is similar to that of Althusser yet maintains some of the original material force of traditional Marxism in his concept of 'habitus', developed in his influential 'theory of practice' (Bourdieu 1977). It is an idea by which the problem of ethnic identity might be examined without the attendant risk of being forced to opt for either instrumentalist or primordialist viewpoints, which are seemingly irreconcilable (see ibid.; Bourdieu 1990). The habitus is the generative principle that shapes the individual's subjectivity and constrains their behavioural repertoire which is displayed in particular 'fields'. Field, for Bourdieu, is a field of forces in which the individual performs. In this sense the dispositions which form the habitus are recognised in the field where the performance of habitual knowledge is demonstrated.

It is a view, which does not suffer from the pitfalls of Marxian and plural society theories that presuppose some inevitable cycle of ethnic conflict or class struggle. Ethnic relations may be viewed as social and historical codes that, while they shape individual identity and behaviour, are not immutable structures. Rather, they are seen as part of a repertoire of strategies that an individual will use, depending on individual as well as communal codes of practice, to make sense of and to negotiate social situations with which they are confronted.

Bourdieu has explained the reflexive concept of habitus as follows:

The habitus, a product of history, produces individual and collective practices – more history – in accordance with the themes generated by history. It ensures the active presence of past experiences, which, deposited in each organism in the form of schemes of perception, thought and action, tend to guarantee the 'correctness' of practices and their constancy over time more reliably than all formal rules and explicit norms.

(Bourdieu 1990: 54)

Bourdieu is suggesting that the objective conditions of existence – material events in social history – generate the habitus which, like a grammar of behaviours, in turn generates certain dispositions, attitudes and behaviours: a lexicon from which each individual may choose. This allows a more inclusive, intersectional view that does not insist on arguing for primacy of either social class or ethnicity. All such influences are part of the habitus and have been ultimately derived from the history of an individual, a group or, indeed, a population. The habitus is most definitely not an idealist or abstract concept: 'the habitus only exists in, and through and because of the practices of actors and their interaction with each other and with their environment: ways of talking, ways of moving, ways of making things, or whatever' (Jenkins 1992: 27).

The habitus clearly has features in common with the Marxian view that material conditions giving rise to a social class will be reproduced in the material practices of those experiencing such conditions. The habitus enables a view of ethnic identity and boundaries that allows a focus on social class and socio-cultural interactions rather than appraising these sets of factors as competing explanatory variables or assigning primacy to one or the other. All acts of ethnic expression can be explained in terms of lived experiences, habitual practices that produce the codes by which people live and inscribe meanings onto the body and psyche of the individual. A corollary of this is that the 'theory of practice' allows for analysis of both individuals and groups.

There are differences in each individual's habitus – unique individuals construct their own. However, the individual has also been steeped in the specific traditions of a group, embodying its social codes. Therefore, while the habitus has a potentially infinite capacity to produce practices, the actual behaviours brought into active practice are 'constrained without violence, art or argument'. The group habitus tends to exclude all 'extravagances' ('not for the likes of us'): that is, all the behaviours that would be negatively sanctioned because they are incompatible with the objective conditions (Bourdieu 1990: 56).

Brackette Williams (1991) applies Bourdieu's concept of habitus to the depiction of the struggle for 'symbolic dominance' in Guyana's ethnically polarised situation. In Guyana it became apparent that the attempt to establish hegemony over the rival group was well marked, and everyday interaction in public life was often seen as a battleground for ethnic rivalry and a struggle for symbolic domination. As Bourdieu and Boltanski note, 'symbolic domination really begins when the misrecognition (meconnaissance), implied by recognition (reconnaissance), leads those who are dominated to apply the dominant criteria of evaluation to their own practices' (Bourdieu and Boltanski 1976: 4).

Bourdieu's 'theory of practice' can readily be used to look at cases of interethnic differences, alienation and conflict. The two major groups in Guyana, in many cases, can be seen to share the same language, speak with enthusiasm about the same aspirations, wear similar clothes and display many other similarities.

Yet, although these superficial similarities are often mentioned, they may be rooted in very different generative structures (see Bentley 1987: 37). Overlaps in the behavioural repertoire of peoples having characteristically different experiences (and habitus) are likely to give rise to invalid assumptions of mutual understanding: what Jürgen Habermas (1970) calls 'systematically distorted communication' (Bentley 1987: 37).

Furthermore, while it must be recognised that some surface structures appear similar (although derived from different habitus), such congruency of codes may be reserved for those public contexts in which collaboration is a functional necessity. Quite different codes will be exhibited in a more private domain. For example, in Guyana many street traders will take on a friendly attitude and communicate freely with members of the different ethnic groups, playing down any differences; yet with cohorts of their own ethnic group they may actively deride their erstwhile associates, borrowing freely from the available lexicon of stereotypes to describe their encounters. In this way Bourdieu's theory of practice helps us to avoid misreadings of ethnic relations in Guyana.

The strength of Bourdieu's approach is its empirical nature and its resistance to the acceptance of abstract categories of 'class'; instead, aspects of social space are understood in terms of fine-grained relationships between types of capital and their distribution between different social groups. Bourdieu (1989a) argues that social space is constituted by three dimensions demarked by our position in relation to social, cultural and economic capital. An individual's position in this social space shapes his or her tastes and preferences, ways of speaking and bodily hexis; indeed, the individual's practical sense that we might see as second nature. The habitus is composed of dispositions which accrue from life experiences, especially those resulting from deep-seated family or cultural conditioning.

The differences in habitus that can lead to conflict and misunderstanding or selective perception of the 'other' may occur within a specific group. That is, if members of a particular ethnic community are exposed to different objective conditions to those of their fellow members their habitus will be shaped by the new experiences and thus their ability to relate wholeheartedly to the values of their fellows will be affected. The differences may be connected to age-group differences, which are commonly noted. For example, if an Indian child attends a local school in which the majority of students are African, their relation to more traditional values will be affected.

So, within a group habitus may be developed differently depending on factors such as education, occupation, regional differences, exposure to different groups and differences in age group. Bourdieu makes the point, however, that the agency of change is the habitus itself rather than the category of experience:

generation conflicts oppose not age-classes separated by natural properties, but habitus which have been produced by different modes of generation, that is, by conditions of existence which, in imposing different definitions of the impossible, the possible, and the probable, cause one group to experience as natural or reasonable practices or aspirations which another group finds unthinkable or scandalous or vice versa.

(Bourdieu 1977: 78)

Here we see the potential of 'theory of practice' analysis to alert us to processes of change in ethnic relations despite the synchronic appearance of ineluctable polarisation of the ethnic groups.

Another compelling reason for pursuing theory of practice is that the approach allows analysis of the dynamics of the ideological field. In nations such as Guyana and Trinidad ethnic relations may be usefully seen as a struggle for symbolic dominance, the need for a group to establish hegemony through the dissemination and acceptance of the dominant values. In Guyana the series of rapid and disruptive changes experienced in socio-political and economic spheres has contributed to 'the loss of coherence between experience and the symbols through which people understand it'. This, in turn, 'causes feelings of discomfort and alienation, of rootlessness and anomie. Both powerful goads to action, hence motives for political mobilisation' (Bentley 1987: 44).

Jenkins states, in his 1992 critique of Bourdieu, that his concept of 'habitus' is uncertain and vacillates between material existence (it purports to embody experiences) and, 'as an explanation of practice, something which exists beyond the realms of appearances' (Jenkins 1992: 94). However, it could equally be argued that Bourdieu provides a workable dynamic because the determinism is never absolute, always tempered by the specific attributes operating in the local field.

In relation to the study of 'race', Walter (2010), following the work of Lareau and McNamara Horvat (1999), suggests that in addition to Bourdieu's three dimensions of social space (the relationship we share with others in terms of social, cultural and economic capital) a fourth should be added, as 'racial capital' is of itself generative:

In four-dimensional social space, life trajectories are determined by intertwined economic, racial, cultural and social capital interactions. What is distinctive about this four way interweaving, as opposed to Bourdieu's three way weave is the recognition of the raced nature of social and cultural capital. Thus race capital, like other capitals, is distributed unequally prefigured as a sphere of relational societal resource: both a predictor and determinant of our social positioning.

(Walter 2010: 47)

The power of this perspective, then, rests on its ability to make fine-grained analyses based on complex interrelation of the dynamics of the social sphere and the individual and group practices which are attested to by the performative aspects of habitus in different fields. By expanding the forms of capital there is greater understanding of the relational positions of individuals to how these resources are unequally distributed. The symbolic, material and social come together in this perspective without recourse to the abstractions upon which others have fallen back.

Malesevic (2004) highlights problems that might arise with attempts to synthesise theory. The concern is that certain combinations are not compatible and should not be utilised just to cover possible aspects of a phenomenon:

> All theoretical positions are incomplete and that is in their 'nature'. But the very fact that they are incomplete enables them to engage analytically and attempt to explain social reality. The theory which can explain everything is not a theory but a mere registrar of events, actions, behaviours and beliefs.
>
> (Malesevic 2004: 168)

However, on the face of it, Bourdieu has provided a number of fertile conceptual tools which permit consideration of how both agency and structure can be included in our understanding of how ethnicity is constituted subjectively as well as revealing the manner in which individuals are positioned by their relationship to different forms of capital.

GENDER, SEXUALITY, RACE AND ETHNICITY

Social divisions are emphasised and represented differently in different times and places; whether along the lines of caste, class, status, gender or sexuality, these are the means by which power is articulated and channelled in societies. Furthermore, the means by which a society constructs difference is liable to periodic shifts, as illustrated in Chapter 2. Social divisions are often intrinsically linked, forming a shifting lantern show of oppressions triggered by social, economic and political realities of the time. Racist beliefs have always been interwoven with ideas of gender and sexuality, as we have seen from our discussion of stereotypes: African-Caribbean men, for example, were portrayed as possessing 'uncontrolled sexual potency' and a 'potential for violence and criminality', whereas Asian women were 'sexually exotic, passive and unambitious – the docile victims of a traditional culture' (Bilton *et al.* 1987: 264).

It could be argued that the black body and the female body are at some level connected as prone to objectification by the 'male gaze' – a characteristic of both patriarchy and colonialist values. Popular culture is permeated with ready-made stereotypes and also with the fascination and fear that black sexualities exert in western societies. Paul Gilroy (1993) and Kobena Mercer (1994) make reference to the immense popularity of black musical genres among white people, Mercer suggesting that this is one example of the ways in which 'black men and women have articulated sexual politics' (ibid.: 140) through the candid expression of sexuality and the long tradition of open emotion, sexual politics, loss and longing expressed in the blues and jazz (see also Waddington 2004).

This ambivalence about the sexuality of the 'other' is deep-seated and began during early periods of colonisation of the globe. Historically, ethnic divisions and the conception of the racialised 'other' were frequently presented in gendered terms. The continents were typically portrayed as women, untamed and bared, virgin territory to be colonised.

Profound links exist between the construction of race, ethnicity, gender and sexuality. Slavery and the colonial regime undoubtedly developed an eroticised power relationship between colonial master and subject, as is attested by the legacy of mixed race in the Caribbean and in India. Concubinage and rape were certainly commonplace among planters and slave-owners, although the fascination and desire for the 'other' was always treated with marked ambivalence. The colonial adventure, with its metaphoric and actual rape and plunder, opened up fantasies of sexual domination and the exotic 'other' that pervade accounts of colonial life in Africa, Asia and the Caribbean. The racism that combines with this colonial obsession leads to what Young describes as 'the familiar structure of sexual attraction and repulsion' (1995: 150). The fascination with exotic differences is attested in the inordinate interest in the anatomical features of African women, who were studied, displayed and discoursed upon in inordinate detail. A case in point was the so-called 'Hottentot Venus', a twenty-year-old Quena woman named Sara Baartman who was taken from Cape Town to London in 1810 and put on public display around Britain and France. Contemporary descriptions of her shows at 225 Piccadilly, Bartholomew Fair and Haymarket in London say that Baartman was made to parade naked along a 'stage two feet high', along which she was led by her keeper and exhibited like a wild beast, being obliged to walk, stand or sit as he ordered (History of Race in Science 1995). She died in France in 1815 and, even after her death, remained the object of imperialist fascination. Baron Cuvier, the eminent social anthropologist and surgeon general to Napoleon, had her sexual organs and brain removed and pickled. They were displayed in the Musée de l'Homme until the mid 1980s. This extraordinary interest in her anatomy indicates the function of such displays to European ideas about black female sexuality and European racial superiority.

The same biological reasoning that legitimated slavery and exploitation on the basis of race was also responsible for male tyranny over women. From at least the early 1800s to before the Second World War a eugenics discourse that borrowed legitimacy from Social Darwinism emphasised a concern with race purity and 'hygiene' and the dangers of descent into moral and genetic decline. Pseudo-scientific ideas were generated by this confluence of racism and sexism. Correlating brain size to race and gender yielded the apparent (although largely spurious) discovery that black people's brains were smaller than white people's, and women's brains smaller than men's. This led to the view that the 'inferior' races were more feminine and that racial mixing would produce children exhibiting increasingly feminine traits. Young articulates this fundamental connection between gender divisions and the development of a racialised discourse as deeply embedded in common-sense views of culture and pre-scientific hierarchical structures:

> Race was defined through the criterion of civilization, with the cultivated white, western European male at the top, and everyone else on a hierarchical scale either in a chain of being, from mollusc to God, or, in the later model, on an evolutionary scale of development from a feminized state of childhood (savagery) up to full (European) manly adulthood. In other words, race was defined in terms cultural, particularly gender difference – carefully gradated and ranked.
>
> (Young 1995: 94)

Tobach and Rosoff cite Pruner's 1866 comment that 'The Negro resembles the female in his love for children and his cabin [...] The black man is to the white man what woman is to man in general, a loving being and a being of pleasure' (Tobach and Rosoff 1994: 70).

Popular discourse about the supposed childlike, undisciplined and indolent state of natives abounded and was published in books such as Moore's *Savage Survivals*, a text that purported to be a serious scientific treatise while making sexist and ethnocentric statements based on crude Darwinist conjectures about indigenous peoples being at an immature stage of development and ruled by capricious id-like tendencies, while clearly suggesting that women share these traits:

> The savage is in many ways a child. He has the same untrained will as the child, the same unsteadiness, the same tendency to be ruled by the impulses that rise within him from moment to moment [...] Women are much more inclined to imitate each other than men are, because they have, on the whole, more of the characteristics of the child psychology.
>
> (Moore 1933: 116)

It seems clear that racialisation of social relations, despite the flimsiest of evidence and under the cloak of Social Darwinism, has also had a marked impact on the representation of gender and sexuality.

BLACK FEMINISM

Black feminism developed from traditions of courage, independence and resistance by black women to the brutal conditions of slavery and institutionalised racism. The challenge of black feminist approaches in Britain, America and elsewhere is their focus upon the simultaneity of oppressions that affect women of non-western origins, especially racism, sexism, class oppression and homophobia. The term 'black feminism' has been criticised for generating essentialist readings of blackness (just as, arguably, second-wave feminisms have tended to universalise concepts of woman and 'sisterhood'). There have been strands of feminism that specifically focus upon female biological differences. Patricia Hill Collins comments:

> for the term black and the accompanying assumption that being of African descent somehow produces a certain consciousness or perspective are inherent in these definitions. By presenting race as being fixed and immutable – something rooted in nature – these approaches mask the historical construction of racial categories, the shifting meaning of race, and the crucial role of politics and ideology in shaping conceptions of race.
>
> (Hill Collins 2000: 405)

Early feminist Sojourner Truth is a cornerstone of black feminist thought. Her vivid evocation of the 'double burden' – sexism and racism (not to mention class oppression) – has become well known through her famous 'ain't I a woman?' speech that so directly addresses the fact that she is not treated as a white woman, as a fragile and delicate woman in need of protection. Her speech still rings out with undiminished power because it underlines the distinctions made between women on the basis of their race, class and gender. Yet, as Aziz comments, it was also a 'powerful admonishment to her audience (a white Ohio congregation), defying them to see her as nothing more than 'a product of racism-sexism-slavery' (Aziz 1992: 2).

The contribution made by black feminists has been to question feminism and draw attention to the divisions between women that make the essentialist viewpoint of a united 'sisterhood' difficult to maintain. Black women faced multiple oppressions and their identity as an oppressed racial group meant that unity with black men was often more important to them as a bulwark against racism than separation from them as a stand against patriarchy. Black women in the USA were concerned that 'feminism' did not concern itself with their struggle and was a vehicle for white and often middle-class women. Alice Walker proposed the term 'womanist' as one that embodied black women's more serious and mature identity in the face of oppression. Walker's much cited phrase 'womanist is to feminist as purple to lavender' (Walker 1983: xii) clearly seems designed to set up this type of comparison – black women are 'womanist', while white women remain merely 'feminist'.

The concerns that afflicted black women in the 1960s and 1970s were of a different order to those that characterised white feminist struggles. White women were traditionally portrayed as delicate, in need of protection and unsuited for hard labour, whereas black women were presented as quite different beings. At the time that white women were making a strong stand about reproductive rights, the pill and limited access to abortion, black women were facing a willingness to prescribe DepoProvera, a contraceptive drug that was known to cause a high incidence of sterility, in addition to more overt eugenic-inspired programmes (as discussed earlier) and differing treatment from policy-makers, who either saw their families as dysfunctional, culturally deprived and in need of state management or were, at least, critical of black women's abilities as mothers (see Knowles and Mercer 1992: 107).

In effect, black feminism must come to terms with both a white feminist agenda blind to racism and black or ethnic nationalist movements that fail to confront their own sexism. In each case the tendency towards a form of 'strategic essentialism' is a distorting effect of striving for political recognition, yet clearly the most damaging oppression at one time can shift and expose others who are equally central to the culture and the combination of class, race and gender can be arranged differently depending on the context. There has often been a danger of reducing black identity to class identity (typically assuming working-class identity). These and many other internal divisions that require identification have rendered older, more universalist politics unconvincing to many.

There is a clear parallel here to the fragmentation of left-wing politics generally. Although inequalities have actually widened, there seems to be a tendency to dis-identify with class (see Bufton 2004), giving way to more subjective notions of identity, cutting across class boundaries and involving other divisions that may be seen as more significant. A similar fragmentation is observable within feminism. However, whether or not some see these disputes as undermining a traditional socialist or feminist agenda, they mark an important critique that recognises the problems of ignoring local differences in the interests of political strength. Black feminists have raised important issues about power relations and inequality. Can women be genuinely said to share a common experience of oppression? What is the relative importance of racism and sexism? Have 'feminists over-concentrated on patriarchy and neglected race and ethnicity as sources of women's oppression?' (Solomos and Back 1996: 13). Do black men share the same positions of patriarchal power as white men? These questions were posed by black feminists in Europe and America as major challenges to the women's movement.

Just as gender politics can deny ethnic differences, there is a danger that, politically, a type of 'ethnic absolutism', a conceptual and political view of ethnic groups that sees them as possessing distinct and separate traditions, fixed and absolute, is supported in a struggle for ascendancy and resistance. Black feminism highlights the complex construction of the subject and serves as a reality check to those who eschew difference for the sake of political strength.

The interview below, conducted by Mark Quah (a British-born Chinese research student), examines one site of the intersection of these discourses in the identity of British-born Chinese. It becomes clear that personal identity develops at the conjunction of several divisive discourses: ethnicity, gender and class, as well as occupational status and generational differences. The negotiated space that Eve and her mother have carved out is sited between traditional patriarchal Chinese views and the incipient xenophobia and racist stereotypes prevalent in Britain.

BOX 4.1 BRITISH-BORN CHINESE

EVE: That's the thing, you also feel like you don't properly belong, like you belong to either set, British or Chinese but they don't see you as part of them so ... Being female, well, the thing is, I don't know if it's just the people in my community back in Wales but they tend to be fairly traditional and quite sexist, I don't know possibly more so than your average English family. I don't know 'cos being an eldest son have always have been better than my younger brothers ... so my dad was 'why can't you be a son, I wish you were a boy' and ... my dad actually has a nickname for me which is a boy's name but he only calls me that when I've been doing really well and he pats me on the head and says 'my boy!' It's quite weird but I know is more important than being the eldest daughter and the thing is ... in terms of my education my results that's only my dad ... my mum does work with my dad as well but it's just that he expects her to be the little housewife for him but my mum's been trying to break free from that ... I mean she goes to college and she does loads of study ... she's quite an inspiration. I'm very proud of her, she's doing all of this and she's doing chairperson of the Chinese society and so she is helping a lot of other Chinese women sort of like, could say empower themselves to be able to make them feel like they can actually not so much break free but feel like they can be more than just the wife.

MARK: Do you think it's a bit confined the roles that they can play?

EVE: The thing is, because of my mum's involvement in this Chinese women's society my dad got very very angry and all of the men in the area got very angry with my mum. And it was like ... she's spending far too much of her time away from the family and she's neglecting us. The thing is, we're all grown up, my brother's at university, my younger brother is at secondary school and we're all fairly – well the eldest two – we're fairly independent and the youngest can look after himself and we don't have to have my mum there all the time to look after us and my dad's just ... thing is, we're all very supportive of my mum and she's doing her best. The thing is, she's got accountancy thing something or other, she's an accountant anyway and she wants to get a job but my dad won't let her and that was fairly disappointing even though she was feeling like she's doing all of this by herself but she's still listening to my father and kind of like doing what she can to please him. It's understandable but yeah 'cos she loves him or whatever (lots of different pressures on) and I don't know – there is a fair amount of pressure on her. And my dad, I wouldn't say he was a tyrant, but I don't know ... oh what has she done, she's also be arranging English lessons for the other Chinese women because that's the thing, the fact that they don't know any English 'cos a lot of them first generation don't know a lot and they're just trapped in the home working looking after the children . A lot of the time it's because they don't know any English and they don't have the confidence to go out, because they may know a little bit or whatever but they don't have the ... and they can't read, they don't have the confidence to kind of go out.

MARK: Seems pretty essential then that they get these other services.

EVE: Mmm, that's the thing – and my mum has been helping, teaching them English I mean, she's been teaching them very basic English but also mm helping the women enrol on courses in the local college. I'm very proud of her ...

MARK: Maybe they should do something with the Sunday schools, teach English as well as Cantonese?

EVE: Yeah well that's what I think, a lot of what she also does is, you know, the Chinese women's society. They meet once a week in the daytime when the men are asleep so you know they don't know the women have gone, you know, snuck out (that's really good, I like that, but maybe it shouldn't be like that). That's the thing, it's like you know the women have to wake up early in the morning to take the kids to school anyway and they ... I don't know about other women, I know my mum does a lot with her day, she zooms around doing stuff you know going to college and I know she's done psychology and biology and accountancy and that's the thing, that's also why I feel like I should excel 'cos my mum's such a good example I can't let her down.

MARK: That's really great.

EVE: Also gives them a chance to ... as well as learn things ... but to actually congregate and just talk and relax and have someone to talk to as well as umm just being cooped up at home working their fingers to the bone and whatever, I think it's just as important to have friends and have people

BOX 4.1 BRITISH-BORN CHINESE (CONTINUED)

to talk to. I think that was the main point of her society: just to have somewhere for the women to go just once a week. To relax and not have to be a mother and a wife, to kind of be themselves and also teach them various skills. I mean I went home the other day and my mum was doing all this stuff on the computer and I was like 'mum how do you know all this' I was so shocked but my mum, I can't pull the wool over my mum's eyes over anything.

Actually I remember ... when you're at school and you do work experience I really wanted to be a doctor! That's another thing about Chinese parents. They want you to be a doctor or a lawyer (laughs) and I told them I want to be an engineer and they were horribly disappointed and I said I want to be a psychologist and they said no! You'll be surrounded by mad people and then you'll turn mad yourself (laughs). And they wanted me to be a doctor and I quite liked the idea as well and I went and did some work experience at the hospital and I did the rounds with the doctor and I had my white lab coat and everything, and then we came round to the bed of this really old woman and she said, she sounded very surprised and she said 'I expected you lot to be working in takeaways'. And at that minute I thought yeah. I can't remember, this was so long ago and it wasn't the most offensive thing anyone's said to me but it was like 'cos I'm Chinese you actually just expect me to work in a takeaway.

MARK: Did you say anything back?

EVE: I don't remember what I said back, I'm pretty sure I said something back but erm ... no I can't remember, it was so long ago, I softly just said yeah my parents are but I'm trying to work my way up. This point brings up issues of how far to respond to these attempts at being marginalised and how far this marginalisation is itself internalised. The latter point refers to the apologetic nature of the comment above by Eve: her reply speaks volumes in terms of the ability of those at the centre to influence the shape of the internal worlds of those at the margins. And I guess part of the problem is that a lot of Chinese people do kind of ...

MARK: ... mix in, keep themselves to themselves?

EVE: Yeah they do keep themselves to themselves and I mean I heard someone say the Chinese people, the Chinese community, are pretty much the invisible people of the UK – 'cos the thing is we have this huge community of Chinese but you never hear anything about them about what they do and ...

MARK: You hear stuff like, oh Chinese food, they cook dogs and stuff like that ...

EVE: Yeah yeah, that's the thing, we do have a huge Chinese community and there are loads of people that don't work in the Chinese takeaways and restaurants or whatever but the few that are out there and doing their jobs they don't speak up for themselves. That's the thing, Chinese people don't speak up for themselves and I guess that's why we're the invisible race.

MARK: You're in our country but we don't want you in the mainstream.

EVE: Yes, I'm sorry about that but I am working very hard.

This interview highlights the struggle of British-born Chinese women. Eve, the young person being interviewed, negotiates the different interpellations of traditional Chinese discourses of femininity and masculinity, stereotypes and expectations about work and cultural dimensions to identity in twenty-first-century Wales. The area is notably monocultural and Eve's mother is a leading light of the Chinese women's association, helping Chinese women to adapt to their surroundings and break away from the traditional housewifely roles. Gender relations, then, are another modality in which ethnicity and class are articulated. Individuals need to negotiate between traditional cultural expectations of gender roles and performances and those that make up the majority culture.

CHAPTER SUMMARY

This chapter has attempted to give an overview of some influential theoretical approaches that have been applied to an understanding of race and ethnicity. This involves explanations of ethnic mobilisation in terms of biological imperatives, class, honour, status, functionality, rational action, pursuit of political or financial power, primordial symbols and concepts of self developed through interaction and the intersection of gender and ethnicity. The twin axes of biological determinism and conscious, strategic manipulation (rational choices) run through the theoretical paradigms which seek to represent ethnic/race identity. In a similar fashion, there are variations between the Marxian emphasis on the exploitation of 'race' as an expedient device to divide the working-class movement and the Weberian emphasis on status and instrumental action. Each explanation can be considered to represent some valid facets of race as social being. The later twentieth century saw refinements of these ideas make use of Gramscian hegemony and the microanalyses permitted by Bourdieu's examination of everyday life; the material, social and symbolic conditions which produce forms of stratification. Foucault's power/knowledge dynamics and the disciplinary formation of discourses along with feminist and culturalist understandings around the body, blood and sexualities further extend our understanding of the complex subjectivities of 'otherness'.

The idea of accepting some synthesis, combining the strengths of each theory, may ultimately prove untenable, as this is at best a mere mosaic of quite contradictory approaches. However, the insights developed by post-structuralists and feminists seem to offer some ways forward in recognising societal discursive structures and their shaping influence on individual subjectivity. It has become clear, in this topology of theories of race, that the degree of primacy given to race, its critical importance as a marker of social position, varies significantly.

EXERCISE 4.1

1   Consider the phenomenon of racist attacks that is constantly in the media. What is the most convincing cause of such apparent hatred in our multicultural society? Which of the above theories offers the most useful perspectives?

2   'The central fact about these gross physical differences is not of course that they are based on genetic differentiation, but that they are clearly visible to the eye. They are what, palpably to the untutored, unscientific eye, makes race a thing we can continue to talk about' (Hall 1996b). Critically discuss this idea and its consequences for identity and equality.

3   How adequate is the traditional Marxist model of base/superstructure when explaining racism?

4   Consider a specific act of racism and analyse its causes, consequences and meanings using the following theories: Marxism, Weberian, symbolic interactionism, black feminism, Bourdieu, Foucauldian, neo-Marxism. Which of the theories is most relevant in the case you chose and why?

5   After considering the case of Sara Baartman, discuss the function of ethnographic displays in museums. Are they a means of educating about other nations and their people or a reaffirmation of European imperialism?

6   Are there other examples of 'human exhibition' that you know of? What function do such displays appear to fulfil? (You might begin to research this issue by reading a short article available at http://postcolonialstudies.emory.edu/museums-and-colonial-exhibitions/; see also Qureshi 2004.)

7   Read the interview with the British-born Chinese woman Eve. What aspects of identity does Eve discuss? How does Chinese identity appear to be a source of both strength and resistance, while at the same time imposing certain constraints on Chinese women?

Further reading

There are a number of books which give an idea of the topology of theoretical thinking around race and ethnicity. Perhaps one of the foundation texts is John Rex and David Mason's *Theories of Race and Ethnic Relations* (Cambridge: Cambridge University Press, 1986). Other works by Rex are also an excellent starting point. More recent titles include S. Malesevic's *The Sociology of Ethnicity* (London and Thousand Oaks, CA: Sage, 2004) which demonstrates that the founding thinkers in the sociological tradition who have often been dismissed as not having presented work on ethnicity are in fact more fully realised even though their terms of reference were different ('ethnicity' was not in common usage until relatively recently). Furthermore, these viewpoints from Marx, Weber, Durkheim and Simmel are at the origins of more fully articulated conceptions today.

Notes

1 That is, explanations for human attributes as developed to meet the needs of their environment.
2 A8 countries are the eight countries with low per capita incomes that joined the European Union during the 2004 enlargement.
3 See Chapter 7 for more illustrations of these divisions in Malaysia.

CHAPTER 5

Identity

Marginal voices and the politics of difference

> You were the first to teach us something absolutely fundamental: the indignity
> of speaking for others.
>
> (Gilles Deleuze in conversation with Foucault, from Foucault 1977b)

In Chapter 4 some of the theoretical landscape was charted and it became apparent that there is more going on within race and ethnicity than can be adequately accounted for by materialist and economic explanations. The movement towards more individualistic and fragmentary views of identity has emerged with increasing emphasis on difference. There has been a 'cultural turn' in theoretical formations of race and ethnicity, and notions of identity have taken centre ground. This more individualistic and context-specific approach is clearly already visible in the work of Rex and others and is affirmed and developed by culturalists such as Hall and Gilroy, who have selectively applied ideas from postmodern and post-colonial theorising, producing finely tuned studies of the cultural terrain in which ethnic identity and unique forms of sexism and racism are generated and circulate as cultural signs to be consumed. Certainly there is a fragmentation and atomism of Left politics. Resistance needs to be retooled to account for the hybrid and local voices that had remained marginal for so long. The fragmentation of the political and social field and the recognition that subjectivity itself is constructed is reflected in the use of terms such as 'postmodern frame' (Donald and Rattansi 1992), 'differentialist' approach (Mac an Ghaill 1999) and 'contradictory plurality' of the subject (Laclau and Mouffe 1985). Such terms recognise that our understanding of the social relations of power no longer allows a straightforward view of authority to be resisted.

POSTMODERNITY: MAPS AND TERRAIN

It is argued that the conventional theoretical frameworks that informed much of the academic study of race and racism in the course of the 1970s and 1980s are now outdated and inadequate to the task of providing an analysis of the complex nature of the operation of racialised discourse in contemporary society: 'postmodernity means coming to terms with ambivalence, with the ambiguity of meanings, and with indeterminacy of the future; yet acceptance of ambivalence can be life-enhancing, especially when contrasted to the driven world of certitudes that modernity used to foster' (Giddens 1994: 349). Terms such as postmodern, post-structural and post-Marxist describe the perception that at some juncture in the twentieth century (although the timing is widely contested) the driving force of modernity – the positivist and rationalist project set in motion in the Enlightenment – has collapsed, folding in upon itself. The map has become the terrain (an image popularised by Borges' work *A Universal History of Infamy* (1975), in which map-makers strive for such accuracy, such verisimilitude, to the land they are charting that they make a map that exactly covers the country's every contour and feature). The representational has become the real and behind the sign there is nothing (see Baudrillard 1983). In marketing terms, the brand identity has taken over from the utility value of the product and, indeed, we can see today that products are often bought because they are a specific 'aspirational' brand rather than merely because they are useful. The signifier dominates and the practice of relating to deeper meanings, connotations, is passé. A world of images flows over us in endless pastiche, superficial and meaningless, corporatised and global, the Gulf Wars as video games or Hollywood epics (see Baudrillard 1991) where tens of thousands of lives lost are 'collateral damage'. Media imagery has an immediacy and omnipresence today that, like Borges' fable of the map, appears to cover every inch of the world. Similarly, this view of global coverage is illusory; the forms that dominant media take are market-driven reflections of the narrow, ethnocentric values of corporate ownership and advertising.

HOLOCAUST AND RELATIVITY

Another feature of the 'postmodern condition' is loss of faith in the validity of science and rationalism. Zygmunt Bauman (2002), among others, has envisioned the Holocaust, the systematic annihilation of six million Jews and 'other' marginalised groups, as the epitome of the use of rational positivism. The argument is that the cold calculation needed to effect murder on such a vast scale is something quite different from the barbarism and brutality of the 'wild justice' (see Gilroy 2004) of colonialism (although the same infrahuman vision of beings as human waste surely underlies these atrocities). Instead, the obsession with order and the use of the most rational systems (IBM punch cards, in the case of Auschwitz, enabled the allocation of the infamous five-figure number tattoos) was necessary to effect this destruction. As Malesevic notes: 'It was the product of modern "dull bureaucratic routine" governed by the principle of instrumental rationality and a hierarchical delegation of tasks' (Malesevic 2004: 147). Like the infernal punishment machine in Kafka's 'In the Penal Colony' (2000), the State inscribes its will onto the bodies of its victims; violence is merely a technical example of the State's omnipotence.

If certainty and mono-cultural dominance can produce such terminally bleak results, then the Nietzchean view of humanity as fatally flawed (as 'all too human') begins to look more plausible. The impact of all this on social theory, along with the parallel collapse of theories of representation and the successive fragmentation of social movements through the process of identity politics, is a tendency towards relativism in the face of what appears to be modernity's attempts 'to transgress hybridity and the fragmented nature of ethno-national narratives' (Malesevic 2004).

Kenan Malik has produced a reasoned scholarly argument against what he sees as a misguided dismissal of the most progressive feature of Enlightenment thought: the striving for universal human rights. Rather than pursuing the argument that universalising rationality leads to the death camps, Malik sees the critical juncture in the Enlightenment as the movement towards making distinctions between human beings rather than recognising their essential humanity. These are differences that are based not on science or rationality but on ethnocentric and romantic notions of the 'other'. Race science, which is (as we have seen) unsupported by any empirical evidence, provided the spurious rationale for racial superiority and the fiction of the primordial destiny of the Aryan races.

Malik (1996) has highlighted the manner in which universalist viewpoints have been condemned as implicitly fascistic and ethnocentric. Postmodernists, cynical about the Enlightenment ideals of reason and universal conception of humanity, have favoured a supposedly more open and tolerant approach that promotes diversity. Malik suggests, to the contrary, that an over-emphasis on cultural difference has the possible effect of encouraging conflict and separation and denying the most important realisation of the Enlightenment, which was an affirmation of the equality of mankind. An obsession with difference evolved later, with pseudo-scientific topologies used to legitimatise colonialist exploitation abroad and class exploitation at home. The achievements of scientific reasoning that came about in the Renaissance and the Enlightenment have led to genuinely superior and innovative technologies and political forms and should not be seen as products of mono-cultural dominance, European superiority and racism.

Frantz Fanon, one of the great voices of post-war developing world nationalism, argued that the problem was not Enlightenment philosophy but the failure of Europeans to follow through its emancipatory logic. 'All the elements of a solution to the great problems of humanity have, at different times, existed in European thought,' he argued. 'But Europeans have not carried out in practice the mission that fell to them' (Malik 2002: 4).

It is difficult not to see the parallels between colonial oppressions and the extermination of a whole generation of European Jews. In the 1970s BBC programme *The Ascent of Man*, Jacob Bronowski squatted in the pond at Auschwitz and, taking a handful of mud, his hands raised in a powerful gesture, he said:

> It is said that science will dehumanise people and turn them into numbers. That is false – tragically false. Look for yourself. This is the concentration camp and crematorium at Auschwitz. This is where people were turned into numbers. Into this pond were flushed the ashes of four million people. And that was not done by gas. It was done by arrogance. It was done by dogma. It was done by ignorance. When people believe that they have absolute knowledge, with no test in reality – this is how they behave. This is what men do when they aspire to the knowledge of gods [...] We have to cure ourselves of the itch for absolute knowledge and power. We have to close the distance between the push-button order and the human act. We have to touch people.
>
> (Bronowski 1976: 186)

Bronowski's is a heartfelt and strikingly potent defence of science, a plea not to abandon rationality but to embrace it and recognise that true adherence to science would never allow callous certainty to triumph but would lead to a more open society. Echoing the words of Oliver Cromwell, Bronowski pleads, 'I beseech you in the bowels of Christ, think it possible you may be mistaken.'

However, it is dangerous to locate the fatal flaw of narcissism and arrogance, of which the Holocaust is an example, as solely a consequence of European modernity. Recent and ongoing blood-soaked rationalisations have taken place in many other parts of the world. Gilroy conjectures that:

> Though it's neither the flipside of a Europe-centred modernity nor something eternal and evil, outside of history and secular morality altogether, it does have something to do with the pathologies of modern development that Rousseau called 'the fatal ingenuities of civilized man'.
>
> (Gilroy 2000: 237)

While Bronowski and others protest that science should not be pilloried for the dehumanisation of which Auschwitz is an especially bleak example, 'scientism', which came to dominate the early twentieth century, changed forever the scale and tone of human potential for persecution. 'We have to deal, not only with the old dangers of occultism and irrationality, but with the new evils represented by the rational application of irrationality' (Bronowski 1974: 186).

IDENTITY POLITICS AND TRADITIONAL LEFT THOUGHT

Postmodernism is a loose amalgamation of theories that attempt to explain the uncertainty, ambivalence and fragmentation which seems to characterise society. While globalisation may increase cultural homogeneity, this may occur at a fairly superficial level and, beneath this veneer of global brand names, other contradictory forces are arguably eroding ethnic solidarity and monolithic national identity. The traditional Left notion of a unified front against racism or capitalism seems to be abandoned as more specific identity projects are being realised. Homi Bhabha captures the unease of our times, the ominous sense that the driving force towards social democratic commonality has been replaced by

> an anxious age of identity, in which the attempt to memorialise lost time, and to reclaim lost territories, creates a culture of disparate 'interest groups' or social movements. Here affiliation may be antagonistic and ambivalent; solidarity may be *only* situational and strategic; commonality is often negotiated through the 'contingency' of social interests and political claims.
>
> (Bhabha 1996: 59)

McGuigan (1999) shows the importance of considering the commitment of identity politics to equality and, indeed, solidarity across different marginal and subordinate social positions – questions that are much too easily dismissed as illegitimately 'universalistic'. While McGuigan (ibid.: 88) stresses the vital role of difference as a 'subversive principle', he highlights some of the concerns that more traditional Left intellectuals harbour about this shift towards identity politics. Hobsbawm writes in defence of the older tradition: 'The political project of the Left is universalist: it is for all human beings' (Hobsbawm 1996: 40), whereas 'Identity groups are about themselves and nobody else' (ibid.: 44).

Clearly the fragmentation recognised in identity politics and postmodern views of identity as fluid and highly constructed are very hard for traditional leftist thought to accept. An end to essentialist categories makes power relations difficult to understand and, as Foucault has shown, undermines traditional Marxist thought: how can there be a class enemy or a ruling class of oppressors?

Despite the apparent contrast between modern and postmodern, others argue that postmodernism is merely the latest chapter in the cultural history of western modernity, not a major shift. Sardar has been a powerful critic of those who portray postmodernity as heralding a new radical liberation movement to oppressed peoples around the world. According to Sardar:

> far from being a new theory of liberation, postmodernism, particularly from the perspective of the 'other', the non-western cultures, is simply a new wave of domination riding on the crest of colonialism and modernity. [...] Colonialism was about the physical occupation of non-western cultures. Modernity was about displacing the present and occupying the minds of non-western cultures. Postmodernism is about appropriating the history and identity of non-western cultures as an integral facet of itself, colonising their future and occupying their being.
>
> (Sardar 1998: 13)

Sardar is suggesting that postmodernity is another form of colonialism in the guise of liberal values. The postmodern 'we' is never inclusive in Sardar's view; it never refers to the non-western 'other'.

CONSEQUENCES OF POSTMODERN THOUGHT

Postmodernity signals a crisis of uncertainty, complexity and chaos, showing the chinks in modernity's armour of certainty and the belief that absolute truths about the world could ultimately be revealed. In *The Meaning of Race* Kenan Malik goes on to critique the post-structuralist and postmodern theories of difference that have become the backbone of contemporary anti-racist discourse and to examine the possibility of transcending the discourse of race.

> The postmodern condition is one in which the 'grand narratives' have become discredited. Grand narratives are attempts to grasp society in its totality, to give coherence to our observations of the objective world. Nationalism is one such grand narrative because it attempts to impose a collective sense of belonging on disparate individuals. Postmodernists reject all the great collective social identities of class, of race, of nation, of gender, and of the West. They reject Marxism too, and in fact any form of emancipatory theory the aim of which is the total liberation of humankind.
>
> (Malik 1996: 218)

Malik goes on to explain that universalism is considered by postmodernists as being inherently racist: a dangerous Eurocentric fantasy that serves to impose European and American culture and values of rationality and objectivity on the rest of the world. Indeed, universalism denies the very possibility of non-European viewpoints. In this view, the endeavours of the natural sciences and social science such as anthropology are dangerously ethnocentric in their outlook and attempt to construct the 'other' – that is, the non-European individual – through their dominant discourses.

However, as we have seen from the analysis of Foucauldian approaches, postmodern views have political consequences. For the very reason that they disallow and decry mass, collective movements they are pessimistic about social change other than through micro-revolutions. Every case of racism is unique, is based on different social, political, cultural and economic subject locations.

> belief in the arbitrary nature of both power and truth leads to an extreme relativism [...] If power is simply the constituting element in all social systems, how can we choose between one society and another? And if discourse makes its own truth, whose validity is given by the strength of an arbitrary power, how are we to distinguish between different representations or discourses?
>
> (Malik 1996: 234)

So the dilemma of the postmodern (and also the post-colonial) becomes clear: based on a Foucauldian notion of power (the collapse of the concept of ideology), relative values are celebrated and the result could be the impossibility of making value judgements about any cultural practices or recognising any universal human values. Malik directs his criticism towards the current trends in valuing diversity at the heart of an ethos of multiculturalism, which he sees as leading away from ideas of equality and encouraging separatism and, far from discouraging racism, providing a fertile ground for racists to gain respectability and legitimatise their views.

Hence Malik maintains 'The philosophy of difference is the politics of defeat, born out of defeat' (ibid.: 265). On the other hand, isn't the celebration of diversity preferable to enforced integration and aggressive ethnocentrism? Yet, when 'valuing diversity' becomes a basis for policy the logical conclusion seems to be divisive policies of education, increasing segregation, hardening boundaries and a divisive strand of competitive ethnic rivalry, political correctness and identity confusion which the extreme right is able to exploit to their advantage.

POST-COLONIAL IDENTITIES

Examining the contentious territory of the post-colonial entails the study of political, social, cultural and literary formations of identity. This section is intended to convey an understanding of what Hall (1994) has called 'diasporization' or 'hybridization'. This indicates that society is moving away from simplistic essentialism in its understanding of ethnic identity. Bhabha, Spivak and others talk about the mythical conception of an essential 'other', which in reality is always divided. Many of our conceptions of race and ethnicity assume an original pure form of being, but this is a claim that has been strongly refuted by the growing voices of post-colonial thinkers, whose key theme could be characterised by the idea that: 'The language of the oppressed has yet to be invented' (Petkovic 1983).

Post-colonialism is a complex field of discourse, constituted by responses to colonialism, slavery and the master discourses of empire, those authoritative and learned discourses that purport to speak for the muted colonial subject: history, literature, philology, anthropology, ethnography, philosophy and linguistics. It is the voice of the oppressed emerging and talking back with well-chosen words – a critical assault on the western conceit that it can constitute the colonial 'other' in its own form. These post-colonial currents in thought have become increasingly important and challenging to the rather ossified theoretical canon. The following quotes give an idea of the features of this new landscape:

> Post-colonial theory involves discussion about experience of various kinds: migration, slavery, suppression, resistance, representation, difference, race, gender, place, and responses to the influential master discourses of imperial Europe such as history, philosophy and linguistics, and the fundamental experiences of speaking and writing by which all these come into being. None of these is 'essentially' post-colonial, but together they form the complex fabric of the field.
>
> (Ashcroft *et al.* 1998: 2)

> Post-colonialism is regarded as the need, in nations or groups which have been victims of imperialism, to achieve an identity uncontaminated by universalist or Eurocentric concepts or images.
>
> (During 1995: 125)

Such a field allows new explanatory paradigms for the radical changes that are occurring and the new cultural forms that are emerging:

> Theories of 'cultural imperialism' and 'neo-colonialism', which reproduce the oppositions of 'centre' and 'periphery', 'dominance' and 'submission' that shaped colonialist thinking itself, have seemed insufficient to account for the fragmentations and redefinitions of national boundaries and the shifting, contingent and hybrid forms of cultural and political identification characteristic of the late twentieth century.
>
> (Bennett and Stephens 1991: 5)

Up until the Second World War, most of the developing nations, with the exception of some Latin American countries, were ruled directly by western colonial powers (see Chapter 3). These powers controlled monopolies of trade, with each European country scrabbling to acquire colonies amongst the developing nations that were both the source of raw materials and captive markets for manufactured products. As already discussed, this colonial situation was aided by popular stereotypes and romantic myths about, for example, 'their' inherent spirituality in contrast to western materialism. The break-up of colonial states occurred from the end of the Second World War onwards. Most of the countries that had been in the hands of European colonists were caught up in a wave of revolutionary thought. India gained independence in 1950; many African countries were not far behind. The war had drained Europe of money and labour and hence the capacity to maintain colonial rule and infrastructure was seriously threatened. At the same time, the growing nationalist movements were becoming an increasing nuisance to the colonial authorities.

This fracture of western dominance and the regaining of pluralist voices across the globe has meant the further destabilisation of our assumptions relating to how the subject is constructed. This is another example of the fragmentation associated with postmodernism. The great modernist trends in thought, which centred on the western rationalist, positivist view of the world, have been shaken by the voices of those previously oppressed emerging from lands liberated from colonial rule. The resulting challenges to the colonial powers led to an unravelling of the global bindings, decentring the omniscience of European thought.

Post-colonialism is a complex set of global cultural formations that brings into question any unifying perspective that foregrounds dominant Eurocentric values. At another level, it can be narrowly defined as a literary movement that emerged mostly from within English departments in western universities which attempts to describe and understand the experience of colonised peoples – before and after colonisation – by an examination of texts, images, movies, advertising and especially literary genres that reflect the colonial condition and imperatives in works by, for example, Rudyard Kipling, Joseph Conrad and George Eliot. Post-colonial scholars re-examine such texts in the light of their portrayals of complex identities created within the colonial experience.

THEORIES OF POST-COLONIALISM

The publication of Frantz Fanon's revolutionary book *The Wretched of the Earth* (1961) could be argued to have marked the birth of post-colonialism. Written at the height of the Algerian war, it has proved an inspiration for worldwide liberation movements. Fanon focuses on the struggle for identity of the colonial subject and the psychological scarring caused by colonialism. It is a rallying cry to the voices of those peoples subjected to the yoke of colonialism to articulate their own destiny:

When the nation stirs as a whole, the new man is not an a posteriori product of that nation; rather, he coexists with it and triumphs with it. This dialectic requirement explains the reticence with which adaptations to colonization and reforms of the facade are met. Independence is not a word which can be used as an exorcism, but an indispensable condition for the existence of men and women who are truly liberated, in other words who are truly masters of all the material means which make possible the radical transformation of society.

(Fanon 1961: 250)

Fanon's work achieved significance as a guiding light for anti-colonial resistance. Fanon believed that there was a redemptive quality in the violent banishing of oppressors from the homeland that more diplomatic and negotiated solutions did not allow: 'colonialism is not a thinking machine, nor a body endowed with reasoning faculties. It is violence in its natural state, and it will only yield when confronted with greater violence' (ibid.: 61). Fanon practised psychiatry in Algeria and saw at first hand the 'internalization of oppression' that scarred not only the colonial subject but also the oppressor; the consequences of the violence of oppression were mental as well as physical. Fanon has been influential theoretically because he was able to see the relevance of Lacanian ideas of the mirror stage to the racialised subject.[1] Like the metaphysical awareness engendered by the mirror stage, the self undergoes a reflective process in which a whole cultural imaginary is constructed in the image of the colonial power.

Perhaps the most influential scholar and literary theorist to have had an impact on the post-colonial terrain is Edward Said, a Palestinian/American professor of literature best known for writing *Orientalism* (1985), the seminal work that examines the western construction and conceptions of the 'Orient'. Said defines 'Orientalism' as a sub-genre of post-colonial obsession with 'others'. It is the construction created by the west to manage relations with the east. Said presents his work not only as an examination of European attitudes to Islam and the Arabs but also as a model for analysis of all western 'discourses on the 'other''. He claims that the discourse of Orientalism preceded and paved the way for colonial possession and exploitation of the east. Said believes that a society builds up its identity more efficiently by imagining an 'other', in the same way that Pieterese illustrated the imagined 'others' of Europe in Table 1.1. Hence western identity is defined in relation to the essentialist myth of Orientalism. In this way the cultural and intellectual superiority imagined by the west was foreshadowed by an imagined east that remained forever culturally static and inferior. A similar process has been applied to the western constructions of all 'others'.

The Orient was viewed, Said claims, as a region outside the influence of western rationalism and science. It was characterised by 'its sensuality, its tendency to despotism, its aberrant mentality, its habit of inaccuracy, its backwardness' (Said 1978: 205). Orientalism was constituted by an amalgamation of complex interwoven discourses of philology, history, sociology and economics, among others, through which Orientalism not only creates but it also maintains; it is, rather than expresses, a certain will or intention to understand, in some cases to control, manipulate, even to incorporate, what is a manifestly different (or alternative and novel) world; it is, above all, a discourse that is by no means in direct, corresponding relationship with political power in the raw, but rather is produced and exists in an uneven exchange with various kinds of power.

(ibid.: 12)

Despite this apparently sophisticated discursive argument (Said relies heavily on a Foucauldian notion of discourse in his work), Said's conception has come under heavy attack more recently as being too simplistic and helping to reify the existence of two monolithic entities: the Occident and the Orient. The colonial reality, it is argued, is much more complex and multifaceted than Said suggested. Nevertheless, Said's work has radically redefined the cultural landscape, while his further texts have developed and refined his initial contentious and ground-breaking thesis. Feminist critics have both criticised and built on Said's work, which initially seemed to give little recognition to the important role women play in colonial discourses.

FEMINISM AND POST-COLONIALISM

In many different societies women, like colonised subjects, have been relegated to the position of the 'other', 'colonised' by various forms of patriarchal domination. They thus share with colonised races and cultures an intimate experience of the politics of oppression and repression, albeit from a very different perspective. This is clearly a reason why post-colonial theories have shared concerns with developments in feminist theory. Both discourses endeavour to examine and reassert marginalised voices. Indeed, Gayatri Chakravorty Spivak's teasingly rhetorical and ironic question 'Can the Subaltern Speak?' (1985) captures perfectly the dual burdens of post-colonial female subjects. The dual colonisation, both patriarchal and imperial, has rendered women mute.

Feminist critiques of Said's *Orientalism* target the fact that he appears to conceive of Orientalism as a unified discourse. As Reina Lewis points out, the only use of gender 'occurs as a metaphor for the negative characterization of the Orientalized 'other' as "feminine" [...] Said never questions women's apparent absence as producers of Orientalist discourse or as agents within colonial power' (Lewis 1996: 18). Arguably, Said did not address one of the key elements in the discursive subordination of the east: the portrayal of women as powerless. It is important to see that the power of colonial discourse may be derived from how it positions women. The veil, the *hijab*, has come to be seen as a symbol of this oppression as well as the signifier of the 'romantic mystique' of the Orient, and is contrasted to the supposed freedoms of western sexuality. These claims can be contested on the basis that such apparent freedoms still favour hegemonic male sexuality are freedoms that still favour hegemonic male sexuality and they are used to uphold the spurious notion that Muslim women are the passive victims of an archaic patriarchal culture.

Into the twenty-first century the veiled Muslim woman has come to represent the ultimate symbol of backwardness and oppression and acts as a visual cue to bolster claims of the 'alarming' rise in Islamic militancy. This discourse of Muslim women as passive bonded subjects was laid down in the nineteenth and twentieth centuries, when European colonialists became obsessed with freeing the 'other' woman in order to subvert and destroy the indigenous cultures over which they ruled, and was further exacerbated by the mistaken belief of feminist discourse that the only true model of emancipation was the western model of feminism (Woodlock 2002).

Meyda Yegenoglu (1998) shows the inability of both Orientalism and feminism to resist these divisive myths of the 'other', leading in turn to an easy acceptance of developing nations as static and ruled by insular and impoverished cultural values. This discourse regarded women of the less democratic, less learned, unstable and poverty-stricken societies as deprived of the possibilities and channels of power that are elsewhere accessible to western women. This 'backwardness' is sustained by an implicit comparison between underdeveloped or developing countries and industrialised ones. Such a comparison betrays a difference that remains central to the discourse disseminated by mainstream feminist practices: it reintroduces the 'west and the rest' opposition, thus constructing the sovereign western female subject endowed with all the privileges and powers reserved solely for her. This opposition also brings us back to the problems posed by post-colonial theory in its analysis of how 'Orientalism orientalizes the Orient' (Erdogan 2000).

Figures 5.1–5.4 indicate some of the ways in which discourses of gender, race and sexuality have been historically combined. In the nineteenth century the preoccupation with race and 'breeding' led to an inordinate focus on sex and reproducing the race. In the latter half of the nineteenth century an outpouring of concerns about race purity and sexual orthodoxy combined eugenics with a growing fascination with psychiatric analysis of sexual perversion. Women were delicate vessels for the raising of healthy babies needed to keep the stock pure; non-reproductive sex and homosexuality were treated as grievous waste of the 'germ plasm' (see McCaskell 1994; Vertinsky 1990) as the potential for furthering the race was squandered through unfeminine and hedonistic practices. As Foucault (1984) claims, this inordinate focus on sex and race can be seen as: 'An entire social practice, which took the exasperated but coherent form of a state-directed racism, [and] furnished this technology of sex with a formidable power and far-reaching consequences' (1984: 119).

Other developing practices, as noted above, reflected this peculiar linking of racism and sexism. Craniology and brain measurement purported to show that blacks and whites had different-sized brains, and the size of the brain was thought to correlate directly to intelligence. Similar findings suggested that women's brains

Figure 5.1 'Bejewelled Beauty of the Kabyle', from J. Hammerton's *Peoples of All Nations* (1933)

Figure 5.2 'Circe of the Sudanese Dancing World', from J. Hammerton's *Peoples of All Nations* (1933)

were slightly smaller than men's. As a result, non-western native peoples were often portrayed as feminine, indolent and passive, or fitting other well-worn stereotypes such as being natural mimics, emulating their superiors, or being simple-minded and treacherous, having no sense of honour.

Figures 5.1–5.4, and thousands of other images like them, are indicative of dominant western discourses. The first three images show the exoticism and sensuality with which western views of the female 'other' are imbued. Figure 5.1, 'Bejewelled Beauty

ARABIA

Unveiled Charms of Beduin Women

This sun-kissed young Beduin mother carries her baby, according to the custom of the East, on her back. The child as it grows older will acquire the dusky hue of its mother. The Beduin woman, right, like most of her fellows wears elaborate ornaments; and her silver ear-rings, breeches, and necklace may represent a good part of her husband's capital.

Figure 5.3 Arabia: 'Unveiled Charms of Beduin Women', from J. Hammerton's *Peoples of All Nations* (1933)

Figure 5.4 Egypt: 'Fleeting Glimpses of Feminine Charms', from J. Hammerton's *Peoples of All Nations* (1933)

of the Kabyle', echoes codes from classical paintings such as Ingres's *The Turkish Bath* and Sophie Anderson's *In the Harem, Tunis*. Lewis's (1996) discussion of gendered Orientalism provides numerous examples of the portrayals of Oriental women by upper-class female artists, and the adornment and posture depicted in these paintings is very similar. The codes by which women are displayed as erotic objects for the male gaze have been discussed at length by feminists and cultural-studies theorists. For example, the screen theorist Laura Mulvey, drawing on Lacanian ideas of scopophilia and the Oedipal male look, notes how 'Woman displayed as sexual object is the leit-motif of erotic spectacle: from pin-ups to striptease, from Ziegfeld to Busby Berkeley, she holds the look, plays to and signifies male desire' (Mulvey 1975: 6–18).

Portrayals of veiled women, as in Figure 5.4, 'Fleeting Glimpses of Feminine Charms', illustrate the voyeurism implicit in presentations of 'exotic otherness'. The male gaze and the desire for the 'other' – to see beyond and into the 'other' – is reflected in these images. The women in these images are displayed in postures that seem to suggest sensuality and availability. The accompanying text empha-sises their colouring: the Bedouin wife (Figure 5.3) is 'sun-kissed', the Kabyle woman has a 'tinge of hue' that 'is but permanent sun burn', the Bedouin's child will acquire the 'dusky hue of its mother'. These markers are, it seems, important when assessing the feminine charms of 'exotic' women. The language used by Hammerton (1933) is both coy and provocative, like the postures and poses that are selected and designed by the photographers. The other theme that emerges is the women's description as being part of the husband's wealth, displaying elaborate adornment which, in the Bedouin's case, 'may represent a good part of her husband's capital.' In Figure 5.1 the arrangement is voyeuristic and stylised, very obviously posed – almost choreographed (like a Cecil B. DeMille biblical water bearer or exotic harem dancer). When I showed this image to students, one or two mentioned the old Fry's Turkish Delight adverts – 'full of eastern promise'[2] – featuring the 'exotic' eastern female of countless adverts, television shows and films. The image employs codes from film, dance, costume, romantic painting and literary traditions. Indeed, she could easily come from the pages of a book by that great Orientalist Sir Richard Burton (translator of *The Rubaiyat of Omar Khayam*, *1001 Nights* and the *Kama Sutra*) or from a silent epic, dancing the Seven Veils, a 'bejewelled beauty' from the Bedouin sheik's harem. The use of the ornate jug and the colour of the fabrics, the richly woven rug and blanket that frame her, are very easily recognised signs of 'Orientalism'. The highly produced character of this image, its deep colours and sumptuous textures, renders it as more than a photograph (or photogravure) and separates the real woman from biographical detail, rendering the image an icon of the Orient.

This mythologising tendency in such books has been discussed in Chapter 1. While this treatment undermines the putative ethnographic task of recording the detail of the life worlds of the 'other' with a degree of objectivity, the fact that these images at the denotative level are photographic, with all the presumptions of unmediated reality, renders them 'innocent' in Barthes's terms, allowing the reader to willingly suspend disbelief and affirm the Orientalist myth of exotic beauty. The discourses that are readily available to replace the anthropological accuracy of these images are compelling ones from popular culture.

The harem has served for the Orientalist as a fantasy stage and the Muslim woman as the anchor that structured this space, enabling colonial discourse to operate on a number of levels. In the past three centuries the 'enslaved woman' was perceived as a sign of the backwardness of Muslim society, in contrast with the situation of the western woman, who was then heading for emancipation (Erdogan 2000).

In Figure 5.5, 'A Pleasing Contrast', interesting transformations are made. The image is at once chaste and innocent, yet the 'pleasing contrast' being drawn is purely one of colour aesthetics, 'the glossy blackness' against 'the whiteness of snow'; such is the language of a paternalistic and imperial gaze, which reminds the reader of colour and the Manichean divisions that accompany these oppositions. A contrast

Figure 5.5 'A Pleasing Contrast' , from J. Hammerton's *Peoples of All Nations* (1933)

would never be drawn in this way of a white person in a black gown, because this girl is closer to the realm of objects than that of human beings, and her colour is her most relevant and distinctive feature.

Racism relies on the invisibility of whiteness and the focus on blackness as particular and deviant. This obscures the fact that whiteness is just as integral to the mechanisms of racism (in the same way that homophobia relies on homosexuality as the defining identity of gays and lesbians and obscures the particularism of heterosexuality). Therefore, as Aziz cogently states:

> white women experience the state (to take one example) as patriarchal, whereas black women experience the state as racist *and* patriarchal: if the state is racist, it is racist to everyone; it is merely more difficult for white people to see this, because part of the racism of the state is to treat and promote whiteness as the norm.
>
> (Aziz 1992: 298)

Gayatri Chakravorty Spivak is another theorist central to post-colonial studies. She is best known for her essay 'Can the Subaltern Speak?',[3] in which she addresses one of the central issues affecting the field – how to represent the subjugated groups in academic discourse. Spivak 'questions whether or not the possibility exists for any recovery of a subaltern voice that is not a kind of essentialist fiction' (Ashcroft *et al.* 1995: 8). In relating the experience of marginalised groups and the disastrous impact on them of western colonialist discourses, she asks whether these groups can speak for themselves or require someone to speak for them. Her frustrating conclusion is that neither option is satisfactory.

Drawing on the post-structural work of Jacques Derrida, Spivak focuses on the impossibility of anyone, even members of the ethnic group themselves, finding a true, unproblematic voice that would adequately express the views of the whole group. To attempt this would be implicitly subjective and, as Derrida contends, all subjectivity is fragmented and therefore tainted. Furthermore, subaltern groups are simply too heterogeneous to allow any one member to realistically represent the entire group. (For example, Australians frequently refer to 'the Aborigines' as a single group when in fact the indigenous peoples of Australia are made up of hundreds of distinct cultural segments with unique languages, customs and belief systems.)

Why can't academics speak for them? Partly for the reason mentioned above but also because, as Spivak argues, those academics (usually from privileged and comfortable western universities) who attempt to speak for the subaltern are unlikely to do more than perpetuate the familiar discourses of domination and rely on 'fictional' voices to represent the whole – just as Said suggested westerners did with their inventions of the 'Orient'. Therefore we are trapped in a catch-22 situation; a Babel of voices limited by the subjective nature of the subaltern speaker who cannot speak for all subalterns or, alternatively, reduced to academic constructions of the developing world that are seeking the inherent 'otherness' of the subaltern and will frequently fall back on theoretical simulacra (the critical apparatus that has already been developed).

There is also debate around how post-colonial discourse should articulate colonialism and neo-colonialism. Should a stark 'master–slave' dichotomy be reinvented to define the characteristics of colonial dynamics, to help 'recover (a) the socio-economic and historical referents of the colonial encounter, and (b) the agency and oppositional impulses of the individual colonised subject and nationalist discourses and movements in general' (Loomba 1993: 308)? Or is 'hybridity', the ambivalence and duality of the colonial subject, more useful and instructive? Bhabha and others suggest that the coloniser–colonised relationship is not a Manichean divide, but deeply fissured from the start (see Williams and Chrisman 1993).

The term 'post-colonial' could be considered problematic in that it might seem to suggest that colonialism is a thing of the past, when in fact many of the nations so dubbed are still subordinated to the affluent industrial states. However, it is clear that in fact the thrust of much post-colonial thought seems well aware of these ironies:

To reveal 'the continuing persistence of colonial discourse', to question the 'post' in 'post-colonial', as Mani wishes to do, is important; at the same time, if we are contesting the stasis attributed to colonised societies by Orientalist discourse, the 'pre' and the 'post' of colonialism deserve equal attention.

(Loomba 1993: 320)

Post-colonialism is not an easy term to define. It represents a new socio-political and cultural space in the aftermath of colonisation, and is an area often charted through complex, hybrid ethnic forms and literatures. Drawing on diverse traditions of criticism – Marxian, psychoanalytical (especially Lacanian) literary and film theory, post-structuralist practices – it is indeed an important aspect of postmodern theory and practice. It is the caesura left after the brutality of colonial rule and decolonisation wars, and it is within this space that the post-colonial subject, hybrid and diasporic, seeks to find an identity and voice.

> Local voices retool the semantics of ethnicity by being specific. Their specificity defeats the manipulation of ethnicity, itself a nexus of power. Failing to hear the subaltern voices, still newer forms of oppression may masquerade as 'ethnic' and be promulgated as such by intellectuals.
>
> (Schoenbrun 1993: 48)

The importance of the local and specific voice had long been reduced to a whisper against the roar of the mainstream, but this specificity invokes the issue of identity politics whereby fragmentation of social movements occur. For some the privileging of 'subaltern' and specific identities involves a theoretical conundrum: are the claims for self-determination and human rights made by post-colonial individuals from, say, Sri Lanka or Vietnam to be assessed as valid because they are Sri Lankans or Vietnamese or on the basis of their common membership of humanity? As Tabish Khair comments in a recent article: 'Our claim to rights is a universal claim, while our oppression is always specific to our particular, relational identities' (Khair 1999: 2). This is not to deny the validity of claims or the very real oppression that colonial regimes have practised. The problem, as Khair astutely notices, is that, again, the discourses of post-colonialism, as with postmodernity, are founded on a negative view of ideas that attempt to essentialise or universalise and instead embrace the relative and fragmented view that no one world view is capable of speaking for all 'others'. However, as Khair notes (in a view echoed by Malik and others), 'exploitation and control work by way of particularities just as much as by way of abstract and false universalisms' (Khair 1999: 2). In addition, the post-colonial focus on literature and what Rorty has called the 'linguistic turn' in theory has been subject to accusations of encouraging 'an idealist reduction of the social to the semiotic' (Callinicos 1995: 111).

Despite the controversy generated and the theoretical complexity of some of these critiques, culture is always 'in the making', never static, and those academics who seek to reduce post-colonial voices to essentialist or determinist categories or outcomes are bypassing the importance of the specific and local. It is here that post-colonial theories offer insights into complex intersectional identities and the relationship between knowledge and power and an understanding of the specific expressions of identity consciousness and belongingness. Colonialism is not a thing of the past, but an aspect of the imperialist urge which takes different forms in different eras.

To complete the examination of theoretical ideas it is important to discuss Critical Race Theory (CRT): that strand, or multiple strands, of thinking stemming from legal and black feminist thinkers in the USA but now actively being pursued in other countries around the world. Some of the criticisms aimed at postcolonialism are also levelled at CRT, which has led to a robust dialogue with Marxist scholars, who, again, see its focus as delusional and prioritising white supremacy over notions of class.

CRITICAL RACE THEORY

In the last few years Critical Race Theory, developing from Critical Legal studies in the USA, has grown in influence in the UK and elsewhere, finding multiple applications. The diverse scholarship of CRT questions some of the foundational issues of the western philosophical canon. The argument, in many ways overlapping with post-colonial thought, is voiced by some of the adherents of CRT – broadly that western thought tends to follow a reductive, objectifying logic: 'Rob the Universe of its richness, deny the significance of the symbolic simplify phenomena until it becomes a mere object, and you have a knowable quantity. Here begins and ends the European epistemological mode' (Ani 1994: 29).

While CRT has no 'canonical set of doctrines or methodologies to which all subscribe' (Crenshaw 1995: xiii), several key unifying interests have been identified: first, its purpose is to understand how a regime of white supremacy and its subordination of people of colour have been created and maintained – this has been theorised particularly in the context of American society. CRT begins with the notion that racism is normal in American society (Delgado 1995: xiv). However, CRT scholars maintain that in western countries more generally racism is 'endemic ... "normal" not aberrant nor rare: deeply ingrained legally and culturally' ... in a way that 'crosses epistemological boundaries' (Gilborn 2006: 12). And, as discussed earlier, in British society a general attitude prevails that racism is an abnormality when in reality there are thousands of cases of racism and it is a daily experience for many people. Second, CRT departs from mainstream legal scholarship by sometimes employing storytelling, for which a particularly strong case was made by Derrick Bell, who uses fantasy parables to model the processes by which racisms are manifest. Centralising the marginalised voice is important to CRT. Storytelling and counter-storytelling methodologies are thus seen as 'race'-centred research that can effectively voice the experiences of black people. Third, CRT puts forward the argument that liberalism is a means for maintaining the status quo: the white supremacy that underpins the thinking and operation of power in western society. The concept of 'interest convergence' (a term coined by Derrick Bell) is used to show that seemingly liberal and progressive policies and legislation are ultimately permitted only because they benefit the white majority. Consequently,

CRT challenges traditional dominant ideologies around objectivity, meritocracy, colour-blindness, race-neutrality and equal opportunities. The facade of liberalism is argued to be a front for the fact that the real beneficiaries of civil rights legislation have been whites. One consequence of interest convergence is particularly of concern for liberal democracies that believe themselves to be moving progressively forward and combating racism through legislation. In the UK, for example, the 2000 Race Relations Amendment Act was, on the surface, a radical marker against institutional racism that was backed up by tough legal sanctions. However, it could be argued that in reality it has made little substantial difference:

> The Race Relations Amendment Act is one of the strongest equality laws in Britain, and one of the strongest protections that working people have ... But despite these strengths, the act is undervalued and underused. Many trade unionists have allowed the issues it covers to drop down their list of priorities. Others have assumed that the law must be so complex that only lawyers can understand it properly.
>
> (NATFHE and UNISON 2004: 1)

Similarly, although there have been some changes in police recruitment of BME groups following this law and a raft of other public enquiries, racism in the British police force appears to continue, prompting the Runnymede Trust to report that:

> we remain unconvinced, despite some small areas of progress and despite the best of intentions, of the effectiveness of such guidance in meeting the overarching recommendation of the Stephen Lawrence Inquiry – to eliminate 'racist prejudice and disadvantage' and to demonstrate 'fairness in all aspects of policing'.
>
> (Rollock 2009: 7)

While the detailed examination of liberal legislation and bureaucratic systems does seem to support in some aspects the argument of interest convergence this would be of little surprise to Marxists, who would argue that liberal democracies support the interests of the status quo and that the maintenance of racism at the social and cultural level is one way in which this is managed while appearing to inoculate these systems from the extremes of racist behaviour: they are merely paying lip service to change.

Finally, CRT has been a focus for anti-essentialist thought, recognising the intersectional reality of social divisions. It is understood that, for example, sexism should be understood and modified by the specific dynamics of race, class position, or sexual orientation through which women or men experience discrimination. These forms of oppression interact and compound one another. The vigour and political acuteness of CRT scholarship, therefore unites feminists, legal scholars, and postmodern thinkers in a compelling and challenging recognition of hybrid and luminal identities. Forms of social oppression do not act independently of one another, but must be understood from the points at which they modify one another. The social effect of these compounded oppressions require a critical rethinking of any particular one. Implicit for some practitioners is that the rational and positivist social sciences must be challenged as depersonalising and dehumanising. The complex etic self of the subaltern must be heard and has inherent validity:

> All of my selves are invested in this work – the self that is a researcher, the self that is a parent, the self that is a community member, the self that is a Black woman. No technical-rational approach to this work would yield the deeply textured, multifaceted work I attempt to do. Nor would a technical-rational approach allow for the 'archaeology of knowledge' (Foucault 1972) that is necessary to challenge the inequitable social, economic and political positions that exist between the mainstream and the margins.
>
> (Ladson-Billings 2003: 423)

In contrast, a Marxist viewpoint considers 'race' as a form of mystification, disguising the structure of exploitation and the severe inequalities within global capitalism, and argues that 'many contemporary race theorists, in their systematic erasure of materialism, have become close (ideological) allies with the economic and political elites, who deny even the existence of classes' (Young 2006: Red Critique No 11). The implied criticism of enlightenment rationality has been criticised as straying into 'radical chic' of subjectivism.

Although Marxists may deny the importance of race as a primary category – as a mere mask of capitalism. This in turn could be criticised as reducing complex human agency to relations of production, which may be too crude a tool when considering ethnicity, family, culture or sexuality.

Despite these various criticisms, CRT has provided a contrast to often blinkered, complacent and laissez-faire views which argue that society is increasingly fair and equal, denying the commonplace racism faced by many on an everyday basis and failing to recognise the inherent racism at the heart of institutions and in our daily lives.

CHAPTER SUMMARY

There has been a shift towards those theoretical approaches to race and ethnicity that deconstruct social meanings and consider the individual subject location, rather than more macro-sociological and materially based theories. Postmodernity has allowed a great many synthetic and experimental approaches to defining identity.

This focus on identity politics has been shown to have some positive value for a closer culturalist understanding of the construction of race and racism(s) as well as of gender and sexuality. Stuart Hall and others have utilised the work of Foucault, Derrida and neo-Marxists to develop an understanding of ethnicity that is fluid and diasporic. The 'postmodern turn' has been opposed by some, who feel that the fragmentation of identity politics and relativism represent a politics of defeat and undermine anti-racist struggles for equality by over-emphasising difference. Both post-colonial and the Critical Race Theories mark a refusal to forget the historical contexts of oppression or the current reality of racism and white supremacy. They provide insights into the complex hybrid identities which are the result of the impact of colonialism. Both also recognise the power of language and the importance of giving voice to those discursively subordinated. As Mcleod puts it:

> We are declaring that the standpoint from where we read the world is both a privilege and a loss, a vantage and a limit. We are admitting that knowledge is inseparable from power, and that one way to help the world is to transform the way we come to know the world.
>
> (Macleod 2000: 313–14)

EXERCISE 5.1

1 Consider the images used in this chapter. What are the initial meanings and values you would associate with them?
2 Can you find similar images of the 'Orient'? Have today's images of the 'other' changed substantially? Why?/Why not?
3 What modern literature are you aware of that develops the narrative of the contemporary multicultural cosmopolitan city?
4 Consider Spivak's question 'Can the Subaltern Speak?' How relevant is it to minority ethnic groups, women, gays and other discriminated groups?
5 Assess Khair's (1999) robust criticism of post-colonialism that 'exploitation and control work by way of particularities just as much as by way of abstract and false universalisms'. Is this view borne out in practice? What does this mean for postmodern/post-colonial criticism?
6 Is 'the philosophy of difference the politics of defeat' (Malik 1996: 265)? Why?/Why not?
7 There seem to be many arguments against postmodern theorising on race and ethnicity, but what are the benefits of such approaches to this area of study?
8 Gloria Ladson-Billings stated that 'CRT never makes claims of objectivity or rationality'. Should we be concerned about the issues of subjectivity and essentialism implicit in the abandonment of a technical rational approach?
9 Much of the argument implicit in the epistemology of CRT is that western rationality has systematically denied other forms of cultural knowledge and has led to a rational disenchantment with traditional symbolic meanings. Do you agree with this view?
10 Is the traditional ethnographer a 'deus ex machina'? How might we avoid this 'god's eye' view in ethnographic research? How do we 'do' valid research which includes different world views?

11 Is 'interest convergence' an analytically useful concept? Could *any* progressive change possibly be claimed as 'interest convergence'? How might the concept of 'interest convergence' be argued in the ascension of Barack Obama to power?

12 Could a more standard Marxian concept explain how legal and other progressive changes are rendered less effective in practice? So, for example, Fiske cites the problem of incorporation:

> On the one hand it can be argued that progressive practices are panaceas allowed by the system to keep subordinate content within it. By allowing the system to be flexible and to contain points of opposition within it, such progressive practices actually strengthen that to which they are opposed, and thus delay radical change that is the only one that can bring about genuine improvement in social conditions.
>
> (Fiske 2010: 152)

13 Is it a lost cause to argue primacy of class or race? How do we proceed out of this traditional impasse between materialism and relativist idealism?

Further reading

A text which gives the reader a critical overview of post-colonialism, John McLeod's *Beginning Postcolonialism*, is a useful introduction (Manchester: Manchester University Press, 2nd edn, 2010). In terms of collected writings the following are of enduring value, giving the reader a sense of the breadth and depth of the field of post-colonial studies: P. Williams and L. Chrisman, *Colonial Discourse and Post-Colonial Theory: A Reader* (London and New York: Harvester Wheatsheaf, 1993) and B. Ashcroft, G. Griffiths and H. Tiffin (eds), *The Post-Colonial Studies Reader* (London and New York: Routledge, 1995).

There is a growing trend in subaltern studies which makes interesting reading about complex intersectional identities. The following titles by Gyanendra Pandey examine the idea of 'subaltern citizenship': Subaltern Citizens and their Histories: Investigations from India and the USA (Routledge, 2010) and Subalternity and Difference: Investigations from the North and the South (Routledge, 2012).

Notes

1 See Glossary.
2 The tagline for advertisements of the 1960s and 1970s for a popular chocolate bar.
3 'Subaltern' is defined here as one subordinated discursively.

CHAPTER 6

Case study

Indigenous Australians

There is no greater sorrow on earth than the loss of one's native land.

(Euripides 431BCE)

The time has now come for the nation to turn a new page in Australia's history by righting the wrongs of the past and so moving forward with confidence to the future. We apologise for the laws and policies of successive parliaments and governments that have inflicted profound grief, suffering and loss on these, our fellow Australians...

(Kevin Rudd, Sorry Speech, 12 February 2008)

Australia's indigenous people have faced more than two centuries of dispossession. Having endured wave after wave of colonialism. First external colonialism from Britain, then 'internal colonialism', which meant policies of 'protection' with the overt intention of protecting them from the damage done by European culture albeit while never restoring Aboriginal culture, which was seen as doomed due to its inherent inferiority (see Hughes 1995). This was followed by post-war policies of assimilation and integration which gave way to self-determination and reconciliation. Yet, despite these shifts in policy, the conditions and treatment of Aboriginal peoples in Australia is uniformly shameful. There has been much made of the apology made by Kevin Rudd in 2008, the much anticipated public 'sorry' which was resisted by previous governments; however, it was not cause for universal celebration. Gary Foley commented afterwards: that 'it [is] inevitable that this as an event will be a part of future white Australian mythology about how wonderfully they have always treated the Aboriginal people. It will become part of white Australia's long history of denial' (McKinnon 2008). This chapter seeks to examine a specific site of the relationship between white and indigenous Australians. First, however, to make this study more accessible, some contextual discussion is needed.

LAND RIGHTS

The Land Rights Movement claims that Aborigines have the right to own large tracts of land on the principle of being the first inhabitants, and yet before Britain colonised this land, Australia was a wilderness, a land going to waste. Although rich in natural resources and pastoral land, the Aboriginal had not, in thousands of years, constructed permanent dwellings or developed the land in any form. Very little real culture was recognisable. Today, with the technology of the European, all Australians have a nation of which they can be very proud. One which has the potential of being the richest and most self-sufficient in the world.

(Tract 'Threat to the Nation', Union of Caucasian
Christian People, Perth 1985)

Perceptions such as those expressed above reflect a popular misapprehension about land rights and is indicative of an inherently racist view that is shared by Australians from varied backgrounds. Such views recall the first settlers' refusal to recognise Aboriginal people as having any prior rights over their land and their using of the term *terra nullius* (empty land) to describe large areas of Australia on early maps (see Figure 6.1). In an ironic reversal, anti-immigration activists in the early 1990s employed graffiti of an outline map of the country with the word 'FULL' printed inside. The ground-breaking Mabo High Court Ruling in 1992 (see Chapter 3) further fuelled public anxiety, already inflamed by media panics about Aboriginal land claims suggesting they threatened suburban gardens and vast areas of public land. These inflated concerns, backed by powerful industrialists and pastoralists, were finally endorsed by what many would see as regressive government legislation. Howard's amendments, known as the Ten-Point Plan, were implemented in response to a rightist campaign to nullify a December 1996 High Court ruling in the Wik case, which legitimised native title claims on pastoral leases – public land leased to farmers and pastoralists (ranchers). But the polarisation over the issue has been a thorn in the side of John Howard's Liberal government.

At the time that this legislation was passed, an infamous series of television ads represented this issue as a direct attack on Australian 'battlers', farmers and other white Australians, who were presented as 'sons of the soil' – every bit as entitled to the land as Aborigines. The effect of this has been to inflate an issue which never in fact presented any threat and to scapegoat Aboriginal people, who compose about 2 per cent of the population.

Figure 6.1 Australia, from *terra nullius*, 'empty', in 1788 to 'full' in 1988

Over the course of this year [1997], the National Farmers Federation (NFF) [...] has spearheaded a campaign asserting that small farmers' right to work the land is in jeopardy from the newly recognized native title rights. This scare campaign is backed by the National Party and sections of the Liberal Party, including the state governments in Queensland and Western Australia. Howard's measures were drawn up under the pressure of these forces.

(Aiken and Poulsen 1997: 2)

LIVING CONDITIONS

Table 6.1 shows just how inequitable life in Australia is for Aboriginal peoples. The figures present a picture of stark contrast. Aboriginal people, as noted, make up only around 2 per cent of the population but are more than seventeen times more likely to be incarcerated, three times more likely to be unemployed and have a chronically shortened life span compared with white Australians. It is important to recognise these details because there is much disinformation about the conditions in which Aboriginal people find themselves.

Figure 6.2 is from the website of the pressure group PARIAH (People Against Racism In Australian Hotels). Aboriginal people in Darwin and other cities in Australia are frequently victims of racist abuse and are marginalised, moved on

Table 6.1 Patterns of indigenous disadvantage

NATIONAL INDICATORS	INDIGENOUS	NON-INDIGENOUS
Life expectancy at birth (2005–2007) (male)	67.2	78.7
Life expectancy at birth (2005–2007) (female)	72.9	82.6
Infant mortality (2003–7) per 1000 live births	9.7	4.4
Home ownership (2008)	29%	72%
Unemployment (2006)	16%	5%
Overcrowded housing	27%	6%
Imprisonment rate per 100,000 (2008)	2,223	129

(Source: Australian Bureau of Statistics 2013 and Australian Institute of Criminology, July 2009)

and barred from hotels and other public places. On the same site there is a protest against the extraordinary rates of incarceration suffered by Aboriginal people in the Northern Territory (NT). The title of the image in Figure 6.2 shows the irony of a legislature that convicts Aboriginal people for the flimsiest of reasons. Because Aboriginal drinkers are refused entry to many pubs they may be seen drinking in public places such as parks or city squares; however, such behaviour is considered

Figure 6.2 'Breathing while Black'. 'Prior to their being "moved on" by NT Police, these people were peaceably assembled in Darwin's city centre, instead of their isolated and (according to ex-NT Chief Minister Shane Stone) "dysfunctional" communities. Don't you love the Aboriginal Art (for the tourists) in the background' (Mick Lambe, PARIAH website)

unacceptable and taboo. As Fiske *et al.* (1987) suggest, there is a cultural boundary for white Australians, who see public drinking as threatening.

> So their drunkenness is more visible and breaks the tacit rule of white drinking; and they get arrested on charges of drunkenness in a vast disproportion to their numbers or even degree of drunkenness and the danger to public order they represent. But the punitive treatment of Aboriginal drinkers in public places serves a double ideological function: it separates them off from full participation and membership of white Australian society (they are 'dirty drunks' whereas whites are 'good boozers'), and it vindicates the magic wall around the pub, which protects white drinkers in their alcoholic anti-society and keeps the subversion and criticism within its safe bounds.
>
> (Fiske *et al.* 1987: 11)

Stephen Muecke investigates how concepts of aboriginality are constructed through discourse. Muecke argues that 'whatever "Aboriginality" is, it has never always been the same thing from one tribal group to another, from ancient times to the present, or even according to some legal definitions, from one state of Australia to another' (Muecke 1992: 19). Although arguing that aboriginality has never had a singular definition or meaning, Muecke rightly notes that, according to humanist thought, 'the essence of what "they" are, is known intuitively by the people themselves, and no-one else can have access to this knowledge' (ibid.: 19). This view has underpinned the movement towards self-determination and makes a nonsense of the idea that aboriginality can be quantified in terms of blood, which was seriously discussed in Australia in the 1990s, when it was considered how Tasmanian and other Aboriginal claimants could be tested as bona-fide Aboriginal.

Muecke's work on aboriginality is an important starting point in a discussion about the historical construction of aboriginality in Australian society. Muecke offers a lucid critique of the ways in which aboriginality is represented as a truthful and authentic object by whoever appropriates it. Aboriginality is socially constructed through various representations in, for example, print media, television, film, politics and music. Muecke's critical and historical approach argues 'that European ways of talking about Aborigines limit their ways of knowing what Aborigines might be' (ibid.: 20). An example of this restrictive discourse at work, which has had long-term consequences, is the legal status of 'public drunkenness':

> This offence was constructed during a period of high moral conservatism in Australia, and its existence now appears to be anachronistic. More insidious though is the fact that public drunkenness is the offence which sees many young black men being placed in police custody – a situation which leads to young black men taking their own lives at a disproportionately high rate compared with the national average for suicides in gaol. It would take a small act of legislative courage

to remove the offence of public drunkenness from the statutes thus reducing the possibility of young black men being arrested and possibly taking their own lives.

(Finnigan 2001: 43)

Aboriginal people, as discussed in Chapter 1 with reference to Hartley's (1998) assessment of how the media divides reality, are marginalised – part of a permanent metaphysical 'otherness' ('Theydom'). Media coverage of Aboriginal issues typically constructs them as a problem, depicting them as:

> agitators, politicos, welfare-funded drunks or as frequent cause of social unrest in 'stable' white communities. In media discourse, an 'educated' and 'articulate' Aboriginal person is quickly labelled a political stirrer, radical activist, or black sympathiser. News crews are quick to cover community brawls, or scuffles at Aboriginal landright marches or protest gatherings outside courtrooms. Wherever and whenever Aborigines (or other ethnic groups) can be captured on film as unruly, disruptive, and (preferably) violent, the media are present.
>
> (Luke 1996: 6)

Australia has a complex indigenous heritage comprising several hundred 'Aboriginal' groups with unique languages and traditions. However, the consequences of invasion, rates of incarceration and the legacy of the 'stolen generation' (forcible removal of Aboriginal children), as well as continuous pressure from developers on already small parcels of land, have had a catastrophic impact on many communities, dislocating them from their traditional areas and leading to many indigenous people being trapped in an impoverished and pressured state. There is often a struggle to obtain even the most basic amenities in the midst of monocultural Australian affluence.

The case study in this chapter focuses on one specific site of this colonial legacy, Darwin in the Northern Territory, and the indigenous Australians who live there. The Northern Territory population has the highest proportion of indigenous people in Australia (recorded at 30 per cent, Australian Bureau of Statistics 2011). Many of these indigenous groups are transient or enjoy an uneasy existence on the edges of the city in a few poorly resourced and crowded housing estates or in informal camps. It is an existence that at times brings them into conflict with the white community and local government's concerns for the image of the city and the burgeoning tourist trade. The strategies employed by Darwin City Council to manage what they call the 'itinerant problem' are reminiscent of the divisive tactics employed by colonial overseers. Certain disparate groups of indigenous peoples have been formed into the Larrakia Nation in pursuit of long-standing land-rights claims in the Darwin area. This group has been encouraged to act as 'cultural ambassadors' to persuade groups of so-called 'itinerant' Aborigines to return to their own homelands. This chapter looks at the contested notion of 'home', citizenship and nation and focuses on what occurs when lifestyles, cultures and financial aims collide.

CONTESTED HOMELANDS: DARWIN'S 'ITINERANT PROBLEM'[1]

Framing the fringe dwellers

The dry season in Darwin: dragonflies fill the air, backpackers fill the streets, Mindil Beach Markets are in full swing, presenting tourists with a multicultural mosaic, and the ongoing campaign to remove homeless Aboriginal people from public view moves up a notch.

Darwin has the largest Aboriginal population of any Australian city at nearly 9 per cent. While the greater majority of the indigenous population in Darwin live in circumstances not unlike their non-indigenous neighbours, a number are, out of necessity, more transient, moving between remote communities and the city, visiting friends and relatives who may be in hospital or prison, seeking work or escaping unenviable conditions in remote communities. It is important to preface the present study with a word on social and historical context, as the representation of indigenous issues in 'the Territory' is founded upon historical and cultural constructions of aboriginality. What underpins this long-running moral panic about homeless indigenous people?

First, the history of Aboriginal people in Australia has been one of dispossession, cultural genocide and displacement.

> During the period of conquest, indigenous people were deprived of their most basic rights, their society and culture were destroyed, and their populations were decimated. Survivors were forced onto reservations and controlled by missionaries and special welfare bureaucracies. They were seen as racially inferior and expected to 'die out'.
>
> (Castles and Davidson 2000: 73)

Second, there is a long-standing and well-recognised cultural defensiveness – the 'cultural cringe' – a deference to European and British culture ('the old country') that has been recently reinvoked with reference to the 'stolen generation' and until recently the government's refusal to make an official apology to indigenous Australians. Prime Minister John Howard, as discussed in Chapter 3, used the term 'black armband view of history' to characterise what he regards as a negative and morose reading of history that reflects 'a belief that most Australian history since

1788 has been little more than a disgraceful story of imperialism, exploitation, racism, sexism and other forms of discrimination' (Howard 1996; see also McKenna 1997; Mayne 1997).

Third, the context of the repositioning of social theory since the 1980s, the exhaustion of the narratives of modernity and the deconstruction of previously unchallenged foundations of national identity, have all thrown into sharper focus historical events that had been buried in a common-sense ethnocentric credo of Australia as the 'lucky country'. However, Donald Horne, who popularised the epithet, made it with pointed irony: 'Australia is a lucky country, run by second-rate people who share its luck' (Horne 1964).

The recent scrutiny and documenting of Australian history has challenged a more ingenuous image of Australia as a land of sunshine and opportunity and has led to debates about the intentions behind (as well as the actual extent of) acts that fit international definitions of genocide (see, for example, Windschuttle 2004a; 2004b). These new readings have also produced works of literature such as Robert Drewe's *The Savage Crows* (1976), which draws on the 1829 journals of George Augustus Robinson, which describe the last days of the Tasmanian Aborigines; Robert Hughes's *The Fatal Shore* (1987), a history of Australia as a penal colony; and, more recently, films such as *Rabbit-Proof Fence* (2002), which powerfully portrays the forced removal of Aboriginal children as part of a systematic eugenics[2] policy.

> large numbers of part-Aboriginal children [were taken] from their mothers, to be raised in Children's Homes or by white foster-parents, a policy introduced on the grounds that the Aboriginal peoples were destined for extinction. This policy of assimilation, which was followed with especial vigour by A.O. Neville the Protector of Aborigines in Western Australia and continued until 1970, continues to cause great distress and hardship for many Aboriginal families, and is a cause of much mistrust.
>
> (Bittles 2004: 3)

Through these and many other works, a more realistic and plural identity began to emerge. At the same time, the multi-ethnic composition of Australia was also being recognised, previously coercive assimilationist policies were being criticised and multiculturalism emerged as a progressive discourse, despite warnings from conservative historians such as Geoffrey Blainey, who argued that it would lead to a weakening of national culture (Blainey 1984).

Fourth, there has been a conservative backlash to these shifts in discourse. It seems that there is a popular, stridently xenophobic sense of being disenfranchised by liberal, multicultural rhetoric that seems to threaten white Australian popular mores. Pauline Hanson's One Nation Party, which had a surge of popularity in the late 1990s, tapped into these very sentiments. In this context the need to demonise Aborigines serves a long-standing function of reaffirming the civilisation and culture of white Australians, particularly in rural areas and away from Sydney and Melbourne. Hanson was able to effectively exploit a streak of resentment and xenophobia by pointing to benefits that Asian migrants and Aborigines received.

> One Nation was a tragedy. By creating a block of 1 million voters strategically placed between Labor, the Nationals and the Liberals, it tempted the parties to pander to its prejudices. The Liberals adopted much of its refugee policy. More importantly, they pursued their own similar agenda against multiculturalism and Aboriginal reconciliation.
>
> (Jupp 2002: 139)

Fifth, at the same time that the national climate concerning indigenous politics has encouraged conservatism, economically Darwin has become a premier tourist spot – the gateway to Kakadu and the much-promoted areas to the south (Uluru, the Olgas, Kings Canyon), and, of course, the crocodile parks and river cruises. Tourism in 2003–4 saw visitor spending increase by 8 per cent (to $1.2 billion), which injected an additional $81 million into the NT. Culturally orientated tourism is heavily promoted as a vital part of this success. Tourists can

> meet members of the local indigenous community for an educational experience in bush land setting. Learn of the Aboriginal culture through the wide range of exhibits. See demonstrations of boomerang and spear throwing and learn about traditional sources for food and medicine. There is opportunity to sample bush foods such as Witchetty Grubs, Bloodwood Apples, Bush Bananas and various seeds. Following a morning tea of damper and billy tea, learn about tribal life, languages, art, dance and music, where you can be taught how to play the didgeridoo.
>
> (from Goway.com; Australia and the South Pacific 2006)

As a tourist to the 'Top End', this is typical of the rhetoric one is exposed to. It appears that the static imagery of traditional lifestyles unchanged and timelessly pursued in remote settings is the preferred image, the one that is thought to attract tourism. The imagery used in the card in Figure 6.3 is very appealing and unproblematic, yet for many Aboriginal people these images of traditional life are far removed from their day-to-day reality, living in urban settings often very similar to those of their white compatriots. However, the visibility of impoverished urban Aborigines runs counter to the images of carefree natives in a bush setting, which is the only available image presented for tourist consumption, and since 2003 the Northern Territory government has stepped up measures to remove so-called 'itinerants' from the city.

Figure 6.3 'Australian Aborigines': typical representations of Aboriginal culture

This is not to deny the survival of rich and varied traditions of indigenous culture – only to state that the culture is one which, like all cultures, grows and develops, adapting, synthesising and making sense of a changing world. Indeed, there is the suggestion that Aboriginal people are imprisoned by a timeless view of culture. This view of culture is romantic and static and highlights the lack of real communication between indigenous and white populations in Australia: 'they are constantly called upon to display this essence, or this or that skill, as if culture were an endowment. This is an enormous burden, and it is the Western version of culture which gives them this, not the Aboriginal' (Muecke 1992: 40).

Sonia Smallacombe (Head of Indigenous Studies, Charles Darwin University), in a recent interview, supported this view of indigenous people tied to a primordial ethnic identity:

> Some of the legislation is so draconian. To satisfy a land claim you've got to have lived a lifestyle that occurred before 1788 – of course we've changed a lot since 1788! But the legislation doesn't recognise it – the Government doesn't recognise that cultures change and also we have to change if we want to survive. They look at indigenous culture as static, they don't look at any other culture, but they certainly see indigenous culture as it has to be static which we're certainly not.
>
> (Spencer 2004b)

Directly racist constructions of aboriginality have used this form of static essentialism based on blood quantum, genealogical test or ideas of an Aboriginal 'race' to define Aboriginal identity and membership and eligibility to benefits (see Gardiner-Garden 2003). It is clear, then, that concerns about developing tourism and prevailing trends of ethnocentric self-interest have developed an approach to indigenous culture that divides the 'timeless cultural values' that seem most marketable from the cultural resistance of 'itinerant' lifestyles that are antagonistic to the aims of profit maximisation. The latter lifestyles and communities are a threat that has attracted an extraordinary amount of concern, such that the NT government has allocated $5.25 million since June 2003 to try and resolve the issue. However, the money has not gone towards improving the accommodation for Aboriginal communities, which are wholly inadequate in area and in gross disrepair.

The 'itinerant problem': community conditions

The ideas of 'home' and of being homeless have powerful cultural and normative power. The less formal aspects of the homes of 'long grass' people (generally referred to in Darwin as 'itinerants', which is another very emotionally loaded term) are a cause for concern to white Territorians and hard to equate with the neat suburban blocks that most Australians inhabit. Homes as temporary, makeshift or transient spaces are seen as a rather threatening concept. Yet from the work of writers such as Bill Day and Marcia Langton it appears that these 'itinerant' camps are highly organised and structured, with complex relationships and rules by which the campers live (see Day 2001a; Langton 1997; Sansom 1980).

The largest official Aboriginal community in Darwin, the Bagot community in the Ludmilla area, began as an Aboriginal Reserve in 1938. Like a few other communities, the Bagot is under-resourced and too small for the needs of an expanding indigenous community. Bagot has been reduced in area, as some land has been taken to build a fast-food outlet. This is in a prime location for passing traffic to the airport and will obviously receive patronage also from local Bagot residents themselves. A recent project to build a fence around the community was promoted by local politicians as an investment in the community:

> Mr Vatskalis said the first stage of the $460,000 project is about to start and will involve the construction of a new fence across the front of Bagot community, a new entrance and associated landscaping. Additional new fencing will also be installed around most of the remaining boundary of Bagot community to improve security and prevent vehicular access.
>
> (Northern Territory Government 2003)

However, the project may well be greeted with cynicism by some members of the indigenous community. One wonders whether the fencing is for their security and the enhancement of the community or to hide the cramped and run-down conditions within the impoverished community from public scrutiny and further stigmatise the people inside. A recent story illustrates the conditions within Bagot: 'A Darwin indigenous community (Bagot) says it does not have the money to remove a run-down house containing asbestos' (ABC Northern Territory 2004). The house could not be quickly and safely removed as the costs of such an operation were prohibitive.

Another smaller community with a less formal status, closer to the city centre, is the One Mile Dam community. The lack of services here was very apparent when I visited in July 2004. The camp was set up for indigenous people in the 1970s and has received little help or improvement since then. It can swell to accommodate nearly 200 people and has only two toilets. Piles of refuse fester in the heat and recent reports have cited faulty wiring, exposing residents to the danger of electrocution. In addition, nearby fuel-storage tanks overlook the community, presenting an ever-present threat from volatile fumes; residents worry about the pollution to the dam, which is considered a place of special significance to the community. The new luxury apartments that overlook the community signify another threat, as developers look to expand and use the community land for future developments.

The continual pressure on these small parcels of land has become intense, as the local government refuses to build new community sites to accommodate so-called 'itinerants'. The resultant overcrowding and other social problems associated with poverty and difficult living conditions have blighted Aboriginal communities for a very long time. Different groups are thrown together in these shrinking communal spaces, and arguments and violence are not uncommon. The excessive consumption of alcohol and high incidences of illness, domestic violence and child abuse have all been associated with communities. While these behaviours are undeniably a part of life in the cramped and under-resourced areas apportioned to 'itinerants', they receive much more public censure than when they occur in the white community. There are a number of possible reasons for this, including the obvious one that this is a group that is much more exposed to public scrutiny – barred from pubs so forced to drink in public, sleeping in the open when accommodation is not available. More than this, however, it appears that any 'official' approach to Aborigines is always from a point of historically constructed paternalism.

Law and order

In 2003 the city council began to look seriously at a number of initiatives that it saw as potential solutions to what had become characterised as the 'itinerant problem'. The government concern reached a peak around early to mid-2003; even an apartheid-style permit system for Aboriginal people, restricting their access to the city, was briefly considered. Draconian policing laws under the previous Liberal government had included mandatory sentencing, which led to some extraordinarily harsh penalties for the most minor offences.

A man from a remote community north east of Darwin stole a packet of biscuits and some cordial... worth $3.00...he received 12 month prison sentence. Similarly a homeless man was given a year sentence for taking a towel from a clothesline 'to use as a blanket'. A 17 year old youth from a remote community east of Darwin who stole $4.00 worth of petrol for sniffing and received a 90 day penalty.

(North Australian Aboriginal Legal Aid Service 1999: 20)

Even with a Labor government in office, the policy of aggressively targeting young male Aborigines who were often unemployed or students has continued. In 2003 over 80 per cent of the prison populations in the Northern Territory were Aboriginal people. A popular NT tabloid presented this fact thus: 'of 756 prisoners in jail in Darwin and Alice Springs, 612 are indigenous. [...] This equates to 82 per cent of the prison population being black. [...] And this means they still show little or no respect for the laws of this country' (Col Newman, NT News, October 2003).[3]

Media manifestations

During 2003 the Northern Territory developed a perennial theme through its daily newspaper the *Northern Territory News*. The theme could fairly be classed as a moral panic in the original use of the term, whereby 'a condition, episode, person or group of persons [who] become defined as a threat to societal values and interests' (Cohen 1987: 9). Indigenous people have been a constantly demonised and, as shown, criminalised group. The news headlines reproduced in Box 6.1 also indicate possible resolutions to the problem. The use of the term 'itinerants', clearly employed here as a thinly veiled euphemism for Aborigines, is cast aside and almost parodied in the second headline. A transparent campaign of moral sanction and censure reached a peak around April 2003, as attested to by the headlines shown here. Many of the stories show the tabloids' tendency to reduce complex stories to rabble-rousing slogans in a manner that is aggressive towards and antagonistic about Aboriginal issues (see Figure 6.4).

BOX 6.1 ABORIGINAL AUSTRALIANS

PERMITS FOR ABORIGINES (*Northern Territory News*, 4 March 2003)

ITINERANTS TOLD BY THEIR OWN PEOPLE: GO HOME (*Northern Territory News*, 15 April 2003)

GANG OF 30 BASHES 3 TEENS (*Northern Territory News*, 16 April 2003, featuring a photograph of an Aboriginal male and the inset box "'Why? Because there was nothing to do", Darren Duncan pictured at court yesterday')

BLACK v WHITE: ABORIGINES TRY TO REMOVE WHITE WORKERS (*Northern Territory News*, 26 April 2003)

Cohen (1987) and others (Young 1971; Hall *et al.* 1978; Critcher 2003) have shown how a desire for moral consensus may underpin moral panics, focusing on a group that comes to embody – for a period – evil or moral corrosion in society. Figures of authority and agents of social control, particularly the police, are seen to 'amplify' the occurrence of deviance. The media is a central agent in this process of amplification (and, at times, sheer fabrication) of deviance and threat to a moral order. The headlines from the *Northern Territory News* present indigenous people as a threat; they are repeatedly portrayed as violent, drunk, homeless beggars who are a civic nuisance.

There is, it could be suggested, an ambivalence about these portrayals because, first, the conditions in which Aborigines are living are in some cases shamefully under-resourced and squalid, yet only a few minutes from the affluent centre of the city. Second, the derogatory stereotypes relating to Aboriginal drinking (which have a long history) may draw attention away from white Territorians' parallel excesses and alarming rates of alcoholism. Third, many tourists visit the Northern Territory to see Aboriginal sites and enjoy the timeless 'cultural performance' of aboriginality. Chas Critcher, in an interview (June 2004), suggested that moral panics often represent the need for moral unity, 'particularly at times when moral consensus is hard to come by'. In Australia it could be argued that the moral consensus about the historical treatment of indigenous populations and about attitudes of white dominance have gradually shifted and have been exposed to critical scrutiny, as has Australia's less than glorious colonial past as a penal colony.

A key element in the construction of urban Aborigines in Darwin is the discourse around public drinking. There is evidence that the perceptions of Aboriginal Australians prevalent today have their origins in derogatory historical stereotypes.

Figure 6.4 Front page of *Northern Territory News*, 15 April 2003

The caricatures from 1887 editions of the *Queensland Figaro* (see Figures 6.5 and 6.6) portray drink as a central and morally corrosive feature of Aboriginal urban culture. The effects of drinking on indigenous culture have clearly been used by white Australians to affirm their place on higher moral ground and as a means of racist ridicule and paternalism in which the loss of noble 'natural' attributes is bemoaned.

The irony, of course, is that it was these very attributes of naturalness that were so despised by early settlers in the frontiers of America, Canada and Australia. As David Sibley suggests, science and Christianity asserted white dominance over indigenous peoples, arguing that

> peoples closest to nature, in a primitive state needed saving. Salvation often involved not only accepting Christianity but also adopting European style of dress and discipline of a Christian education in the mission school [...] The civilizing mission distanced them from nature.
>
> (Sibley 1995: 25)

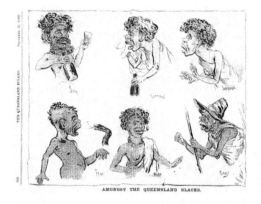

Figure 6.5 'Amongst the Queensland Blacks', *Queensland Figaro*, 10 December 1888

Figure 6.6 'Nature – Civilization', *Queensland Figaro*, 6 August 1887

However, there is also the suggestion here that Aboriginal people are, at best, poor mimics of white society. They are portrayed as so far removed from the civilised mores and refined etiquette of English culture that the very suggestion of Aborigines adopting such a lifestyle is ridiculous (as shown in Figure 6.7).

This contrast between the raw 'nature' of Aboriginal existence and 'civilisation' (Figure 6.6) recalls another popular discourse, that of Rousseau's 'noble savage', a romantic discourse stemming from a strand of Enlightenment thought. The suggestion that Aboriginal people should remain true to their 'nature' is, as I have illustrated, very much alive and well and is still the abiding 'safe' image of indigenous Australians that white Australians and tourism affirm. These visions of Aboriginal people as depraved drunks are obviously the basis of the gross stereotypes available to white Australians who often have little or no contact with indigenous people throughout their lives. As discussed, Aboriginal drinking is always looked at as a problem. Yet there is a contradiction involved when the Northern Territory (especially) is clearly proud of a frontier tradition of excessive drinking. Sonia Smallacombe drew out this point in a recent interview: 'It's basically a

Figure 6.7 'England – Blackfellows at home: They are kindly received in fashionable circles – ladies play the piano to them etc.' *Sydney Punch*, 15 August 1868

contradiction. It's quite celebrated, the fact that the city has a huge consumption of alcohol, [...] while they're celebrating, they're also saying that indigenous people are the ones who should really control their drinking' (Spencer 2004b).

In Darwin, the Beer Can Regatta is a public celebration in which rafts and boats constructed from thousands of beer cans (see Figure 6.8) are raced at Mindil Beach. Aboriginal people (as well as other ethnic groups) are notably absent. Anthropologist Bill Day suggests that the festival serves a crucial function:

> In the Beer Can Regatta the Darwin non-Aboriginal settler society conceals its cultural dislocation and dispossession of Aboriginal people, while constructing settler myths on the urban landscape. In my analysis, I suggest that the festival mediates the disjunction between culture and place typical of immigrant people. In contrast, I suggest that Darwin fringe dwellers believe that they are at home on their own land, while their drinking is associated with Aboriginal resistance to dispossession.
>
> (Day 2001a: 1)

Further, Day suggests that the regatta reflects the British origins of the 'regatta' (as in, for example, the regatta at Henley-on-Thames) and further imbues white drinking behaviour with 'civilised' values, in contrast to the image of Aboriginal drinking, which is presented as out of control. The Beer Can Regatta is presented as a purposeful and constructive reason for drinking. Originating in the 1970s as part of the Keep Australia Beautiful campaign, as a creative solution to the mountains of tin cans strewn around the city, the regatta was then founded on the idea of a constructive and civic-minded activity that would improve the environment. Day suggests that the act of drinking and hence making more cans available for this family-orientated

181

Figure 6.8 'Purposeful drinking'. Beer can boat at the annual Beer Can Regatta, Darwin

activity is given a positive value, and heavy drinking was excused as preparation for the regatta. One team said they had drunk 3,000 cans of beer in a week. 'If we win we'll get rid of a few more cans of beer – to use in next year's race, of course' (*NT News*, 6 August 1997, as quoted in Day 2001). Day makes the point that the festival serves as an unspoken affirmation of white domination, especially as it takes place at Mindil Beach, an area that has significance to local Larrakia (an umbrella term which includes several different groups indigenous to Darwin) people as a burial site.

> In post-colonial Darwin where public expressions of racial superiority are illegal, the festival makes a powerful unspoken statement authorising task-directed white drinking in public places. Aborigines, who are noticeably absent from the Mindil Beach festival, are further displaced by the appropriation of the supposedly empty landscape for the predominantly White festival.
>
> (Day 2001b: 13)

Drinking, then, is at the heart of the construction of the 'itinerant problem' and of dominant perceptions of Aboriginal people in Darwin. Aboriginal drinking is seen as an example of the corruption of Aboriginal culture (see Pearson 2000), a view that accords with dominant white constructions of Aboriginal culture as tainted by contact with 'civilised' values. Conversely, a number of analysts have equated heavy-drinking cultures among 'itinerant' communities as a form of resistance to white hegemony (see Day 2001a: Chapter 9). This is not the place to speculate about this, but suffice to say that the treatment of Aboriginal people for very minor offences such as public drunkenness (to which a blind eye is turned if the person is white) appears to be out of proportion and suggests that urban Aborigines are seen as a threat, perhaps at a symbolic level. This is a feature of the moral panic that has led the white authorities in Darwin to focus on 'itinerants'.

Deconstructing the 'itinerant problem'

In June 2003 the Northern Territory government announced a $5.25 million budget allocation to develop a strategy dubbed the 'Community Harmony Strategy'. The overarching aims of the strategy were a significant reduction of the incidence of anti-social behaviour by 'itinerants' in all major Territory centres and the delivery of infrastructure, intervention programmes and health services responding to the identified needs of 'itinerant' groups (Northern Territory Department of Community Development 2004). While the ostensible aims of this strategy seemed laudable – a focus on health and well-being and a sort of assisted passage back home for people stranded and penniless in city areas – the terms of reference and the definition of implicitly inclusive and exclusive categories of citizenship raise several concerns.

First, the term 'itinerant' entails assumptions of degradation and exclusion that are never made explicit. 'Itinerant' appears to be a euphemism for Aboriginal Australians who stray into the city limits and do not choose to live in the ghettoised suburban developments where social housing is provided. Mick Lambe, a vocal opponent of local government schemes and racist attitudes towards indigenous groups in the Territory, commented that the term 'itinerant' signified 'Territory-speak for Aboriginal people who choose to live traditionally' and 'Aboriginal people who have escaped from their remote Communities' (Lambe 2003).

Second, the term 'itinerant' is applied to groups who are relatively settled in areas around Darwin city centre. There are a number of camps that have been established since the 1970s with some basic dwellings that are now in a state of disrepair: One Mile Dam (also known as Railway Dam), with between 90 and 150 people, and larger communities such as the Bagot in the outer suburbs of Darwin, with over 300 people. In addition, there are a number of 'long grass' camps that are more transitory but nevertheless have been a feature of Darwin's foreshore for many years. As Sonia Smallacombe told me, 'The Government has labelled these people as itinerants, although a lot of them have been around twenty or thirty years so they're actually not itinerants' (Spencer 2004b).

Third, the term 'itinerant' clearly reflects judgements about lifestyle as well as origins and length of habitation. Indeed, those people known as itinerant appear to maintain some vestiges of a traditional lifestyle and to be resistant to the model of citizenship offered by the representatives of the Larrakia Nation. Sonia Smallacombe commented:

They're a group of people who for various reasons are not keen to live in houses, and a lot of people will say things like 'The reason I don't want to go and live in a state house or a housing commission flat is because I can't – I'm not allowed to have my extended family visit me or stay with me – I'm not allowed to have my animals.' Aboriginal people like to have their dogs, they're not allowed to have their dogs with them.

(Spencer 2004b)

Anthropologist Bill Day suggests that 'itinerant' is a signifier that removes the threat the privileged white society of Darwin feels towards Aboriginal people: in Darwin it would seem that homeless Aboriginal people become less threatening as 'transients' or 'itinerants'. These categories are often used as the equivalent to the iconic 'drunken "Abo"', as described by Langton (1993a). However, as Cowlishaw (1994: 80) claims, the refusal of Aborigines in towns to be passive and silent 'stimulates the fears and feeds the paranoia' that many town residents feel towards the significant minority.

Fourth, the term 'itinerants' disguises (effectively denies) the agency of dominant white Australians in dispossessing Aboriginal groups from their traditional lands, forcibly removing groups to missions and removing children from their families. Ironically, the approach stemming from the euphemistic 'itinerant problem' is arguably related to the earlier policies characterised by the title 'Aboriginal problem'. 'The aim of these assimilationist policies was that the Aboriginal "problem" would ultimately disappear – the people would lose their identity within the wider community, albeit through continuing restrictive laws and paternalistic administration' (*Northern Territory News* 1996).

The government approach to homeless Aboriginal people today appears to be of the same order, removing Aboriginal people from the city centre and using a variety of coercive methods to return them to their 'homelands'. Local government has mooted the use of permits for 'itinerants' to control their access to the city area in Darwin. When this approach did not work – and, as stated in the *Northern Territory News* editorial (11 March 1996), 'Pulling down of makeshift camps and moving people on certainly doesn't work. The itinerants just shift to another spot in town. Disliking them and their lifestyle won't make them go away. Positive ideas are needed' – the most recent scheme has involved the collaboration of the government with a newly formed Aboriginal group, the Larrakia Nation, to give the job of policing itinerants a more ethical and apparently culturally sensitive approach.

Larrakia Nation

The Larrakia Nation, founded in 1997, represents a newly incorporated umbrella group of collectively defined groups who have long-standing land-rights claims in the Darwin area and the Cox Peninsula.

The Larrakia are unique in the sense that we are identified as the traditional owners and custodians of the greater Darwin area, Palmerston area, rural area which is unique in the sense that most large urban areas, particularly city areas, throughout Australia share a joint ownership of two or more aboriginal groups but we're certainly recognised as the only aboriginal group in the greater Darwin area as custodians/traditional owners: within that there are 8 identifiable family groups that represent the 1700 Larrakia people.

(Calvin Costello, Head of Larrakia Nation, interview July 2004)

These are people who have struggled for many years for recognition of their lands and, as with all Aboriginal groups, are marginalised and impoverished. After a 23-year struggle, in December 2000, the government's Land Commissioner, Justice Grey, recommended with regard to the 'Kenbi Land Claim' that a large area of land on the Cox Peninsula should be handed back to the Larrakia.

After its formation the Larrakia Nation received backing totalling $500,000 from the state government. Teams of 'Larrakia Hosts' were formed, their function being to persuade 'long grassers' or itinerants to go home and to attempt to reduce 'anti-social behaviours'. Cultural protocols were foregrounded, asking non-Larrakians to respect traditional values when on Larrakia land. The host scheme was fairly ineffective, but signs were put up around the centre setting boundaries and times for public drinking. This approach was supplemented by intensive policing of Aboriginal people in the park, although, to an outsider it seems hard to imagine that Darwin has a significant population of indigenous people, as they are noticeably absent from the city centre. During my visit I saw a few groups of Aboriginal people in the Bicentennial Park on the Esplanade; small clusters sat conversing and sharing beers. It was hardly the riotous assembly the tabloids had portrayed. There was a very significant police presence in the park; one evening fifteen officers with motorbikes and patrol wagons gathered informally near the Esplanade. Police wagons move in and out of the park during the day checking on the small knots of Aborigines, especially where white tourists are sunbathing. Mission Australia also patrols the park, stopping to investigate Aboriginal needs, distributing fresh water and giving contact details in case they want to use any of the services that the Mission provides, including an assisted passage back home (tickets are purchased for them and the money is reclaimed from their social-security allowance). In short, this surveillance and monitoring seemed inordinately focused on a few transient people who were causing very little fuss. The focus is on public drinking and the harassment of tourists and retail businesses in the city from 'itinerants' begging or 'humbugging'. These are the issues that city aldermen insist require drastic measures to counter.

There is a general suspicion, however, about the Larrakia's involvement in city-council schemes to send itinerants home, with its founding being viewed by some as a political bargaining tool. And now members act as 'hosts' who inform other Aboriginal people of the sort of behaviour that is respectful on Larrakia land. The same message was disseminated via a video that features Larrakia elders exhorting other Aborigines to return to their homelands. This is perceived by some 'itinerants' as divide-and-rule tactics by a group who have been lured into collusion by the promise of shared bounty.

The scheme was featured on the ABC's *7.30 Report* (6 January 2004), where it was portrayed as an effective way to help Aboriginal people who get marooned in Darwin and cannot afford the fare back home. No mention was made of the long-standing 'long grass' and other communities in Darwin. The Larrakia scheme was presented as a brilliant enterprise that avoids the rough handling that was associated with the Liberals' attitude. The story was presented in the usual magazine style, with commentary by the presenter Murray McLaughlin and a few indigenous voices, although, interestingly, these were never involved in dialogues or exchanges, but gave only unitary utterances in terse, almost broken, English. The coordinated and orderly work reported as performed by many service providers renders the story one of success for the voice of reason, civic pride and responsibility. The itinerants are described as befuddled natives who can think no further than their immediate needs. Keeping them actively employed making paintings and carvings might keep them off the streets. It is paternalism dressed up in the discourse of timeless aboriginality. There was no attempt to highlight or even address the issue of 'itinerants': they have no voice here and are contrasted unfavourably with the Larrakia 'leaders' and white Australians. However, the division between Larrakia and others is certainly not clearly defined in reality. Sonia Smallacombe commented that the Larrakia

> had somehow been recruited by the Government – not all of them, I've met a lot of Larrakia people who don't agree with it – being recruited by the Government to tell other indigenous people that your behaviour in our country is not good enough, and you really should respect Larrakia ways of doing things – when you going up here and drinking, and going up and asking tourists for money… Fortunately it's not been a decisive policy; a lot of Larrakia people actually support the itinerants, and there is an itinerant organisation that's been set up – and there's a lot of Larrakia people in that …. I think indigenous people are aware that the Government uses those kind of strategies to try and divide indigenous groups.
>
> (Spencer 2004b)

The attempt to use Larrakia claims and voices strategically could be seen as neatly sidestepping the criticism that this is the will of a powerful and aggressive Territory government, protecting tourist revenue. Instead a relatively powerless group, and only selective members at that, provide an argument that there are 'cultural protocols' to restrict 'itinerants' from seeking refuge in Darwin.

The apparent divide between two relatively underprivileged groups further amplifies the deviance of the more loosely defined 'itinerants', while the Larrakia 'Nation' becomes a viable partner with the state government and council and shares in financially lucrative schemes. Furthermore, as with any effective colonial administration, it sets subject 'races' in an antagonistic relationship, reaping the benefits and maintaining control while disguising the true conditions of domination.

Despite the desperate needs of other indigenous groups around the outskirts of Darwin, Costello takes a pragmatic view of their welfare and struggles with officialdom. He is quick to point out a different side to the plight of One Mile Dam, explaining that they haven't paid rent on the site for over four years. One might feel that the suggestion of 'rent' was an insult given the appalling conditions they have to contend with, but Costello gives a wry smile and suggests that they also have choices – moving into public housing is also an option available to them. There are two sets of values informing this divide, two discourses that give competing readings of the role that itinerants play in Northern Territory society.

Realistically, this situation is not a simple polemic; the waters are much muddier. The Larrakia have struggled for over two decades for the recognition they have achieved, but the issue of lifestyle is extraordinarily divisive. Even within the ranks of Larrakia people there is a diversity of views; certainly, many Larrakia are keen supporters of groups such as the Kumbutjil Association, established by the One Mile Dam Community to run their own programmes and projects for a safer, active and healthier community.

However, Larrakia people, Costello argues, make up a tiny minority of less formal communities such as the Bagot (he claimed that only two Larrakia people lived there; see Rawlinson 2013). Instead, they have been dispersed into public housing. I asked him about the Community Development Employment Programme. Marcia Langton has called this 'labour apartheid'. Costello simply stated the popularity of the scheme and the fact there was a waiting list of several hundred. If skills and experience are needed, does this scheme provide these? Some have argued that the scheme is merely a means of providing labour under the minimum wage and that the majority of the tasks are menial, degrading and hardly constitute growing a skilled community. Sonia Smallacombe emphasised that developing skills and growth in the community is the only way out of the appalling conditions faced by generations of indigenous people in the Northern Territory.

For the 'Larrakia', who are portrayed as being cooperative and willing to negotiate with the state government, membership of the Larrakia Nation appears to have potential benefits. Calvin Costello, Larrakia Nation Coordinator, proudly showed me a model of the proposed cultural facility that is planned to be built on Larrakia land near the airport. The multi-million-dollar development is designed to attract tourists to share in Aboriginal culture and will offer employment possibilities for large numbers of Larrakians. This development, however, is not for outsiders or 'itinerants', as the promotion for a 'multi-purpose cultural facility' makes clear: 'All Larrakia people are encouraged to attend a viewing of the concept model for the proposed Larrakia Multi-Purpose Cultural Facility. All Larrakia Nation Members and Non-member Larrakia Families are invited to provide input into the development of this major Project' (www.larrakia.com/the website/future.html). Such projects represent a financially lucrative arrangement between some of the Larrakia, Councillor Ah Kit (himself of Larrakian origin) and the Labor government. 'Essentially a plan to remove "itinerants" (Territory-speak for Aboriginal people who choose to live traditionally) has been given a politically correct fillip by the use of some of the less "traditional", but far wealthier Larrakians' (Lambe 2003).

The implications of this are clear when aligned with a policy of policing the boundaries of shared ownership and disseminating information about cultural protocols. There are effectively two competing groups: one defined by homelessness, poverty, dispossession and anti-social behaviours; the other, with official approval and recognition, has bargaining power, a successful land claim and relative affluence, but a less traditional lifestyle. When I asked Costello about the contrast in lifestyles he reinforced the fact that the negative impacts of alcohol on 'long grass' communities were affecting young children, with, he suggested, rising levels of the violent abuse of women and the sexual abuse of children. He was unequivocal about the need for indigenous people to move into housing to gain employment and hence self-respect. To him a pragmatic approach was probably one positive antidote to a very hard and demoralising existence. However, there are other ways in which a state with genuine concern for cultural values could give Aboriginal people of all origins and lifestyles a sense of belonging, rather than casting some of them as pariahs. A suggestion made by several groups is to re-zone areas that include the less formal camps and to allow those who wish to live less formally with extended family and their animals to do so.

Postscript

Since my visit in July 2004 several events have occurred that clearly show the acquisitive motives which intervene and prevent reasonable compromise. The Larrakia Nation and the Aboriginal Development Agency appear now to have joined forces to develop the One Mile Dam area into a profit-making four-star hotel. Larrakia chief executive Ilana Eldridge appears willing to involve the long-term residents in the scheme:

Plans have emerged for a 242-bed hotel and an aged care facility at One Mile Dam – the indigenous community in the heart of Darwin.

Aboriginal service provider Larrakia Nation is negotiating with the Aboriginal Development Foundation for the leases on One Mile Dam, Knuckey Lagoon camp and the Palmerston Indigenous Village.

... Aboriginal Development Foundation boss Bernie Valadian, who controls the lease, said yesterday he didn't know much about what Larrakia Nation had planned. But he did meet with Ms Eldridge yesterday.

She said the idea was to work collaboratively with residents to improve their futures and housing options. That approach contrasts with Deputy Chief Minister David Tollner's plan to 'normalise' city Aboriginal areas such as Bagot ...

(Bevege 2013: 1)

As always, the displaced people in such fringe areas are subject to complex political and economic forces, making the future for the community at One Mile Dam uncertain.

The events and rhetoric described in this chapter could be seen as the persistent demonisation of Australia's most vulnerable groups, a historically maligned 'other', as Hartley has suggested:

Aborigines who are stereotyped as outsiders or as tribal cannot be seen as citizens with rights. More often they are treated as subjects of welfare, or in connection with crime stories...as outsiders with a 'they' identity they are newsworthy for their economic, security or welfare impact on 'our' community.

(Hartley 1992: 209)

'They' are thus voiceless and largely nameless: 'they are representative of their race, not of their persons' (Hartley 1992: 207). There is clearly a danger of 'blaming the victims' and scapegoating the highly visible dysfunctions of these struggling communities, but this is not to suggest, however, that isolated communities should be abandoned to their own devices and that the serious issues of violence, rape and child abuse that are documented should not be acted upon. Such crimes, resulting from an inflammatory combination of poverty, unemployment, alcohol, drugs and the influx of often different and incompatible groups into small and under-resourced areas, are a real problem in indigenous communities.

In May 2012 it was reported that in the Toomelah Aboriginal community in New South Wales sexual attacks on children younger than five had become a horrific feature of the community (ABC *7.30 Report*, 30 May 2012). Mal Brough, who was the Minister for Indigenous Affairs under the Howard government, led a policy of 'intervention' in Aboriginal communities – in some cases sending in the army to police and protect children who were seen as at risk across the Northern Territory. On the ABC programme *7.30 Report* (30 May 2012) Brough railed against the apparent indifference of Australians to the plight of Aboriginal people, suggesting disconcertingly that much more furore was kicked up about the mistreatment of cattle in Indonesia. He went on to argue for a 'colour blind' approach:

CHRIS UHLMANN: But do you think that Australians are inured to this or do they just think that it's such a hopeless situation that there's no point in commenting on it?

MAL BROUGH: I wish I had an answer. I think a lotta people are desensitised, and I think the other thing – and jaded. I also feel that – I was speaking to a friend not long ago this evening and he said, 'Oh, I turned it off.' Sometimes these things are just too tough for us to deal with, and I think if we can strip away the fact that they're Aboriginal children and just call them children, just take away the colour, take away the race altogether, maybe we'd re-engage again as a public and we would say, 'No, we can't allow this to happen.' We need to show leadership as a society. We need to show leadership as politicians and political leaders and as community leaders. And if we do that, it's not beyond our wit to be able to address these issues.

(ABC TV *7.30 Report* 2012)

Later in the interview Brough made a comment about the sense of isolation experienced by these forsaken fringe communities and their disconnection with the economic system:

Your story last night: the nurse, 18 years a nurse, as credible as you can get, said there isn't a family in Toomelah that hasn't been touched by that abuse. That is a society almost beyond repair by just another programme, another intervention. We need to look at root and cause; why we have Aboriginal people living in isolation almost on top of the rest of society, but on their own in almost what you'd call an apartheid fashion, and say, 'What message is that sending to those children? Why are they being so isolated? And how much better can we do this?'

(ABC TV *7.30 Report* 2012)

While it is heartening to hear such sentiments being expressed, and one can only concur with the thrust of Brough's remarks, it represents a postscript to the continued failure and inability of governments to get to grips with the real causes of this psychic distancing by the white Australian community – a resigned (and perhaps worryingly functional) 'othering' of an entire people – whether it is 'cultural cringe', denial of the 'black armband' or deep-seated romantic and racist values embedded in the collective history of the nation, its manifestation is through this inability to communicate other than through the two interlocking tribes of 'Wedom' and 'Theydom'.

The posting of signs such as the one shown in Figure 6.9 followed from the 'intervention' policy, adding to the moral panic and stigma which appear to have been generated about Aboriginal communities. The sign draws a line beyond which alcohol and pornography are prohibited, suggesting that Aboriginal people are especially vulnerable to alcohol and pornography. Arguably there was some genuine concern behind these actions despite the paternalism that is inherent in treating every indigenous community in this way.

Since these observations were made, several changes have occurred in Australia, including a change in federal government with, first, Labor's Kevin Rudd and then Julia Gillard in office, followed once more by Rudd, who supported the

Figure 6.9 Sign posted outside the One Mile Dam Community near Darwin 2009

intervention policy and staged a public government apology for the historical treatment of Aboriginal peoples. It is hard not to feel cynical about the sporadic and inconsistent actions of government; years of laissez-faire neglect punctuated suddenly with the rhetoric of high moral outrage. In terms of the broader stories of abusive relationships within the cramped confines of fringe communities in Australia, the situation for children is precarious and statistically alarming – only 33 per cent of Aboriginal children stay in the system to Year 12, compared with 76 per cent of other Australian students (Fleming and Southwell 2005).

Conclusion

I read somewhere during the Bosnian war ... I think about 'ethnic cleansing' – well I'm beginning to think that that's what's happening here.

(Spencer 2004c; Figure 6.10)

Figure 6.10 David Timber, Coordinator of the Kumbutjil Association at One Mile Dam Community near Darwin

Initially it seemed extraordinary to me, an outsider from the cramped confines of urban England, that such vast areas of land could not accommodate a few thousand indigenous people who wish to determine their own lifestyle and to resist being squeezed into new and regulated suburban spaces. However, I came to the conclusion that the recalcitrance of the city authorities is more purposeful and is fuelled by the need for a moral consensus, that the affluent white population wishes to reaffirm its hegemony and that the result has been a moral panic which, over the decades, has demonised and pressured this group. Aboriginality is being used as a 'floating' signifier (see Hall 1997), drawn upon expediently where there is cultural or economic capital to be gained cultural and economic capital to be gained: a lucrative tourism market is enhanced by the image of unchanging indigenous culture, not signs of dispossession and neglect. Aboriginal people are portrayed, when it suits, as noble custodians of the outback and the embodiment of ancient traditions or dirty drunks who are an embarrassment to the civic authorities and a potential threat to businessthat must be banished from the city environs. The signifier of collective guilt and collective denial of that guilt is never far away, because what happened in the past is still happening today. There can be no solution to this situation until the reality of Aboriginal identity is realised and the history of what has really taken place in the Northern Territory and in the rest of Australia, is confronted.

THEORETICAL FRAMING

In this section the case study above is used as a way of exploring different theoretical readings. Students may find it easier to comprehend the possible uses of these conceptual frameworks when they can see them as parallel and complementary approaches, and when the details of a specific case are presented. These are not intended to be exhaustive analyses but only to suggest how these approaches might be applied.

Plural society theory

The Aboriginal diaspora is a direct consequence of colonial dispossession of Aboriginal lands and the disruptive removal of Aboriginal children. The complex and clannish groupings of Aboriginal people have followed a pattern that would seem to support Furnivall's (1948) contention that market forces can have a divisive and shaping effect on ethnic enclaves. Collective identities are to an extent mobilised in response to the possibility of economic bargaining. In this case it appears that Aboriginal people were able to mobilise under the newly formed banner of 'The Larrakia Nation'. The outcome seems to have consequences for those who are pigeon-holed as 'itinerants', a euphemism for Aboriginal people who are not welcome in the area. Interestingly, the prohibitions and aggression of the colonial era clearly shaped practices in ways that administrators did not foresee: alcohol as a sign of citizenship, a communal sacrament to be shared and a form of resistance to the white authorities, all of which condemn Aboriginal drinking but promote white drinking.

Similarly, the antagonism between different indigenous groups is fuelled by an institutional system in which economic and social privileges are permitted to a few groups, such as those with successful land-rights claims, thus dividing fellow 'countrymen' and, in this case, labelling one group as 'itinerants' – interlopers who might upset the negotiated settlement for the Larrakia people (which included the building of an extensive cultural centre and shares in tourist revenues). From the conversations with different protagonists in this complex case it would be fair to say that most ordinary Larrakians (a term that was little used before the land-rights victory united a number of groups under a shared banner of success) had a great deal in common with these 'itinerants' and even shared similar informal spaces with them, supporting their common cause. Others were clearly made aware of the political situation in which displaced indigenous people from other parts of Australia were rocking the applecart. As a result there was the rather surreal spectacle of certain Larrakian 'ambassadors' recording video messages asking them to go home.

Marxist approaches

Conflicts between the white community and indigenous Australians have a long and dismal history. The elite white population is predominantly affluent, and it is common knowledge that the remoteness and 'frontier spirit' of the Northern Territory may serve as a filter to collect people who tend to be like-minded and generally conservative. Certainly, attitudes expressed in the state government would be less likely to be heard in the larger urban centres. These are attitudes akin to those of the aggressive colonial history of the region. Marxist approaches could show that the colonial strategy of divide and rule is still very much in place, now involving the co-opting of the Larrakia people into a favoured position as a bulwark against 'itinerants' (shorthand for Aboriginal people who do not project the correct image required for tourism in the city). The conceptual framework employed by each strand of Marxist reasoning could produce articulate readings of the Darwin issue. In terms of hegemony, media resources aggressively demonise Aboriginal people (using the term 'itinerant' to highlight undesirable civic values). Tourism plays a role in both the further exclusion of urban Aborigines and the construction of mythical views about Aborigines. It is a major form of capital for the Territory and Aboriginal culture is one of the aspects that draws tourists to the state. The visible presence of Aboriginal people in Darwin city centre is almost entirely associated with the production of Aboriginal art and artefacts, which would suggest that traditional arts and crafts and, indeed, the objectification of people themselves are dominant aspects of the capitalist mode of production.

Althusser's conception of failed 'repressive state apparatus' giving way to 'ideological state apparatus' clearly seems to be applicable here. Under the former Liberal government the policy for dealing with 'itinerants' was to destroy their temporary dwellings and to confiscate their possessions. Shane Stone, Former Chief Minister, recommended that the police should 'monster and stomp' on them: 'People who are out there causing havoc on our streets, who are defecating in our car parks and our shopping centres, deserve to be monstered and stomped on' (ABC *7.30 Report*, 1 June 2004). In addition, the mandatory sentencing scheme operating in the Northern Territory saw a prison population in which nearly 80 per cent were Aborigines. None of these schemes worked: no sooner had shelters been pulled down in one area than they were erected again elsewhere. Furthermore, the 'itinerant' problem and the harsh treatment of Aborigines risked bringing unwanted attention to the government of the day. Hence, the Northern Territory's Labor government has pursued an apparently more culturally sensitive approach.

In terms of the dynamics of ownership of the land there was a dramatic shift in the means of production. Indigenous peoples who had been living for thousands of years in a variety of tribal hunter-gatherer modes experienced the rapid and systematic enclosure and grazing of the land by pastoralist first settlers. In the broadest terms it could be argued that although Marxism may call for a levelling of social hierarchies it nevertheless shares a materialist view which sees people as producers and consumers and a view of nature that sees it as very much to be dominated and shaped through collective struggle. Progress, for bourgeois and for Marxist thinkers, is measured by the degree to which nature is pacified. Aboriginal critics of Marxism see in such an attitude a disrespect for nature, an almost erotic attachment to domination identical to that of bourgeois society. '"Marxists," writes Frank Black Elk, "are hung up on exactly the same idea of 'progress' and 'development' that are the guiding motives of those they seek to overthrow"' (Bedford 2013).

This point is worth raising as it demonstrates the contention that Marxist views are not compatible with traditional beliefs about nature and in a way denies the possibility of other forms of understanding, as some Critical Race Theorists have argued. The problem, however, is that such belief systems are frequently dismissed as mysticism or a form of indulgent postmodern view which in rational terms appear to be a relativistic cul-de-sac.

However, while it is clearly important to recognise that Marxist ideas generated in late nineteenth century were influenced by ethnocentric conceptions of progress and social Darwinism, there is evidence that the understanding of capitalism is relevant to both indigenous and non-indigenous people and hence some Marxist concepts used alongside the knowledge of Aboriginal people, particularly about the environment, might provide a more autonomy for indigenous people and be instructive for the whole of society (see, e.g., Scott 2011: 6–9).

Weberian notes

The Weberian traditions, as articulated by Rex and Tomlinson, among others, are very much germane in this case study. The more complex social structures that are autonomous of class are clearly in operation here. Ideas of 'imagined community' (Anderson 1983) and citizenship are an important part of the subjective identity of the groups involved. The anthropologist Bill Day recognised the importance of drinking alcohol to Aboriginal people, who, he claims, associate it with citizenship because for many years there was a specific prohibition on Aboriginal people drinking in the city environs: 'Remembering the era of prohibition and the campaigns for change, Aboriginal people in the Northern Territory and elsewhere equate achieving the right to drink with "citizenship rights"' (Day 2001a: 4).

This presents a very different function behind drinking and the status attributed to it by whites and indigenous people. Some observers have assessed the Beer Can Regatta in terms of class and masculinity, but Day suggests that this is a misreading, that it is really a ritual affirmation of dominance over and separation from Aboriginal inhabitants and a way of stressing the legitimacy of drinking for white Australians. Certainly the fact that alcohol is a key social problem for non-Aboriginal Australians could be damaging to the identity of rugged individualism on which the Northern Territory prides itself. 'With Aboriginal citizenship, non-Aboriginal Northern Territory drinkers were faced with the contradiction of deploring uncontrolled Aboriginal drinking while praising the frontier tradition of drinking to excess' (ibid.: 4).

Taking issues such as this into account highlights the importance of status and social honour as well as monopolistic social closure. A Weberian approach maps social groups and their value systems without the reduction to relationships of production. However, in most cases, neo-Weberian analyses such as those of John Rex and David Mason (1986) could be said to allow that social contexts are underpinned by economic relations.

Nevertheless, there are clearly times when social honour, citizenship rights and other aspects of identity and resistance in the face of dispossession exert more influence than class. Again, Day and others have commented that, ultimately, Aboriginal drinking, wherever it takes place, is returning a profit for white Australians. Alcohol is aggressively promoted in areas where Aboriginal people have access to it. Furthermore, the revenue on alcohol could be seen as one means of recouping welfare benefits to Aborigines:

> One submission to the Royal Commission into Deaths in Custody (Langton *et al.* 1991: 319) stated: 'everyone is just trying to make more and more money from these outlets, and take money from the people'. For some Aboriginal people 'alcohol is seen as a deliberate component of the invasion of traditional lands and the destruction of traditional culture and law'.
>
> (Day 2001a: 18)

This less deterministic view of class opens up the possibility of more subtle overlapping analyses in which 'ethnicity overlaps with status in one situation, and with class, caste or estate in other cases' (Malesevic 2004: 129).

The competition between groups of Aborigines indicates competition for scarce resources and is reflected in differential market positions (in Weberian terms). In this case, one group has achieved a different market position by forging allegiances with the state government and by providing assistance in projects which encourage Aboriginal endeavour as part of the lucrative tourist market. Conversely, other groups (the 'out-groups' who have been dubbed 'itinerants') have a relationship to the state characterised by purposeful resistance: heavy drinking and living a so-called itinerant lifestyle rather than living in public housing. Cultural identity, therefore, can be a divisive force. On the one hand there is the retention of attachments to the land and to practices of food preparation, communal patterns of behaviour, extended family and dogs (incompatible with state housing in Australia); and, on the other hand, there are aspirations to some of the material rewards of white Australian culture, albeit the price is having to relinquish or modify previous cultural practices.

So it becomes apparent that in some instances an analysis that refuses to give any credence to cultural values and status issues that exert influence on ethnicity could be one that misses the complex variables that are contributing to the situation. Interpretations of conflict and cooperation in terms of race and ethnicity (cultural difference) are frequently used by the state to disguise the powerlessness of groups and their disadvantage in the marketplace – a disadvantage that is frequently extremely marked and of long duration.

Elite theory

Classical elite theory reaffirms the Marxist emphasis upon sectional interest (in other words, elites) in determining the distribution of power in the state and civil society. There are clear examples that give credence to the role of elites in constructing the political structures of the state and in guiding policy in many democratic states (not least the US and UK administrations). The theory would encourage us to look at the motives of the power holders in the Northern Territory government and in other organisations that have a stake in the issues. John Ah Kit (the Minister for Community Development, Sport and Cultural Affairs, himself a Larrakian) has certainly been instrumental in the policies. There are indications that the Larrakia Nation and its social-harmony plans, which are directly funded by the government, have the potential to be very lucrative to Larrakians higher in the hierarchy. Furthermore, stakeholders in other hierarchies are clearly not above sacrificing the 'itinerant' communities, who, they feel, have persisted in negative and self-destructive resistance. For example, the Aboriginal Development Foundation, which holds the lease to the One Mile Dam site, is willing to hand it over if the government pays them $1 million, while at the same time the Larrakia Nation is negotiating with the government to turn the camp into parklands.

Symbolic interactionism

In this perspective the way in which the divisions between and within ethnic groupings are affected is a result of outside categorising and an intersubjective relationship between the in-group and the out-group. Individual identity is formed through interactive encounters with other individuals and groups and is given authority and reach when transmitted through mass media channels. Media often broadcast ideas about common cultural identities and differences which can easily become generalised labels (like the euphemistic term 'itinerants'). Interactionists say that the world we experience is socially constructed. In this view, ethnic groups are seen as products of social interaction. Ethnicity arises when communication channels between groups are limited and the different groups develop different systems of meanings. In this case, there are certainly different conceptions of what it means to be an Aborigine, each concept derived from different social histories and relations to dominant white society and different economic and political meanings, which have led to quite different and contradictory strategies for survival.

As Fenton argues:

> the 'cultural stuff' of ethnicity is grounded in social relationships. In a more or less conscious way, it is a feature of daily practice. This cultural content – the shared ancestry, the claims to a shared inheritance, the common customs and language – are also 'drawn upon' by ethnic group members, to give substance to. It may be drawn upon, too, by those who do not belong and do not share the cultural inheritance – that is, to mark them off from us.
>
> (Fenton 1999: 63)

Hence, in the case of Darwin there are clearly quite different perceptions of each group vis-à-vis the 'other'. While the lifestyle and outlook of white Australians will have very little in common with those of Aboriginal people (in or out of the Larrakia Nation), a pragmatic decision was made permitting a few individuals to have some share in the bounty from white tourism in exchange for some of their lands and for their complicity in being the reasonable face of the government in dealings with 'itinerants'. Conversely, the tangible dissatisfaction of itinerants is aimed at the lifestyle of some Larrakians, which they see as falsely claiming indigenous credentials when in reality it illustrates a sort of cultural amnesia.

Rational-choice theory

The actions of all protagonists could be partly explained from a rational-choice perspective. The premise is that all action is determined by assessment of gains and losses and rational calculation indicates the best strategy. Larrakians, whose land claims are, at least in principle, recognised, have formed into a united group despite considerable differences among their members. This could be seen as a rationalist approach to mobilisation around a common claim of ethnic unity, a sort of strategic essentialism on the part of the influential indigenous leadership. Similarly, the government viewpoint is clear in this perspective. The state (Northern Territory) requires increased funding and tourism holds great potential for an area that is often forgotten, owing to its relatively small population base and the aridity of much of its land area. Tourism provides the Northern Territory with high profits and increased global status. In order to capitalise on this niche, all efforts are prioritised to promote the tourist benefits of the Northern Territory. Its great resources are the unspoilt wilderness areas, the proud frontier image of the area and, of course, the increasing interest in Aboriginal culture and art. However, negative images, bad press about racism and the appalling conditions in which urban Aboriginal people are forced to live are not conducive to the success of green and cultural tourist agendas, hence the remarkable efforts made to remove or disguise the problem.

Postmodernity

Postmodern approaches would typically stress the discursive construction of the relationship between Aboriginal and white Australians. The nature of the dominant white discourse on Aboriginal people is one which locates them in the past as part of a static, timeless culture (in fact, their sign is 'nature' rather than 'culture'). This discourse, the so-called 'bush myth', has a function in the urban capitals as a romantic marker of white superiority that glorifies the frontier traditions of Australia and white dominance over adversity. Although the fierce wars and conflicts with the original inhabitants are not part of this history, the rugged individualism epitomised by Banjo Patterson's poems, and recent films based on them (e.g. *The Man from Snowy River*), definitely is. Furthermore, the discourse of Aborigines as romantically attuned to the bush and to ancient mystic traditions is a source (especially in the Northern Territory) for the burgeoning tourist trade, worth nearly $1 billion a year. Hence there are clear motives for disguising the poor conditions into which displaced Aborigines are forced near the city: makeshift camps and beggars are not compatible with the image of Australia being broadcast. Postmodernist perspectives might also consider the situation in terms of identity politics. Competing factions assert their subjectivities, and the fragmentation of indigenous groups into their regional identities is an example of an awakening sense of giving voice to identities too long subsumed under the 'subaltern' term 'Aborigines'. Identities are malleable in this view and constantly in the process of being formed. Discursive practices, as Muecke (1982) has shown, constitute the available discourses by which whites can talk about 'them'. Taking this analysis further, Marcia Langton writes:

> 'Aboriginality' [...] is a field of intersubjectivity in that it is remade over and over again in a process of dialogue, of imagination, of representation and interpretation. Both Aboriginal and non-Aboriginal people create 'Aboriginalities' [...] This opens up further possibilities for the development of understanding and communication between cultures traditionally located in such isolation. This process appears to be one to strive for but how realistic is this when the average white Australian is highly unlikely to even exchange the time of day with an Aboriginal person?
>
> (Langton 1993b: 33)

Bourdieusian analysis: habitus and symbolic violence

This case and many like it demonstrate the deeply problematic nature of paradigms which might fall into the universalising grand narrative categories or, conversely, the errant relativism that is sometimes the unfortunate consequence of the postmodern rejection of rationality. A Bourdieusian approach, however, allows a micro-analysis of the complex combination of social, economic and cultural factors which are operating in the particular field. Crucially, Bourdieu 'submits that the correspondence between social and mental structures fulfils crucial political functions. Symbolic systems are not simply instruments of knowledge, they are also *instruments of domination*' (Bourdieu and Wacquant 1992: 13). The situation for Aboriginal people has many strands of symbolic oppression which have already been alluded to here. Education, for example, reproduces the dominant power relations in society and there is a historical psychic legacy about the treatment and perception of Aboriginal families:

> Reynolds argues that in the late nineteenth century '...many of those responsible for, or just interested in, Aboriginal education had come to accept the view that Aborigines should acquire no more than practical skills and rudimentary literacy.' In 1883 the Aborigines Protection Board was established, with the power to take children away from their families, and this they often did while the children were at school.
>
> (Fleming and Southwell 2005: 2)

The case, as discussed, demonstrates several levels of social division which might well follow from Bourdieu's guiding terms. Habitus and field provide important tools for an understanding of the contrasting and mutually exclusive systems of white Australians and Aborigines. Bourdieu's particular use of social capital is very relevant to an understanding of the complex relationships in this case. Bourdieu argues that it is 'impossible to account for the structure and functioning of the social world unless one reintroduces capital in all its forms and not solely in the one form recognized by economic theory' (Bourdieu 1986: 242).

Different levels of and access to social capital clearly mark out the different players in this field. The Larrakia have brokered links with the financial, legal and political elements of the Northern Territory and through their successful land-rights case they have effectively been clawed into the system, whereas the homeless or 'long grasser' groups are outside the boundaries of the Territorian collectivity. Larrakians were ready to act as 'hosts' to ask these 'itinerants' to go 'home' and to ask for respectful behaviour on their land. The quick coalescing of several different tribal groups into Larrakia Nation was noted by other Aboriginal observers as a political act, and with the bounty of half a million dollars for a cultural centre. Hence the rupture between the different Aboriginal players in the arena of Darwin demonstrates clearly that the social capital plays a vital role here. Membership enabled the Larrakia to obtain

> the backing of the collectivity-owned capital, a 'credential' which entitles them to credit, in the various senses of the word. These relationships may exist only in the practical state, in material and/or symbolic exchanges which help to maintain them. They may also be socially instituted and guaranteed by the application of a common name (the name of a family, a class, a tribe, a school, a party, etc.).
>
> (Mignone 2009: 101)

Furthermore, other types of capital are also important in this case. An examination of cultural capital is very revealing because there are interlocking and nested sets of cultural hierarchies here. The Territorians themselves are somewhat isolated from the metropolitan standards of culture and taste associated with the cities of Melbourne and Sydney. They are part of 'outback' Australia, more invested in the traditions of the rugged individualism of the bush. So the 'cultural cringe' factor (a defensiveness in the face of disdainful European standards of high culture) may be felt more strongly or rejected altogether here. There is an irony that traditional Aboriginal culture is seen as viable capital for the tourist trade in Australia, yet different indigenous tribal societies and their unique cultural forms are struggling to survive in the face of wave after wave of destructive colonialism. On the one hand the traditional untainted cultural imaginary of 'aboriginality' is a draw for the very lucrative tourist trade, yet the presence of itinerant Aborigines who are not cultural producers does not project the decorative image that their artefacts do. It seems inevitable, then, that the Larrakia who have a bona fide claim on the land are also seen as viable cultural producers. Yet, as several commented, many of those subsumed under the 'Larrakia' umbrella lived in the very same deprived conditions as the so-called 'itinerants' and saw no differences between their own plight and that of their less supported 'countrymen'.

Critical Race Theory – a case of interest convergence?

The possibility of applying a Critical Race Theory approach clearly follows from the above. These stories can be seen to lend themselves to some of the broad emphases of CRT in several ways, first of which is the need to examine the succession of western constructions of aboriginality which have always worked in the interests of the white majority. The Mabo legislation and, more recently, Philip Rudd's supposedly historic 'official sorry' can arguably demonstrate interest convergence, providing the state with the apparent liberality which had been absent historically and seeming to mark a turning point in this negative aspect of Australian history, when in fact the resistance to actual land claims has been stiffened, with unrealistic caveats placed on the onus of proof of a tribal group being historically static. Meanwhile, indigenous people continue to face the corrosive effects of a harsh penal system in which they are disproportionately incarcerated and an education and employment sector in which they are consistently failed and denied access. Finally, the success of land-rights claims per se and the case of the Larrakia Nation as described above in particular also demonstrate the convergence principle at work. Possibly a few individuals will benefit locally, but the vast majority of Aboriginal people are homeless and suffer from the same problems of poverty and exclusion. The grounds for achieving land-rights claims present a catch-22 situation, as to prove prior ownership and worthiness to be granted such rights the claimants have to demonstrate they have remained culturally static, thus fulfilling the stereotypes of Aborigines being unable to change from some primordial ethnic image, which again sustains the dominant suite of prejudices.

CHAPTER SUMMARY

As can be seen from these analyses, the case presented in this chapter is complex and cannot easily be understood without reference to the historical context. Initially the author imagined that the case of urban Aborigines in Darwin was a simple case of persistent racism mirroring the inglorious history of displacement and dispossession. Indeed, there is continuity with historical perceptions of aboriginality, but the situation is further complicated by the fractures within the apparently similar Aboriginal groups in Darwin. The rapid mobilisation of several Darwin-based indigenous groups (under the umbrella of Larrakia Nation) was spurred by the successful land-rights claim over much of the Darwin area. This successful claim led members of this group to serve as 'ambassadors' to encourage indigenous people from other regions to return to their home turf. Furthermore, the case shows that the sense of oppression is multi-layered and embedded in the cultural codes, practices and institutions of Australia. On one hand, tourism demands romantic and unchanging images of indigenous Australians as valuable cultural producers, but on the other hand this image is grossly at odds with the everyday reality for people dislocated from their cultural origins and land. This chapter has examined the historical, socio-cultural and political constructions of aboriginality that are manifest in this case. The paternalism of the intervention has latterly been recognised to contain some elements of a solution but couched in the extreme form of a moral panic; as ever, there seems to be little will to really address the serious social problems stemming from years of neglect and repressive legislation unless it can be turned to political capital.

EXERCISE 6.1

1   How does the situation of indigenous peoples differ from those of other groups within plural societies such as Australia?
2   Why might Aboriginal people be disinclined to take part in (or wish to be recognised as part of) Australian multiculturalism?
3   Can the situation of Aboriginal Australians be understood without recourse to what John Howard called the 'black armband view' of Australian history – in which extermination, expulsion and exploitation of indigenous people played a significant role?
4   How do lifestyles become a key issue in this case and separate people who otherwise have much in common?
5   Consider Steven Muecke's 'Available Discourses on Aborigines'. How do the discourses of the romantic and anthropological operate in this case?
6   What are the signs that there is a moral panic taking place?
7   What paternalistic views are disseminated about Aboriginal people? Why are these views so prevalent and long-lasting?

8   What strategies could be put into place to improve the situation in the Northern Territory and elsewhere?

Further reading

It is all too rare to find Aboriginal writing promoted, but Aboriginal writers have
provided insights into the conditions of life trapped between different cultural
expectations. Some key moments in forging and expressing Aboriginal identity
include Sally Morgan's *My Place* (London: Virago, 1987). Also see the poetry of
Oodgeroo Noonuccal (Kath Walker) and Marcia Langton's critical analyses of film
and ethnographies (some of her work is listed in the bibliography).

Another source is the series of Working Papers in Australian Studies, including
Chris Weedon's *Culture, Race and Identity: Australian Aboriginal Writing*, Working
Paper No. 59 (1990), available online at www.kcl.ac.uk/artshums/ahri/centres/men-
zies/research/Publications/Workingpapers/WP59ChrisWeedon.pdf; which gives a
fascinating insight into growing up in white Australian contexts.

Media representations of Aboriginal people are another area of interest. See, for
example, John Hartley's *The Politics of Pictures* (London: Polity, 1998), which has
been referred to several times in this book.

Steve Mickler is a West Australian academic who has written a number of influential articles, including 'The Perth press and problematising Aboriginal status', which is
available online at www.mcc.murdoch.edu.au/ReadingRoom/dreamtime/press.html

More recent critical discussions of Aboriginal identity and public life
include J. Mignone's 'Social Capital and Aboriginal Communities: A critical assessment. Synthesis and assessment of the body of knowledge on social
capital with emphasis on Aboriginal communities', *Journal de la santé autochtone* (November 2009) and Crystal McKinnon's 'Duplicity and Deceit: Rudd's
Apology to the Stolen Generations, an interview with Gary Foley', *Melbourne
Historical Journal* 36 (2008).

Notes

1   This section is adapted from Spencer 2005b.
2   In fact, whether the policy pursued was actually an example of eugenics is hotly contested, as miscegenation with inferior stock (as Aboriginal people were considered) would
seem unthinkable in a strictly eugenicist policy (see Windschuttle 2004). However, the
notion that 'half caste' children were to be salvaged from a race destined for extinction
appears to be the reasoning behind the forcible abduction of children. The legacy of the
stolen generations is one of misery and has been considered a form of cultural genocide
by some (see Manne 2003). Eugenics was deeply embedded in early twentieth-century
thinking and promulgated such myths.
3   These laws were repealed and modified by the new labour government in 2001.

CHAPTER 7

Conflict

The primary threat to nature and people today comes from centralising and monopolising power and control. Not until diversity is made the logic of production will there be a chance for sustainability, justice and peace. Cultivating and conserving diversity is no luxury in our times: it is a survival imperative.

(Vandana Shiva)

Human diversity makes tolerance more than a virtue; it makes it a requirement for survival.

(René Dubos 1981)

Peace is not unity in similarity but unity in diversity, in the comparison and conciliation of differences.

(Mikhail Gorbachev 1991)

These and a hundred other quotes proclaim this very reasonable view that we are 'all leaves on the same branch', all in the same boat, a united humanity on a fragile world. Everyone from the Dalai Lama to John Lennon and the bloke next door may have lucid moments when they recognise this, and such sentiments can be cited from the earliest times. Recognising the importance of embracing diversity and difference in any real way, though, may be more difficult. The causes of inter-ethnic violence are complex and often have deep roots. This chapter reviews some sites of inter-ethnic conflict, examining the historical, political and socio-cultural dynamics of these cases. There are no ready solutions to ethnic conflicts, but understanding the complex nature of these sites of conflict is a necessary part of any strategy. Similarly, easy formulas to understand how conflicts over ethnicity come into being, play out or resolve are lacking. The seeds of many such conflicts are sown in earlier periods of colonial administration in which antagonisms between subject groups were functional, keeping the exploited dissatisfied with each others' contributions so that consensus against the colonialists was disabled. The legacies of this type of divisive approach are the development of opposed ethnic habitus and an internalised hegemonic sense of 'otherness' which may lead to intractable competitive relations with the other ethnicities within the divided state. The sense of injustice experienced across the ethnic divide is often felt trenchantly and may lead to outbreaks of violence. In Guyana, the first case discussed here,

> Social and political upheavals in the early 1960s resulted in hundreds killed in spasms of ethnic violence that pitted neighbour against neighbour and village against village and left indelible memories of violence on the psychic landscape. Historical ethnic identity tensions have been kept alive by politicians and fuelled by subsequent political contestation at the national and regional levels.
>
> (Myers and Calder 2006)

The following narrative captures the ironic and bitter conflicts that led to segregation and hardening of attitudes in Guyana in the early 1960s, but the story, apocryphal or not, illustrates well the way that anger and irrationality have come to characterise this self-destructive conflict.

BOX 7.1 INTERVIEW WITH MARTIN CARTER

Interview with Martin Carter, Georgetown, Guyana, 29 April 1991. Martin Carter was one of Guyana's most famous poets and also a political activist in his day; he was imprisoned by the British colonial government as part of the independence movement. Martin died in 1999.

MC: When a crisis comes, belonging to a different race becomes a resource. So I am making the two terms 'crisis' and 'resource'. That is to say that when something happens that an individual of one racial group cannot cope with, he regresses towards his racial stock ... as a resource, as a vision to help him ...

SS: So the crudest stereotypes emerge ...

MC: And dreadful things will be said ...

SS: I'm hearing this every day when people start talking in taxis, terrible tirade of abuse ...

Continued.

▌ BOX 7.1 INTERVIEW WITH MARTIN CARTER (CONTINUED)

MC: You make a very sharp observation about the taxi. For instance, in a taxi you may not see it too easily, but it happens. Let us assume that the taxi driver is a man of Indian descent. There is a tendency for him to ignore the person who is of African descent and vice versa. So that would therefore mean that the people in a taxi would more likely be of one group ... and so again you will get what you just described – like-minded people you see, who are really reinforcing their perceptions. And it is worse now, it never used to be like that until ten years ago ... but in the debasement it has now become a sort of protest against ... and it can get ugly – at least verbally.

As I said, when it becomes a critical imbalance – and I've seen this in 62 and the dimensions of it are horrendous. I'll give you an example and one which sticks in the mind. In 1962 this very street – not here but further up, in which a man, a young man, riding his bicycle, he's wearing a hat, so his head is covered (and in those days people attacked one another, especially if they were in a disadvantaged situation). So this young man came along, and some young dark boys came out of a shop or something and attacked him, started belabouring him with sticks. Now the young man who is riding the bicycle realises what is going on very clearly, because he lives here – and the problem was that he was normal dark brown, but his features were more aquiline than average. So he instinctively realised that these chaps had attacked him because of his apparent resemblance to an East Indian. Realising this he tore the hat off his head – and said to them 'What you beating me for? Look at my hair' (for he had negro-type hair). And then when they paused – only momentarily – he said in explanation, 'My mother was an Indian and my father was a blackman.' And the reply was as follows, which is the real horror, they said: 'Oh so your mother was an Indian and your father was a blackman – well we beat the East Indian within you.'

When you reach that state of irrationality you understand that is why I say it is a resource. That has gone beyond politics, it's no longer a disagreement with a party, it's now become existential – in the worse sense of the word.

Martin Carter's tale (regardless of the veracity of the events) is an indication of the post-colonial psyche. The violence is *existential* because it is partly perpetrated on the self – the 'enemy within'. The colonial system in Guyana and elsewhere, through its imposition of repressive segregation and persistent devaluation of non-white ethnicities, has succeeded in creating a bifurcated consciousness: a contempt for the 'other' who is also oneself. After my visit to Martin Carter I heard a very similar story, except that this time the ambiguity was stressed from the other side of the ethnic divide – it was the African within that was beaten – but the chilling punch line remained the same.

This theme of the enemy within, the seeking of an 'other' to scapegoat, to punish, is a theme which has run through the studies in this book. The guarantee of difference strengthens belonging and affirms identity. This can take the form of an insistence on unquestioned white superiority. But in post-colonial settings such as Guyana, Malaysia, Rwanda or Fiji the struggle for ascendancy often appears to resurrect the stereotypes ingrained in the hierarchical ordering and labour roles of the once subject groups. These reflected differences in cultural practices that perhaps seemed negligible when there was a common oppressor – these groups were once comrades in arms, *strategically* united, but with the withdrawal of colonial administration and the relative orderliness of that exploitative system, the uncertainty of life may lead to a situation of unremitting competition.

The people in this and similar stories in Guyana have probably lived in close proximity, been to the same schools and shared many aspects of culture in their everyday lives. In many ways much Guyanese culture is 'creolised': that is, a synthesis of both African and Indian traditions and their unique adaptation to an alien culture. However, ethnic rivalry since colonialism has reached an intensity which threatens at times to again blow up into inter-ethnic violence.

In everyday exchanges in Guyana it was observable (as Premdas has suggested (1981; 1986; 1996)) that there was a ritual performance of inter-ethnic harmony in which deep-seated grievances were held back in a tacitly stage-managed farce of conviviality, but I felt that at any moment the mask might fall away and expose the violent emotions beneath. Indeed, the fragile veneer of inter-communal amity was soon exposed when one talked to either group away from the 'other'; the bitter stereotypes that emerged drew directly from the nation's curly apostrophes colonial past.

Here and in other divided post-colonial nations the 'other' has been shaped by political, economic and historical processes. For example, in the run-up to independence in 1966 parties began to unite along ethnic lines. *Apanjat*, Hindi for 'race vote', was employed by leaders of both ethnic enclaves. Other factors in these situations have been fears and tensions relating to the Cold War and military intervention by the USA and Britain to secure countries such as Guyana under the rubric of liberal democracy, especially where natural resources and useful markets exist within the country. In the case of Guyana this meant deposing the elected candidate and installing a more favoured statesman.

Figure 7.1 is a photograph taken in a thriving market in Georgetown, the capital of Guyana. Although Georgetown is predominantly an African town, social spaces such as this market are areas where all groups come together to buy and sell. Publicly, members of different groups may be observed making transactions and mixing without any outward signs of conflict, but the boundaries are there and are

Figure 7.1 'Only believe all things are possible': scene in the Stabroek Market, Georgetown, Guyana

expressed fervently when the groups are 'offstage'; within the private bounds of their ethnic enclave they will drop the stage-managed calm of the public arena and often express deep resentment about the other groups.

The nature of boundary-making and the consequences of difference reach extremes in nations that are split into dependent and interlocking ethnic enclaves. These examples of bipolar ethnicity are largely the legacy of colonial divisions fostered by administrators to maintain a competitive workforce and to prevent a unified front being forged between subject 'races'. Donald Horowitz (1985: 36–40) usefully defined ethnic systems as belonging to two major categories: 'centralised' or 'dispersed' forms of multi-ethnic state. A 'dispersed ethnic system' includes states in which the population comprises many small ethnic groups, too small to be able to take control of the centre. Horowitz argues that this fragmentation of dispersed groups encourages inter-ethnic harmony and consensus. States such as India and the former Yugoslavia, he suggests, showed a 'benign complexity'. However, as the bonds that have held the nation together begin to unravel this complexity is lost and the result is fragmentation and the creation of separate national boundaries, each with a single dominant ethnic group.

The situation in Guyana fits with Donald Horowitz's definition of a 'centralised' state. This form of state occurs when the ethnic blocs are so large and strong that the problem of their interactions is ever present and central to the political and economic life of the nation. The situation in Guyana (and countries such as Trinidad, Fiji and Latvia) is one of bipolar ethnicity, which is always likely to be the most problematic. In Guyana the swing between ethnically partisan political parties has led to catastrophic shifts, each change accompanied by allegations of electoral fraud (which was certainly true in the past) and street violence. The state is locked into internal conflict with no end in sight owing to the sectoral divisions that have been embedded since the end of the colonial regime. Indians (who now have ascended to power with their People's Progressive Party) are the backbone of the country's rural-based economy as well as being the most successful entrepreneurs. The Africans, on the other hand, are heavily represented in the civil service, police and army.

Guyana has been blighted by bitter and protracted ethnic conflict. This conflict may be viewed as a manifestation of a long historical process of ethnic-boundary construction rather than a recent post-colonial eruption of primordial ethnic difference. Indeed, 'ethnic boundaries are constructed from the interaction between groups with shared historical experiences and cultural values and their social environment' (Turpin 1990: 73). Ethnicity is socially constructed and subject to constant re-evaluation. It may well be that the conflict helps to shape and affirm identity on both sides. In Guyana there exists considerable institutionalised inequity in the distribution of power between the two ethnic communities.

Early in the history of indentureship (the transportation of indentured labourers to replace the vacuum left by the abolition of slavery), planters recognised the value of having a working population segmented racially and rarely missed the opportunity to 'play… off the two principal races – by using one to put down any overt resistance by the other' (Rodney 1981: 188). Rodney also quotes evidence given at the West Indian Royal Commission, clearly showing that this manipulative attitude was commonplace in the colony.

> The two peoples do not mix. That is, of course, one of our great safeties in the colony when there has been any rioting. If the negroes were troublesome every coolie on the estate would stand by one. If the coolies attacked me, I could with confidence trust my negro friends for keeping me from injury.

> (ibid.: 188)

This active separation of ethnic groups can have long-term consequences. Malaysia, Guyana, Trinidad, Fiji and Rwanda, among other countries, have experienced intense and bitter post-colonial conflicts in which inter-ethnic enmity erupts in the competition for political or financial power. Often the people who are most reviled are the people who straddle the divide: those of dual heritage who are treated as pariahs because they embody a transgression against the imperative of the divide.

THE STRUGGLE FOR SYMBOLIC DOMINANCE

The manner in which ethnic groups face off over historical divisions and stalemates frequently entails the symbolic use of ethnicity or of cultural associations central to the group. Symbolic domination or violence can take many forms, such as, for example, parading significant achievements in sport, cultural capital, the arts, economics, a dominant linguistic tradition and so on. Many forms of cultural capital can affirm one group as a superior rival; so, for example Greek Cypriots place an emphasis on 3,000 years of Greek culture and the connotations of Greek superiority implicit in classical traditions. The former Yugoslavia is claimed to be a conflict in which 'all the symbolic power that ethnicity can provide was manipulated in such a way that fanned the flames for an aggressive ethnonationalism to emerge as a force that finally led to chaos' (Sotiropoulou 2002: 9). In Guyana and Trinidad cricket (once a sport that gave heart to colonial subjects, as the West Indies team showed their mastery over the British) has also become an arena for the divided ethnic politics of the region. The West Indies team regarded Guyana as an 'away match', as the support during World Cup events was directed to the visitors. Many Indian-Guyanese spectators were jubilant in cheering the Australians when they played in 1991 and projectiles and abuse were thrown at the all-Afro-Caribbean team (see Spencer 2007). 'In Guyana, as in many plural societies, one form of establishing or attempting to establish such hegemony is to deny the reality of ethnic inequality and division and to attempt to instil Guyanese identity among *all* Guyanese' (ibid.).

The following interviews illustrate one dimension of the divide. Ethnic stereotypes that were produced a century ago are reactivated in these two vignettes and the basic elements are seemingly unchanged. The maintenance of boundaries through the use of stereotyped images is not a peripheral activity governed by caprice but rather an activity central to one's own identity and security in a recognisable social world. Classifying the 'other' by reference to their body, size, shape, diet, economic behaviours and so on is essential in defining one's own social space: 'Nothing classifies somebody more than the way he or she classifies' (Bourdieu 1989c: 19). Such images are the boundary markers of identity for the individual member of an ethnic group. They are ways of envisaging the 'other' and, hence, oneself.

BOX 7.2 CONVERSATION WITH TWO AFRICAN-GUYANESE PROFESSIONALS

During a conversation with two African-Guyanese professionals, Lenny and Griff, in the emotionally charged atmosphere of the Demico House bar in central Georgetown, the following exchange took place after a discussion about a high-profile Indian businessman, Yesu Persaud. Neither of my companions rated this figure highly. Griff said, 'You see, in the land of the blind, the one-eyed man is king.' Lenny called him a 'lackney'. Then they took turns in attacking his credibility. He was given his house by President Burnham as part of an immoral deal. Without any prompting on my part the invective started to flow; both men seemed suddenly excited, even needled, by my off-hand question about this much-lauded Indian entrepreneur. There was much thumping of the table. Griff reached for my empty bottle and said, 'Say the Indian wants your bottle – or wot not. He will be so nice – so very good to you, you would never know. He will offer you money, and if that doesn't work – he will send his daughter to you, and if you don't want her he will send his wife! And as soon as he achieve this end – he take it away, then you know he never speak to you again – never! He only interested in the money. That's how they are.'

I ventured that this was perhaps a generalisation and that surely some Indians had other motives, but Lenny could barely contain his impatience. 'It *is* general, mon! They all the same – *ALL!*'

(Georgetown, 5 March 1991)

THE PERSISTENCE OF ETHNIC STEREOTYPES

Such vehement expressions of resentment are commonplace and reflect the Indians' apparent ease, relative to many Africans, at managing financial matters and property, causing jealousy and condemnation. 'The single-mindedness of the Indians in terms of saving money and foregoing present comforts and the good life for future improvement and security was condemned as avarice and caused irritation to whites and Africans alike' (Vasil 1984: 243).

African-Guyanese stereotypes

The fears of many Indian-Guyanese seemed to focus on the common perception of the African as overly physical, perhaps also in terms of their dominance manifest in the state itself (especially through the use of coercive force to maintain their power base). This stereotype was notably strong around Georgetown, the seat of government, where African-Guyanese are in the majority. There was a widespread feeling among the Indians that they were vulnerable to attack by Africans. The blame for all muggings, known as 'choke and rob', and break-ins, known as 'kick down door', was always assigned to 'blackmen' by Indians.

BOX 7.3 CONVERSATION WITH INDIAN-GUYANESE MAN

The following is an extract from an encounter with a Georgetown East Indian man in his early twenties who worked as a mini-bus 'conductor'. The exchange took place on an empty bus; the only other person present was the East Indian driver.

SS: Do you feel that there is any racist attitude …?

EAST INDIAN MAN (EI): Racist. Yes! Racialism – there is! Yeah very strong. You see the Negro people – them don't – them ain't got this kina way – like you know, building a future. Them only brek it – them ain't got dis ting so. They people aven't got the stronghold over this country – is East Indian people and Portuguese – people like Peter D'Aguair …

SS: Right I see …

EI: … like Cayman Sankur and Jose Persuad. Majority is Indian or Portuguese – but no you don't find no black people getting capital investment in this country. Any investment they got – they responsible for is drug pusher …

SS: … drug pusher – yeah?

EI: Yeah, they jus getting the money – look you'd ah seen em on the streets, riding the most fanciest bike, the most fanciest car to drive in. They dress their self in gold right?

SS: Uh huh. Yes.

EI: They dress their self in gold – Indian can't wear gold and the Negro would wear them in town on the skin. Why? They bully – cause if you wear it they come an choke you. They don't do this no more (here he demonstrated a choke and rob hold on my neck). Years ago they used to choke you ...

SS: Choke and rob – yeah?

EI: ... and rob you. Now. Now. They cutting you off! They cutting your finger off and they walking alongside you on the pave and they just take out the knife of the pocket ... and dis 'don't move' – one on one side – now you can feel something sharp sticking in your side – 'now don't move' – a sudden movement [he became increasingly agitated here] Very bully – black people very very very bully! Black people travelling in this veekle – they arlways shart of money and they need music – they need spacious seat – and they arlways short of money. Yes.

(Georgetown, 13 April 1991)

This sense of vulnerability appears to have, if anything, increased. Since the People's Progressive Party achieved government in 1992 there have been allegations that a great number of aggravated assaults and murders in Guyana are racially motivated and largely perpetrated by African-Guyanese against Indians. Apart from the overt sense of physical threat here, which illustrates the common stereotype of the African as a physical aggressor, there is also reference to another popularly voiced view, that of the African as profligate, flashy and lacking in sound financial judgement. For Indians, the 'economic irresponsibility' stereotype is not peculiar to a segment of the African population, but is true of all Africans generally (Premdas 1972: 290–1).

THE 'OTHER' – THEFT OF LEGITIMATE PLEASURES

Slavoj Žižek uses the phrase 'theft of enjoyment' to explain the complex psycho-social perception of the 'other'. In his article 'Eastern Europe's Republics of Gilead' (1990) he related this notion to the growing tensions in Yugoslavia. Žižek equates national movements and 'causes' with the manner in which ethnic groups 'organise their enjoyment through national myths' (ibid.: 53). Furthermore, he presents the notion of the 'other' constantly impinging on our senses because of their perceived lack of restraint in the practice of their pleasures.

In short what really bothers us about the 'other' is the peculiar way in which it organises its enjoyment: precisely the surplus, the 'excess' that pertains to it – the smell of their food, their 'noisy' songs and dances, their strange manners, their attitude to work (in the racist perspective, the 'other' is either a workaholic stealing our jobs or an idler living on our labour, and it is quite amusing to note the ease with which one passes from reproaching the 'other' with a refusal to work to reproaching him for the theft of work).

(ibid.: 54)

The two views of the 'other', as related by Žižek above, can equally be seen in the stereotypes African and Indian-Guyanese hold about each other. Indian-Guyanese often fear the African population, believing that they are responsible for robbery and street crimes, which are especially grievous when related to the loss of their pleasure in adorning themselves with gold and jewellery in public, which was once an important aspect of their culture. Conversely, African-Guyanese feel the Indians' success and facility with money and property is a direct trespass on the pleasure and privilege to which they were entitled through their traditional status as public-service workers. Indians are seen as workaholics; their ambitions are often viewed as avaricious and their willingness to save money single-mindedly and to sacrifice the comforts of the good life for the present as meanness (Vasil 1984: 243).

Žižek states that: 'What sets in motion this logic of the "theft of enjoyment" is of course not immediate social reality – the reality of different ethnic communities living closely together – but the inner antagonism inherent in these communities' (Žižek 1990: 56). This is very much the case in Guyana, where tension and suspicion between the groups is deeply ingrained but rarely voiced openly (see Chapter 4). Žižek compares the theft of enjoyment to Lacan's notion of 'imaginary castration'. Certain aspects of cultural identity, those unique features which seem to characterise a group, such as a long association with the land or a type of traditional work practice, are felt to be inaccessible to the 'other'. Yet when the 'other' is seen as a rival for these scarce resources the result is a constant state of distrust. This is perhaps the central contradiction of Guyana and other ethnically divided states. Žižek's identification of the psychological threat seen to be embodied in the culture of the 'other' can be recognised in many nations with a marked ethnic divide.

The next example is drawn from another ethnically fractured state, Malaysia, which experienced a catastrophic eruption of ethnic rivalries in 1969 that provided justification for some overt political manoeuvring.

BOX 7.4 CHINESE MALAYS, INTERVIEWS RECORDED JUNE 2004, SHEFFIELD HALLAM UNIVERSITY

Proportionately Malaysia has the largest Chinese community in the region, constituting 27 per cent of the population. When the British departed when independence was achieved in 1957, they left a socio-economic and political system divided along ethnic lines. Since racial riots in 1969, the government has vigorously promoted the advancement of ethnic Malays. This has involved a quota system and other restrictions on ethnic Chinese in religion, business, education and employment. Chinese Malaysians nevertheless control about half the private-sector economy and, in spite of such restrictions, have actively preserved their culture. There is, since the violence in the late 1960s, a sense of inter-ethnic suspicion and the recent protests in the run-up to the elections have demonstrated the deep-seated distrust of the country's ethnic minorities for the ruling Barisan Nasional (BN) government and in the fairness of the electoral system. There has effectively been a one-party state since 1957 (UMNO, the party which represents indigenous Malays), with little freedom of expression and tight state control of alternative comment in the Malaysian media. The recent victory of the UMNO-led coalition BN in the polls, based on only 47 per cent of the vote (to the opposition party's 50 per cent), but with a majority of seats in parliament, proved controversial, with allegations of gerrymandering being widespread (see Campbell 2013; Freedom House 2013). In the wake of this close electoral scrape, the ruling party has announced even more measures to support indigenous Malays (the so-called Bumiputera Economic Empowerment (BEE) programme) which promises to provide benefits of around $10 billion (see *The Economist* 2013).

Fenton gives examples from Malaysia where differences of custom and practice between Indians, Chinese and Malays are reflected in language, religion and cuisine. In Malay Islamic practice halal meat restricts the practice of commensality (i.e. sharing a table), which is the basis for much social exchange. These routine patterns of behaviour and preference are reproduced in everyday social interaction, just as in the Guyanese example. Also similar to the situation in Guyana are the marked economic and political divisions between the three main groups. Everyday examples of difference are exacerbated and collect a negative charge as any marker of difference becomes operationalised as a marker of domination or a reminder of political or economic struggles between the ethnic enclaves.

In Malaysia the political dominance of the native Malays has been formally ascribed into constitutional law. The Bumiputera Movement creates quotas and systems of positive discrimination for these 'sons of the soil' who have maintained political ascendancy. Meanwhile, the Chinese have maintained their dominance of the economy and Indians make up the workforce of the nation.

However, to ensure that Malays are not left out of the mainstream economic system, laws were passed that allowed Malays to take a slice of all businesses in the country (even though their role in these businesses could be said to be negligible). Malays also make up the main student body of public

BOX 7.4 CHINESE MALAYS, INTERVIEWS RECORDED JUNE 2004, SHEFFIELD HALLAM UNIVERSITY (CONTINUED)

universities as 60–70 per cent of places are reserved for them, whereas Chinese and Indians have to compete for the remaining places, take up positions in expensive private institutions or, of course, study overseas. In a conversation with three Chinese Malay students, we discussed their feelings about the current social and political relations within the republic.

SS: Could you talk a little about the dynamics and perhaps the boundaries of ethnicity in Malaysia. How does that work for you?

PUENG: We have to come back to during our colonial times under the British. The differences are that the Malays more to the political side, Chinese more on the economic side and Indian is more on the labour side. But after the so-called 1969 May 13th incident[1] – because of the economic gap between these three – the riot arise. So government has come up with our new policy – Desai Economic Baru – a new economic development plan to try and get the three races closer within the main economic trend ...

SS: Do you feel this harmonising programme is working out?

KAREN: I don't think it's working – it's still improving.

SS: So it's got a way to go yet to achieve its goals?

JAS: But you can still see that some Malays have more politicians and the Chinese, they are still a lot of business and, as for the Indians, they are still maintained as labour.

SS: Could you please explain to us about the Bumiputeras?

PUENG: Er ... Bumiputeras ... you can refer to two groups, OK? We can divide it into two categories: one the Malay Malay – the native *orang asli*, someone who has been in the motherland before the Malay immigrants from Indonesia or Philippine Islands came to the peninsula of Malaysia.

SS: Like an indigenous people?

PUENG: Yeah, like the natives in Australia before the English moved there.

SS: How do non-Malays feel about this possibly privileged group? How do you feel about the Bumiputera movement?

PUENG: I must say that they enjoy some sort of privilege ...

KAREN: A lot!

PUENG: A lot that we don't enjoy – like when purchasing a house they enjoy a 5 per cent discount on any house off the total value – and they enjoy the quota – the education quota in the local public university. Maybe 60–70 per cent of the places are left for them and the rest we have to share among.

KAREN: Well basically Malays are the majority and for Chinese and Indians is a minority – but of course among the three races we feel sometimes it's quite unfair – but that's how it is …

PUENG: They can get into the local university easy even though their results may be not as good as the Chinese …

JAS: And they can easily just get a loan.

SS: So it's not based on merit?

JAS: No it's much more to quotas.

PEUNG: No it's based on quotas.

KAREN: No …

JAS: … which most of us find unfair and dissatisfaction.

PUENG: And those companies – if you like to do your business you have to take in at least 30 per cent of bumiputera to work in your company – directors also, 30 per cent – if you want to get involved in a company government project you must have at least one or two Malay directors in your company.

SS: Has the system arisen because there was seen to be some disadvantage for Malay people – in other words, that they were poorer at one stage? And this was to reset the balance – was there some of that motive or …?

PUENG: I must say that this kind of system exists because of the new economic development, because as I mentioned, most of the Malay they focus on the political side and lose their power in economic side – so that's why the government, after the riot, they want to get balance, so they must move the company, move the Malay into the main economic stream – so that they set such rules to encourage the Malay to get involved in the economy.

SS: So because the government itself was heavily represented by Malay Malays.

PUENG: For us you can say it has both advantage and disadvantage as well – because its advantage is to promote the unity among the races. Because our country without those policies might be the next Indonesia where …

KAREN: … there's no democratic …

PUENG: There's no democratic … and they treat Chinese very bad like what happened in 19[69]…

KAREN: Yes, very racist.

PUENG: Yeah, very racist, not like today we can share the unity peaceful life in Malaysia.

---

[1] The incident of 13 May 1969 referred to here was a major riot in Kuala Lumpur at the time of the federal elections. Long-standing tensions erupted and, in the aftermath, the government imposed emergency powers, suspended the press and the parliament and established a National Operations Council which ultimately functioned as a de facto government for nearly two years. When the parliament finally reconvened in February 1971 it announced that certain racially sensitive issues,

BOX 7.4 CHINESE MALAYS, INTERVIEWS RECORDED JUNE 2004, SHEFFIELD HALLAM UNIVERSITY (CONTINUED)

now known as *isu-isu sensitif*, were henceforth not to be openly discussed under any circumstances. This amounted to a decree which forbade any further questioning of the special privileges of the Malays. A contemporary European analyst commented that 'perhaps the most serious consequence of May 13 [...] is the apparent decision of the Malaysian rulers to render Malay status inviolable by thought, word, or deed' (Short 1970: 1089).

The alignment of class relations with ethnicity is very marked in the case of Malaysia, as Fenton (1999) convincingly shows. The post-13 May New Economic Policy (NEP) was designed to reduce poverty (especially to redress the balance in favour of the rural peasantry, who were mostly Malays), to break up the ethnicity/class structure and to avoid the threat of future violence. The NEP was undoubtedly successful, although it has not managed to significantly change the predominant ethnic class sections. The problem of rural peasantry in poverty is deeply entrenched and Malays are still highly represented in this sector. The other problem, a source of hurt and resentment, articulated by these young Chinese Malay students is the pursuit by the government of draconian policies disallowing any criticism of the inequalities enshrined in state policies. There has been a good deal of criticism both within Malaysia and around the world about the effective gagging of any sort of a free press in the federation, as well as of the Internal Security Act.

Clearly, the Chinese Malays interviewed here, while they recognise the injustices of the Malay-dominated state bureaucracy, find this preferable to the open and violent confrontations that occurred in the past (not dissimilar to the extreme anti-Chinese ethnic cleansing under Suharto in 1960's Indonesia) in which many thousands were killed. Some have equated ethnic conflict with ethnic loyalties based on kinship and extended kinship. This produces a hardening of boundaries and leads to antagonism, violence and conflict. The frustration with the present regime was apparent in these students' concerns and also evident in their comments about the Internal Security Act, which suggested that taking part in political debate in a public place in Malaysia could have severe consequences:

BOX 7.4 CONTINUED

SS: OK, I understood from what you said before that these issues are very sensitive and really not spoken of publicly. And that there is some problem if people speak too publicly about this. Is this the case? What would be the situation in everyday life? Are people concerned? They wouldn't talk publicly?

KAREN: They'd be thrown into prison ...

JAS: [*laughs*]

KAREN: [*nudges Pueng*] Tell them about the ... ISA.

PUENG: Oh yeah ISA is still not the worser if you don't talk openly. OK if you want to talk in the café with your friends – have a normal conversation – chit-chat – that is OK but you don't try and influence the public on a certain policy ...

KAREN: ... go on a demonstration ...

PUENG: ... go on a protest – all those things OK. If you want to openly influence the public you will be retained under the ISA, with which they will detain you ...

KAREN: ... without any reason for two years – and after two years you will only be put to court.

PUENG: ... not without *any* reason – they suspect you. If you get involved in certain activities that may bring harm to the public ...

KAREN: Ahh, still they don't have to prove it to put you in the prison ...

PUENG: Yeah, they put you into prison – no visitor – no judgement.

SS: So obviously people are reluctant to demonstrate ...

PUENG: Yeah, especially those opposition party leaders, they're always being detained under ISA ...

SS: So it's not really tolerated – too much criticism about the government?

KAREN: They won't tolerate at all ...

It would appear that in Malaysia the dominant cultural interests are protected by racial quotas and overtly partisan legislation; the ISA

provides for preventive detention for up to two years with the possibility of renewal every two years. Any police officer may, without a warrant, arrest and detain anyone he has 'reason to believe' has acted or likely to act in 'any manner prejudicial to the security of Malaysia'. The act also allows for restrictions on freedom of assembly, association, and expression, freedom of movement, residence and employment. It allows for the closing of schools and educational institutions if they are used as a meeting place for an unlawful organization or for any other reason are deemed detrimental to the interests of Malaysia or the public.

(Human Rights Watch 2001: 2)

In situations such as this the state often imposes constraints on democratic freedoms: the press becomes a mere mouthpiece for government viewpoints, and opposition parties as well as individual expression and association are heavily restricted. Malaysia is a remarkably intractable, racially polarised society. Wan Husin (2012) recently invoked the 'clash of civilizations' argument (which has been influential in the USA following Huntington's thesis (1998)) as the root of the 1969 violence, but it has also been suggested that, far from a spontaneous ethnic clash, this was a coup d'état by the ethnic Malays that enabled the establishment of a state capitalist ruling party that can invoke the fear of the street violence and mayhem of the 1960s to effectively promulgate their dominance in terms of counteracting demands from non-Malay communities for civil rights (Soong 2008).

RELIGION

In 2001 the former prime minister Dr Mahathir Mohammed declared Malaysia an Islamic state. The reaction to 9/11 in Malaysia has led to a watershed of opinion between moderate and more radical Islamic elements:

> on the one hand, some Malay Muslims may see it fit to de-emphasise their Muslim public image and, on the other, some may now be motivated to profile their Muslim image more strongly, either openly or silently. It is the latter that may worry the Malaysian government which is doing its best to fight against Islamic fundamentalism and extremism. It is not improbable that the opposition Parti Islam would take up this issue and turn it into political capital to attack the ruling party, especially UMNO [United Malays National Organisation], and demonstrate that its strategy to please the West by declaring Malaysia a 'moderate Islamic state' has backfired and could be seen a dismal failure in international diplomacy.
>
> (Shamsul 2002: 3–4)

The increasing power of the Islamic lobby and its impacts on non-Malays had also been noted by my respondents:

BOX 7.4 CONTINUED

SS: And I heard that in some states holding hands in public would be frowned upon …

KAREN: Right, it was a year ago …

PUENG: Yeah, it's true – it's already happened to some Chinese students.

KAREN: Yeah, I heard the rumours that one of the victims, *tashens*, they were just holding hands in the park, in a public park, when they were confronted by Islamic officers that you are charged with public holding hands. That is not right. Some people are very unsatisfied – because I'm not a Malay – first of all and I'm not under Islamic ruling, so practically this rule does not apply to me – but still they get a fine for it. They got a fine for it – they were lucky they weren't thrown into prison.

The Malaysian government has been accused of a form of internal colonialism; policies of containment and control based on ethnic origins have been practised since the 1960s. While tacit calm may be viewed as preferable to out-and-out violence, as one of the students suggests, the unrest and frustration of those subjected to the dominant political culture is tangible in these interviews. Malaysia has developed affirmative action and a quota system that, as the interviewees recounted, require businesses over a certain size to have Malay partners and that 'ring-fences' 80 per cent of the spots in the public university for Malays (Human Rights Foundation 2011). Clearly, a governing class of Malay technocrats has been created. The bitter memories of the violence of 1969 live on, and there is a tense stand-off, which may be more fragile in the face of increasing Islamic militancy. Recent demonstrators in the Bersih ('clean', as in clean and fair elections) movement have called mass rallies in Kuala Lumpur in protest against the autocratic nature of the state and called for electoral reforms in actions considered similar to the Arab Spring protests.

ETHNIC CLEANSING

Conflict can take many forms, from the tense stage-managed inter-ethnic 'harmony' of, for example, Guyana and Malaysia – where struggles for symbolic domination manifest in a game of cricket, in the capping of places at the local university, in political and economic rivalry, in censorship of negative media about the ruling party, in electoral fraud – through to full-scale inter-ethnic violence. The causes are many and complex and often (as in the cases reviewed) have a long and inglorious history that has been marked either by colonial rule (Malaysia, Guyana, Rwanda, Egypt, Algeria) or superpower intervention (Guyana, Afghanistan, Iraq, Iran and scores of others). The possible solutions to conflicts where there is a desire for self-determination are of two kinds: coercive and non-coercive.

Secession is rarely successful. There are a number of movements currently: Chechens in Russia, Basques in Spain, Quebeckers in Canada, Sikhs in India. The majority ethnic group which forms the state fights to retain those territories in question. The coercive means of resolving conflicts are all too familiar and the consequences of such approaches show that they are unworkable and lead to increased violence and human suffering (international involvement is often necessary) as a result of elimination, ethnic cleansing, forced assimilation, containment and control.

Ethnic cleansing has been witnessed in the ongoing murder of southerners in Sudan; in the killing in Rwanda in 1994 of an estimated 800,000 of the Tutsi minority by the Hutu majority; in the massacre of 200,000 Bosnian Muslims by the Serbs in the former Yugoslavia in the early 1990s; in the slaughter of 1,700,000 Cambodians under the Khmer Rouge in the 1970s;[1] and in the extermination of 300,000 or more East Timorese by Indonesia at about the same time (a total estimated as being as much as one third of the pre-invasion population: see, for example, Powell 2006).

The list is very long before as well as after the Nazi regime. Ethnic cleansing also takes the inhumane form of forced assimilation or homogenisation. In the 1980s ethnic Turks in Bulgaria were forced to take on Bulgarian names, while mosques were closed and ethnic ceremonies and practices outlawed. Similarly, the mixed children of Aboriginal parents in Australia were removed (often forcibly) from their parents, given new names and placed with white Australian families. Containment policies can starve minorities of resources or oppress them politically or culturally by refusing to accept their languages (e.g. Basque, Catalan, Welsh). These types of policy may take place within a situation of what Hechter has called 'internal colonialism', and often become the focus of resistance movements.

It seems that many commentators, when reporting conflicts in the developing world (especially in African countries) are too ready to invoke ethnocentric (or blatantly racist) notions of tribal hatred characterised as an unreasoning primordial force in the blood or an ineffable part of ancient cultures. The then BBC Africa Correspondent Fergal Keane suggested that such hatreds as those behind the genocide in Rwanda were better understood as 'a complex web of politics, economics, history, psychology and a struggle for identity' (Keane 1996: 226) – the catalyst in this case being Machiavellian action by members of the government:

> What happened in Rwanda was the result of cynical manipulation by powerful political and military leaders. Faced with the choice of sharing some of their wealth and power with the [insurgent] Rwandan Patriotic Front, they chose to vilify that organization's main support group, the Tutsis ... The Tutsis were characterized as vermin. Inyenzi in kinyarwanda – cockroaches who should be stamped on without mercy ... In much the same way as the Nazis exploited latent anti-Semitism in Germany, so did the forces of Hutu extremism identify and whip into murderous frenzy the historical sense of grievance against the Tutsis ... This was not about tribalism first and foremost but about preserving the concentration of wealth and power in the hands of the elite.
>
> (Fergal Keane quoted in Misir 2000: 2)

This wielding of power, the power over life and death, is what Foucault referred to as biopower.[2] These frenzied genocidal actions are carried out when a population is seen as a dispensable substratum whose demise is considered a salutary thing.

Foucault describes the racial aspect of biopower thus: 'racism justifies the death-function in the economy of biopower by appealing to the principle that the death of others makes one biologically stronger insofar as one is a member of a race or a population' (Foucault 2002: 258). Reducing a people to 'unpeople' (a term coined by Mark Curtis), to insects or vermin that steal from the healthy body of the state, justifies their eradication. Andrea Smith pursues this concept in a discussion of the US policy of exterminating indigenous peoples who were seen as 'a pollution of which the colonial body must purify itself' (Smith 2003: 72).

'RACE RIOTS' OR SOCIAL AND ECONOMIC EXCLUSION

The phenomenon of ethnic conflict is often the negative context in which the dominant culture reflects on the vicissitudes of ethnicity. The designation of conflicts as racial or as 'race riots' is frequently contentious. A simple clash between a group of people in an inner-city area and the police or right-wing demonstrators does not necessarily have anything to do with the mobilisation of ethnicity, although such events are often all too quickly portrayed in such a light, which has the effect of locating them within the dominant discourse of law and order and thus marginalising the participants. Such is the case with the so-called 'race riots' of 2001 in the UK, in which predominantly Asian youths clashed with police in Oldham and Bradford (Lancashire), causing significant damage to property, and again in Australia in Sydney's Redfern district, where Aborigines clashed with police in 2004. In each instance the feature that was emphasised was race. However, neither the long-standing tensions in these areas nor their extremes of poverty were stressed. The area of Lancashire affected by these disturbances is among the least economically active areas in the country, and the Block area of Redfern is a run-down ghettoised area with, again, some intractable poverty situated at the edge of the affluent city of Sydney. In Lancashire the response from the state:

> was variegated and involved promoting a discourse which constructed Asian and Muslim communities as having a surfeit of alterity which interrupted closure of the nation (Grillo, 2007) thus necessitating a broader critique of multiculturalism and a promotion of 'community cohesion' and a blunt response from the criminal justice system.
>
> (Patel and Tyrer 2011: 100)

It is not new to suggest that there is a tendency to 'blame the victims'. The point is that the victims live a precarious existence where entrenched unemployment has fostered welfare dependency, removed from the amenities and services of the wealthier white community. These areas are, also owing to their often stigmatised character, more heavily patrolled by police (despite not always being areas of higher than average crime).

The anger of the Redfern community was sparked by the death of an Aboriginal boy, TJ Hickey, who died in suspicious circumstances that were rumoured to have involved his being chased on his bike by a police vehicle; he was found impaled on railings. A police spokesperson who was interviewed on British television described instead the role Aboriginal drinking might have played in the riot. (This discourse has a long history, as discussed in Chapter 6.) TJ's mother was quoted as saying: 'It's got to stop the way they treat our kids ... They treat our kids like dogs ... They manhandle them' (Gail Hickey, mother of 17-year-old Thomas Hickey, quoted in Connolly 2006: 41).

However, while the riots are perhaps not racial in the way they are glibly asserted to be in sensationalist reporting, they are certainly a consequence of constructions of race. Both Oldham in Lancashire and Redfern in New South Wales are highly segregated and among the most impoverished areas in each country. This is not coincidental; both groups involved in confrontations with the police are the most disadvantaged minority groups. Pakistani and Bangladeshi population groups are self-segregated from the white population in Oldham, as are indigenous people in the Sydney suburb of Redfern.

> The level of residential self-segregation is great in Oldham, with Asian and white communities concentrated in specific housing areas which all suffer from poverty and lack of opportunity. This has restricted day-to-day social contact between people from different ethnic groups. Some primary schools in central Oldham feature pupils from only one ethnic group, when the area as a whole has a very diverse community.
>
> (Metropolitam Borough Council of Oldham 2006: 14)

The segregation of Aboriginal people in Sydney and other cities (as discussed in Chapter 6) is the result of entrenched inequalities that amount to being excluded from the relative affluence of mainstream Australia. Redfern is an area with a long-standing sense of social exclusion that

> dates much further back than the modern preoccupation with Sydney's gentrification might suggest. According to Morgan (2004: 4), for example, when the Queen visited Australia in 1954, local authorities were so concerned about the sight of Redfern's Aboriginal districts on the approaches to Central Station they erected 'great hessian screens to obscure her view'. It is hard to imagine a measure better calculated to engender a collective sense of exclusion from the dominant culture and all it stands for.
>
> (quoted in Weatherburn 2006: 27)

In 2000 the UN made unprecedented criticisms of the Australian government's outdated policies, which had not improved the circumstances faced by the 2 per cent Aboriginal population, who were seventeen times more likely to be arrested, fourteen times more likely to be imprisoned and sixteen times more likely to die in custody than non-Aborigines. Economic disadvantage in each case is underpinned by histori-cal patterns of exclusion. These outbreaks of violence reflect general trends of disad-vantage across the country and in the case of Australia these relatively rare indigenous riots are almost always associated with perceived injustices on the part of the criminal justice agencies. In the same year there was an inquiry into the riots on Palm Island, which had occurred after the death of a local man in police custody; violence had broken out, the police station had been burned to the ground and the court rooms had been badly damaged. In both the Redfern and Palm Island riots these causes are significantly played down: 'the dominant representations by media and politicians steer clear of these understandings, preferring to focus on either the irrationality of lawlessness, or the passive victimhood of disadvantage' (Cuneen 2008).

At times marginalised and impoverished communities explode, usually as a result of perceived injustices. Such resistance is often dealt with disproportionately, as was the case in the Bradford and Oldham 'riots'. At the same time other causa-tive factors were downplayed, including the neglect of socio-economic disadvan-tage, aggressive policing and provocation from far-right groups (see McGhee 2005; Patel and Tyrer 2011). Clearly, punitive measures lead to greater violence and suf-fering and do not address the roots of the conflict. Less coercive approaches, how-ever, require the active recognition of the group in question and can include the development of autonomy, forms of power sharing or multicultural approaches. The outbreaks of violence in the heart of cities in Britain and Australia are sympto-matic of forms of urban segregation and exclusion, but have routinely been blamed on multiculturalism and lack of cultural integration. In Britain the discourse of 'community cohesion' was highlighted in the official inquiry into the 2001 'riots' (Cantle 2001). The report suggested that these outbreaks were symptomatic of a deeper malaise in the heart of ethnically diverse cities in Britain (Thomas 2007; McGhee 2005). Parts of the Cantle Report made important points, recognising:

> The extent to which physical divisions were compounded by so many other aspects of our daily lives, was very evident – separate educational arrangements, community and voluntary bodies, employment, places of worship, language, social and cultural networks, means that many communities operate on the basis of a series of parallel lives.
>
> (Cantle Report 2001: 9)

However, ultimately the analysis tended to ignore the often complex causes of these violent clashes and located the problem instead at the Pakistani/Bangladeshi com-munities' lack of acculturation:

> The reports into last summer's disturbances in Bradford, Oldham and Burnley painted a vivid picture of fractured and divided communities, lacking a sense of common values or shared civic identity to unite around. The reports signalled

the need for us to foster and renew the social fabric of our communities, and rebuild a sense of common citizenship, which embraces the different and diverse experiences of today's Britain.

(Home Office 2002: 10)

In addition, these events have been the catalyst for a raft of policies aimed at vigorously reinserting ideas of responsible citizenship into the national agenda. The emphasis pursued by the then home secretary David Blunkett was the need for immigrants to achieve a better understanding of citizenship (this became a key requirement for immigrants seeking to become British); Citizenship also became a compulsory part of the school curriculum. Several writers have seen this as a basic misunderstanding of the situation for these mostly young, second-generation migrants, who were very much assimilated into the local culture and fully understood the meaning of citizenship. Indeed, Back *et al.* suggest that these were, in fact, riots about failed or 'thwarted citizenship' (Young 2003: 449; McGhee 2005). Rather than lacking a cohesive sense of British culture and citizenship skills, these young people

had the same accents and expectations as the white youths who rioted on the other side of the ethnic line. They scarcely needed teaching citizenship or English – they knew full well that bad policing was a violation of their citizenship just as was a drastic exclusion from the national job markets.

(Young 2003: 458)

A serious concern here is that the discourse of failed or 'weak integration', which misrepresents the issue, has had a significant influence on policy for asylum and immigration as well as in the approaches to counter-terrorism (see McGhee 2005: 6.1).

Ten years later, in August 2011, Britain again experienced disorder in many urban centres. The discussion of the nature of these disorders has covered almost every theoretical base, but discussion of race and racialised conflict was muted, somewhat surprisingly, as it is well known that the shooting under uncertain circumstances of an African-Caribbean man in Tottenham has been acknowledged as the catalyst for what ensued. Clearly the riots in 2011 were markedly different: there was the very visible involvement of young white men and, as Murji and Neal (2011: 2.8) argue, different spatial references, with disturbances in affluent white and 'unracialised or only selectively racialised geographies' including Gloucester, Enfield and Ealing. In addition, the composition of the centres in question demonstrates the progressive super-diversity (Vertovec 2007) of British cities. Finally, while the bonds of community appeared to be very significantly at play during the 2001 riots, in 2011 the opposite seemed to be the case:

Where Cantle indicated 'too much community' as a core problematic of the 2001 disturbances (in that he saw those communities as silos with their separate populations living 'parallel lives'), in 2011 it is the breakdown and loss of communities and community values – 'not enough community' – that is being mobilised as the core moral problematic.

(Murji and Neal 2011: 4.2)

Taken as a whole these different examples of conflict and civil disturbance demonstrate different principles at work. At the national level there are the legacies of colonial regimes and their inherited stereotypes of ethnic 'others'. In the cases of Malaysia and Guyana ethnic fault lines lead to violent incidents of conflict akin to ethnic cleansing while, in addition, the ethnic seizure of political power (through blatant or suspected vote rigging) allowed the ruling party to promulgate draconian laws to constrain and penalise the 'other', who is seen as a thief whose contribution is not valid and whose share in the bounty of the state must be curtailed. By contrast, the eruption of violence in the multicultural UK is a consequence of the experience of long-term socio-economic deprivation, the so-called 'ethnic penalty', which is measured in terms of structural disadvantage in employment and discriminatory patterns of policing. The Australian case is similar, as the indigenous people at the centre of the 'riot' were responding directly to a case of a young member of their community dying in suspicious circumstances. Most cases of violent battles with the police, like this one in Redfern, stem from perceptions of injustice and police action. It is worth considering these 'riots' as manifestations of a 'moral economy', a concept introduced by E. P. Thompson (see Cunneen 2008) in which people react by rioting as a viable means of protest against infractions of deeply held traditional rights.

CHAPTER SUMMARY

Conflict situations can be of several kinds depending on the form of ethnic system. Where there are multiple 'dispersed' groups too small to individually take control of the centre a tacit harmony may exist, but this may dissolve into ethnic rivalry (as witnessed in the Balkans and in the former Soviet territories). Centralised states such as Guyana, Trinidad and Fiji may experience increasing polarisation as ethnically based enclaves become mutually exclusive and ethnic competition for political and economic power becomes a zero sum game. The solution may be to struggle towards a grand coalition which breaks the division into race-based constituencies and refocuses on an earlier creolised national character. Horowitz (2003) suggests that, despite the enthusiasm of many politicians for secession and separation, they do little to create long-term harmony and tend to exacerbate conflict. Living together is fraught with difficulties but the alternatives are much worse.

The causes of ethnic conflict can be complex; there is no quick-fix solution, no unique theoretical understanding which can unlock and solve these problems. In many cases the historical roots of inter-ethnic violence are very deep and there is a condensation of relations of difference into the very grain and texture of the cultures and in the creation of dispositions, attitudes and practices which make up the individual's habitus. While political intervention may be part of a solution, this can be viable only if it leads to an acceptance of heterogeneity rather than division. All too often the political system itself is a key cause of ethnic marginalisation, leading to disaffection and resentment.

In polarised states such as Guyana, electoral competition became part of the cycle of ethnic violence as allegations of vote rigging and politicisation of ethnic constituencies further polarised the divide (a functional part of the colonial system). A thorough and realistic analysis of the sources of the conflict is essential and must take account of the unique features of the rivals involved and make direct reference to the socio-political structures of the society.

The situations discussed in urban UK and Australian locations demonstrate the hegemony of dominant values. The term 'race riot' seems to be easily provoked, the victims of segregation and oppression too easily blamed and a careful examination of the complex circumstances behind these violent conflicts is too often not carried out.

EXERCISE 7.1 GUYANA

1 What are stereotypes? What purpose do they serve?
2 List stereotypes you are aware of about ethnic groups. Where did they come from?
3 Consider the Guyanese interviews in this chapter. In what way are the stereotyped views that are expressed functional?
4 How might these images of the 'other' be considered mutually dependent, even complementary?
5 The process of 'creolisation' is a form of cultural adaptation very visible in Caribbean cultures. Why do you think this has not led to a more harmonious culture in Guyana?
6 Ethnic conflict such as that in Guyana has many possible causes. Which are the most plausible?

EXERCISE 7.2 MALAYSIA

1 Do you recognise key similarities and/or differences in the Guyana and Malaysia cases of conflict?
2 What aspects of the situation are most likely to appear to be threatening to the Chinese Malays?
3 What aspects of the situation are most likely to appear to be threatening to the Malay Malays?
4 What is your opinion of 'affirmative action' policies as adopted in Malaysia?

5   How might colonialism have played a role in sowing the seeds for future con-
    flicts in both countries? (This question may require further research.)

EXERCISE 7.3

1   What policy initiatives might improve the situation in both countries?
2   How far are conflicts such as those in Guyana and Malaysia concerned with
    class and the relationship to the means of production?
3   How far are the conflicts in Guyana and Malaysia to do with what Žižek has
    called 'theft of enjoyment'?
4   Look at the definitions of genocide and ethnic cleansing. Are there other acts,
    crimes against humanity, that should be included?
5   When could the United Nations intervene in a situation of ethnic cleansing
    or genocide? How much power should the UN be given? Should such inter-
    vention be brokered with other regional organisations?

EXERCISE 7.4

1   Why is it likely that the UK government has mistakenly pinpointed a lack of
    cultural integration/citizenship as the root cause of the 2001 riots?
2   In what way have news and popular media represented the Asian communities?
3   To what extent is there a common set of codes and responsibilities for British
    citizenship, or for that of other nations?
4   How are the causes of the inner-city riots discussed in this chapter (in Sydney
    and various sites in the UK) different or possibly similar?
5   Can the idea that 'Nothing classifies somebody more than the way he or she
    classifies' (Bourdieu 1989: 19) be significant in these cases? What might the
    insistence on deflecting attention from socio-economic structures of racism
    tell us about the dominant culture?

Further reading

The following works provide some follow-up sources for the discussions in this
chapter and some more general reading.

Australia

The consequences of punitive policing for the remote Aboriginal community on
Queensland's Palm Island was powerfully documented by Chloe Hooper's *The Tall
Man: Death and Life on Palm Island* (Jonathan Cape, London, 2009).

Chris Cunneen's 2008 article, 'Riot, Resistance and Moral Panic: Demonising the Colonial other', *University of New South Wales Faculty of Law Research Series* 29, available online at http://law.bepress.com/unswwps-flrps08/art29, gives an insight into the history of the inner city area of the Block and the distorting representation of such events in the popular media.

UK

See the following:

Ash Amin (2003) 'Unruly Strangers? The 2001 Urban Riots in Britain', *International Journal of Urban and Regional Research* 27(2): 460–63.

L. Back, M. Keith, A. Khan, K. Shukra and J. Solomos (2002) 'The Return of Assimilationism: race, multiculturalism and new labour', *Sociological Research Online* 7(2): 1–13.

P. Bagguley and Y. Hussain (2003) 'Conflict and Cohesion – Constructions of Community in the 2001 "Riots"', Paper presented to the Communities Conference, Trinity and All Saints College, University of Leeds, 18–20 September 2003.

P. Bagguley and Y. Hussain (2008) *Riotous Citizens: ethnic conflict in multicultural Britain* (Aldershot: Ashgate).

T. Cantle (2001) *Community Cohesion: a report of the independent review team*, Home Office, available online at www.homeoffice.gov.uk/comrace

M. Farrar (2003) 'Community, Social Capital and Identification in the Multi-ethnic Inner City: Reflections on the violent urban protest in the north of the UK in 2001', Paper delivered to the Communities Conference, Trinity and All Saints College, University of Leeds, 18–20 September 2003.

D. McGhee (2005) 'Patriots of the Future? A Critical Examination of Community Cohesion Strategies in Contemporary Britain', *Sociological Research Online* 10(3), available online at www.socresonline.org.uk/10/3/mcghee.html

P. Thomas (2011) *Youth, Multiculturalism and Community Cohesion*, New York: Palgrave Macmillan.

J. Young (2003) 'To these wet and windy shores: recent immigration policy in the UK', *Punishment & Society* 5(40): 449–62.

Malaysia

These are a few of the available sources which get under the surface of the ethnic tensions in Malaysia. Particularly useful are essays in Steve Fenton and Stephen May (eds) (2002) *Ethnonational identities* (Palgrave, London).

In addition, several articles are also revealing, including: D. K. Mauzy and R. S. Milne (2002) *Malaysian Politics Under Mahathir*; W. N. Wan Husin (IACSIT Press, Thailand, 2012) 'Cultural Clash between the Malays and Chinese in Malaysia: An Analysis on the Formation and Implementation of National Cultural Policy'; and K. K. Soong (2008) 'Racial conflict in Malaysia: against the official history New Era College', *Malaysia Race & Class* 49: 33–53.

Caribbean

Here are some suggestions for texts which examine Guyana and Trinidad's bipolar ethnic make-up and provide analyses of the conflicts that have colonial roots. Guyanese conflict was also aggravated by US and UK interventions in the country's politics in the 1960s.

P. Misir (2002) *The Social Construction Of Race-Ethnic Conflict in Guyana* (University of Guyana, Georgetown).

R. Myers and J. Calder (2006) 'Toward Ethnic Conflict Transformation: A Case Study of Citizen Peacebuilding Initiatives on the 2006 Guyana Elections', Occasional Paper in *Peace Building Series,* 4 November 2011 (Partners for Peace and Development, Guyana).

R. Premdas (1998) 'Identity in an Ethnically Bifurcated State: Trinidad and Tobago', in S. Fenton and S. May (2002), *Ethnonational Identities* (Palgrave, London).

W. Rodney (ed.) (1979) *Guyanese Sugar Plantations in the Late Nineteenth Century* (The Argosy, Georgetown, Guyana: Release Publishers).

S. Spencer (2007) *A Dream Deferred: Guyanese Identity & the Shadow of Colonialism* (Hansib, London).

I. D. Sukdeo (1982) *The Emergence of a Multiracial Society of Guyana* (Exposition Press, New York).

General

The discussion of biopower as a means of social control and of potentially ethnic cleansing or genocidal power over populations derives from the few pages Foucault wrote about the concept in *History of Sexuality* I, but also from the following:

M. Foucault (2002) *Society must be defended: Lectures at the College de France, 1975–76* (New York: Picador).

P. Rabinow and N. Rose (2006) 'Biopower Today', *BioSocieties* 1: 195–217 London School of Economics and Political Science, available online at http://imap. anthropos-lab.net/wp/publications/2007/01/rabinow-rose.pdf

S. Powell (2009) 'UN verdict on East Timor January 19, 2006', in Yale University, *Genocide Studies Program*, 2010, available online at www.yale.edu/gsp/east_timor/unverdict.html

Notes

1 Despite the global outcry over the slaughter by Pol Pot's Khmer Rouge, this would not have easily occurred without the carpet-bombing of Cambodia by the USA, which killed an estimated 2.5 million people (see Herman and Chomsky 1995). There are also claims that the USA covertly supported Pol Pot as the Prince Sihanouk regime did not want to become another US client state.

2 See Glossary.

CHAPTER 8

Living the Contradiction

Identity politics must be based not only on identity, but on an appreciation for politics as the art of living together.

(Phelan 1989: 170)

DIASPORA AND HYBRIDITY

BOX 8.1 BUXTON, GUYANA 1991

'Dis-en-chant-ment. Disen-chant-ment'. Louis dreamily segmented the word, savouring its nuances, speaking it like a spell into the gathering dusk of Buxton. Goats, chickens, assorted croaking, bleetings, yelps, late kiskadees, laced in the mellow lugubrious musak spilling from the rumshop; an over-drowsy saxophone waltzes from the horn of a drunken b-side busker. Two gangly Indian figures worked by the roadside husking coconuts and collecting for copra, exhausting endless work.

Louis's apparent worldly musings on the word seemed to embody a history of broken dreams, not especially his, but of the country itself – if not the world. Yet enchantment – the bonds of colonialism and empire – a misty nostalgia for the 'mother country' was alive and pulsing in his voice, in the faraway look he cast across cane fields, the polders. The spell still cast its magic deep in the folds and resonances of his voice.

(S. Spencer, field notes, 1991)

The above sketch from rural Guyana attempts to capture the poignant feeling of the colonial (post-colonial) subject for whom there may be many layered memories of the lost but dreamed-of communities, never seen but imagined and ingrained in family history, in tales of the brutality of slavery, and constantly remembered in the broken and dissolute condition of the towns and in the origins of the sugar cane: a sad and distant memory indelibly stamped with the trauma of removal and dispossession. Its populations have been removed from their cultural background, divested of traditions, prey to a sort of cultural forgetting. African-Guyanese people, like Louis in the above example, are the descendants of slaves, part of a *victim* diaspora.[1] The Indian-Guyanese, as in the example on pp. 212–13, make up what has been named *labour* diasporas; their forefathers arrived as part of the waves of indentured labour that replaced slavery. Both groups could also be considered part of a *hybrid* diaspora, as they are the result of creolised influences of colonialism.

Diaspora: the term which has come to be used for this post-colonial sense of dislocation has also come to convey the dream of a homeland, a shrine of the past where the flame of memory is kept alive for the migrant group. Yet the return to some idealised pre-colonial culture is perhaps more a symbol than an attainable reality. A number of religious and messianic cults embody this idealised culture: Rastafarianism and Kali Mai sects in the Caribbean have been influential for their promises of deliverance from the increasingly difficult reality of grinding poverty as international debts have bitten hard into the economies of the region. As conditions have deteriorated the growth of these forms of religion has been seen to increase (see Bassier 1987). 'Thus, colonised peoples cannot simply turn back to the idea of a collective pre-colonial culture, and a past "which is waiting to be found, and which when found, will secure our sense of ourselves into eternity"' (Hall 1994: 182).

Hall maintains that this aspect of diaspora is not a romantic naïveté that stubbornly holds fast to an imagined idealised past but rather a symbol of a new becoming:

> it is no mere phantasm either. It is something – not a mere trick of the imagination. It has its histories – and histories have their real, material and symbolic effects. The past continues to speak to us. But it no longer addresses us as a simple, factual 'past', since our relation to it, like the child's relation to the mother, is always-already 'after the break'.
>
> (Hall 1994: 183)

Grossberg suggests that 'diaspora emphasises the historically spatial fluidity of identity, its articulation to structures of historical movements (whether forced or chosen, necessary or desired)' (Grossberg 1996: 92). The 'diaspora space' is a critical concept created by the tensions of power between old and new identities, in which the parameters of inclusion, exclusion, 'otherness' and belonging are challenged. This may be a useful way of envisaging post-colonial relations, as it places both natives and migrants in the same conflicted and negotiated space: 'diaspora space as a conceptual category is "inhabited" not only by those who have migrated and their descendants but equally by those who are constructed and represented as indigenous' (Brah 1996: 181). This is a space that recognises the reciprocal effects for those established 'natives' as well as for migrant groups, hence it is a radical reconfiguration of the centre/periphery relationship implicit, as Soysal argues (2000), in the common use of 'diaspora', which reaffirms the centrality of the nation state with all its ethnocentrism and chauvinism. However, the 'diaspora space' developed by Brah subverts this meaning, for although migrants and established communities are not equal they are each recognised to be in flux, destabilised and hybrid.

In our pluralistic societies there are now several generations of migrant groups. This section looks at issues of belongingness, citizenship, sense of home and the forming of identities across boundaries. Colonialism displaced millions of people forcibly or for the promise of a better life, under indentureship, which in many cases was not far removed from slavery. This 'body snatching', as Sharrad (1993) has described it, has had a profound and continuous impact on the world. How do those children of many diasporas see themselves and their place in society? How easily are they accepted by the mainstream culture?

The concept of hybridity has come to be one of the cornerstones of post-colonial thought. In his essays Stuart Hall suggests that there is something significant developing within our multicultural diasporic communities. Posed next to the globalising forces that seem to be suturing together world cultures, creating more homogenous 'third cultures', there are equally powerful social processes that, quite to the contrary, seem to be unravelling these global certainties; unitary definitions of nation and identity are eroded away. Hall, Gilroy and Bhabha have all been proponents of a fluid, hybrid conception of ethnic identity, which insists that the notion of 'rooted' identities is a delusion. Instead, discussion centres around the celebration of more marginal, creolised, diasporic voices, which recognises 'the transgressive potential of cultural hybridity' (May *et al.* 2004: 132). In *Signs Taken For Wonders* Bhabha identifies post-colonial hybridities as a source for new subjectivities and as locations for alternative strategies of resistance to colonial power. He borrows from a number of lexicons expressing the subtle and elusive nature of hybridity, which is also the reason for its power:

> Hybridity is the sign of the productivity of colonial power, its shifting forces and fixities; it is the name for the strategic reversal of the process of domination through disavowal (that is, the production of discriminatory identities that secure the 'pure' and original identity of authority).
>
> (Bhabha 1985: 153–4)

The state of being in between cultures is a reality for migrants, as we have seen, but, by the same token, the flow of migrants has a reciprocal influence on the indigenous population in the diaspora space, where struggles and adaptations take place. In Britain the notorious 'rivers of blood' speech made by Enoch Powell in 1968 mobilised native fears of a lost (yet always hard to define) 'British way of life' and, as Gilroy (2004) suggests, provided the justification for many a pre-emptive strike, such as the one that took Stephen Lawrence's life in 1993. 'Racist violence provides an easy means to "purify" and rehomogenize the nation' (Gilroy 2004: 111). Challenges to the idea of hybridity come not just from the mainstream culture: for example, there have been strands of ethnic separatism operating in the midst of these pluralities and, as we have seen, there is resistance to mixing; 'mixed race' or hybrid identities are often seen as transgressive and at times are treated as a threat (perhaps a threat to the collective power of ethnic essentialism).

Despite much conjecture about a 'multicultural drift' in the UK, the insistence on the preservation of a nation state is certainly strong in recent western governments. Recent debates about the consequences of 9/11, global politics and the ensuing 'war against terror' in the west, and about identifications of members of the Muslim community in our inner cities, have yielded some interesting pictures of these dynamic and fluid identities.

In a number of articles and broadcasts the journalist Sarfraz Manzoor (2005) has examined the politics of identity among young British Asians. It seems that the events of 9/11 and the wave of recriminations that followed against Muslims as a visible minority has led to a resurgence in interest in Islam among Muslims, reaffirming their religious identity. However, as Manzoor notes, Asians generally are re-examining their identity as 'Asian' and drawing boundaries based on *their* religious identities. Indeed, all Asians have been prone to the effects of this indiscriminate halo of alterity which seemed to mark anyone Asian out as a potential terrorist. Manzoor reminds us that the first victims of indiscriminate violence following 9/11 were not Muslims but Sikhs, their very particular visibility marking them out.

September 11 changed the type and nature of racial abuse – instead of 'Paki' the new term of abuse became 'Bin Laden' and 'al-Qaida', and the abuse was motivated not by race, but by religion. Hindus and Sikhs, frustrated at being mistaken for Muslims, resolved to assert their own religious identity. In doing so they were sending a message to the rest of the country: we had nothing to do with terrorism and riots – that's the work of those troublemaking Muslims.

(Manzoor 2005: 2)

There seems to be a trend for some Asians to emphasise their religious identities in reaction to the stigmatised identity of Islam, which they had experienced as a spoiled identity. Merely looking Asian could inspire racist abuse. This is not a sudden change, however, as many Asians have been critical of this homogenised cultural branding for years. It was enough to bring down the ire of one of Britain's respected black spokesmen, Darcus Howe, who saw this as another fragmentation of lost essentialist identity and even as undermining Britain's secular society. The remnants of the old Left – among which Darcus is clearly proud to be counted – find identity politics (whether to hyphenate or not) ideologically unpalatable. Howe commented in the *New Statesman*:

> And what of the vast number of young Asians who are Sikhs, Hindus, Muslims only in name and do not wish to be saddled with a religious label? [...] Manzoor is going down a rocky road. Those of us who came from former colonies to the UK first defined ourselves as 'black', presenting a united front as we entered the struggle against racism. Margaret Thatcher led the demonisation of our communities; she claimed that we had swamped this country with an alien culture. The pace of the struggle quickened, and successful Indians and Pakistanis demanded to be known as 'brown'. They were saying to our detractors that they were closer to white people than to us darkies and therefore merited better treatment.
>
> (Howe 2005: 1)

Howe is well known for courting controversy, and his hyperbole is probably only slightly tongue-in-cheek. Certainly, the strategic value of the term 'black' was recognised by a spectrum of Asians and 'others'. In the US even Koreans and Cypriots have been known to align themselves strategically in this way. It seems clear that the reasons why people identify with religion or with more secular descriptors or politically motivated standpoints can be many and various. Certainly some identities become stigmatised and the reality is that to be a Muslim in Britain today is to be treated as an embodiment of a tradition characterised as fundamentalist and anti-western. The suggestion that religion divides more than common ethnicity unites may be regarded as politically unsound by some, but it may be an inevitable consequence of a divisive 'war on terror' when religion is projected onto the global arena.

Hybridity, as a theoretical concept, also receives criticism from many directions. It is accused of presupposing 'the prior existence of pure, fixed separate antecedents as with the race theorists in the Nineteenth Century' (Young 1995: 25). Young's critique (1995) suggests that the new cultural theory of hybridity implicitly legitimates race thinking. Others, such as Stephen May, suggest that advocating hybridity encourages the view 'that all group-based identities are essentialist', and, further, that while the world is increasingly fragmented into fractured identities these identities are generally *not* hybrid – just the opposite, in fact (May 2004: 133). Mercer argued that the 'subversive potential once invested in notions of hybridity has been subjected to pre-millennial downsizing. Indeed hybridity has spun through the fashion cycle so rapidly that it has come out the other end looking wet and soggy' (Mercer 2000: 510). Meanwhile, Modood comments that the reaction against essentialism can lead to excesses in the other direction that are 'inherently destructive' because, 'Reconciled to multiplicity as an end in itself, its vision of multiculturalism is confined to personal lifestyles and cosmopolitan consumerism and does not extend to the state, which it confidently expects to wither away' (Modood 2000: 178). Valdaverde (1995) commented in a book review that Gilroy and other hybridity writers' discussions of hybridity tend to be weakened by a 'romanticism of the in-between that is perhaps more politically palatable but no more theoretically sound than the romanticism of identity politics'. And again May (2000: 134) argues that 'hybridity fails to address adequately the social and political continuities and transformations that underpin individual and collective action in the real world.' Indeed, in the real world, Ahmad (1995: 14) suggests that political agency is historically anchored to time, place and a sense of 'stable commitment to one's class or gender or nation'.

These theorists draw up a reality checklist, warning against self-congratulatory discourses of hybridity which, carried away by a sort of anti-essentialist euphoria, seem to float away from the realities of everyday material existence in multicultural societies. However, as Les Back reminds us, at some level hybridity *is* a fact. By using the term 'the fact of hybridity', he is insisting that hybridity is not a mere intellectual construct but reflects the truth that human lives are inseparably intertwined, that there are overlapping histories that make the total separation of the self an impossibility (Back 2000: 450). The following conversations present some of the real-life experiences of living 'between cultures', not as a romanticised concept but as a challenging and at times painful negotiation between attitudes and values that are resistant to merging.

BOX 8.2 BRITISH-BORN CHINESE

The experience of hybridity, as we have explained it, relates to the sense of dislocation. This sense of being in between cultures is a complex one and, as can be seen, relates also to generational, gender and class differences. Mark Quah's interview demonstrates the manner in which individuals attempt to navigate their place in the culture, drawing on some concepts that they feel reflect their developing identity and dis-identification with others who may seem to want to trap them in stereotypical roles.

BOX 8.2 BRITISH-BORN CHINESE (CONTINUED)

British-born Chinese, border crossings
Interviews by Mark Quah

This case study is based upon interviews with British-born Chinese people. It brings attention to the tenacity necessary to negotiate cultural boundaries and the confusion that ensues when boundaries are regarded as closed or impassable. The interviews were conducted with the aim of uncovering shared experiences among second-generation British-born Chinese that had, up to this point, often been hidden from view even among and between British Chinese people themselves.

Win lives in Sheffield. He is twenty years old and a full-time student, and also works part-time in his parents' takeaway. He attends Chinese school, where he learns how to speak, read and write Cantonese.

MARK: Do you think it's a positive thing, having a British perspective and a Chinese perspective? Or do you find it confusing?

WIN: Probably confusing at times, because you don't know where you fit in, it's difficult. You need to find an answer for yourself I think, where do you think you belong? Which is right for you, and if you think that's right you're just gonna go for it … Like where do you belong? where's your identity? Is it disappeared? It's like disappearing in the western world isn't it? The more you think about it … It's like the next generation and the next generation … and get worse … like Americans they've lost it. Like whenever I go on holiday it's like, or any British-born Chinese, the first thing they want to do is eat British food, isn't it? Not Chinese food, so where's the first place they look? … McDonald's, and they want to eat it every day. like my brother, he just eats McDonald's, McDonald's, McDonald's when he could eat something else, but he doesn't want to 'cos he wouldn't know it … his taste is all British.

WILL: If you're in a Chinese community, you just naturally go into a sort of Chinese community state, a Chinese state, when you're with English people in English society you just act more English type. So it's not really I can do this in a Chinese community and then I can change over to that in an English community, it just comes naturally to you.

At the time of this interview Eve was twenty years old and a full-time student. As she described it, there was a sizeable Chinese community in the places where she grew up.

EVE: I'm very much part of this British society but also I very strongly identify with being Chinese and more specifically with Hong Kong ... you feel like you don't properly belong, like you belong to either set British or Chinese, but they don't see you as part of them so ...

MARK: Win, what's life at home? Did your parents stress to you you're Chinese? Act this way ... or you're Chinese you shouldn't act that way?

WIN: At home like your parents try to bring you into Chinese but if you don't want to learn they can't make you, basically it's for yourself to sort of like judge if you want to learn, like. When you're like brought up accustomed to all these things isn't it? You're brought up to like, say dating they prefer you to marry your own race isn't it?

MARK: yeah, my mum says that ...

WIN: ... whereas if you don't they'll be disappointed but when you have kids like they'll probably forgive you innit?

MARK: Yeah.

WIN: In Hong Kong you get called banana boy! *laughs*

MARK: One thing with me is one girl from Hong Kong, she was speaking to me and she's speaking English with a Chinese accent, and fair enough it's not her first language, I don't take the piss ...

WIN: ... yeah we don't take the piss ...

MARK: ... and I say a few words in Cantonese to her, she laughs, yeah.

WIN: That's ... the way it is.

MARK: Sometimes that makes me feel like giving up why should I make an effort if ...?

WIN: You can laugh at them, if you want ...

MARK: It's not me though ...

WIN: 'Very good!' *Chinese accent* 'Very good!' ... We don't really do that though, we're less likely to take the piss out of them ...

MARK: There's something strange, here we get taken the piss by the English guys and Chinese but we don't take the piss out of either, yeah ...

WIN: Both of them think they're better than us ...

MARK: Did your parents say to you be proud to be Chinese?

WIN: Yeah, they say it's good to be Chinese – I think it's good to be Chinese but there's some, I know some, Chinese people that reject ... they don't like being Chinese and stuff like that, which is weird if you're brought up that way.

MARK: What does being Chinese mean to you?

WIN: Everything, basically, life, the way I study, the way I talk, characteristics, everything – so I'm proud to be Chinese.

Mark and his respondents have a strong, if conflicted, sense of identity and are conscious of navigating between cultures. The middle ground is hard to find, as it is constantly clawed back by each culture. In Hong Kong terms such as 'banana boy' may be used by some who are grounded in the home culture to suggest that the hybrid individual has a veneer, an outward appearance, of 'Chineseness' which, if scrutinised, will reveal a white English core. However, the social mores that the Hong Kong Chinese person aspires to may, it is suggested, be those very white European attributes and cultural knowledges that the above respondents cannot disguise.

The next interview further strengthens this assessment of hybrid identity. Stuart is a British-born Chinese in his twenties. Articulating a strong sense of his Chinese identity, which endures despite his Englishness, Stuart recognises identity as almost physically ascribed, similar to the way in which Mauss talks of the habitus as internalised dispositions or bodily orientations (Mauss 1979). He also notes the automatic nature of racisms that employ well-worn stereotypes and assumptions about Chinese people.

BOX 8.3 BETWEEN TWO CULTURES

SS: First, could you tell us a little about yourself, Stuart?

STUART: OK, I was born in England in Leicester, spent most of my life in the UK, went over to Hong Kong when I was about seven for a year so I adapted to the culture then, but most of my life I've been in the UK. But I feel that – even though I've only lived in Hong Kong for a year, in my heart I still feel Chinese. Even though my behaviour is very English – I still feel inside my heart I'm very Chinese. I have friends in Hong Kong who are totally Chinese, when they come to England they want to be English – even though their experience of life is Chinese – they want to be English, whereas me I'm opposite: I'm totally English behaviour and in my heart it's very Chinese.

SS: That's interesting, then, that there are these different aspirations that people from Hong Kong have got, the English side of it – they've got the colonial thing – and you've been over here …

STUART: … yeah I'm the opposite …

SS: … you're looking over that way …

STUART: … but I strongly believe that this is me, I'm one individual, everyone's different – OK, my experiences have brought me the person I am, yeah, even though I was born in Hong Kong or China I would be the same, but even so my environment would have shaped me to a degree to the person I am – my inner self – I still believe would have been the same but different like, maybe slight differences outside in what I perceive, but inside my heart I still believe I'd be a Chinese human being.

SS: Have your parents had a big influence on the fact, do you think? I mean do they keep the cultural traditions going quite strongly?

STUART: I personally think that Chinese as a whole whether you're born in the UK, America, Hong Kong, China, the values, morals are very deep rooted, it's passed on from generation to generation. That's the bottom line, the bottom line, the basis for Chinese humanity, the bottom values and like, the cornerstone to build it on. So whether you're born in UK, Hong Kong, China, you still have this deep-rooted tradition, culture which is embedded. It's hard to like to disassemble, it's deep rooted. *Makes building motions with his hands, simulating bricks and mortar.*

SS: Yeah ... so presumably you've learnt some of the languages which embody the culture as well. I mean having to learn that – I mean that embodies all of the cultural traditions presumably?

STUART: It's true what you say because like in psychology, I can't remember who it is now – they say the language itself will shape the personality. We have words like rice that is cooked and uncooked, you only have rice (you don't know if it's cooked or uncooked). Your mum's brother or your dad's brother there's different words for it you just say 'uncle', what can it be? So we have more different sorts of words that can add to the meanings and that – icy, rainy, cold – we have different words and that – so obviously that's going to affect your vocabulary and your knowledge of how you say things in life. But that's just a part of it – I think mostly it's to do with the individual, yourself, you as a person. ... It's like with me my experiences in the UK people say that there's no racism. Then in the end I believe I'm Chinese, whether I'm black or white, I believe that we're human beings and we live in this world and you cannot possibly as a human being put yourself above another human being – not everyone is like that, some people are more narrow-minded, some are like, I don't know, disturbed in the head, I don't know, but some people are like that. In this world we are seen as one thing – we can't just get on with one another – people just resent you – jealousy, envy, I don't know, it's just human nature to be like that, irrespective of your colour. So in my upbringing – I went to school in England – but lucky for me I had brothers and they all just assume that because your brothers do kung fu that you do kung fu. It's like a stereotypical thing about Chinese ...

BOX 8.3 BETWEEN TWO CULTURES (CONTINUED)

SS: ... What? The kung fu?

STUART: Yeah, it's always the case, always the case ...

SS: Do you ever feel that you're stuck in between two cultures?

STUART: Yeah yeah – because people always assume black white, black white, but it's not. The way I look at it is black, green, non white and white, ethnic minorities and white. On the exterior say it's cosmopolitan, equal opportunities but in the heart, deep rooted, there's still that resentment, that hatred for colours, that's the bottom line. OK ... First, I see myself as a human being then I see myself as an Oriental, Far East, not an Asian, Far East – Oriental, Middle East is like Arabs and that. Then I see myself as an ethnic minority. So I see myself as a human being, Chinese, oriental, ethnic minority, then coloured, non-white. So when I see an Oriental with a white European, an Asian, a black African, I don't give a shit, if they're happy they're happy.

(Recorded 16 February 2005)

Stuart's identification with a primordial sense of Chineseness comes through strongly as a foundation that is structured in the language but arguably, as Stuart says, goes further, suggesting an embodied sense of being Chinese. Equally, the interview communicated Stuart's frustration at the stereotypical categories, the colour codes and ethnic straitjackets which people are prone to impose on one another.

Many migrants are only short-term: they travel for work or education and return after a period of months or years to their countries. However, this temporary immersion in a culture so different may, at times, bring about transformations. Inhabiting the 'diaspora space' may enable unique perspectives and comparisons for both the visitors and the people they associate with. This is certainly the case in the next interview, in which a Mexican subject, Diego, who was a research student in the UK, developed, after several years, a critical detachment. There are several points of comparison made throughout the exchange and Diego was able to recognise flaws with his country (as well as with the UK) despite an obvious pride and a deep-seated sense of the country as a moulding influence. Diego expresses the sense that ethnic identity is not an issue in his community owing to its relatively homogenous composition (at least superficially). However, the issue of the Chiapas uprising has allowed many Mexicans such as Diego to consider a side of themselves that Diego suggests is typically denied.

BOX 8.4 CONTRASTING NORMS BETWEEN THE UK AND MEXICO

SS: You will soon be back in Mexico – and I was wondering what contrasts you expect to notice having lived here in the UK for several years?

DIEGO: When I arrived here, if there is a health problem and you have to go to the doctor, here in the UK you have to wait because there is a queue and you have to respect this, and you cannot make use of other people – we call this 'traffic of influence' when you make use of other people in order to take advantage of this. And for me this represents a big impact – because in Mexico it's very common that you should have something like a file and each record in the file represents a contact, maybe I should say 'traffic of contacts', I'm not sure, a contact for medical problems, for example, and a contact for education problems, a contact for administrative problems, a contact for tax problems ... a contact for everything.

SS: Right, so people in influence who can help you out ...

DIEGO: Right and that doesn't exist here, and now when I go back – I hate that – I prefer to go to the tail of the queue – I just want the same treatment or the same deal as everyone else. So this was a big impact for me ... [*laughs*] My Mexican friends disagree with me, they think this is not the real situation. At the end I do not fit in my country – in the Mexican culture – of course I love my country, but I hate corruption, I hate all of those things so ...

SS: You suggested there is a language of this corruption, you call it *la transa*?

DIEGO: Yes, of course, *la transa* is part of our lifestyle – it's part of us. I'm sure if you were able to remove this habit of our culture, I'm sure that we'd be a very different culture – I think we should speak like English, German, American, Gringos. For example you can go to an academic meeting, a conference, you can ask many many questions and there isn't any problem if you disagree with the guy. In Mexico it's a bit different. If you express your disagreement there is a problem – my impression is that we are very sensitive persons.

SS: So things are taken personally?

DIEGO: Yes, yes we take things personally.

SS: Just talking about identity again, Mexico has quite interesting different layers of ethnic identity. What's your impression of how that operates in everyday life – is it a big factor – the ethnic identity of people?

DIEGO: In this aspect it's very difficult for me to give an opinion to you. I live in the northern part of the country, and I think you can perceive

BOX 8.4 CONTRASTING NORMS BETWEEN THE UK AND MEXICO (CONTINUED)

this in the capital and the south of the country because in the capital and the south it is very common that you can see these groups, but not in the north.

SS: Do you think the history of people all over Mexico is really the history of these different mixtures of groups in the country? I'm just wondering what impact that has on personal identity and how people look at themselves?

DIEGO: At the end we all know that we are a mixture of indigenous and Spanish people, but my perception is that we are racist persons. There is a racism, my perception is that we don't want to recognise that there is indigenous in each Mexican – that's my perception. Maybe the origin, part of the problem in Chiapas. The conditions in which indigenous people live in Chiapas was very, very poor, ten years ago with Zapatism.

SS: Do you think the Zapatista movement actually had an impact on the average Mexican's feelings about these things?

DIEGO: Yes, yes, I think that the problem's still there. The current President claimed in his campaign that he would be able to solve the problem in just five minutes, and in four years he hasn't solved anything. But yes I think it's not the same Mexico as before and after Zapatism – even when many people don't agree with the movement. I think it's not the same. At least we are conscious about the problem that indigenous people have, but before we ignored all these things.

(Recorded June 2004)

This interview implies that Mexicans tended to deny their own indigenous heritage, and the treatment of the indigenous population has long been harsh and unjust. The indigenous groups in the border region of Chiapas live in appalling conditions with few rights over the land, although some communities exercise considerable local control over economic and social issues. They continue to remain largely outside the country's political and economic mainstream and, in many cases, they have minimal participation in decisions affecting their land, their cultural traditions and the allocation of natural resources. The powerless and impoverished indigenous people of the Chiapas region became a national focus during their resistance in the early 1990s, which captured global attention. An armed uprising in 1994 (by the Zapatista Army of National Liberation (EZLN)) linked up issues of indigenous rights in the Chiapas region with demands for democratisation in Mexico and a global struggle against neo-liberalism. The capture of four towns in the Chiapas region by the EZLN held world attention, as an unlikely challenge to the hegemony of global marketing. The uprising was timed symbolically to the day the North American Free Trade Agreement (NAFTA) came into effect (1 January 1994).

The impact of the agreement was perceived as a death sentence to indigenous cultures as in order for Mexico to receive loans from the World Bank it had to conform to Structural Adjustment Programs which insisted on the break-up and privatisation of all land. This had severe consequences for the poorest indigenous farmers who survived on land which had been used collectively (*ejidos*).

It is hardly surprising that Emiliano Zapata (a leading figure in the 1910 Mexican Revolution) is still a potent symbol for the disenfranchised peasantry in Mexico. Zapata's call for 'Tierra y Libertad' (land and freedom) as well as his partly indigenous roots, would have resonated strongly with the movement. The Zapatistas became a focus for cultural renewal and identification with the origins of Mexican society. This illustrates how aspects of a country's shared traditions can revitalise ethnic identification and can become the focus for a deep re-examination of the hybrid nature of the country, a truth that has been denied and an identity which has been derided as 'primitive'. The image of Zapata is a deeply pervasive one in Mexican culture; in Mexico City it forms a station sign for the underground train and is present in the murals by Diego Rivera at the Presidential Palace in the Zocalo (see Figure 8.1). It was in this vast central square that the Zapatistas' historic march from Chiapas culminated:

Figure 8.1 Zapata sign for underground station in Mexico City

On 13 March 2001 the Zapatista column came to Mexico City. It was the culmination of an extraordinary three-week march through Mexico, accompanied by tens of thousands on its way. The delegation attended the Indigenous People's Conference before moving on to the capital, where it was met by a huge crowd in Mexico City's main square – the Zócalo. The British media contemptuously described the crowd as 'several thousands strong' – but anyone who has ever stood in that vast colonial square knows that 'several thousands' would barely occupy one corner. There were hundreds of thousands there.

(Gonzalez 2001: 1)

Indeed, estimates of 300,000 or more have been given. This was undoubtedly an event of enormous symbolic importance, even if the conditions in Chiapas have changed little apart from a small measure of autonomy and accommodation from the government, including the removal of some of the troops from the region. As Mike Gonzalez (2001) suggests, this event was extraordinary in enabling the 'representativity' of indigenous peoples on a global platform because of the advocacy of Sub-Commandante Marcos.

There was no doubt that this was a historic victory for Mexico's indigenous people. But it had other consequences and implications. The Zapatistas, above all through the prolific writing of Subcomandante Marcos, claimed a representativity – a right to speak for a movement of many struggles united against globalisation and its impact. This is the central reason why the Zapatistas have come to symbolise the anti-capitalist movement worldwide. Yet the negotiations behind the accords, and the agreements themselves, narrowed and limited the nature of the Zapatistas' demands. Slowly, imperceptibly, and with the collusion of many of their external supporters, the Zapatistas were redefined as a movement exclusively concerned with indigenous rights.

(Gonzalez 2001: 2)

The plight of indigenous people in Mexico may not have changed in any substantial way as a result, but it could be suggested (as the interview with Diego affirmed) that there is now a new popular perception of the plight of native Indians and a way of broaching the question about a facet of most Mexicans' hybrid identity that was always denied before the Zapatistas. This was a movement that captured popular imagination and reinvoked images from Mexico's revolutionary foundations.

More recently there have been further disruptions to the collective psyche of Mexicans. A book by Marco Polo Hernández Cuevas (2004) suggests that Mexico may have a strong African heritage, as an estimated 300,000 African slaves were brought to Mexico during the colonial era. The suggestion made by Hernández

Cuevas is that this large number was absorbed into the population and that some prominent national leaders during Mexico's revolution were black. However, it seems that there has been a policy to systematically erase African heritage (as well as indigenous antecedents) from national memory. Hernández Cuevas recognises the importance of reclaiming lost histories in forging identity and links this shared heritage to peoples throughout the Americas: 'Mexicans, Hispanics, Latinos and African Americans will recognize one another in our common African heritage and bridge the gap that divides us' (ibid.: 2). Someone who so effectively portrayed Mexico's rich culturally mixed heritage without recourse to 'whitening' the makers of Mexican history was Diego Rivera, who painted the extraordinary series of murals depicting Mexico's turbulent history that surround the walls of the National Palace in Mexico City.

The struggle for 'Tierra y Libertad' was reignited by the Zapatistas in 1994. This time the enemy was the global forces of capitalism (see Figure 8.2) and the struggle became an exciting rallying point for Left politics worldwide. However, slightly removed from some of the leftist rhetoric, but equally significant, is the emergent identity of a post-colonial society still in the shadow of a European self-image – a self-image that is apparently beginning to unravel.

Figure 8.2 Beginning the struggle: Zapatistas in San Cristobal de Las Casas, 1991

The way that national identity is forged, as we have seen, often involves attempts to disguise or revise significant historical occurrences and to excise aspects of colonial history that seem to reflect badly on the proud image of nationhood. However, the past thirty years have seen increasing awareness of the multi-ethnic, plural nature of cities in many western countries. There is a new confidence and a more mature expression of diversity than before, but how pluralism should be managed is an issue for considerable discussion and disagreement. Furthermore, much of the debate around multiculturalism in Europe is set against an increasingly open racism based around anti-Muslim sentiments. In France the meteoric rise of far right politicians Jean-Marie Le Pen, and his daughter Marine Le Pen demonstrate a worrying growth of intolerance which is prevalent across several countries in Europe.

MULTICULTURALISM

In the 1980s the discourse of multiculturalism was being consecrated and enshrined in policy in several western countries. In Australia a new ministry, Immigration and Ethnic Affairs, was instituting educational and other policies at the local level, and significant amounts of research and academic concern with the new ethos made it a very public and highly respected approach. In the UK, which was in the grip of Thatcher's radical Right, Labour councils were sites for research into pluralism in ethnicity, gender, sexualities, age, disability and combinations of these. The rate-capping of these outposts eventually curtailed some very interesting research.

The discourse of multiculturalism attained respectability as it was seen as progressive and a positive break from the ugliness of nationalism. In Australia, where a White Australia Policy had been in place up to the 1970s, multiculturalism seemed to be an antidote to the essentialist views that tarnished Australia's image. But today multiculturalism is frequently seen as more problematic and as a less positive force.

History and the conception of the multicultural state

The trajectories of Britain, France, the USA and Australia are broadly comparable since the 1960s. All have largely abandoned their policies of 'out-and-out assimilation' (Grillo 1998: 168) and now embrace more pluralistic solutions described variously as 'integration', 'insertion' or 'multiculturalism' (ibid.). This movement in Britain was partly a response to the degree of jingoism and patriotic fervour noted in political discourse during the 1980s, including the Conservative government's rhetoric over the Falklands War and the output of the tabloid press, especially when commenting on the European Union. As Grillo suggests, 'Britain seemed an increasingly ugly, nationalistically minded society. The lager-swilling young men rampaging through the cities of Europe dressed in Union Jack shorts and T-shirts may have been untypical, but they offered a compelling, and repellent, vision of the new Britain' (ibid.).

What is multiculturalism?

Fleras defines 'multiculturalism' as 'a set of principles, policies, and practices for accommodating diversity as a legitimate and integral component of society' (Fleras 1994: 26). The way these policies come about and how they are manifest varies considerably, depending on national context. For Canada, the USA and the UK, the term is implicitly linked with questions of racialised differences. In Canada and Australia official policies have been launched (Australia in 1978–9 and Canada in 1988), while in the UK there has simply been an unofficial 'multicultural drift' (Hall 2000). In Australia and elsewhere, as Gunew comments:

> While there have always been migrations and disaporas, after two world wars and many other conflicts this century the mix of people within borders increasingly rendered traditional national models anachronistic. Multiculturalism has been developed as a concept by nations and other aspirants to geo-political cohesiveness who are trying to represent themselves as homogeneous in spite of their heterogeneity.
>
> (Gunew 1999: 1)

Further, Gunew correctly notes that the concept, as a result, is considered a revisionist one that implies

> an identity politics based on essentialism and claims for authenticity which automatically reinstate a version of the sovereign subject and a concern with reified notions of origins. Thus it becomes impossible, it seems, to mention multiculturalism and socially progressive critical theory in the same breath.
>
> (Gunew 1999: 1)

Hall suggests that multiculturalism functions in a similar way to diaspora – as a means of reifying and fixing cultural distinctions and of drawing hard-edged boundaries to demarcate ethnicity. Hence, an ostensibly well-meaning approach to diversity may create similar divisions to one that is founded on racist principles: 'this is what my friend Farand Maharaj has called sometimes "a spook look-alike apartheid logic": apartheid coming back to meet you from the "other" side' (Hall 2000).

It is important to recognise that the ideal and intent of multiculturalism may be confused with experiences in everyday life. Racism still exists in spite of multiculturalism, and ethnic inequalities in income and political participation have not been removed. There is still very unequal treatment of some minorities in education, employment and the justice system. While these are legitimate complaints, however, multiculturalism is not responsible for racism. Malik has argued that discourses of diversity and difference have tended to lead to segregation rather than to more robust anti-racist strategies confronting examples of racism within a mixed community. Racism is able to flourish within the divided communities, cloaked in a politically correct gloss. Separation occurs both spatially (cities such as Bradford have become as segregated as ghettoised areas in the USA) and mentally, creating not cooperative communal structures but stark internal as well as external divisions. However, to blame such divisions on multiculturalism would be mystifying for people who live there and may have very little sense of being part of a multicultural diverse community. Indeed, it could just as well be argued that there is not *enough* multiculturalism.

Promise and reality: life in a multicultural society

The gradual movement of multiculturalism, which has been fomented by the struggle and strife of nearly 50 years of migration, is not a formally constructed policy like those launched in other nations, but what Stuart Hall calls:

> *multicultural drift*, that is to say the unplanned, increasing involvement of Britain's black and brown populations visibly registering a play of difference right across the face of British society. However, this creeping multiculturalism remains deeply uneven. Large areas of the country, most significant centres of power, substantial areas of racially differentiated disadvantage, are largely untouched by it. Outside its radius racialised exclusion compounded by household poverty, unemployment and educational underachievement persist, indeed multiply.
>
> (Hall 2000: 1–2)

In America, as well as in Australia and Europe, there are sporadic concerns over the effects of migrant populations on national identity, security and economy. In the last thirty years the Hispanic population has grown dramatically – from 14.6 million in 1980, to nearly 53 million as of 2012 (United States Census Bureau 2013). Popular concerns about these changing demographics are often expressed in terms of the groups' separatism and refusal to properly assimilate 'American values'. In Australia the very hard-line stance taken against immigration has threatened the country's reputation as a land of the 'fair go'. There has been little change from the harsh treatment of 'asylum seekers' reported by John Pilger in 2002:

Those Iraqis and Afghans who have succeeded in reaching Australia receive treatment which, for a society proclaiming humanist values, beggars belief. Many are imprisoned behind razor wire in some of the most hostile terrain on earth, deliberately isolated from population centres in 'detention centres' run by an American company specialising in top-security prisons. In their desperation, the refugees, many of them unaccompanied children, have resorted to suicide, starvation, arson and mass escapes.

(Pilger 2002: 2)

Successive governments have maintained this approach to refugees, fuelled increasingly by the rhetoric of the 'war on terror', which seems to suggest there is such a thing as 'illegal immigrants' or 'bogus asylum seekers'. In more enlightened times such terms might seem corrosive of basic humanitarian principles.

However, despite the rhetorical shifts and the bad faith in former notions of equality, which have been distorting aspects of the 'multicultural brand', multiculturalism is a concept that is evolving and that requires a more mature response to the embedded diversity that characterises our cities (see Figure 8.3). As Lord Parekh stated:

Multiculturalism basically means that no culture is perfect or represents the best life and that it can therefore benefit from a critical dialogue with other cultures. In this sense multiculturalism requires that all cultures should be open, self-critical, and interactive in their relations with each other.

(BBC News 2004b: 1–2)

This positive affirmation of diversity is one parallel strand of the rhetoric about multiculturalism. The CRE poster shown in Figure 8.3 demonstrates the sense of difference as an enrichment to be valued.

However, over ten years on, the debate about multiculturalism needs more careful scrutiny. Understanding the shifts in this 'empty signifier' indicates the trends in thinking about difference in popular consciousness. What follows here is a discussion of some of the implications of multiculturalism and the ways that it is being defined and redefined against a backdrop of social and political change. The clear and progressive values which constituted a healthy basis for understanding the inclusion of many different groups in a society, providing an antidote to insularity and xenophobia, seem to have been muddied, perhaps because the term has become heavily overused, rendered mere rhetoric by commentators on every side of the political debates which flare around the very different experiences of diversity. It has been unfairly linked to extremism and terrorism as well as, at times, evoked as an eternal expression of diversity in all its forms. This restless shuttle of political expediency is evident in David Cameron's speech at the 47th Munich Security Conference in 2011, where he argued that:

Figure 8.3 Celebrating diversity: Commission for Racial Equality poster, 2004

we have allowed the weakening of our collective identity. Under the doctrine of state multiculturalism, we have encouraged different cultures to live separate lives, apart from each other and apart from the mainstream. We've failed to provide a vision of society to which they feel they want to belong. We've even tolerated these segregated communities behaving in ways that run completely counter to our values.

(UK Government 2011: 3–4)

However, it is arguable whether there has ever been a 'doctrine of state multiculturalism' and the concept may be over-stressed by its rhetorical everyday use. Indeed, conversely, it can be argued that recognising diversity in this way has led to real gains that are still being made. The essence of multiculturalism lives on; it permits a critical dialogue about serious issues which affect society, such as expressions of cultural identity, the experience of diaspora, cultural adaptation and an increasing recognition of human rights as ideals to work towards.

The equation of multiculturalism by both ends of the political spectrum with a superficial celebration of diversity (the 'samosas, steel drums and saris' discourse: see, for example, Gorman 1996; Alibhai Brown 2000) that actually encourages a fragmentation based on competitive claims for difference to be recognised rather than an equality agenda belies the increasing integration of many groups. Indeed, it may represent, rather, the last gasp of exhausted notions of Britishness. Integration is a less visible dialectical process and one which has been operating in many parts of the world for a very long time.

Les Back makes a case for multiculture as a lived reality, rejecting the idea of multiculturalism as a mosaic or a beehive, where society has impermeable cell-like ethnic enclaves with little cultural cross-over, and instead suggesting a much more nuanced process of transformation:

in my mind, multiculture – which is a term I prefer – really describes the diversity of traces that we all carry, whether we know it or not, whether our skins are pale or whether they are black or brown. Because the experience of modernity, even European modernity, is an experience of multiculture; of collision, sometimes terrible, sometimes brutal, between people around the world. And sometimes that connection has been about exploitation and sometimes it's about struggles against those exploitations. So in a sense I don't think we can understand contemporary forms of life in Britain (or anywhere else for that matter) without understanding the traces of the past in the present and the far in the near.

(Interview with Les Back, Roehampton University, 15 July 2006)

Back's conception of multiculture as the ever-widening ripples from those profound colonial impacts permeating our everyday lives has an intuitive validity but is much more difficult to represent. These are processes which are not part of the spectacle that holds attention and sells newspapers. Back reminds us that culture is replete with diverse cultural influences that may be too quickly forgotten when there is a constant political and media rhetoric that seems intent on narrowing our focus and reasserting an ahistorical conception of 'Britishness'. Multiculturalism can quickly be demonised as associated with Muslim extremists, 'bogus asylum seekers' and conflicts in inner cities that are repeatedly cited as a result of years of multiculturalism that has led to 'parallel societies' and segregation. In Chapter 7 it was seen how the flashpoints of ethnic conflicts in Britain were dubbed 'race riots' and rather than examining the economic deprivation, heavy-handed policing and active provocations by extreme right-wing groups in the areas in which they occurred, multiculturalism was once again portrayed as a malign ethos which had somehow infected the minds of those who took part.

How multiculturalism stole Christmas!

The debate about loss of British identity and fears of extremism have been described by some as consequences of the relativism implicit in multiculturalism (see, for example, Malik 2005). Persistent voices in the media have been quick to deride multiculturalism as weak-willed liberal thinking. In 2007 Trevor Phillips was at the forefront of this debate, first as head of the CRE, where he helped to champion a policy of 'community cohesion' that sought to redress the perceived divisiveness of multiculturalism, and latterly as the head of the Equality and Human Rights Commission. In his new role he recently suggested that nativity plays ought to be compulsory at all British schools and that:

> Schools which are deliberately shying away from the true story of Christmas are just plain wrong. What they should do is make sure that all of their children have access to this very important fundamental, national celebration and tradi-tion. Otherwise they're robbing their children of really being part of what it is to be British.
>
> (BBC Radio 4, *Today*, podcast 10 December 2007)

What Phillips says here must be put in context. Earlier he had railed against the popular press spreading disinformation about ethnic 'others' as embittered aliens determined to undermine heartfelt British traditions. But he also, as shown above, reinforced anxieties by suggesting that schools which choose not to perform nativ-ity plays are 'robbing' children of an essential part of Britishness. At other times he has highlighted other imaginary facets of Britishness including Shakespeare and cricket. Certainly, the British media has been very economical with the truth; Muslims are routinely portrayed as threatening the precious institutions of Britishness. Roy Greenslade exposed a number of spurious headlines: 'Hogwash:

Now the PC brigade bans piggy banks in case they upset Muslims (no they didn't); Christmas is banned: it offends Muslims (no it wasn't); Now Christ is banned (no he wasn't)' (Greenslade 2011).

Phillips is correct about the manner in which certain media sources decry the loss of national culture, frequently arguing that this stems from an assault by zealous, politically correct pedants who insist that plural traditions must be imposed in the interests of multiculturalism. However, it seems likely that Phillips overestimates the actual interest that indigenous Britons have in nativity plays, and his comments could be seen as merely fuelling the cultural angst. It is another case of what Žižek has called 'theft of enjoyment'. Žižek (1990: 53) equates national movements and 'causes' with the manner in which ethnic groups 'organise their enjoyment through national myths' and presents the notion of the 'other' as constantly impinging on our senses because of their perceived lack of restraint in the practice of their pleasures. By saying 'if only it wasn't for them life would be perfect and harmonious again', Žižek argues, society is always already divided, with or without the contentious groups. Indeed, Žižek suggests that if they weren't here we would have to invent them. The eruption of moral panics over the veil or over asylum seekers, for example, illustrates the function of such stories to broker a consensus which is valuable in the marketplace for the media as well as for political platforms.

This discussion demonstrates the inherent proclivity of human groups to seek markers of difference as a source of identification. On the one hand it is important to note that this discursive shuttlecock that is rhetorical multiculturalism is a thing of semiotic interest. The rhetoric vacillates between sporadic reports of the 'death of multiculturalism'[2] to its rediscovery and resurrection as a surprisingly fresh expression of Britishness. The 2012 Olympics in Britain were a case in point, demonstrating the rhetorical meanings of the term and its effects on either side of the political spectrum. Some right-wing politicians seemed to object to Danny Boyle's opening ceremony, with its focus on black and mixed-race Britons as being key players in British culture and history. Conservative politician Aidan Burley could barely contain his resentment at this portrait and tweeted that the event was 'multicultural crap'. This view was mirrored in some newspapers, with the *Daily Mail* headlines reaffirming the notion of multiculturalism as errant separatism that leads to the erosion of British life: 'Multiculturalism? Nonsense. The Olympics are a victory for patriotism and common British values' (*Daily Mail*, 7 August 2012). Some avowedly left-wing commentators also reflected that patriotism and pageantry were possibly acceptable after all (e.g. *New Statesman*'s Baxter blog, 28 July) and suggested that the Left should 'lighten up' and stop being 'wet blankets'.

The fluctuating discourse of multiculturalism reflects the manner in which group boundaries are constantly being drawn, discussed and redrawn, and rhetoric such as these media examples play an ongoing 'bardic' role (Fiske and Hartley

1978) in affirming and challenging the shared values associated with inclusion and segregation, in-groups and out-groups. Such boundaries are dependent on how 'social space' (in several dimensions, including ethnicity and class) defines groups through their relative positions within it. For Bourdieu the social space is 'a field of forces', social, symbolic and material, which suggest that the agent is:

> defined by the positions he occupies in the different fields, that is, in the distribution of the powers that are active within each of them. These are, principally, economic capital (in its different kinds), cultural capital and social capital, as well as symbolic capital, commonly called prestige, reputation, renown, etc., which is the form in which the different forms of capital are perceived and recognized as legitimate.
>
> (Bourdieu 1985: 724)

In this way, analyses of ethnic relations and individual expressions of these that were illustrated in previous chapters have clearly developed over time. The manner in which the multicultural situation plays out is determined by the interplay of these forces within the field. In Malaysia and Guyana, for example, some ethnicities are defined by their affluence and their entrepreneurial and trade skills, while others have a strong sense of social and political status as the indigenous people or an imagined community of those most deserving, the 'sons of the soil' (the meaning of Bumiputera, the term used for the Malay Malays).

Beneath the fluid dimension of change and shared destiny that may dominate the political and diplomatic language of these nations there are sharply dividing rivalries which reassert hierarchical thinking. Some groups feel threatened by the successes of their compatriots across the ethnic divide and, in Malaysia for example, other groups face restrictions and disadvantages, as they are perceived as being less deserving of the benefits of the state. These perceptions stem from the persistent attributes and identifications formed under the yoke of colonialism, shaping each enclave's dominance in mutually exclusive fields.

Multiculturalism has been criticised by some key thinkers as a distraction from more progressive efforts to reclaim global consensus and, in particular, from the importance of universal human rights. In an interview Michael Banton stated that:

> there's a lot of strength in the protection of human rights. By contrast, multiculturalism is political rhetoric. Now political rhetoric is necessary, it's good, it's got its own function, but it is different, you know, and to my way of thinking it cannot have the same priority as the protection and promotion of human rights, so I think that's where we should start.
>
> (Interview with Michael Banton, Roehampton University, 15 July 2006)

The idea of cultural enclaves which maintain their integrity and autonomy may make genuine agreement on issues of rights problematic, but the alternative, which stems from reluctance to uphold one cultural view as inherently superior, makes moral consensus impossible. Lemert pointed out that 'If the world is multicultural in any plausibly real sense, then the world is many worlds. Otherwise, the term cultural is being used figuratively and not with complete empirical seriousness' (Lemert 2004: 48).

Indeed, it seems that when different migrant groups appear to challenge the integrity of the state in different ways, support for multiculturalism drops away. Kymlicka (2012) notes that the fluctuation in support for multiculturalism rests on several factors. These include whether migrants are perceived as a security threat (this particularly relates to fears of terrorism after 9/11 and 7/7 and fears of loss of control of border security); whether migrants show commitment to universal human rights; whether there is evidence that migrants are economic contributors (being givers, rather than merely takers); and whether migrants are from diverse backgrounds rather than overwhelmingly from one area. The evidence seems to suggest that when these concerns are not foregrounded multiculturalism is seen as a viable and low-risk approach, but

> [m]ulticulturalism tends to lose support in high-risk situations where immigrants are seen as predominantly illegal, as potential carriers of illiberal practices or movements, or as net burdens on the welfare state. However, one could argue that rejecting immigrant multiculturalism under these circumstances is in fact the higher-risk move. It is precisely when immigrants are perceived as illegitimate, illiberal, and burdensome that multiculturalism may be most needed.
>
> (Kymlicka 2012: 2)

Furthermore, these fears are often subject to gross exaggeration in popular culture. Stories which emphasise loss of border control, loss of opportunity and identity and apparent terrorist threats in recent years have reached a feverish level in the popular press in Britain, the USA and Australia, among many other countries.

Kymlicka, among others, argues that multicultural policy initiatives are, despite the rhetorical claims, making genuine contributions to incorporating diversity within a benevolent dominant culture that will allow for gradual non-coercive integration over time. Multiculturalism, which teaches tolerance, acceptance and even celebration of diversity, is certainly a step forward, despite the dangers of tokenism and structural inequality (political and economic power is typically a 'next wave' phenomenon). We must be cautious about the supposedly homogenising effects of globalisation. Theories of cultural and media imperialism assume that 'local cultures are necessarily battered out of existence by the proliferation of consumer goods, advertising and media programmes stemming from the West (largely the United States)(Featherstone 1995: 115). Featherstone is making the point that we must be careful not to over-simplify the complex negotiation, absorption, assimilation and resistance strategies within the culture, as well as the mediating influence of the nation state,

> but the shape and identity of existing national societies are being challenged from within and from without by ethnic and regional expressions of difference and parallel demands for autonomy and independence, as well as by global population movements, transnational communication network.
>
> (Smart 1993: 136)

An inordinate emphasis on cultural difference may run counter to the necessity of working towards a genuine equality within respectful diversity and instead encourage a hardening of boundaries rather than a bridging of them. Guyanese anthropologist Brackette Williams (1992) notes that Guyana's polarised ethnic relations have a dual nature: on the one hand there is an egalitarian and unifying tradition forged under the oppression of colonialism, but on the other hand there is also a deep-seated hierarchical order (another colonial legacy) in which different groups are measured in terms of their relative contributions – who gives most and who takes the most. As we have seen, ethnic communalism operates by closing ranks and accepting a general vision of the other group as a potential threat to prosperity or political power.

Perhaps a crucial point here relates to the perception of what constitutes a 'mixed-race' identity. In many plural, post-colonial societies mixing is an inevitable fact of life; the hybridity of colonial existence entails a heritage of cultural synthesis. An interview I recorded in Guyana demonstrated this. The respondent, an Indian-Guyanese man, related his experience of a relationship with an African-Guyanese student. The little narrative below demonstrates the reflexivity of the identity categories separating the two ethnic groups, the conversation presenting a playful negotiation indicating numerous points of crossing and perhaps almost an arbitrary ritualism in the exchange.

▌ BOX 8.5 GUYANA: BOUNDARY CROSSING

This chapter has discussed the recognition of 'otherness' and the possibility of forming contingent identities based on mutually exclusive categories of difference. However, in situations where different cultural enclaves live side by side there is a mutual ownership and recognition of these differences in trait and practice – and there are numerous examples of border-crossing. The following story was taken from an interview with Dr Dennis Bassier, a Guyanese anthropologist, which highlighted this intense awareness of ethnic hierarchy. In his student days, he told me, an African girl became attracted to him. The manner in which their relationship developed highlights not only the intense awareness of ethnic difference, but also the fact that such differences can be negotiated and overcome.

DENNIS: Umm, I was a student here in the early 70s and there was a black girl who would sit in class with me and so on. And she became attracted to me, but her orientation was so strong that she could not accept that she was falling for an Indian – and she looked at me and said: 'You know you're not Indian.' I said 'Yes, I am Indian.' She said, 'Oh no no, your hair is kinda curly, wavy when it's long.' And I said, 'No, Indians do have wavy hair – look at the Madrasees, for instance, the Dravidians?' She said 'Ah no no – do you eat roti in the morning?' (Now this is Indian food.) I said, 'No, most mornings I eat bread, crackers, what have you.' She said 'Oh OK, then you're not Indian.' She said 'When you eat, before you eat do you feed your dog or cat?' (And this is true, this is very very marked among Indians – they would take a little of their food and give it to the dog or cat before they eat themselves.) I said, 'No I don't, whatever is left I give.' 'Oh then you're not Indian – all Indians do that …' [*laughs*] So what I say is, it comes back to the stereotypes we have of these categories … and since I don't do those two things among the others then, OK I feel satisfied to myself that this man is not Indian so I can go ahead [*laughs*].

(Interview, 9 April 1991)

In this instance two forces – egalitarianism in recognition of the Indian as desirable and hierarchy in the recital of markers of ethnic status – seem to be the site of an individual struggle to transcend prescribed boundaries. What is extraordinary here is, first, that the young African-Guyanese woman should feel it necessary to put the object of her affections through this test when it seems unlikely that, at least on surface appearance, there could have been any mistaking his 'Indianness'. Second, the recital of cultural markers is surprising in that it seems so fluent and detailed an inventory that, had even these been thwarted, one imagines she would have been able to continue the litany of distinctive features until she struck one that would have achieved the desired result. This aspect of boundary-crossing points to the possibility that subjects are not constrained by any simple determinism, and they may be knowledgeable and able to consciously manipulate elements in the social world.

The manner in which hybrid categorising operates and the social meanings that circulate vary in relation to the existing ethnic divisions and the social and political tensions between these groups. In Guyana's ethnically polarised situation, mixed African and Indian offspring are called '*doogla*' – a term sometimes considered somewhat demeaning given the negatively charged political rivalry between African- and Indian-Guyanese. However, at times 'awl ahwee a Doogla' ('everyone is a Doogla' – that is, of mixed race) is adopted as a catch cry to recognise that a shared history of colonialism means that people have much more in common than is suggested by skin colour or cultural traditions (see Williams 1991: 185; and Spencer 2007: 77).

CHAPTER SUMMARY

This chapter has discussed some of the dynamic and contradictory experiences of identity at the personal as well as the ethnic community level. Diasporic communities exist in an uncertain space that is dynamic and reciprocal in its effects on flows of migrant groups as well as on the indigenous 'locals'. This is not a utopian situation in which hybridity offers new post-racial reality, but it is a space where boundaries may be challenged and broken down or shifted. Individuals may increasingly find themselves, owing to circumstances of birth or migration, between two or more cultures and facing conflicted and contradictory views of themselves, their lifestyles and their identity. These hybrid patterns of ethnic identity, articulated as 'border lives' by Bhabha and existence within 'diaspora space' by Brah, are identities in constant transition which pose a challenge to foundationalist thinking. Much of the writing about hybridity suggests that fluid postmodern ethnicities are the emergent form. Now, while this may be, it is as well not to ignore the reality of our increasingly diverse cities, where there is often all too little cultural mixing between the diverse groups. However, as the examples given here have shown, boundary crossings happen all the time as people forge relations across the sometimes hostile boundaries of traditional divides.

EXERCISE 8.1 HYBRIDITY AND MULTICULTURE

1   Being between cultures, like the people in the interviews in this chapter, may actually provide a stronger, more realised sense of national identity(s) than the identity of a white English person. Discuss.

2   The Zapatista uprising has implications for the world as well as for Mexico. Discuss.

3   Assess the contribution of two contentious terms in the understanding of post-colonial identities: diaspora and hybridity. What are the benefits and drawbacks?

4   Both diaspora and hybridity appear to promise a world in which racism is a spent force. What is the problem with such celebratory discourses?

5   Looking at the quotes and the concerns about multiculturalism in this chapter, what signs can you see that multiculturalism leads towards separatism rather than a more holistic society?

6   Which view of multiculturalism do you see as the most realistic and why?

EXERCISE 8.2 BOUNDARY CROSSING

1   What were the boundary markers apparent in the Guyana example? In what instances do you imagine that such attributes of distinctiveness might be used to reaffirm distance rather than to lower boundaries?

2   Can you cite other examples of ethnic boundary markers from your personal experience? From the media? What was the context in which these differences were raised?

3   Have you ever experienced a boundary crossing? If so, what form did it take?

4   Conversely, have you ever experienced ethnic differences being brought forward to strengthen boundaries?

5   What about other social divisions: age, gender, class, sexuality? In each case, list the distinctive features that are at times used as barriers. How can these be overcome? Are they substantially different from (or similar to) racial/ethnic boundaries?

Further reading

There are a number of texts that are especially useful when considering complex issues of multiculturalism, diaspora and hybridity. Kivisto's work, which is clear and concise, examines the persistence of ties of race and ethnicity and how these relationships have been thrown into sharp relief by processes of political, economic and cultural globalisation. See Peter Kivisto (2010) 'Multiculturalism and Racial Democracy: State Policies and Social Practices', in *Handbook of Race and Ethnic Studies*, Patricia Hill Collins and John Solomos, eds (Sage Publications, Thousand Oaks, CA).

In the specifically British context, the books below capture the ongoing struggle with the implicit contradictions of multiculturalism in a state where immigration patterns largely define ideas of diversity and where the tensions between ideas of live and let live diversity and the periodic resurgence of imagined British identity in political and rhetoric demonises diversity, denigrating the 'm word' as a laissez-faire liberal ideal.

Tariq Modood (2007) *Multiculturalism: A Civic Idea* (Polity Press, Cambridge, UK).

Pathik Pathak (2008) *The Future of Multicultural Britain: Confronting the Progressive Dilemma* (Edinburgh: Edinburgh University Press).

Ben Pitcher (2009) *The Politics of Multiculturalism: race and racism in contemporary Britain* (Palgrave Macmillan, Basingstoke).

In more theoretical mode, *Diaspora and Hybridity* (2005; Sage, Thousand Oaks, CA) by Virinder Kalra, Raminder Kaur and John Hutnyk offers visions of the world's complex cases of intersectional diasporic identities and perceptions of 'otherness', relations between hosts and guests, home and away, in terms of cross-border theory and post-nationalism.

Notes

1 Cohen (1997) gives five types of diaspora. See Glossary.
2 For example., as proclaimed by Angela Merkel in Germany in 2010 and by David Cameron in 2012.

CHAPTER 9

Futures

Our challenge should now be to bring even more powerful visions of planetary humanity from the future into the present and to reconnect them with democratic and cosmopolitan traditions that have been all but expunged from today's black political imaginary.

(Gilroy 2000: 356)

Titling this chapter Futures is not to suggest that anything prescient about race or ethnicity can easily be said. One thing that a study of history might teach us is that the future will not conform to our expectations and predictions are often little more than a projection of current conditions. Throughout these chapters I have consistently used the terms race and ethnicity together, although some attempts to show their divergent and problematic meanings have been given. In the social sciences we are almost unanimous about the non-existence of race – and in this limited sense as Paul Warmington suggests:

We are post-racial in having moved beyond pseudo-genetic notions of race; however, we are not 'post-racial' per se. Therefore we must make creative use of the paradox of race-conscious scholarship: working both with and against conceptual tools that have yet to be effectively replaced.

(Warmington 2009: Abstract)

It is important to remember, while scholarly dismantling of the concept of race is achieved, that it is, nevertheless, culturally woven into global contexts, where it still generates division, conflict and hatred. Racism stemming from concepts that have been held up to scrutiny and found to be invalid nevertheless has real consequences. Similarly, while ethnicity is a term which avoids some of the danger-ous legacy of race, it is constantly drawn back to essentialist meanings, standing in as a de facto term for race. The shifting meanings of these terms are contingent on social and political realities. There is a danger that discussions of race may be passed over as abstract theoretical musings, however, and there is a need for a more pragmatic approach.

The opening quote from Gilroy suggests that a collective vision is required to strive for a renewed global democracy. On the face of it this might seem obvious, but without collective vision and actions to underline the divisive nature of race/racism or of other forms of inequity they remain unchallenged, forms sliding seam-lessly and unspoken into the habitual and institutionalised practices and language of everyday life:

> So injustices may not be perceived as injustices, even by those who suffer them, until somebody invents a previously unplayed role. Only if somebody has a dream, and a voice to describe that dream, does what looked like nature begin to look like culture, what looked like fate begin to look like a moral abomina-tion, For until then only the language of the oppressor is available, and most oppressors have had the wit to teach the oppressed a language in which the oppressed will sound crazy – even to themselves – if they describe themselves as oppressed.
>
> (Rorty 1995: 126)

This unspoken and complicit consensus, which is a habitual presence in our culture, is similar to Marcuse's notion of 'repressive tolerance': 'A comfortable, smooth, reasonable, democratic unfreedom prevails in advanced industrial civilisa-tion' (Marcuse 1968: 19). The impetus to believe in change may also be eroded by the inoculating authority of the media, which has interpenetrated social life more than ever before. Marcuse recognised that the media forms an extension of eco-nomic and political power that cultivates certain moral and political values, effec-tively preventing or marginalising dissent. However, what does Gilroy's 'planetary humanism' really imply? Gilroy's is a plea for a 'credible, post-anthropological, and resolutely nonracial humanism', meaning the end of race as a category and hence the last gasp of racial thinking.

The central theme of this text, with its regard to the representation of race and ethnicity, is to show how the appearances of 'otherness', in their myriad representational forms, operate to naturalise relationships of power and submis-sion. Only by exposing the everyday signs and expressions of difference is their ideological hold broken. Previous chapters have illustrated the manner in which representations of race and ethnicity construct and position identities. It has been emphasised that there are always consequences to these portrayals, and that they are often used expediently in relationships of power. In the UK, Malaysia,

Guyana, Mexico and Australia local conditions have been cited and a little of the historical narrative of complex relations of difference has been revealed. Several points can be usefully made about these examples and what they have shown to have in common in terms of indications of the deep structure of race/ethnicity and the presence and uses of difference.

First, it is important not to reduce race/ethnic difference to functionalism – to, as Martin Carter suggested, 'race as a resource' (although at times it is clearly used in this way). Neither is the aim to posit some inner psychological need for a guarantee of difference which satisfies the ego's need for security, a sense of worth and belonging or its fear of dark 'otherness' (again, this is not to suggest that there are no psychological aspects which manifest).

The argument which has emerged from these sketches is more than essentialist fears and fancies and instrumental rationalism. Another challenge is the tendency to emphasise the symbolic at the expense of the material. Some insist that social life has become overtaken by simulacra, or that postmodern relativism makes reasoned criticism impossible, or that we are in a post-class, post-industrial postmodern state at the 'end of history'. Inevitably the pace of change and the succession of new cultural forms can appear to present life as incessantly reflexive, an implosion of forms of representation, but these transitory forms do not negate the force of history; the dialectical process of change which underpins our material social reality. Post-colonial writers have, on the contrary, shown the importance of not forgetting the historical roots of oppression and the legacies of colonialism: the ripples from colonial impacts are still very much with us. The 'new world order' is characterised by apparently benign economic regulation through the global strategies of the wealthy nations, punctuated by military interventions in oil-rich states under the pretext of policing terror or humanitarian concern for those under dictatorial regimes.

The issues which form our values are those everyday incidents, images and conversations which this book has tried to draw upon. Race can be thrown into sharp relief by political campaigns, media stories, incidents in our workplaces, discussions between students in a seminar or an argument about racism in a pub. At times differences are over-emphasised, while at others a 'colour-blind' approach is adopted in the face of clear inequity and discriminatory practices.

The strands of theory which focus on race as flows of social meanings should not be mutually opposed to a keen recognition of the political and social realities of racism or the embedded structural inequalities which divide our cities. In much of the world, difference – whether it is equated with essentialist myths of 'race', gender, sexuality, religion or other cultural practices – is a cause of division, exclusion and impoverishment; in extreme cases, differences can lead to deadly, even genocidal, consequences.

Such relationships, as we have seen in previous chapters, often have a long and complex history entangled with colonialism, where divisive identities were promulgated. To understand the dynamics of these forces it is necessary to question and deconstruct ideas of subjectivity without losing sight of the necessity of supporting those who are disadvantaged as a result of our society's discourses of exclusion. Differences of race or ethnicity are modified and experienced very differently depending on positionality as expressed through class, economic position, gender, sexuality, ability and so on.

What trends are recognisable and likely to shape our conceptions of race and future ethnic identities? At the beginning of this book we showed the apparently functional necessity of relationships of 'otherness' in determining and affirming identities. Pieterese's work suggests that 'others' of one sort or another have always been with us, but that the basis for 'othering' does not need to be embodied by the concept of race. Indeed, we have seen that 'race' is a fluid and floating signifier which is parasitic on the political and social realities of the day. Such 'in-groups' and 'out-groups' result from social and political discourses and vary considerably over time and between cultures.

GLOBALISATION

The impact of colonialism dividing and dispossessing its subjects, shaped the course of history and set up adversarial relationships with powerful aftershocks today. Not only are these impacts part of ethnic memory but they are also part of the daily reality for most of the non-western world. The expansion of global capitalism and the logic of domination and exploitation of human resources has widened the gap, leaving developing nations in a situation where their debts, brokered in the 1970s and 1980s, have produced auto-colonialist regimes, allowing the wealthy western nations to dictate terms at a distance and create puppet economies from Washington, London, Berlin and Paris. The increasingly obvious fragility of global capitalism and the ensuing economic crises which have overtaken us in the last few years have further encouraged this process. The poorest nations in Europe face a new level of austerity.

Furthermore, one cannot talk about the likely scenarios for the future without recognising the strategic geopolitical goals of the world's superpowers, particularly as regards successive US military interventions – more than fifty since the Second World War (see Blum 2004) – which have had a dramatic effect on ethnic relations within those countries. While there is little space here to discuss this in detail, it must at least be recognised that the long-term picture of race, ethnicity and global relations is deeply affected by market competition and forces of economic and cultural globalisation.

Globalisation is an elusive concept and definitions frequently deal with only economic or easily discernible global processes. Cultural and sociological aspects are far more complex and contradictory. Bringing about profound and sweeping changes, globalisation:

> is a process that transforms existing everyday routines and local rhythms (time) as well as the cultural locations, institutional and social structures, and political forms (space) in which such everyday routines and rhythms are situated. Globalization is thus a socioculturally transformative force in the sense that it de-situates or 'distanciates' – de-temporalizes and dis-locates – everyday life from the temporal–spatial contexts in which it was pre-globally embedded and couples it instead to 'the global'.
>
> (Lewandowski 2003: 117)

Through the agency of transnational corporations, the opening up of global trade and production has led to homogenising patterns of consumption and cultural identification. As a result, owing to the symbolic agency of products, the impact of consumption on lifestyle practices and the immediacy of communicating these (through technological advances unthinkable a few years ago), cultures have become disembedded from their origins. Waters (1996: 157) outlines the principles behind the process of social change in these arenas as governed by the tendency 'that material exchanges localize, political exchanges internationalize, and symbolic exchanges globalize'. The more symbolic and fluid the exchange, the more rapidly it will span the globe. Therefore, it was no wonder that financial exchanges were rapidly globalised but flows of people seeking work were resisted, and in some cases boundaries have been tightened against those seeking work. In many cases this may be based on irrational fears (too often politically exploited) that the country could be 'swamped' with migrants or on the virulent asylophobia which is exploited by politicians from across the political spectrum.

But are we placing too much faith in the dominant western view of globalisation? Is this, in fact, such an inexorable process that affects cultures so profoundly and permanently? This is a difficult question but at least asking it cautions us not to be swept along by what may seem to be the inevitability of homogenising forces and to look critically at other processes that may operate in the opposite direction or despite globalising trends.

Conservative critic Francis Fukuyama takes a more circumspect line on the effects of globalisation, suggesting that much of globalisation has been relatively superficial and that the claims about global media homogenising the world are without foundation. Indeed, the impact of such media might, on the contrary, present a less favourable image of 'western' culture:

> [Forty] years ago, in the 1950s and '60s, Asia looked up to the United States as a model of modernization. Now, Asians look at American urban decay and the decline of the family and they feel that America is not a very attractive model.

Communications technology has allowed both Asians and Americans to see each other more clearly, and it turns out they have very different value systems.

(Fukuyama 2000: 2)

Robertson captures the duality of the global processes in play, again not merely homogenising culture to a dominant western model but a '...twofold process of the particularisation of the universal and the universalisation of the particular' (1992: 177–8). In order to reconcile these social processes Robertson coined the term glocalisation, suggesting the unity as well as the difference between the local and the global. Smart also recognises the duality of global processes:

> the fragile unity ascribed to national societies has begun to dissolve, to fragment, as transnational and global exchanges and communications have gathered momentum, and infranational differences expressed in the form of 'local, regional, and ethnic cultures' have been reconstituted or regenerated.

(Smart 1993: 135)

Giddens is optimistic with regard to the process of globalisation. He takes the view that globalisation is something of an equalising process, since it gives hitherto disempowered groups and nations the potential to realise their goals. Indeed, he (2000) has even spoken of globalisation generating what he calls 'reverse colonialism' – the movement towards supranational entities loosening the bonds that have prevented the expression of local ethnic identities.

At one level the current acceleration of globalisation could be seen as destabilising in relation to ethnicity, perhaps suggesting that ethnic identity will not easily survive. However, globalisation does not necessarily entail homogenisation or integration – it means greater connectedness and deterritorialisation, a term that implies that ethnicity is increasingly removed from its traditional base and becomes a floating signifier divorced from its origins, its roots in a homeland replaced by identities in 'diaspora space' (Brah 1996) and a more hybrid and plural sense of ethnic origins. Waters (1996: 136–7) usefully summarises the impact of globalisation on ethnicity thus:

- Globalisation is both a differentiating as well as a homogenising process. It pluralises the world by recognising the value of cultural niches and local abilities.
- It weakens the putative nexus between nation and state, releasing absorbed ethnic communities and allowing the reconstitution of nations across former state boundaries.
- Centre moves to periphery, introducing possibilities of new ethnic identities to cultures on the periphery (via electronic images and affluent tourism).
- Periphery moves to centre: for example, flows of economic migrants and black culture taken up by white suburban youth.

These processes can be seen as having impacts for expressions of ethnicity. Media imagery and consumer products are reaching the periphery more and more rapidly, while information also flows back from the outer edges with increasing rapidity. Media and mobile communications that link up people accelerate dissemination. More recently in the 2010 Arab Spring uprisings the use of social networking technologies increased the efficacy of protests across the Arab world. However, media messages are increasingly unified by ever-growing global media monopolies, which suggests that, despite the apparent variety of media channels, the message is becoming more politically homogenised and market directed.

Hall (1992) notes two possible adaptive responses by ethnic groups to globalisation. First, translation (syncretistic response): such practices can be seen in many post-colonial societies in which a process of creolisation has occurred that has formed syntheses of cultural values and social practices (hybrid ethnic identities and the possibility of boundary crossing discussed in the previous chapter). Second, tradition (ethnic fundamentalism): this could stem from a sense of cultural values being under threat from outside 'foreign' influences. Since 2010 those popular protests which swept across the Arab world led to changes of long-standing, authoritarian regimes in Libya, Egypt and Tunisia. Such changes may turn out to be at odds with the neo-conservative globalising desires of US administrations to democratise and open up the region to further influence and trade. As in these three cases they have led to the emergence of popular official Islamist parties. Indeed these changes seem likely to create a more multipolar Middle East and diminish the power of US and Israel's interests in the region. Bahjat (in Fawcett 2013) argues though, that interestingly there has been little significant change to the patterns of international relations mostly because the 'post-cold war global system is much less polarised along ideological lines' (p.95).

It seems globalisation can increase local communal unification strengthening and releasing regional identities. However, it is cultural, social and political global processes which may fuel and enable the breaching of traditional and oppressive forces within the state. The rapid development of new media tools has been a crucial aspect of the acceleration and immediacy of global communication, Facebook, Twitter, and other forms of social networking are bringing about changes at both the micro and macro level. There are increasingly liberatory potentials and as Chen (2012: 3) suggests:

Dialectically dynamic, universally pervasive, holistically interconnected, culturally hybridized, and individually powerful characteristics of globalization enhanced and deepened by the stimulus and push of the emergence of new media has led to revolutionary changes in people's thinking and behavior, redefined the sense of community, and restructured human society.

However, while they provide the impetus for these freedoms and flows of information, it may be all too easy to forget their countervailing effects of more intrusion into every area of life, and potential for the greater social control through media management and surveillance. Perhaps the promise of a world without boundaries for a supranational citizen is still a utopian dream.

The pace of change since the 1980s has steeply increased and emergent technologies have accelerated these processes further and now the mobility and immediacy of global information has reached an unprecedented peak. What does this mean in terms of representations of ethnicity? Three issues which contribute to this cultural circulation of meanings about ethnic identity and difference are briefly examined in what follows to indicate the changing global representations of race and ethnicity: mixed-race relationships, the Internet and cyberidentity, and terrorism and global risk.

MIXED RACE

'Mixed race' is a misleading term since it implies that a 'pure race' exists. Like its alternatives, 'multi-racial', 'mixed parentage' and 'dual heritage', it refers to people who are visibly identified as embodying two or more racial or ethnic groupings. It appears to emphasise physically hybrid features but also broader ethnic and cultural syntheses. The concept highlights the borderlines between the terms 'race' and 'ethnicity' and the inadequacy of existing terms to articulate hybrid identities. It seems that there is always this tendency to imagine the world in absolute terms, but 'mixed-race' individuals are a living challenge to this absolutism. Britain currently has one of the highest rates of interracial relationships in the western world, with 50 per cent of all black children born having one white parent. In the 2001 census the controversial new 'mixed' category attracted 400,000 ticks. Ten years later the number of mixed-race people had gone above a million for the first time (see *Guardian* Datablog 2012).

The labels of hybridity and diaspora, other terms such as Bhabha's 'third space' and Brah's 'diaspora space' and Stuart Hall's influential writings on 'diasporization' and Caribbean cultural identities are valuable because they do offer a sense of the fluidity of the individual identities which constitute the 'mixed-race' individual's experience. Similarly, it is argued that identity has become more reflexive and malleable; the individual is able to make individual decisions which reflect the loss of traditions and the increasing plasticity of identity. However, it is nevertheless important, as Christian points out, not to be carried away by 'a celebration of "hybrid forms"' (Christian 2004: 308–10), which he argues avoids the issue of historical interracial identities and the coded persistence of white supremacy inculcated in the hierarchical colour codes of countries such as Jamaica.

Furthermore, as a result of this children born with dual or multiple ethnic heritage may feel ambivalent in terms of their identification. Incipient racism suffered from an early age from peers and teachers might lead to a fluctuating identification. Tizzard and Phoenix cite experiments that have explored young children's racial identifications. The earliest example was the 1939 'Clark Doll Experiment'. When asked to choose between a black and a white doll – and asked to choose the doll that looked 'bad' – half of the black children chose the black doll. Even more worryingly, a third of the same children selected the white doll when asked to 'Give me the doll that looks like you' (Tizzard and Phoenix 1993: 29). These studies were used in arguments that black children suffered from low self-esteem and identity confusion because they internalised negative views of black people from the white community, leading to calls to desegregate American schools. However, more recent studies in 2005 and 2009 showed varying and contradictory results, and it is perhaps ill-advised to set great store by such experiments when there are so many other variables in the way the experiment is conducted that might come into play.

The following observations (Box 9.1) come from Yvonne Howard-Bunt, an academic and mother who asks some pertinent questions about the meaning of 'mixed race' for herself, her family and wider society. Her examples indicate that we are at the cusp of change, in the uneasy borderlands between the reliance on clear 'colour-coded' boundaries and the realisation of a new hybridised social reality.

BOX 9.1 INTERVIEW WITH YVONNE HOWARD-BUNT

I am careful about how I define/label myself and to whom. It changes according to the overall context and purpose, and whether it is for data collection, subject discussion or simply responding to an individual querying my 'racial, ethnic' background. I have difficulty with defining myself within these narrow parameters because I find them misleading and inappropriate. What does 'mixed race' mean when 'pure races' do not exist as a discrete biological entity? 'Black' is a conceptual term of historical social, economic and political significance. Aside from this factor, does the term 'mixed race' have any lesser or greater definitive validity than 'black' and 'white' classifications? At what point and in what way do generational time frame and genetic-distribution factors impinge upon definitions of 'mixed race'? Does the possession of the gene for colour automatically preclude 'mixed-race' people from certain categories? If it does, then the construction of 'race' in terms of 'whiteness' and genetic 'purity' must be unravelled. What would be the implications of a heritage

BOX 9.1 INTERVIEW WITH YVONNE HOWARD-BUNT (CONTINUED)

link to 'black' Africa measured in declining genetic kinship percentages? For example, parent, grandparent, great-grandparent, great-great-grandparent, and so on.

And where on the continuum of 'race' and ethnic classification would I place my 'white'-complexioned, straight-haired, blue-eyed babe of dual 'mixed-race' and 'white' heritage? Three of his grandparents are 'white' UK citizens and one is a 'black' African UK citizen. Is my child 'black', 'white' or 'mixed race'? What are the parameters of defining my child within these subjective constructs? Should I consider his identities in terms of colour, citizenship or inaccurate and outmoded concepts of 'race' and ethnicity?

The issue of colour symbolism as a conceptual determinant of classification blurs boundaries and influences understanding at a 'grass roots' level. For example: my brown-pigmented 'mixed-race' brother was out with his 'white'-complexioned child, the baby's 'white' mother and a 'white' male friend of theirs. A stranger walked up to them, peered into the pushchair and established eye contact with the 'white' parties he presumed to be the parents. The man said, 'What a lovely baby, how old is she?', paying no heed to my brother who was not perceived as the father of the child.

In another situation, a mother enrolled her child in school and was cautioned against classifying her 'white'-complexioned child within a 'white' category. The mother, of dual 'Indian' and 'white' UK heritage, positively identifies herself as 'mixed race', but did not define her daughter in this respect.

She stated that this would not have been an issue if the child's 'white' father had enrolled the daughter in her absence. Caution is required here in the view expressed by some authors. This position labels the mother as misguided in terms of defining her child's identity and attributes simplistic notions of identity confusion and self-esteem.

These cases are indicative of the borderlines where assumptions and common-sense perceptions are challenged. However, such confusion often accompanies major shifts in social dynamics and the mixed-race category is clearly the fastest-growing ethnic grouping certainly in the UK, but also in the USA, where it is also breaking records and meeting certain forms of resistance. There appear to be important and contested issues below the surface of the celebratory discourses. A *US Today* report from 1992 suggested that US resistance to the mixed category may be motivated by powerful lobbying from other ethnic groups, who may consider the creation of a new and rapidly growing group to be a threat and a drain on resources they might expect; a reminder, again, that how boundaries are drawn can have political and economic consequences.

In addition, the struggle for identification as black or Asian has led some groups to embrace a relatively essentialist viewpoint, partly as a strategic means by which to gain recognition. As Hall comments:

> I have the feeling that, historically, nothing could have been done to intervene in the dominated field of mainstream popular culture, to try to win some space there, without the strategies through which those dimensions were condensed into the signifier 'black'. Where would we be, as bell hooks once remarked, without a touch of essentialism? Or, is what Gayatri Spivak calls strategic essentialism a necessary moment? The question is whether we are any longer in that moment, whether that is still a sufficient basis for the strategies of new interventions.
>
> (Hall 1993: 104)

Where at least at the official level categories of ethnicity exist which are considered relatively unmixed, at the pragmatic everyday level it seems that these may be less fixed and more easily negotiated. However, by contrast, as Parker points out, 'in Central and South America those who are "mixed" predominate with often incalculably fine-grained pigmentocracies crucial to the operation of social hierarchies in Brazil for example' (Parker 2004: 109).

Terms such as 'black', 'brown' or 'white' are political and social boundary markers rather than iconic signs representing actual categories, and function in an interlocking fashion to raise or lower boundaries, to exclude or to unite. In a 2001 BFI TV documentary, *Brown Britain*, Pauline Black (a mixed race actress and lead singer with the ska band The Selecter) commented on her self-designation as 'black':

> I will still continue to define myself as black, until white people turn around to me and say, 'Hey I'm mixed race as well.' You know – the Vikings came over one time, the French came over one time – and actually recognise that everybody on this planet is really a mixture.
>
> (Channel 4, *Brown Britain* 2001)

This is a clear example of Hall's 'necessary moment', when individuals make a conscious choice of a strategic way of dealing with the obdurate whiteness of the majority culture that defines identity by difference of colour. People of mixed race are in an anomalous situation – pigeon-holed by others, sometimes in a racist or disparaging way. However, while the figures suggest high levels of violence against mixed-race adults, experiences vary and they are a rapidly increasing group, which perhaps suggests an growing acceptance of inter-ethnic relationships and people of multiple heritage more generally. Such experiences of incipient or confrontational racism may start very early at school, depending on class and gender: so racism is less likely to be directed towards middle-class girls than towards working-class males. One student described the racist taunts as 'constant dripping'; racist language was used in a joking yet pointed way.

Tizzard's and Phoenix's (1993) subjects report that mixed-race boys found name-calling racist and tiresome, but coped with this by laughing it off and, in some cases, by indulging in racist jokes about black people themselves. Their research found that 85 per cent of the mixed-parentage sample had experienced racism in one form or another – most frequently name-calling in primary school. Crime figures reveal the high frequency of assaults on people of mixed race:

> The 2010/11 British Crime Statistics showed that the risk of being a victim of personal crime was higher for adults from a Mixed background than for other ethnic groups. It was also higher for members of all BME groups than for the White group.
>
> (Ministry of Justice 2011: 23)

SIGNIFICANCE FOR THEORISING RACIALISATION

David Parker points out the unique opportunity that 'mixed race' allows for a perspective on the process of racialisation. Mixed-race people are the fastest-growing ethnicity in the UK and, while multi-racial or mixed-heritage populations are clearly increasing rapidly in the USA, the official figures do not allow for a mixed category. 'There are three ways in which "mixed race" has been conceived: as a stable social identity in its own right; re-expressed as "multiracial"; and a temporary pre-figurement of a post-racial future' (Parker 2004: 115).

In Britain the term 'mixed race' is now widely recognised as the identity of self-designation by people with mixed ancestry (Tizzard and Phoenix 1993). Older and more derogatory terms such as 'coloured', 'half-caste' and 'half-breed', although still in circulation, have been displaced. For all the difficulties of invoking a concept 'race', which it then places under erasure, the notion of 'mixed race', by drawing attention to the permeability between so-called races, may have a role in weakening the hold of racialised forms of thought and action in the years ahead. However, as Parker also notes, some restraint is required when we look at the worrying level of racism that exists. A more radical shift in perceptions of identity is needed because, currently, '[t]he social constructions of norms of physical appearance still decisively influence identity formation. In the light of the continuing salience of this and other forms of racialisation, the declaration of post-racialism seems premature' (Parker 2004: 118–19).

Also, as discussed in the previous chapter, the underlying values in British society seem to advocate separation based on difference around a core culture of Britishness rather than a future in which mixed race reflects a view of society which is not dominated by any one cultural tradition but rather allows 'a free flow of contributions from all possible sources'. Rather than having to assimilate (a word which means to be absorbed, swallowed up) to one dominant culture there would be individual freedom to experiment and choose whatever cultural style one felt was most meaningful. The cultural practices within such a state would develop organically from the mixture and interaction amongst myriad cultural forms; this holistic vision would mean that new synthetic forms might emerge over time.

(Bramann 1999: 5)

Is Bramann's vision of a world in which humanist ideals supersede nationalism, where society is open enough to gradually adapt to incorporate new cultural forms, utopian? Perhaps it is significant that Britain shows a marked tendency towards mixing, despite the influence of those who perpetuate segregationist ideas of culture and wish to draw rigid boundaries between ethnicities: Britain 'has the highest number of interracial relationships in the world' (Harlow 2000, quoting Professor Richard Berthoud of the Institute for Social and Economic Research). However, with mixed-race groups now making up an estimated 3 per cent of Britain's population and recognised as one of the fastest-growing groups, these concerns may be over-emphasising the problems (Easton 2011). This is a population in rapid flux and one which represents a different, more positive generational attitude, with evidence that mixed-race identities are becoming more recognised and accepted in their own right. Ethnicity may be of less importance than even ten years ago and, despite the studies and attitudes recorded above, there is a sense of optimism about the social opportunities and resilience of mixed-race individuals. As Mark Easton states: 'They are the faces of new Britain – the poster boys and girls for a multicultural nation. Myleene Klass, Lewis Hamilton, Leona Lewis, Mark Ramprakash, Ryan Giggs, Kelly Holmes, Alexandra Burke, Nasser Hussain, Rio Ferdinand' (Mark Easton, BBC 2011). Furthermore, they are not just prominent in entertainment, music and sport; it appears that they are over-represented in a range of high-level professions, while recent research (Lewis 2010) suggests that they are perceived as being more attractive than people who are not mixed race. This supremely natural and healthy state of affairs is, however, not due to multiculturalism but in spite of it, for multiculturalist ideology, which believes that 'culture makes man' rather than the other way around, sets its face, on principle, firmly against miscegenation, integration and assimilation (Reilly 2001). However, these are clearly trends which open up discussion of the possibility of a world which is not riven by ethnic conflict and racism. The rhetoric at least, if not the reality, recognises the desire to be part of a post-racial world.

This brief review of ideas about mixed-race identity highlights the legacy of the past and the tendency to misunderstand or misrecognise identity based on over-simple visual markers of difference. The notion that a new pluralistic habitus is being created might suggest that the drive to constantly resurrect racial boundaries could be losing ground to a gradual realisation that we are all far from pure identities and that mixed-race individuals are an embodiment of this, providing physical evidence of tolerance and change.

RACE IN CYBERSPACE

The development of Internet-based cultures and communities is certainly a new cultural form that is worthy of research. Virtual environments raise a host of interesting questions and baffling metaphysical issues about the meaning of such encounters, the nature of being and of reality. Inevitably, rather grandiose predictions have been made: cyberspace has been heralded as a post-racial utopia. According to some media advertising, there is no race, gender or disability online: 'There is no race. There is no gender. There is no age. There are no infirmities. There are only minds. Utopia? No! ... The Internet!' (MCI television commercial, 'Anthem'). There is perhaps a sense of promise in the idea of a new commonwealth that can allow a true democracy, divested of the physical coercion and conceits of the earthly one. There was even a 'declaration of independence':

> Fri, 9 Feb 1996 17:16:35 +0100
>
> To: barlow@eff.org
>
> From: John Perry Barlow <barlow@eff.org>
>
> Subject: A Cyberspace Independence Declaration
>
> http://w2.eff.org/Censorship/Internet_censorship_bills/barlow_0296.declaration
>
> We are forming our own Social Contract. This governance will arise according to the conditions of our world, not yours. Our world is different.
>
> Cyberspace consists of transactions, relationships, and thought itself, arrayed like a standing wave in the web of our communications. Ours is a world that is both everywhere and nowhere, but it is not where bodies live.
>
> We are creating a world that all may enter without privilege or prejudice accorded by race, economic power, military force, or station of birth.
>
> We are creating a world where anyone, anywhere may express his or her beliefs, no matter how singular, without fear of being coerced into silence or conformity.
>
> Your legal concepts of property, expression, identity, movement, and context do not apply to us. They are based on matter. There is no matter here.

This promise of value-free cyberspace, a metaphysical space in which diverse subjectivities can reinvent themselves away from the male, straight, ethnocentric gaze all too prevalent in everyday life, is far from being borne out in reality. There are a number of problems with the Internet as a socially transformative force. Cyberspace has the ability to connect people across the globe, but also disseminates dichotomies that exist within our culture. Identities can be invented and individuals can cross (virtual) boundaries, but is this a substitute for, or of any relevance to, the real world? There is the chance of being unmasked for those who practise deception, and the sense of betrayal seems to be just as trenchant as in real life.

Nakamura (2000: 716) discusses the way in which Internet fantasists often adopt Asian female identities (males tend to be the most prevalent in cyberspace). This is another example of how the Internet, while it arguably allows people to experiment with fantasy personalities, cross-dressing and some vicarious pleasure from masquerading as a desired object, may also reinforce racist stereotypes by 'exploiting and reifying through performance notions of the Asian female as submissive, docile, a sexual plaything' (ibid.).

The example of stereotypical avatars and other virtual encounters suggests that claims that the Internet opens up a prejudice-free, colourless realm are very doubtful. An article by Susan Zickmund (2000) shows that, on the contrary, cyberculture allows another channel for the articulation of extremist ideas. Members of the US radical right, the Ku Klux Klan and other Nazi-inspired organisations, have found a collective voice using websites. Zickmund's belief that confronting the radical right on a newsgroup is a 'step towards forcing subversives into open interaction with society' (ibid.: 252) is not very convincing. Far from the Internet becoming 'an ally in the struggle against bigotry and racism' (ibid.), there is the danger of its leading to accelerated membership of such groups and of groups becoming less open (hermetic isolation is achieved by use of passwords and so on) and much more organised.

However, Les Back argues that while cyberspace appears to be making diverse forms of fascist activity accessible across a wide range of forms, from Aryan dating to White Power-based music sites, the Internet, with its compression of time and space, 'seems to have accelerated the tendency towards factionalism, which has mercifully haunted postwar fascism' (Back 2002: 132).

Cyber terrorism

Terrorism, according to Baudrillard, is an 'ecstatic form of violence' – it exists as a spectacle. Rather than opposing state violence with meaning it has to extinguish meaning itself – that is, the meaning that sustains the State. Baudrillard goes on to suggest that the spectacle of terrorism is in the production of senseless acts that serve to accelerate the senselessness of power (see Horrocks and Jevtic 1996).

The term 'terrorism' generally brings to mind physical acts of violence; bombings, shootings and kidnappings. However, forms of terrorism, both of the traditional physically violent kind and associated with the dissemination of messages to instil fear or propaganda to cultivate ideas of dissent, have changed with the advent of information technologies and especially the visual capabilities of the Internet, enabling the virulent enhancement of terror. Aside from being simply a conduit for ideas and the rallying of supporters, the Internet has also become a battleground itself. The increasing incidence of 'cyber terrorism' have seen, for example, the hacking of sites to expose State secrets or cyber attacks on the infrastructure of the economic system. Banks, for instance, can be vulnerable to attacks by flooding the system with information which forces system collapse and the loss of millions of dollars. Moreover, a number of extremist websites have apparently featured live footage of hostages being beheaded in Iraq. The Internet is clearly an enormously powerful tool, but it seems very questionable whether the escape into the virtual will provide 'real time' solutions for intractable ethnic and ideological conflicts.

A PAIR OF BROWN EYES

Before reading this section look at the poster (Figure 9.1) and consider how you would interpret its message.

These visions can assail us in the most ordinary and mundane social spaces. This time it was a shopping trip to the city centre. Through an arcade we were passing a well-known catalogue shop when my partner stopped me and drew my attention to the poster that was stuck in the window of the store. A pair of brown eyes stared out from a cutaway like a pill box slot in a black poster; below, the words 'Life Savers' were set in large type; above the eyes, smaller print read 'terrorism: HELP US DEFEAT IT'. The immediate impression this gave us was that it signified the face of a Muslim woman wearing traditional garb. The dilated hyper-real eyes captured my attention in just the way that those ads do that are said to have enlarged the pupils to make you feel the woman in the picture is interested in you. The accompanying text also seemed weird and incongruous: 'Terrorists need places to live and make plans … they need vehicles and people to help them. If you have any suspicions about terrorist activity DON'T HESITATE … call.'

It has been suggested that the purpose of highlighting the eyes was merely to indicate a person who was alert and vigilant to the threat of terrorism, but this is not likely to be the interpretation most people would arrive at. To test this assumption I walked less than 100 yards from the shopping arcade where the poster was seen, to where a small group of Muslims at a table set out with books and leaflets asked us to 'Discover Islam'. I asked them for their opinion of the poster. To my surprise they were not especially concerned about it, although they immediately noticed the similarity of the image to a 'sister' wearing a veil; they felt that, rather than being an intentional anti-Muslim campaign, it represented an error of judgement and perhaps a lack of sensitivity. They also mentioned that there were two other posters, one of a white woman and another of a black man, which suggested that there was no intentional focus on Muslims.[1] However, the *Guardian* reported that the posters caused a storm of protest from Asian and Muslim groups around the country:

Abdur Rahman Jafar, who represents the Muslim Council of Britain on the safety forum, said: 'We are quite infuriated by it. It looks like a woman with a niqab on, which is one version of the veil where women cover up their face and the top of their head.'

(Dodd 2004: 1)

Figure 9.1 'Life Savers': Metropolitan Police anti-terrorist poster

Post 9/11, the climate of fear in the west has – it appears – led to greater victimisation of Muslims. When I first saw this poster, in 2004, I felt that it was adding needlessly to a climate of fear and a growing moral panic about terrorism and Islam, a view which has been echoed by others in this text. And after the events of 7 July 2005 in London the implicit assumption in such images is no more useful. Indeed, locating repugnant terrorist violence as a feature of Islamic cultural difference only adds fuel to the fire and inflames the sense of alienation that engenders such actions. The impact of such campaigns is especially felt where Asians are a small minority. As Dodd explains:

> Kauser Ahmed, of Exeter's Mosque and Islamic Centre, refused to put the poster up.
>
> She said that in her area 'there are very few people of colour or who are Muslim, so they stand out, and we will be the target of suspicion and hostility.
>
> 'We already feel very marginalised, ignored by the authorities until it suits them. It was very obviously Asian eyes.
>
> 'During the IRA bombings in the 1970s and 80s the posters did not depict someone's eyes, they had a picture of a bag.'
>
> (Dodd 2004: 2)

Dodd goes on to note that after the September 11 attack the Exeter mosque was desecrated by youths who placed severed pigs' heads outside it (ibid.).

The Metropolitan Police have since withdrawn this poster after many complaints from Muslim communities around the country. This poster clearly performs interpellation, as discussed earlier: its implicit message hails the reader as a particular audience member. We could argue that it is open to different semiotic interpretations and easily misinterpreted, but there is little doubt of its intended message or preferred reading. One of the features of life in a multi-ethnic society is the need to develop a keener awareness of these relations of dominance and the sensitivity or empathy to avoid 'default' notions of the normative, the 'Wedom'. It is important to expose the myth of consensus and listen to other voices that are effectively marginalised.

The unfolding issue of terrorism is having an unprecedented and distorting effect on perceptions. Some, like Samuel Huntington (1998), draw the battle lines of the future based not on ethnic identifications or desires for empire but on the 'Clash of Civilizations' (as if these are real and separate bases). Further, he suggests that the west is the only civilisation to value individualism, democracy, equality, liberalism and so on, and that the main threats stem from Islamic states and Confusianism (China). These are ultimately inviolable, essentialist categories that are intrinsically opposed. The west must therefore be prepared to use military force to deal with the threat of these dangerous civilisations. This strand of unreasoned cultural pessimism represents real concern when it is apparent that the world's only real superpower (the USA) has advisers who genuinely believe in the right-eous dominance of American culture (see, for example, the Project for the New American Century, a neo-conservative think tank that promotes an ideology of total USA world domination through the use of force. This was reputedly a strong influence on the Bush administration of the time). Huntington's error is similar to the attributions made by the eighteenth and nineteenth century categorisers who posited invoilable traits based on skin colour. To argue that Islamic nations are 'in essence' opposed to individualism, pluralism and democracy, ignores the role of context and the shared origins and qualities of all human cultures. Paul Gilroy, in *After Empire*, states that:

> The resolute enthusiasm of postmodern ethnic cleansers and absolutists appar-ently knows no colour lines. Hendrik Verwoed, Samuel Huntington, Ariel Sharon, Slobodan Milosevic, Osama Bin Laden, Condoleezza Rice, and a host of others have contributed something to the belief that absolute culture rather than colour is more likely to supply the organizing principle that underpins con-temporary schemes for racial classification and division. These distinctions may be far removed from the warring totalities of blackness and whiteness but are nonetheless likely to be scarred by the Manichean relationship they exemplify.
>
> (Gilroy 2004: 39)

One arena which has fuelled these absolutist sentiments is terrorism. The recog-nition of global risk (Beck 1992; 2002) resulting from terrorist attacks such as 9/11 has served to reinforce the autocratic state. Yet, as Beck comments, terrorism diminishes the nation-state, leading to greater transnational cooperation as a neces-sary means of increasing internal security (Beck 2002: 14) – perhaps the opposite of what the 9/11 terror attack had intended to achieve.

Beck envisages two types of transnational cooperation emerging. On the one hand, states could become even more fortress-like – an all too believable prospect given the heightened surveillance post 9/11. Such states would be rigidly resist-ant to external cultural influences. Such states would dispense with freedom and democracy and become increasingly authoritarian. Conversely, Beck believes that some states could become what he calls 'open world states' that emphasise the necessity for self-determination and take a proactive role in terms of not only com-bating terrorism but also addressing the causes of terrorism. Such an imaginary state would be based on openness and a belief in the need for unification between its own citizens and foreign nationals, rather than use of rigid and ethnocentric protocols to oppose terror.

Clearly, the initial reactions to 9/11 have followed a course similar to those that would characterise Beck's suggested 'surveillance state'. The excesses of Guantanamo Bay and Iraq are the brutal mirror held up to the 'other'. The perpetuation of imperial high-handedness finds its reflection, in turn, in live beheadings broadcast via the Internet and the desperate rage of suicide bombers and other urban jihadists. The gross disparities of power between those reaping the benefits of the new world order and those who are excluded from a share will not be healed by military might, but at present it is hard to imagine the open state approach Beck advocates being adopted. Neo-colonial exploitation has been the road map which seems to lead inexorably towards the 'war on terror', and western nations seem reluctant to relinquish this dominance.

In late 2013 the western reaction to continued terrorist attacks (the Madrid, Bali, London and Boston bombs) has been to further accelerate the process of political globalisation. The perpetrators of terror, whether individuals who cynically plan bombings in the name of religion or western governments perpetrating terror through economic or military might, are locked into an ideological impasse. The actions of each side merely reinforce their sense of righteousness and moral outrage.

As I write this in 2013 the events at the Boston Marathon and, in Britain, the Woolwich killing are still sending out waves of unease. The enemy in these cases was not an outsider, although the perpetrators were drawn as alien and disaffected. While these were shocking events that encourage heightened rhetoric, reasserting core cultural values, other stories do not even make it into the national news. In 2006 police discovered the biggest cache of chemical explosives ever found in mainland Britain in a Lancashire town – but the story was aired only in a regional paper (Hewitt 2006).

These constant attempts to position others – those whose views are violently opposed to the west – as so totally alien are not surprising, as fear is at least then positioned across a boundary. How much more terrifying, then, to consider such elements as part of the 'Wedom' of culture and an 'enemy within' – the term Margaret Thatcher used to describe the militant unions in the early 1980s. Yet it might be that terrorism is exactly this: an enemy within, a mercurial Jekyll and Hyde, a product of the meeting of different world views that can bring about profound transformations, meaning that the old certainties of an easily recognisable 'other' are a thing of the past, and creating profound anxieties about what a firm national identity really is.

The manner in which post 9/11 conceptions of terrorism have become manifest seem very much concerned with this sense of 'otherness' associated with Muslims, but the focus is also on perceptions of these perpetrators as 'home grown', as insiders who cannot so easily be securely located as an invasive outsider against whom boundaries can be secured. McGhee refers to 'converging sites of anxiety that have emerged in the post 9/11 paranoia tend to include terrorists, young Muslim males and asylum seekers in chains of articulation that seem to be another "order" of panic' (McGhee 2005: 76). Such uncertainty seems to suggest that behind the veneer of everyday life there are fears of destructive forces. It is hard not to think of John Griffin's self-perception of 'otherness' under the skin (see Chapter 1).

If, indeed, these phenomenon are about the 'other' inside it is easy to see how this erodes the easier sense of knowable boundaries and controllable borders. The criminologist Claire Valier uses the term 'gothic' (2002; 2004) to signify the nature of risks that transcend the local and threaten terror in the most mundane settings. These 'inner terrorists' (McGhee 2005: 76) cannot be contained and give rise to anxieties about those who appear unremarkably ordinary but harbour malign intent. The gothic nature of social reality was never more apparent than in the aftermath of the Woolwich killing in May 2013 in which two disturbed and radicalised men ran down and butchered soldier Lee Rigby in the street. The spectacle of the assailant holding a bloody cleaver as he was filmed talking to other members of the public suggested to some a new and darker form of terror as spectacle. Although this was clearly a vicious and barbaric act, causing palpable outrage and shock across the nation and giving rise to tough Churchillian talk from politicians, there needs to be a sense of proportion too. Does this have nothing to do with the perception of Britain as a steady partner in the ongoing invading, occupying and bombing of Muslim countries, the setting up of prisons where the usual ethical standards do not appear to apply, the using of drones which have routinely killed civilians, and the imposing of harsh and tyrannical regimes? None of this excuses bloody jihadist actions but it certainly provides a rationale in the minds of the terrorists. Indeed, the Woolwich attacker cited the everyday murder of Muslim civilians as the reason for the attack.

CONCLUSIONS

The images, news items, theory and dialogues presented in this book were chosen in an attempt to expose and problematise conceptions of race and ethnicity. Representation is central to how we form our own identities and perceive those of others, and in turn reaffirm the mediated forms of our culture. This is very much how Foucault suggests discourse (a dyad of power/knowledge) creates us as beings. Forms of representation are how we act out, perform and express our identities. In a similar vein these are expressions of habitus, a sort of ritual condensation of the everyday, habitual nature of lived culture. This book has suggested that by the very habitual nature of these signs of our culture – pictures, photographs, literature, film, all of the historical back pages of our culture, the available symbolic capital – ethnic and racial identities are formed, challenged and resisted. It is not to suggest that the individual agent disappears but that agency is expressed through the mediated resources of culture, not necessarily passively and often through confrontation, resistance and transformation.

No single theoretical explanation of racial or ethnic divisions appears to entirely account for the diverse phenomena contained by these terms. Most theoretical frameworks are too crushing in their generality, too reductionist or else too abstract and fragmentary to recognise the complexity of ethnic relations or capture their vivid lived reality. Nevertheless, these varied explanations are of interest not only for the extent to which they are able to account for race/ism and ethnic identity but because their emphases are instructive and highlight the historical ideas which have shaped our perception of difference. Neither ethnicity nor race can be understood without reference to other social relations and changing contexts. Ethnic identity is recognised by and contingent upon divisions of class and gender, as well as the religious, political and economic contexts in which social relations take place. It turns out that people in very different cultural settings have one thing in common; they all have complex multiple selves, and circumstances have a lot to do with the type of identity which is manifest at any given moment.

Ethnic conflicts have been briefly discussed in areas as diverse as Georgetown, Kuala Lumpur, Oldham and Sydney. They are labelled as 'race riots' or cases of 'bipolar ethnicity', but in every case they have a history which links them to patterns of colonialism, diaspora, indigenous displacement or social exclusion. The social and economic forces which create divisions, drawing and reaffirming or breaking boundaries, are in motion all the time. Currently many cities in Europe are experiencing an explosion of support for far-Right neo-Nazi parties such as the Golden Dawn (Greece), Jobbik (Hungary), National Front (France) and, in the UK, the English Defence League (as well as the more 'respectable' anti-immigration UK Independence Party (UKIP)). This upsurge bears witness to the climate of austerity facing millions of people and shows how visible minorities – refugees, new migrants and Romany families in Eastern Europe, for instance – have become vulnerable scapegoats in the fallout from the banking crisis.

The USA and other western nations may identify certain groups as legitimate targets, as terrorists or freedom fighters, and may quietly but implicitly condone (and practise) the use of extreme measures such as torture (recently dubbed 'enhanced interrogation') as legitimate against prisoners in the 'war against terror'. The ideological rightness of their actions is presented as tacit, as almost beyond question. In reality, although the western powers are not beyond scrutiny, their hegemonic power over news values and their ownership of media sources allows them to foreground their values; dissent is marginalised and can be ignored. But, more than this, while minority extremist viewpoints are often given undue emphasis which helps to exacerbate the sense of threat and make the narrow jihadist pronouncements or far right wing sentiments of a tiny minority seem to have more currency than they do.

So caution is needed: power may move in complex and contingent ways, and the postmodern micro-analysis of culture is important for a heightened realisation of how subjectivity is constructed. Oppressed minorities need to be recognised, their struggles given a voice, but the focus must not preclude analysis of the powerful elites: the encompassing ideologies of the state need to be recognised for what they are, their motives and impacts on vulnerable groups exposed and resisted. An over-zealous pursuit of relativism as a reaction to the excesses of western imperialism may constitute a defeat of enlightened and universal values of humanism.

If race was an invention of modernity – it had a beginning – then is a time imaginable where race will pass into insignificance, become a difference that doesn't make a difference? Will newer divisions arise and take the place of race? Or, as Gilroy suggests, will the legacy of Manicheanism persist in the way any new scheme of cultural distinction is drawn? The form and focus may change, but it is a delusion to assume that we will stop drawing boundaries, whether they are based on blood quantum, colour, cultural differences, citizenship, employment or something else: the one thing that seems certain is that the identification of 'others' will continue to shift and reflect the political and social trends of the time. Difference is part of social unity. However, to deny difference and naturalise traditions of dominance by segregating and staying within defensive cultural boundaries may mean the avoidance of confrontation, and confronting injustice is necessary if we are serious about finding mutual solutions and sharing the future.

EXERCISE 9.1

1 Is 'mixed race' a sign that we are transcending the boundaries of race and entering a post-racial era?
2 What signs suggest that this is an overly optimistic interpretation?
3 Is the Internet a genuinely radical space in which identities can be detached from their material origins?
4 Consider the image used in the anti-terrorist poster (Figure 9.1). What are your impressions of this image?
5 Several other posters showing white, blue-eyed faces were also used. Does that then justify the use of the one shown here?
6 Considering the global shifts commented on briefly in this chapter, give examples of these processes in your own town.
7 Assess Huntington's theory of the 'clash of civilizations' are national cultures represented by Western, Hindu, Islamic and Confucian cultural heritages really so different that there is an impossibility of real communication and rapprochement between them?

EXERCISE 9.2

1 Consider the 'terror' incidents mentioned in this chapter. What might they tell us about changing perceptions of 'otherness'?
2 Assess Valier's conception of the gothic nature of contemporary threats.
3 Is it possible to imagine a society free from racism?

4   How might society be changing to accommodate the changes in the mix of the population?
5   Is a knowledge of the intersections of class, gender, religion and other divisions essential for a better understanding of social divisions? If so, in what way might it help?
6   Why might a traditional Marxist see intersectionality as muddying the water and unnecessary when understanding how social being is formed?

Further reading

Among several texts that present diverse discussions of 'mixed race', especially useful is Jayne Ifekwunigwe's *'Mixed Race' Studies: A Reader* (2004; Routledge, London). The link to terrorism and ethnicity is captured well in San Juan Jr.'s *The Wake of Terror: Class, Race, Nation, Ethnicity in the Postmodern World* (2007; Lexington Books, Lanham, MD). Keenan Malik's gripping political history of the Rushdie case in *From Fatwa to Jihad* (2009; Atlantic Books, London) is an insightful examination of the birth of 'radical Islam' in Britain ignited by the publication of Rushdie's *The Satanic Verses*. Finally, it is essential to develop a balanced understanding of the movement of Islam and how this has continued to shape attitudes about diversity. Two excellent texts to be recommended are Tahir Abbas's *Islamic Radicalism and Multicultural Politics: The British Experience* (2011; Routledge, Abington and New York) and Max Farrar, Simon Robinson, Yasmin Valli and Paul Wetherly's edited volume *Islam in the West: Key Issues in Multiculturalism* (2012; Palgrave Macmillan, Basingstoke). The former gives a detailed and scholarly account of the complex historical, socio-cultural and political causes of radicalism and the latter collection provides a realistic analysis of freedom of speech, politics, religious dialogue and gender issues in the lived realities faced routinely in Britain's multi-ethnic communities.

Note

1   This is certainly true, although I haven't met anyone who saw these in an urban centre.

GLOSSARY

aberrant decoding   A term coined by Umberto Eco (1980) which highlights the problems of interpreting (decoding) a message by means of a different code from that used to encode it. In effect, whenever there are social or cultural differences between the encoder and the decoder of a message then the reading (decoding) of the message will be 'aberrant'. Fiske (1990: 78) gives the example of an interviewee wearing a pair of jeans at a job interview. The subcultural status of jeans, he argues, might have high value to the young man, but to the employer they may seem to be an inappropriate code and represent non-conformity. Many examples of aberrant decoding are apparent when there is an ignorance of cultural codes in a multicultural society. For example, members of some Aboriginal groups may find direct eye contact with a person in authority to be disrespectful and will look away in deference. However, the white European (and Australian) codes for eye contact may read this as a sign of guilt or dishonesty.

affectivity   Primordial attachments are in essence emotional and based upon strong **affective** ties (this is akin to the belief that kinship exerts a powerful influence; the 'blood is thicker than water' argument), which makes such bonds quite impermeable to other social influences.

apriority   This is an idea which, in contrast to sociological views, posits primordial attachments as part of an individual's make-up, given or prior to all social interaction.

biopower/biopolitics   A term used by Foucault to designate a form of power that marked the beginning of a historical era (beginning in the eighteenth century) in which 'there was an explosion of numerous and diverse techniques for achieving the subjugation of bodies and the control of populations' (Foucault 1984: 140). The rapid development of educational, criminal justice, military, medical and labour-management systems of discipline and organisation and their control over the body are mentioned by Foucault. The control of the body, rather than level of consciousness or ideology, is an important and neglected theme for Foucault. While he recognises the insight of Marx, he views the state-centred model of power as self-defeating because, to succeed, the forces of resistance will need to mirror the very state they wish to overthrow. Instead, Foucault's writing traces the biopolitics – the discourses or technologies of power by which bodies and indeed whole populations are controlled. (He particularly focused on punishment, surveillance, medical technologies and sexology.) Many have found Foucault's articulation of power unsatisfactory as it allows for no clearly defined force to oppose.

commodification   A term that indicates the transformation of items, activities, concepts and relationships, which would not previously have been considered as the object of trade or exchange, into commodities and can, for example, include ideas, aesthetics, spirituality, the family, gender relations, cultural ceremonies and artefacts. This process was noted by Marx and Engels in the *Communist Manifesto* in 1848:

> The bourgeoisie, wherever it has got the upper hand, has put an end to all feudal, patriarchal, idyllic relations. It has pitilessly torn asunder the motley feudal ties that bound man to his 'natural superiors', and has left no other nexus between man and man than naked self-interest, than callous 'cash payment'. It has drowned out the most heavenly ecstasies of religious fervour, of chivalrous enthusiasm, of philistine sentimentalism, in the icy water of egotistical calculation. It has resolved personal worth into exchange value, and in place of the numberless indefeasible chartered freedoms, has set up that single, unconscionable freedom – Free Trade. In one word, for exploitation, veiled by religious and political illusions, it has substituted naked, shameless, direct, brutal exploitation.
>
> The bourgeoisie has stripped of its halo every occupation hitherto honoured and looked up to with reverent awe. It has converted the physician, the lawyer, the priest, the poet, the man of science, into its paid wage labourers.
>
> The bourgeoisie has torn away from the family its sentimental veil, and has reduced the family relation into a mere money relation.

In Chapter 6 the commodification of sacred and ceremonial places, art and objects associated with the traditions of Aboriginal people and, indeed, the people themselves, is discussed.

creolisation   The concept of cultural creolisation, introduced in anthropology by Ulf Hannerz (see Hannerz 1992: 264–5), refers to the intermingling of two or several formerly discrete traditions or cultures. In an era of global mass communication and capitalism creolisation can be identified nearly everywhere in the world, but there are important differences in the degree of mixing. The concept has been criticised for essentialising cultures (as if the merging traditions were 'pure' at the outset).

cultural capital Bourdieu made the ground-breaking realisation that 'capital' in its broadest sense is the key to understanding the structure and function of the social sphere. He believed that economic theory had served to create a false dichotomy between exchanges that could be counted as purely financial and self-interested and all others, which were then considered non-economic and hence disinterested. However, cultural capital is deeply intertwined with economics, although disguised as immaterial and disinterested. It can be embodied in the form of 'long-lasting dispositions of the mind and body' or objectified through consumer products of all kinds and especially, perhaps, those which have an aesthetic or status value (books, music, pictures, interior design, electronic gadgetry and so on). However, Bourdieu also makes particular reference to the acquisition of cultural capital through education (various linguistic and cultural knowledges and competencies), which is attained by middle-class children particularly and is restricted and channelled away from working-class children (or, in many cases, children from non-white ethnic backgrounds) (see Bourdieu in Halsey 1997: 46).

cultural imaginary This concept 'refers to the intersections of fantasy images and discursive forms in which cultural communities mirror and articulate themselves, and which act as points of reference for their collective identity formations' (Lykke 2000); also defined as 'those vast networks of interlinking discursive themes, images, motifs and narrative forms that are publicly available within a culture at any one time, and articulate its psychic and social dimensions' (Dawson 1994: 48).

culture Considered by many to be one of the most complex concepts and one which divides opinion broadly, from ideas of culture as: 'the best which has been thought and said in the world' (Matthew Arnold, *Culture & Anarchy* (1869)), which suggests an elite conception of 'high culture' as reflected in literature and philosophy, to conceptions of culture as inclusive and everyday: 'the set of human practices that produce meaning and the objects that are the result of those practices. It encompasses all forms of human engagement in those practices, and their effects on humans acting together as a "culture"' (Kress 1988: 182). Further analysis yields other complex distinctions within 'culture':

> Culture is ordinary: that is the first fact. Every human society has its own shape, its own purposes, its own meanings. Every human society expresses these, in institutions, and in arts and learning. A culture has two aspects: the known meanings and directions, which its members are trained to; the new observations and meanings which are offered and tested. These are the ordinary processes of human societies and human minds, and we see through them the nature of a culture: that is always both traditional and

creative; that it is both the most ordinary common meanings and the finest individual meanings.

(Williams 2011: 6)

This definition conveys the understanding that culture is dynamic and always in the making rather than static and elitist (which was implicit in traditional notions of High and Low culture).

deconstruction A term first used by the post-structuralist Jacques Derrida to refer to the way in which the deeper and multiple meanings within a text can be deduced (these meanings may contradict and undermine the ostensible surface interpretation of the text). For example, in the headline 'Five die in riot', the agency is effectively removed and hence we have an incomplete understanding of the context – did the five die of sun stroke, heart attacks, old age? Were they killed by other demonstrators, army or police? Similarly, there are assumptions in the word 'riot'. Drawn from a paradigm of similar words, 'riot' is different to 'demonstration', 'fracas' or 'street battle' (a careful study of the ideological basis of media presentations of reality can be found in Kress and Hodge 1979). Hence the deconstruction of the surface manifestations of cultural codes can yield insight into the choices and preferred readings of such texts.

deterritorialisation The process by which identity becomes detached from its location and material base. The process of diaspora and hybridisation are elements in the radical displacement of 'rooted' identities, becoming 'routed' in Bhabha's description of the 'border lands' of ethnicity. More generally in postmodernity, the term indicates the compression of time and space suggested by Harvey (1989) and the erosion of meanings from a foundationalist base to becoming free-floating signifiers. The process of globalisation is certainly accelerating the pace at which physical location is decreasing in importance for social relationships.

diaspora A complex term often associated with migration and dispersal of peoples over time. The 1989 edition of the OED traces the etymology of the word 'diaspora' back to its Greek root and to its appearance in the Old Testament (Deut. 28:25). As such, it references God's intentions for the people of Israel to be 'dispersed' across the world.

'Diaspora' now also refers to 'any body of people living outside their traditional homeland.' Victor Hoboken (2004: 202–3) cites the five types of diaspora. These are:

1 The 'victim' type includes communities that have been forced to leave their homeland as a result of political, ethnic or religious conflicts. Among them are Armenians, African captives in Americas and Palestinians.

2 'Labour' diasporas (Italian, Chinese, Japanese, Turkish communities) emerge when the movement of people is caused by unsatisfactory economic conditions in their home countries.

3 'Trade' diasporas do not necessarily mean an escape from home, but are the result of both an individual and a collective (state-sponsored) effort. Chinese trade communities in many countries of South East Asia illustrate this form.

4 The 'imperial' or 'colonial' type of diaspora – for example, Europeans who found themselves outside their countries of origin after the collapse of colonialism, such as the British in Africa or Russians in the former Soviet republics of the USSR.

5 The 'cultural' or 'hybrid' type of diaspora is best illustrated by the Caribbean peoples abroad. The peoples of the Caribbean are the descendants of the European colonists (imperial diaspora), the Indian migrant workers (labour diaspora) and the African slaves from west Africa (victim diaspora).

differance In this term (from Derrida) 'meaning is always deferred, never quite fixed or complete, so there's always some slippage' (Woodward 1997: 21). Meaning is derived from both identity and difference – it is a continuous dialectic between the two and hence never complete, always open. 'Differance' is Derrida's attempt to combine these aspects of the process of sense-making in one word that combines both difference and deferral (see Appignanesi and Garrett 1995: 80). As we have seen in the early chapters, meaning and identity are always contingent on the 'other' or the subaltern; this is a necessary and destabilising force within the identity of the dominant term. In other words, the marginalised and subordinate term is functionally opposed and a negation of the dominant term, yet actually constitutive of it. This is easy to see in terms such as gay/straight, black/white, male/female, sane/insane.

discourse Discourses are those broad patterns of institutional thought, or, as Foucault suggested, 'regimes of truth' that define and limit what can be said about a specific topic. Muecke (1982) suggested that white Australians were limited to only four ways of speaking about Aborigines: via the anthropological, the romantic, the literary and the directly racist (see Chapter 6). Discourse in Foucault's conception is the manner in which power is constituted. This was a radical departure from the notion of power as a possession installed and wielded by (for example) an all-powerful authoritarian state. Foucault, instead, sees power as the result of the association of various disciplinary practices and knowledges and the resistances to these. His analyses traced the origins of the asylum (*Madness and Civilization*), the prison and regimes of punishment and surveillance (*Discipline and Punish*), and the different social formations around sexualities (*History of Sexuality I, II, III*).

Discourse is an elusive term which refers to overarching canons of meaning which constitute knowledge and lived experience. Discourse affects and is affected by subjectivity and directs and focuses complex power relations. It is constituted by language but also by the apparatus of the state (as shown in Foucault's analyses of prisons, torture and asylums) and the ideas and practices of resistance movements. It can be manifest in linguistic structures: the examples given in this book of 'race' and 'ethnicity' illustrate that these terms are the complex surface of many historical discourses (see Chapters 2 and 3).

essentialism   The belief that categories or individuals and groups of human beings have innate, defining features exclusive to their category (for example, the belief that different races have inherent characteristics that differentiate them from other races). Essentialism has been challenged by social constructionist theories which have shown that, while there may be some biological predispositions, identity and meaning are culturally produced. There is evidence that socialisation and the discursive practices of a society will shape our sense of self and that this is being constantly modified by a dialectic process. It is quite clear that ethnicity and race, age, gender, sexuality and other aspects of culture are interpreted differently and the practices associated with social divisions vary between cultures.

ethnic cleansing   'the attempt to create ethnically homogeneous geographic areas through the deportation or forcible displacement of persons belonging to particular ethnic groups. Ethnic cleansing sometimes involves the removal of all physical vestiges of the targeted group through the destruction of monuments, cemeteries, and houses of worship' (www.britannica.com/EBchecked/topic/194242/ethnic-cleansing).

> Ethnic cleansing is the use of force or intimidation by a government to expulse members of an ethnic group, race, nationality or religion from a territory, usually their homeland. It used to be called 'mass deportation'. The goal of perpetrators is to render the territory ethnically homogeneous for the majority of the dominant group.
>
> (Caliendo and McIlwain 2011: 144)

Ethnic cleansing is distinguishable from genocide because its intent is the expulsion rather than the physical destruction of a group, but genocidal massacres are a common tactic in ethnic cleansing. Genocide and ethnic cleansing are not mutually exclusive. A common misconception about genocide is that it requires the intent to destroy an *entire* group, but the Genocide Convention (1948) clearly states that it only requires that a *part* of an ethnic or racial group be destroyed for the term genocide to apply. If the victims of mass murder are selected solely because they are members of an ethnic or racial group, that is genocide. For example, both genocide and ethnic cleansing of non-Arab Sudanese began in Darfur in 2003 and continue today (2013), with estimates of several hundred thousand being killed, as with most cases (e.g. Turkish massacres of Armenians during WWI or Serbian ethnic cleansing of Albanians in the First Balkan War of 1912–13), the origins of the conflict in Sudan go back to disputes over territory. Cultural genocide can also be practised, as occurred in Australia with the 'stolen generation' (as a result of eugenic ideas practised there since the nineteenth century Aboriginal children of mixed ancestry were taken away from their indigenous families and adopted out to white families).

Cases of genocide are often hotly contended (as with the claims of genocide in Tasmania in the early nineteenth century (see Chapter 3) this may be because perpetrators of such crimes take care to disguise their actions. Indigenous peoples continue to be the most vulnerable to genocidal policies. As Madley (2004) reminds us:

> During the twentieth century, dozens of states implemented policies intended to physically destroy indigenous populations. In the age of the UN Genocide Convention, signatory nations waged campaigns of genocide against the Cham of Cambodia, indigenous peoples in East Timor and the Amazon basin, Iraqi Kurds, the Maya of Guatemala, and others. Today, perpetrators employ sophisticated weapons delivery systems, advanced communications equipment, and overwhelming firepower to kill indigenous people. No evidence suggests a waning in this trend.
>
> (Madley 2004: 1)

ethnocentric   The attitude that one's own culture is superior to others, that one's own beliefs, values and behaviour are more correct than others and that other people and cultures can be evaluated in terms of one's own culture. A tendency to understand the world only from the viewpoint of one's own culture.

eugenics   Meaning literally 'normal genes'. Sir Francis Galton (1822–1911), Darwin's cousin, was the founder of the eugenics movement. Eugenics aims to improve the genetic constitution of the human species by selective breeding. There are several forms:

1 **positive**: selective breeding using 'superior' genetic material (for example, sperm donated by a Nobel scientist);
2 **negative eugenics**: forced sterilisation, ethnic cleansing, genocide;
3 **intra-societal eugenics**: this refers to a genetic cause for problems such as crime, poverty and disease that occur within a society. The essentialist eugenics view is that such phenomena are the products of less highly evolved genes;
4 **inter-societal eugenics**: by contrast, this form of eugenics extends the notion of a genetic basis for dominance to imperial notions of 'progress' and 'civilisation' which are explained as being based on evolutionary principles. In other words, the conquerors or exploiters are vindicated because

they are superior genetically. Furthermore, this view inculcates an aggressive focus on the need to compete and defeat other nations. War is seen as a biologically necessary and 'natural' aspect of existence.

Although Darwin was anxious that evolutionary theory was not used in a negative way, certain readings of his work can be seen to have set such discourses in motion. 'When a species increases inordinately in numbers in a small tract, epidemics often ensue; and here we have a limiting check independent of the struggle for life' (Darwin 1979: 72). Darwin does seem to have believed that the mechanisms of natural selection are thwarted by human civilisation. One of the objectives of civilisation is somehow to help the underprivileged members, and it is therefore to be opposed to the natural selection responsible for extinction of the weakest.

ex-nomination   A term used by Roland Barthes (1972) to identify one of the ways in which the dominance of the ruling class goes unexamined precisely because it is not named as such: the process of ex-nomination ensures that we see the values or attributes of dominant groups not as the product of particular class interests but simply as apolitical, intrinsic human values that are, therefore, as unsuitable for critique as a grapefruit or any other 'real thing'. Ex-nomination also works to legitimate the dominance of specific racial and cultural groups by failing to acknowledge or 'mark' their distinctive qualities (for example, white, heterosexual) and thereby assuming their universality.

genocide   The Genocide Convention defines genocide as 'the intentional destruction, in whole or in part, of a national, ethnical, racial, or religious group' (Stanton 2004). The formal definition came in the 1948 Convention for the Prevention and the Punishment of the Crime of Genocide. Genocide is defined in the Convention as any of the following acts committed with intent to destroy, in whole or in part, a national, ethnic, racial or religious group, as such: a) killing members of the group; b) causing serious bodily or mental harm to members of the group; c) deliberately inflicting on the group conditions of life calculated to bring about its physical destruction in whole or in part; d) imposing measures intended to prevent births within the group; e) forcibly transferring children of the group to another group (Becker 2000).

habitus   A concept originally suggested by Marcel Mauss (1979) to designate both the living space and how social groups internalise their environments, forming sets of dispositions including material effects, bodily attitudes and behaviours. The culture is expressed through a range of bodily functions (similar to Foucault's techniques of the self): basic activities such as sleeping, eating, sitting, walking, having sex, giving birth, and so forth. These are thought of as natural functions but they are performed quite differently in different historical periods and cultures. The term has come to prominence in the work of Pierre Bourdieu (1977). Bourdieu extended the concept, demonstrating the relationship between habitus and social class. It has also been applied to various other social contexts, such as ethnicity and gender relations.

hegemony Developed by the Italian Marxist Antonio Gramsci in the 1930s, hegemony refers to the way in which dominant groups in society are able to maintain their dominance over the less powerful groups without recourse to force or coercion, but instead are able to actively gain their consent. This has the effect of making the dominance of certain groups appear legitimate and natural, 'the way of the world'. Hegemony, in Gramsci's view, is never total but operates by constant negotiation with other emergent forms of resistance: see, for example, the 'moral panics' which operate sporadically in western society.

hybridity The 'in-between' stage between the pre-colonial subject's identity and the identity internalised through colonialisation. Hybridity describes the process of cultural translation that is inevitable in a world where communities, peoples, cultures, tribes, ethnii, are no longer homogenous self-sufficient autochthonous entities tightly bound within by kinship and tradition and strongly boundaried in relation to the outside world (Hall 2000). Similar is the concept of 'border-crossing', in which the lack of fixed identities, uncertainty, mobility and the possibility of negotiating boundaries is emphasised.

ideal reader A term that suggests that every text is presented with a particular class of reader in mind, making preferences, values, attitudes and beliefs implicit in its reading. Kress states:

> Every genre positions those who participate in a text of that kind: as interviewer or interviewee, as listener or storyteller, as a reader or a writer, as a person interested in political matters, as someone to be instructed or as someone who instructs; each of these positionings implies different possibilities for response and for action. Each written text provides a 'reading position' for readers, a position constructed by the writer for the 'ideal reader' of the text.
>
> Kress (1988: 107)

These reading positions can give the reader the clear impression that he or she is part of an 'Us' or 'Them'. Take, for example, the sample news headlines in Chapter 6. In this instance, and many like it, a group is presented as a threat to the moral order; the language used about them is in sharp contrast to that used about white citizens, tourists or the police. The values which emerge from a glance at these headlines are firmly white and middle class and imply that 'itinerants' are a problem because of their drinking, begging and bothering of local business people and tourists. The same positioning is discernible (although not always as overtly) in all texts.

identity politics Postmodernism's culturally relative stance challenged and displaced the 'grand narratives' of history, meaning that old certainties associated with the project of modernity appeared untenable – such absolutes lead to the horrors of monocultural dominance. Instead, the previously essentialised opposition to the state became fragmented; unified notions of black, feminist or working-class resistance to oppression, for example, are suggested to have been undermined by this 'cultural turn' in which relative values come to define groups through more and more finely drawn distinctions. This notion of identity politics has become something of a bête noire to Left-leaning intellectuals and scholars as it embraces the notion of increasingly diffuse power relations making mass resistance impossible. The recent debate on multiculturalism (see Chapter 8) is a case in point. Kenan Malik, commenting on an article by David Goodhart entitled 'Too Diverse', which questioned whether diversity was compatible with social cohesion and a genuinely shared social system, made the following rejoinder:

> the real problem is not a surfeit of strangers in our midst but the abandonment over the past two decades of ideologically based politics for a politics of identity. The result has been the fragmentation of society as different groups assert their particular identities – and the creation of a well of resentment within white working class communities who feel left out.
>
> (Malik 2004: 2)

ideological state apparatus Althusser (1977) argues that ideology is a 'system of representations' that mediates people's understanding of themselves and their relationship to society. Ideology actually forms social subjects, manipulating their unconscious desires as well as their rational interests in order to 'interpellate' them – that is, in order to gain their identification with certain social and cultural roles or identities. Ideology offers people particular identities with which they then identify. Althusser makes the point that there is a gap between what constitutes real conditions of the subject and an ideology.

> it is not their real conditions of existence, their real world, that 'men' 'represent to themselves' in ideology, but above all it is their relation to those conditions of existence which is represented to them there. It is this relation which is at the centre of every ideological, i.e. imaginary, representation of the real world.
>
> (Althusser 2006: 339)

James Kavanagh argues that this more sophisticated version of ideology might pave the way for highly sophisticated forms of criticism taking into account multiple social and cultural differences:

> Ideology is less tenacious as a 'set of ideas' than as a system of representations, perceptions, and images that precisely encourages men and

women to 'see' their specific place in a historically peculiar social formation as inevitable, natural, a necessary function of the 'real' itself. Notwithstanding its roots in a class-based understanding of history, contemporary ideology theory also recognises that perceived forms of social 'reality' and subjectivity are constructed within more than one system of differences. In various socially specific ways, differences of sex, race, religion, region, education and ethnicity, as well as class, form complex webs of determinations that affect how ideology works up in a 'lived' relation to the real.

(Kavanagh 1995: 310–11)

ideology An underlying set of values or beliefs, but frequently ones that are not consciously questioned or even visible as such. The ideological process tends to normalise and naturalise, covering its tracks. Stuart Hall defined ideology as: 'images, concepts and premises which provide frameworks through which we represent, interpret, understand and "make sense" of some aspect of social existence' (Hall 2000: 271).

imagined communities Benedict Anderson's (1983) term for the way people's speculative realisation is all that really exists of an ethnic group or a nation state. Groups are often united by a powerful image of the nation that may be at odds with the current reality but provides an idealised or hoped-for state to which the group will return. Politicians are in the business of conveying this imagined holistic vision of the nation as it should be. The plurality of many modern states may seem a threat to these visions and may make their core values harder to articulate. This can lead to break-away movements devising newer, more satisfying images of the community.

ineffability The notion that primordial attachments exert a powerful and unchangeable influence (are in fact ineffable). Hence such attachments are inescapable – outside of social influence.

institutional racism Discriminatory racial practices built into such prominent structures as the political, economic and education systems.

Institutional racism deprives a racially identified group, usually defined as generally inferior to the defining dominant group, from equal access to education, medical care, law, politics, housing, etc.

(Knowles and Prewitt 1969)

One of the perennial criticisms about the way racism has been addressed is the tendency to excuse it as an example of a few 'bad apples' in other words racism operating at an individual level, which is easier then to dismiss.

For too long racism has been thought of in individual psychological terms, reducible to the actions of prejudiced individuals. The concept of institutional racism draws attention to the structural workings of institutions, which exclude people, regardless of individual attitudes.

(Commission for Racial Equality 1985: 2–3)

In 1999 the Macpherson report for the first time officially accepted the concept was at the root of the police failure to properly investigate the 1993 Steven Lawrence murder.

Macpherson defined institutional racism thus:

The collective failure of an organisation to provide an appropriate and professional service to people because of their colour, culture or ethnic origin. It can be seen or detected in processes, attitudes and behaviour which amount to discrimination through unwitting prejudice, ignorance, thoughtlessness and racial stereotyping which disadvantage minority ethnic people.

(Macpherson 1999: para. 6.34)

Arguably the use of the term 'unwitting' was still allowed some margin of excuse. Institutional racism is more subtle, less visible, and less identifiable but no less destructive to human life and human dignity than individual acts of racism.

internal colonialism   A form of colonialism in which the dominant and subordinate populations are intermingled, so that there is no geographically distant 'metropolis' separate from the 'colony'. An explanation of society based on situations where there is a minority persistently exploited by capitalism. Some sort of de facto segregation and exclusion is part of the equation. The concept was first developed with respect to England and its 'internal periphery', mainly Wales and Ireland. The dominant culture uses the 'peripheral' areas to maintain supplies of cheap labour for industry. Other examples would include Turks within modern Germany, blacks in South Africa (Bantustans) and Indians in Mexico (see Hechter 1995).

interpellation   Althusser (1977) describes interpellation as a process of identification by which a subject (mis)recognises him or herself in an 'identity' or role which is offered them in society. Althusser uses the analogy of an address, or 'hailing'. An educator or a policeman, for example, might 'hail' me, by saying 'Hey you'. I might then turn around and recognise myself as the addressee. Thus Althusser hopes to show how ideologies either 'recruit' people to particular, acceptable subject positions in society or else transform individuals into subjects who learn to identify with certain representations. Thus the agent addressing me might equally be a representation in a cultural text. Books, advertisements, TV programmes and films all contain representations of characters and situations with which we might identify; and bound up with such representations are certain societal norms, gender roles, attitudes towards certain groups, etc., which may be disseminated and normalised or satirised.

intersubjectivity   The term implies that the individual's subjectivity is dependent on networks of relationships. In a very real sense our identity is constantly negotiated and renegotiated through communicative encounters with others. There are shared communicative codes within a culture. While we interpret images and other cultural codes uniquely through our own personal experiences and socio-cultural make-up, we nevertheless recognise shared cultural meanings and interpretations. Examples of the 'myth' of whiteness and the contingent meanings of blackness in this text highlight the intersubjectivity of interpretations of race and ethnicity.

intertextuality   This term refers to the interrelationship between texts: usually one text's reference to another. This location of a cultural reference point (most often a historically prior one) usually takes the form of diffuse memories, echoes and reworkings of other texts. Intertextuality is particularly prevalent in 'postmodern' texts, which often play on the notion that everything is a reworking of something else to produce a 'pastiche aesthetic' (such as the hotchpotch of historical styles visible in postmodern architecture).

Kali Mai   Literally, 'black mother'. Kali and Durga are two of the sisters or manifestations of a unitary power which is central to the beliefs of North Indians. The worship of Kali was brought to the Caribbean by North Indians during the indentureship period (1830s–1870s). A major feature of the religion is spirit possession and healing. Bassier (1980) argues that there has been an upsurge in the movement of Kali Mai, with African-Guyanese increasingly joining the church. The growth of the church in the 1990s reflected the need to transcend the political and economic realities in Guyana. Similarly, Rastafarian cults in Guyana have increased since 1978, again for the reason that the practices free the individual from the bonds of society and raise consciousness (by use of the sacred herb and practices that resist the materialism of society). 'The Rastas, like the Kali worshippers, express disenchantment with the establishment and are incapable of having access to the scarce resources of society' (Bassier 1980: 37).

Manichean divide   The Manicheans are adherents to a form of religious or philosophical dualism. Stemming from a religious dualism originating in Persia in the third century AD, Manicheans are said to have considered the universe as two irreconcilable forces of light and dark – hence the use of the term to mean a divide between irreconcilable opposites such as those listed below. These structural oppositions are considered by some structuralists to mirror the human psyche. Lévi-Strauss suggested that cultural patterns had developed from the largely unconscious human proclivity to categorise between stark oppositional categories, actually mirroring cognitive processes. Anomalous categories such as the serpent in the Garden of Eden are considered either magical or disturbing as they do not fit neatly into the existing categories. The tendency to divide the world in these terms, as expressed in the *Clash of Civilizations* (Huntington 1988), can be found in speeches by US presidents (Reagan/Bush references to an 'evil empire') particularly since 9/11 ('in the aftermath of 11 September George W. Bush moved to stifle dissent with the positively Procrustean pronouncement that "either you are with us or you are with the terrorists". There can be no middle way, for criticism is "unpatriotic"' (Macklin 2002)).

WHITE	BLACK
Culture	Nature
Good	Evil
Male	Female
Master	Slave
Adult	Child
Purity	Pollution
God	Satan
Reason	Emotion
Law and order	Chaos
Civilisation	Savagery
Us	Them

mirror stage A Lacanian stage of development in the construction of the self. The child has no initial grasp of the boundaries between the self and others and the external world. Lacan (1977) argues that, during this phase (between the ages of 6 and 18 months – significantly before the acquisition of speech), the sight of oneself in the mirror creates a powerful embodied sense of self as an integrated whole, an 'illusion of a coherent and self-governing personal identity', yet the duality inherent in the experience is significant. Fanon (1967a) gives the example of the French child identifying (reinterpellating) him as a 'black man', thus shattering his illusory holistic self that had been formed within a colonial hierarchy.

misrecognition A term which stems from Lacanian speculation about the development of the ego. The child at a certain stage of infancy makes a primordial identification with his/her reflection in a mirror – this is the recognition of an ideal 'I'. The ego is seen emerging from the child's desire to completely identify with the reflected image (see mirror stage).

The term has also been applied to nationalism and the manner in which the migrant or the colonial subject identifies with the distorted mirror image the nation reflects back, internalising the misrecognised self (often manifest in a negative or contemptuous view of one's own kind). Misrecognition is defined in this instance as the opposite of recognition, and occurs when groups of people suffer because the people or society around them mirror back to them a confining, demeaning or contemptible picture of themselves (Taylor 1994: 25).

moral panic A recurrent feature of modern society, moral panics occur when society becomes convinced that it is under threat from some form of evil, usually in human form. Stanley Cohen (1967) coined the term in reference to the clash between mods and rockers in the 1960s. Central to the concept are the instrumental actions of media in directing a spotlight on what are seen to be threats to the moral order or stability of society. Typical examples are street crimes and muggings (examined by Hall *et al.* in 1978) and more recently ecstasy and rave subcultures, video 'nasties' and paedophiles (Critcher 2003). Moral panics are frequently a reflection of society's anxiety, insularity and ignorance about others. Examples more directly relevant here are Islamophobia, news stories about terrorist activities in the UK and exaggerated images of black gang culture and gun crime.

multiculturalism A term for an ethos, practices and policies through which the state manages diversity. There are several versions of multiculturalism; Lord Parekh's recent statement embodies the more progressive view:

> Multiculturalism is sometimes taken to mean that different cultural communities should live their own ways of life in a self-contained manner. This is not its only meaning and in fact it has long been obsolete. Multiculturalism basically means that no culture is perfect or represents the best life and that it can therefore benefit from a critical dialogue with other cultures. In this sense multiculturalism requires that all cultures should be open, self-critical, and interactive in their relations with each other.
>
> (Parekh 2004: 1–2)

More conservative interpretations reflect a concern that there should be a dominant strand of, for example, Britishness, as commented upon by Ruth Lea:

> every culture has the right to exist and there is no over-arching thread that holds them together. [...] That is the multiculturalism we think is so destructive because there's no thread to hold society together. It is that multiculturalism that Trevor Phillips has condemned and, of course, we are totally supportive. There is another way to define multiculturalism which I would call diversity where people have their own cultural beliefs and they happily coexist – but there is a common thread of Britishness or whatever you want to call it to hold society together.

myth This term is used in contemporary cultural and social studies to address the circulation of complex social meanings which have become embedded in the normative value system of the society. In a similar way to the underlying ideas and beliefs which constitute ideology, myth operates to disguise the process of construction which underpins cultural values. Easily recognisable in the sphere of advertising for example, highly processed food stuff may be presented as 'natural'. In particular the concept has been associated with structuralist linguistics and anthropology. Roland Barthes' Mythologies (1957, 1972) presented a linguistic-based theory of myth as the movement between levels of signification: 'The final term of the linguistic system becomes the first term of the mythical system' (Barthes 1972: 117).

Hence such signs create a double fold of meaning making them unobtrusively commonplace, received 'iconic' ordinary in their use and occurrence. Barthes' examples in Mythologies include – 'Einstein's brain' margarine, steak and chips, wine and milk, striptease, wrestling and the face of Greta Garbo.

In addition political rhetoric frequently uses these commonsense constructions. This is very apparent in the language used about 'Britishness' or 'Frenchness' as if there is a consensual and unified view about national identity. Cultures are not static or finished, they are made up of the varied people who live in that society at any one time. So when politicians decry multiculturalism as a form of apartheid or a cul-de-sac or eroding British values, they are ignoring the point that plurality/multiculturalism is a social fact, and alluding to some timeless view of what constitutes Britain or France or any other nation.

> And that is clearly what I would support because you do accept that people have different cultures and you accept them. It's a positive acceptance not a negative tolerance.
>
> (BBC News, 5 April 2004, see Parekh 2000: 1–2)

the 'other' A term which reflects the metaphysical self-referential perception of people who are seen as fundamentally different; especially used to signify people from other cultures and non-hegemonic sexualities, gays or lesbians, those transgressing gender norms – transsexuals, third sex, and so on. It is a concept that stems from existential thinkers such as Sartre and recognises the contingent nature of self-identity as formed in relation to other alien subjectivities.

plural societies A plural society is one whose population is divided into two or more sub-populations in which the members of each enclave are characterised by distinctive sets of values, beliefs and occupational and social groups. In some cases political preferences may be drawn along ethnic lines. These societies are frequently the result of colonialism, where different nationals have been transported as a labour source. Guyana, Trinidad, Surinam, Mauritius, Fiji and Malaysia are examples of societies where pluralism was created by migration for labour supply for sugar estates and other colonial production. The UK is a plural society owing to the diaspora of subjects from former British colonies.

punctum The term Barthes uses to explain the situation when a particular detail of a photograph (sometimes a seemingly insignificant one) catches the viewer's attention and can bring about a radical change in the reading of the image. In *Camera Lucida* he states: 'a "detail" attracts me. I feel that its mere presence changes my reading, that I am looking at a new photograph, marked in my eyes with a higher value' (1984: 42). The 'punctum' to Barthes is that which 'rises from the scene, shoots out of it like an arrow, and pierces me' (p. 26). The example in Chapter 1 highlights the possibility that a detail in a photo can emerge to dominate the image.

scopophilia A term used by Laura Mulvey (1975) to describe voyeurism and 'the look' in cinema. Derived originally from Freud's theoretical canon, Mulvey has convincingly shown that the look defines and possesses the 'other'; furthermore, by viewing films we are positioned as the voyeur. Some feminist theorists have employed the term as a way of discussing the 'male gaze' and the patriarchal and colonial view of the colonial female body.

'sous rature' [under erasure] Derrida's (1976) concept which recognises the contested and problematic nature of certain concepts. Derrida developed a method of using such terms scored through to demonstrate that they were used out of necessity to convey a meaning which is in circulation but that this use is far from satisfactory. 'Race' in particular (and, owing to its almost synonymous use, 'ethnicity' too) is a prime candidate for this treatment.

REFERENCES

Abbas, T. (2011) *Islamic Radicalism and Multicultural Politics: The British Experience*, London: Routledge.

ABC Northern Territory (2004) 'Funds squeeze prevent asbestos house's demolition', 20 November. Available online at www.abc.net.au/nt/news/200411/s1247891.htm

ABC *7.30 Report*, 30 May 2012, Former Minister reflects on Aboriginal affairs.

Ahmad, A. (1995) 'The Politics of Literary Postcoloniality', *Race and Class*, 36(3): 1–20.

Aiken, R. and R. Poulsen (1997) 'Australian Gov't Tries To Gut Aboriginal Rights', *Militant*, 61(44): 15 December.

Ali, T. (2002) *The Clash of Fundamentalisms: Crusades, Jihads, and Modernity*, London: Verso.

Alibhai Brown, Y. (2000) *After Multiculturalism*, London: Foreign Policy Centre.

Althusser, L. (1971) *Lenin and Philosophy*, trans. Ben Brewster, London: New Left Books.

Althusser, L. (1977) 'Ideology and Ideological State Apparatuses (Notes Towards an Investigation)', in L. Althusser, *Lenin and Philosophy and Other Essays*, London: New Left Books, pp. 127–86.

Althusser, L. (2001) *Lenin and Philosophy and Other Essays*, trans. Ben Brewster, New York: Monthly Review Press.

Althusser, L. (2006) 'Ideology and Ideological State Apparatuses', in J. Storey, *Cultural Theory and Popular Culture: A Reader*, 3rd edn, London: Pearson, pp. 336–46.

Amin, A. (2003) 'Unruly Strangers? The 2001 Urban Riots in Britain', *International Journal of Urban and Regional Research* 27(2): 460–63.

Anderson, B. (1983) *Imagined Communities: Reflections on the Origin and Spread of Nationalism*, London: Verso.

Anderson, S. E. (1995) *The Black Holocaust for Beginners*, London and New York: Writers and Readers.

Ani, M. (1994) *Yurugu: An African-Centered Critique of European Cultural Thought and Behaviour*, Trenton, NJ: Africa World Press.

Ankomah, B. (1999) 'The Butcher of Congo', *New African*. Available online at www.hartford-hwp.com/archives/35/181.html

Anon. (1985) 'Threat to the Nation', unpublished tract, Perth: Union of Caucasian Christian People.

Anthias, F. and N. Yuval-Davis (1992) *Racialized Boundaries*, London and New York: Routledge.

Appadurai, A. (1990) 'Disjuncture and Difference in the Global Cultural Economy', in M. Featherstone (ed.), *Global Culture*, London: Sage, pp. 295–310.

Appignanesi, R. and C. Garrett (1995) *Postmodernism for Beginners*, Trumpington: Icon.

Arundhati, R. (2002: 40) The Algebra of Infinite Justice, New Delhi: Penguin, p. 40.

Ashcroft, B., G. Griffiths and H. Tiffin (eds) (1995) *The Post-Colonial Studies Reader*, London and New York: Routledge.

Ashcroft, B., G. Griffiths and H. Tiffin (1998) *Key Concepts in Post-Colonial Studies*, London and New York: Routledge.

Aung San Suu Kyi (1994) 'Empowerment for a Culture of Peace and Development', address to WCCD in Manila, 21 November. Available online at www.burmalibrary.org/reg. burma/archives/199411/msg00067.html

Australian Bureau of Statistics (2011) Regional Statistics, Northern Territory, March 2011. Available online at www.abs.gov.au/ausstats/abs@.nsf/Latestproducts/1362.7Feature %20Article1Mar%202011?opendocument#Components

Australian Human Rights Commission (1997) *Bringing them Home: Report of the National Inquiry into the Separation of Aboriginal and Torres Strait Islander Children from Their Families*. Available online at www.humanrights.gov.au/publications/bringing-them-home-report-1997

Aziz, R. (1992) 'Feminism and the Challenge of Racism: Deviance or Difference?', in H. Crowley and S. Himmelweit (eds), *Knowing Women: Feminism and Knowledge*, Cambridge: Polity Press, pp. 291–305.

Back, L. (2002) 'The Fact of Hybridity: Youth, Ethnicity and Racism', in D. T. Goldberg and J. Solomos (eds), *A Companion to Racial and Ethnic Studies*, Oxford: Blackwell, pp. 439–54.

Back, L. and Solomos, J. (2000) *Theories of Race and Racism: Reader*, London and New York: Routledge.

Back, L., M. Keith, A. Khan, K. Shukra and J. Solomos (2002) 'The Return of Assimilationism: Race, Multiculturalism and New Labour', *Sociological Research Online* 7(2): 1–13.

Bagguley, P. and Y. Hussain (2003) 'Conflict and Cohesion – Constructions of Community in the 2001 "Riots"', Paper presented to the Communities Conference, Trinity and All Saints College, University of Leeds, 18–20 September 2003.

Bagguley, P. and Y. Hussain (2008) *Riotous Citizens: Ethnic Conflict in Multicultural Britain*, Aldershot: Ashgate.

Bagnoli, A. (2004) 'Researching Identities with Multi-method Autobiographies', *Sociological Research Online*, 9(2). Available online at www.socresonline.org.uk/9/2/bagnoli.html

Balandier, G. (1974) 'The Colonial Situation: A Theoretical Approach (1951)', in I. Wallerstein, *The Modern World System: Capitalist Agriculture and the Origins of the European World Economy in the Sixteenth Century*, London and New York: Academic Press, pp. 34–61.

Balibar, E. and E. Wallerstein (1991) *Race, Nation, Class: Ambiguous Identities*, London and New York: Verso.

Banton, M. (1967) *Race Relations*, London: Tavistock.

Banton, M. (1987) *Racial Theories*, Cambridge: Cambridge University Press.

Barker, C. (2011) *Cultural Studies: Theory and Practice*, 4th edn, London: Sage.

Barker, C. and D. Galasinski (2001) *Cultural Studies and Discourse Analysis: A Dialogue on Language and Identity*, London: Sage.

Barth, F. (1969) *Ethnic Groups and Boundaries: The Social Organization of Culture Difference*, London: George Allen & Unwin.

Barthes, R. (1972) *Mythologies*, selected and trans. from the French by Annette Lavers, London: Cape.

Barthes, R. (1977) *Image, Music, Text*, selected and trans. by Stephen Heath, London: Flamingo.

Barthes, R. (1984) *Camera Lucida*, trans. by Richard Howard, London: Flamingo.

Bassier, W. M. Z. (1987) 'Kali Mai Worship in Guyana: A Quest for a New Identity', in I. J. Banadur Singh (ed.), *Indians in the Caribbean*, London: Oriental Press, pp. 269–93.

Baudrillard, J. (1983) *Simulations*, New York: Semiotext.

Baudrillard, J. (1991) *La Guerre du golfe n'a pas eu lieu*, Paris: Galilee.

Bauman, Z. (2002) 'Holocaust', in D. T. Goldberg and J. Solomos (eds), *A Companion to Racial and Ethnic Studies*, Part 1, Oxford: Blackwell, pp. 46–63.

Bevege, A. (2013) 'Hotel Plan for One Mile', NT News, 26 September. Available online at www.ntnews.com.au/article/2013/09/26/325361_ntnews.html

BBC News (2004a) 'Debate call on "multicultural" UK', 5 April. Available online at http://news.bbc.co.uk/1/hi/uk_politics/3599925.stm

BBC News (2004b) 'So what exactly is multiculturalism?', 5 April. Available online at http://news.bbc.co.uk/1/hi/uk/3600791.stm

BBC News (2012) 'Philippines profile', 7 October. Available online at www.bbc.co.uk/news/world-asia-15581450

BBC World Service (2001) 'Mixed race, mixed feelings', 1 September. Available online at www.bbc.co.uk/worldservice/people/highlights/010831_mixedrace.shtml

Beard, J. R. (1970; first pub. 1853) *The Life of Toussaint L'Ouverture, the Negro Patriot of Hayti: Comprising an Account of the Struggle for Liberty in the Island, and a Sketch of Its History to the Present Period*, Westport, CT: Negro Universities Press.

Beck, U. (1992) *The Risk Society*, London: Sage.

Beck, U. (2002) 'The Silence of Words and Political Dynamics in the World Risk Society', *Logos*, 1(4). Available online at www.logosonline.home.igc.org/beck.htm

Becker, K. *Genocide and Ethnic Cleansing*, Model United Nations Far West, 50th Session Issues. Available online at www.munfw.org/archive/50th/4th1.htm

Bedford, D. (2013) 'Marxism and the Aboriginal Question: The Tragedy of Progress', *The North Star*, 16 January. Available online at www.thenorthstar.info/?p=4715

Belchem, J. (ed.) (2006) *Liverpool 800: Culture, Character, and History*, Liverpool: Liverpool University Press.

Bell, D. and B. M. Kennedy (2000) *The Cybercultures Reader*, London and New York: Routledge.

Benedict, R. (1961) *Patterns of Culture*, Boston, MA: Houghton Mifflin.

Bennett, D. and J. Stephens (1991) 'Postcolonial Critique', *Arena* 96: 5.

Bentley, C. (1987) 'Ethnicity and Practice', *Comparative Studies in Society and History* 29(1): 24–55.

Bhabha, H. (1985) 'Signs Taken for Wonders: Questions of Ambivalence and Authority Under a Tree Outside Delhi', *Critical Inquiry* 12(1): 144–65.

Bhabha, H. (1994) *The Location of Culture*, London and New York: Routledge.

Bhabha, H. (1996) 'Culture's In-Between', in S. Hall and P. du Gay (eds), *Questions of Cultural Identity*, London and Thousand Oaks, CA: Sage, pp. 53–60.

Bhabha, H. K. (1998) 'The White Stuff', *Artforum* 36(9): 21–24.

Bilton, T., K. Bennett, P. Jones, M. Stanworth, K. Sheard and A. Webster (eds) (1987) *Introductory Sociology*, 2nd edn, London: Macmillan.

Bittles, A. (2004) 'Review – Eugenics in Australia: Striving for National Fitness by Diana Wyndham (2003)', *Galton Institute Newsletter*. Available online at www.galtoninstitute. org.uk/Newsletters/GINL0403/Eugenics_in_Australia.htm

Black, E. (2001) *IBM and the Holocaust*, London: Little Brown.

Blainey, G. (1984) *All For Australia*, North Ryde: Methuen Haynes.

Bleakley, J. W. (1929) *The Aboriginals and Half-Castes of Central Australia and North Australia*, Trove, National Library of Australia. Available online at http://trove.nla.gov. au/work/19457444

Blum, W. (2004) 'Killing Hope US Military and CIA Interventions Since World War II'. Contents available online at http://williamblum.org/books/killing-hope

Bonnett, A. (1996) 'Anti-Racism and the Critique of White Identities', *New Community* 22, 97–110.

Borges, J. L. (1975) *A Universal History of Infamy*, trans. by Norman Thomas di Giovanni, Harmondsworth: Penguin.

Bourdieu, P. (1977) *Outline of Theory of Practice*, Cambridge: Cambridge University Press.

Bourdieu, P. (1986) 'The Forms of Capital', in J. Richardson (ed.), *Handbook of Theory and Research for the Sociology of Education*, New York: Greenwood, pp. 241–58.

Bourdieu, P. (1989a) *Distinction: A Social Critique of the Judgement of Taste*, London and New York: Routledge.

Bourdieu, P. (1989b) *The Logic of Practice*, Cambridge: Polity Press.

Bourdieu, P. (1989c) 'Social Space and Symbolic Power', *Sociological Theory* 7(1): 14–25.

Bourdieu, P. (1990) *In Other Words: Essays toward a Reflective Sociology*, Oxford: Polity.

Bourdieu, P. and L. Boltanski (1976) 'La production de l'idéologie dominante', *Actes de la Recherche en Sciences Sociales* 2(3): 4.

Bourdieu, P. and L. Wacquant (1992) *An Invitation to Reflexive Sociology*, Chicago, IL: The University of Chicago Press.

Brah, A. (1996) *Cartographies of Diaspora, Contesting Identities*, London and New York: Routledge.

Bramann, J. K. (1999) 'Multiculturalism and Personal Identity', preliminary draft of the Philosophical Forum presentation for 26 October. Available online at http://faculty. frostburg.edu/phil/forum/Multicult.htm

Bronowski, J. (1974) *The Ascent of Man*, London: BBC Books.

Brown Britain (2001) BFI documentary directed by Yasmin Dellal.

Bufton, S. (2004) 'Social Class', in G. Taylor and S. Spencer (eds), *Social Identities: Multidisciplinary Approaches*, London and New York: Routledge, pp. 14–34.

Caliendo, S. M. and C. McIlwain (eds) (2011) *The Routledge Companion to Race and Ethnicity*, London: Routledge.

Callinicos, A. (1995) 'Wonders Taken for Signs: Homi Bhabha's Postcolonialism', in M. Zavarzadeh, T. Ebert and D. Morton (eds), *Post-Ality: Marxism and Postmodernism*, Washington, DC: Maisonneuve Press.

Campbell, C. (2013) 'Malaysia's Multiracial Promise Marred by Bigotry and Political Persecution', in *World Time*, September 19, 31. Available online at http://world.time. com/2013/09/19/malaysias-multiracial-promise-marred-by-bigotry-and-political-persecution/#ixzz2iUOds8jQ

Cantle, T. (2001) 'Community Cohesion: a report of the independent review team, Home Office'. Available online at www.homeoffice.gov.uk/comrace

Caplan, P. (2005) 'In Search of the Exotic: A Discussion of the BBC 2 Series *Tribe*', *Anthropology Today* 21(2). Available online at www.savan.nl/data/ PatCaplanonTribeinAnthropologyToday.pdf

Carmen, L. (1996) 'Reading Gender and Culture in Media Discourses and Texts', in G. Bull and M. Anstey (eds), *The Literacy Lexicon*, New York and Sydney: Prentice-Hall, pp. 196–208.

Carnegie, C. V. (2002) *Postnationalism Prefigured: Caribbean Borderlands*, New Brunswick, NJ, and London: Rutgers University Press.

Carrera, M. M. (2003) *Imagining Identity in New Spain: Race, Lineage, and the Colonial Body in Portraiture and Casta Paintings.* Austin, TX: University of Texas Press.

Cashmore, E. (1988) *Dictionary of Race and Ethnic Relations*, 2nd edn, London and New York: Routledge.

Cashmore, E. and J. Jennings (eds) (2001) *Racism: Essential Readings*, London and Thousand Oaks, CA: Sage.

Castles, S. and A. Davidson (2000) *Citizenship and Migration: Globalisation and the Politics of Belonging*, London: Macmillan.

Castles, S. and G. Kossack (1985) *Immigrant Workers and Class Structure in Western Europe*, 2nd edn, Oxford: Oxford University Press.

Centre for Contemporary Cultural Studies (1982) *The Empire Strikes Back*, London: Macmillan.

Centre of International Studies (2001) 'Resolving Self-Determination Dispute Through Complex Power Sharing Arrangements Workshop', Cambridge University 9–10 February. Available online at www.polis.cam.ac.uk/research/cps/download/background1.pdf

Chandler, D. (1994) *Semiotics for Beginners.* Available online at www.aber.ac.uk/media/Documents/S4B/semiotic.html

Chen, G.-M. (2012) 'The Impact of New Media on Intercultural Communication in Global Context', *China Media Research* 8(2). Available online at http://digitalcommons. uri.edu/cgi/viewcontent.cgi?article=1012&context=com_facpubs

Chin, U. H. (2000) *The Chinese of South East Asia*, London: Minority Rights Group.

Chinweizu (1987) *The West and the Rest of Us: White Predators, Black Slavers and the African Elite*, 2nd edn, Lagos: Pero.

Chludzinski, K. (2009) 'The Fear of Colonial Miscegenation in the British Colonies of Southeast Asia,' *The Forum: Cal Poly's Journal of History* 1(1). Available online at www. digitalcommons.calpoly.edu/forum/vol1/iss1/8/

Christian, M. (2004) 'Assessing Multiracial Identity', in J. O. Ifekwunigwe, *'Mixed Race' Studies: A Reader*, London: Routledge (first published 2000, in M. Christian, *Multiracial Identity: An International Perspective*, London: Macmillan).

Cinema Paradiso (2012) 'The Battle of Algiers', synopsis. Available online at www.cinema-paradiso.co.uk/rentals/the-battle-of-algiers-2114.html

Clark, G. (2002) 'Native Title System Means Legal Dispossession of Indigenous People', *Aboriginal & Torres Strait Islander Commission (ATSIC).* Available online at http:// archive.eniar.org/news/yortayorta1.html

Cohen, R. (1997) *Global Diasporas*, London: UCL Press.

Cohen, S. (1967) *Folk Devils and Moral Panics: The Creation of the Mods and Rockers*, London: MacGibbon and Kee.

Cohen, S. (1987) *Folk Devils and Moral Panics*, 2nd edn, Worcester: Basil Blackwell.

Cohen, S. and J. Young (eds) (1981) *The Manufacture of News: Social Problems, Deviance and the Mass Media*, London: Constable.

Comaroff, J. (1995) 'Ethnicity, Nationalism and the Politics of Difference in an Age of Revolution', in J. L. Comaroff and P. C. Stern (eds), *Perspectives on Nationalism and War*, Luxembourg: Gordon and Breach Publishers.

Comaroff, J. and J. Comaroff (1992) *Ethnography and the Historical Imagination*, Boulder, CO: Westview Press.

Commission for Racial Equality (1985) *Swann: A Response from the Commission for Racial Equality*, London: Commission for Racial Equality.

Commonwealth of Australia (1978) *Migrant Services and Programs: Report of the Review of Post-arrival Programs and Services for Migrants*, Canberra: AGPS.

Connell, R. W. (1987) *Gender and Power*. Stanford, CA: Stanford University Press.

Connolly, S. (2006) *Racial And Ethnic Equality*, North Mankato, MN: Smart Apple Media.

Cooper, F. and A. Stoler (1989) 'Introduction: Tensions of Empire: Colonial Control and Visions of Rule', *American Ethnologist* 16(4): 609–21.

Cooray, M. (1988) 'Multiculturalism in Australia'. Available online at www.ourcivilisation.com/cooray/multcult

Cornell, S. and D. Hartmann (1998) *Ethnicity and Race: Making Identities in a Changing World*, London and Thousand Oaks, CA: Pine Forge Press.

Cottle, S. (ed.) (2000) *Ethnic Minorities and the Media*, London: Allen & Unwin.

Cowlishaw, G. (1994) 'Policing the Races', *Social Analysis* 36: 71–91.

Cox, O. C. (1976) *Race Relations: Elements and Social Dynamics*, Detroit, MI: Wayne State University Press.

Crenshaw, K. (ed.) (1995) *Critical Race Theory: The Key Writings That Formed the Movement*, New York: New Press.

Critcher, C. (2003) *Moral Panics and the Media*, Milton Keynes: Open University Press.

Crowley, H. and S. Himmelweit (eds) (1992) *Knowing Women: Feminism and Knowledge*, London: Polity Press.

Cuff, E. C., W. W. Sharrock and D. W. Francis (1990) *Perspectives in Sociology*, 3rd edn, London and New York: Routledge.

Culler, J. (1983) *Barthes*, London: Fontana.

Cummins, T. B. F. (2006) 'Casta Painting: Images of Race in Eighteenth-Century Mexico' (book review), *The Art Bulletin* 88(1): 185–9.

Cunneen, C. (2008) 'Riot, Resistance and Moral Panic: Demonising the Colonial Other', in University of New South Wales Faculty of Law Research Series 29. Available online at http://law.bepress.com/unswwps-flrps08/art29

Curtis, L. (1984) *Nothing but the Same Old Story: The Roots of Anti-Irish Racism*, London: Information on Ireland.

Curtis, M. (2001) *Web of Deceit*, London: Verso.

Curtis, M. (2004) *Unpeople: Britain's Secret Human Rights Abuses*, London: Vintage.

Cuvier, B. (1890) *The Animal Kingdom*, London: W. H. Allen.

Dabydeen, D. (1991) 'On Cultural Diversity', in M. Fisher and U. Owen, *Whose Cities?* Harmondsworth: Penguin, pp. 97–106.

Dabydeen, D. and B. Samaroo (eds) (1987) *India in the Caribbean*, London: Hansib.

Daily Mirror (1980) 'Mirror Comment: They Eat Horses Don't They?' 10 September, p. 2.

Darwin, C. (1979) *The Illustrated Origin of Species*, abridged and introduced by Richard Leakey, London: Faber and Faber.

Dawkins, R. (1989) *The Selfish Gene*, 2nd edn, Oxford: Oxford University Press.

Day, W. B. (2001a) 'Aboriginal Fringe Dwellers in Darwin: Cultural Persistence or Culture of Resistance?' PhD thesis, University of Western Australia Department of Anthropology. Available online at www.drbilldayanthropologist.com/resources/THESIS%20fINAL%20COPY.pdf

Day, W. B. (2001b) 'Race or Race: The Darwin Beer Can Regatta as a Statement of Racial Superiority. From Bill Day (2001) Aboriginal Fringe Dwellers in Darwin: Cultural Persistence or Cultural Resistance?' PhD thesis, Department of Anthropology, University of Western Australia. Available online at www.drbilldayanthropologist.com/resources/Race%20or%20Race_beercan%20Regatta%20article.pdf

de Torres, Sheila (2002) 'Understanding Persons of Philippine Origin: A Primer for Rehabilitation Service Providers', CIRRIE University of the Philippines. Available online at http://cirrie.buffalo.edu/culture/monographs/philippines/

Deans-Smith, S. (2011) 'Visualizing Racial Mixing in Colonial Spanish America', *Not Even Past*, November 9. Available online at www.notevenpast.org/discover/casta-paintings

Defoe, D. (2001; first published 1719) *Robinson Crusoe*, London: Penguin Classics.

Delgado, R. (1995) *Critical Race Theory: The Cutting Edge*, Philadelphia, PA: Temple University Press.

Derrida, J. (1976) *Of Grammatology*, trans. Gayatri Chakravorty Spivak, Baltimore, MD, and London: Johns Hopkins University Press.

Dickinson, G. and K. V. Anderson (2004) 'Fallen: O.J. Simpson, Hillary Rodham Clinton, and the Re-Centering of White Patriarchy', *Communication and Critical/Cultural Studies* 1(3): 271–96.

Dobbin, M. (1998) 'Unfriendly Giants', *ROB Magazine*, July. Available online at www.globalpolicy.org/socecon/tncs/unfriendlygiants.htm

Dodd, V. (2004) 'Muslim Groups Infuriated by Anti-Terrorism Poster', *Guardian*, 14 May. Available online at www.guardian.co.uk/terrorism/story/0,12780,1216410,00.htm

Donald, J. and A. Rattansi (eds) (1992) *'Race', Culture and Difference*, London and Thousand Oaks, CA: Sage.

Dreaper, J. (2013) 'Union claims nursing hit by "hidden workforce crisis"', Health correspondent, *BBC News* 12 November 2013.

Drescher, S. and S. Engerman (1998) *A Historical Guide to World Slavery*, Oxford: Oxford University Press.

Drewe, R. (1976) *The Savage Crows*, Sydney: Collins.

Du Bois, W. E. B. (1897) 'Strivings of the Negro People', *Atlantic Monthly* 80: 194–8. Available online at http://eserver.org/race/strivings.html

du Gay, P., S. Hall, L. Janes, H. Mackay and K. Negus (1997) *Doing Cultural Studies: The Story of the Sony Walkman*, Thousand Oaks, CA: Sage/Milton Keynes, UK: Open University Press.

During, S. (1987) 'Postmodernism or Post-Colonialism Today', *Textual Practice* 1(1): 32–47.

During, S. (1995) 'Postmodernism or Post-colonialism Today', in B. Ashcroft, G. Griffiths and H. Tiffin (eds), *The Post-Colonial Studies Reader*, London: Routledge.

Dustmann, C., T. Frattini and C. Halls (2010) 'Assessing the Fiscal Costs and Benefits of A8 Migration to the UK', *Fiscal Studies: The Journal of Applied Economics* 31(1): 1–41.

Dyer, R. (1997) *White*, London: Routledge.

Easton, M. (2011) 'Britain: More mixed than we thought', BBC News, 7 October. Available online at www.bbc.co.uk/news/uk-15164970

Eco, U. (1980; first published 1965) 'Towards a Semiotic Enquiry into the Television Message', in J. Corner and J. Hawthorn (eds), *Communication Studies: An Introductory Reader*, London: Edward Arnold, pp. 131–50.

The Economist (2013) 'Bumi not Booming', 28 September.

El Nasser, H. (1997) 'Measuring Race: Varied Heritage Claimed and Extolled by Millions', *USA Today*, 8 May, p. 1A.

El Nasser, H. (2013) 'Census rethinks Hispanic on Questionnaire', *USA Today*, 4 January. Available online at www.usatoday.com/story/news/nation/2013/01/03/hispanics-may-be-added-to-census-race-category/1808087/

Equiano, O. (2005) *The Interesting Narrative of the Life of Olaudah Equiano*, Gutenberg Project.

Erdogan, N. (2000) 'Veiled and Revealed: Review of Meyda Yegenoglu, *Colonial Fantasies: Towards a Feminist Reading of Orientalism*'. Available online at www.iath.virginia.edu/pmc/text-only/issue.100/10.2.r_erdogan.txt

Essed, P. and D. T. Goldberg (eds) (2002) *Race Critical Theories*, Oxford: Blackwell.

European Network for Indigenous Australian Rights (2002) 'Native Title System Means Legal Dispossession of Indigenous People', ATSIC. Available online at http://archive.eniar.org/news/yortayorta1.html

Fanon, F. (1961) *The Wretched of the Earth*, Harmondsworth: Penguin.

Fanon, F. (1967a) *Black Skin, White Masks*, New York: Grove Press.

Fanon, F. (1967b) *Toward the African Revolution*, Harmondsworth: Pelican.

Farrar, M. (2003) 'Community, Social Capital and Identification in the Multi-ethnic Inner City: Reflections on the Violent Urban Protest in the North of the UK in 2001', Paper delivered to the Communities Conference, Trinity and All Saints College, University of Leeds, 18–20 September 2003.

Farrar, M., S. Robinson, Y. Valli and P. Wetherly (2012) *Islam in the West: Key Issues in Multiculturalism*, London: Macmillan.

Fawcett, L. (2013) *International Relations of the Middle East*, 3rd edn, London: Oxford, pp. 77–103.

Featherstone, M. (1991) *Consumer Culture and Postmodernism*, London and Thousand Oaks, CA: Sage.

Featherstone, M. (1995) *Undoing Culture*, London and Thousand Oaks, CA: Sage.

Featherstone, M., S. Lash and R. Robertson (eds) (1995) *Global Modernities*, London and Thousand Oaks, CA: Sage.

Felluga, D. F. (2011) *Introductory Guide to Critical Theory*. Available online at www.cla.purdue.edu/english/theory/

Fenton, S. (1999) *Ethnicity: Racism, Class and Culture*, London: Macmillan.

Fenton, S. (2003) *Ethnicity*, London: Polity.

Fenton, S. and H. Bradley (eds) (2002) *Ethnicity and Economy: 'Race and Class' Revisited*, Basingstoke: Palgrave.

Fenton, S. and S. May (eds) (2002) *Ethnonational Identities*, Basingstoke: Palgrave.

Finnigan, G. (2001) *City of Port Phillip Aboriginal Resource Primer*. Available online at www.portphillip.vic.gov.au/default/GovernanceDocuments/Aboriginal_Resource_Primer.pdf

Fiske, J. (1987) *Television Culture*, London: Routledge.

Fiske, J. (1990) *Introduction to Communication Studies*, 2nd edn, London and New York: Routledge.

Fiske, J. (2010) *Understanding Popular Culture*, 2nd edn, London: Routledge.

Fiske, J. and J. Hartley (1978) *Reading Television*, London: Methuen.

Fiske, J., B. Hodge and G. Turner (1987) *Myths of Oz*, London: Allen & Unwin.

Fleming, R. and B. Southwell (2005) 'An Investigation of Some Factors in the Education of Indigenous Australians', University of Western Sydney. Available online at http://publications.aare.edu.au/05pap/fle05489.pdf

Fleras, A. (1994) 'Multiculturalism as Society-Building: Doing What is Necessary, Workable and Fair', in M. Charlton and P. Barker, *Cross-currents: Contemporary Political Issues*, 2nd edn, Scarborough, ON: Nelson, pp. 26–42.

Foley, G. (1997) 'Muddy Waters: Archie, Mudrooroo and Aboriginality'. Available online at www.kooriweb.org/foley/essays/essay_10.html

Foucault, M. (1972) *The Archaeology of Knowledge*, London: Tavistock.

Foucault, M. (1977a) *Discipline and Punish*, London: Allen Lane.

Foucault, M. (1977b) 'Intellectuals and Power: A Conversation Between Michel Foucault and Gilles Deleuze', trans. D. F. Bouchard and S. Simon, in D. F. Bouchard (ed.), *Language, Counter-Memory, Practice: Selected Essays and Interviews by Michel Foucault*, Ithaca, NY: Cornell University Press, pp. 205–17.

Foucault, M. (1980) *Power/Knowledge: Selected Interviews and Other Writings 1972–1977*, edited by C. Gordon, Brighton: Harvester Press.

Foucault, M. (1984) *The History of Sexuality: An Introduction*, London: Peregrine Books.

Foucault, M. (2002) *Society must be defended: Lectures at the College de France, 1975–76*, New York: Picador.

Frankenberg, R. (1993) *White Women, Race Matters: The Social Construction of Whiteness*, London and New York: Routledge.

Fredrickson, G. M. (1981) *White Supremacy, A Comparative Study in American and South African History*, Oxford: Oxford University Press.

Fredrickson, G. M. (2002) *Racism: A Short History*, Princeton, NJ: Princeton University Press.

Freedom House (2013) 'Irregularities in Malaysian Election Must Be Investigated', Washington 8 May. Available online at www.freedomhouse.org/article/irregularities-malaysian-election-must-be-investigated

Fukuyama, F. (2000) 'Economic Globalization and Culture', in D. Held (ed.) *A Globalizing World? Culture, Economics, Politics*, 2nd edn, London: Routledge.

Furnivall, J. S. (1948) *Colonial Policy and Practice: A Comparative Study of Burma, Netherlands and India*, New York: New York University Press.

Galton, F. (1996) *Essays in Eugenics*, Washington DC: Scott-Townsend Publishers.

Galtung, J. and M. Ruge (1973) 'Structuring and Selecting News', in S. Cohen and J. Young (eds), *The Manufacture of News: Deviance, Social Problems and the Media*, London: Constable, pp. 62–72.

Gans, H. J. (2005) 'Race as Class', *Contexts* 4(4): 17–21.

Gardiner-Garden, J. (2003) 'Defining Aboriginality in Australia', *Current Issues Brief* 10: Social Policy Group, 3 February. Available online at www.aph.gov.au/About_Parliament/Parliamentary_Departments/Parliamentary_Library/Publications_Archive/CIB/cib0203/03Cib10

Geertz, C. (1973) *The Interpretation of Cultures*, New York: Basic Books.

Giddens, A. (ed.) (1994) *The Polity Reader in Social Theory*, Cambridge: Polity.

Giddens, A. (2000) *Runaway World: How Globalization is Reshaping Our Lives*, New York: Routledge.

Gifford, Lord (1996) 'Slavery: Legacy', in Lords Hansard text for 14 March 1996. Available online at www.publications.parliament.uk/pa/ld199596/ldhansrd/vo960314/text/60314-24.htm

Gillborn, D. (2006) 'Critical Race Theory and Education: Racism and Antiracism in Educational Theory and Praxis', *Discourse: Studies in the Cultural Politics of Education* 27(1): 11–32.

Gilroy, P. (1993) *The Black Atlantic*, London: Verso.

Gilroy, P. (2000) *Between Camps, Nations, Cultures and the Allure of Race*, London and New York: Routledge.

Gilroy, P. (2004) *After Empire: Melancholia or Convivial Culture*, London and New York: Routledge.

Glasgow University Media Group (1976) *Bad News*, London: Routledge.

Glasgow University Media Group (1980) *More Bad News*, London: Routledge & Kegan Paul.

Goffman, E. (1972) *Interaction Ritual*, Harmondsworth: Penguin.

Goffman, E. (1984) *The Presentation of Self in Everyday Life*, London: Pelican.

Goldberg, D. T. (1992) 'The Semantics of Race', *Ethnic & Racial Studies* 15(4): 543–69.

Goldberg, D. T. (1993) *Racist Culture*, Oxford: Blackwell.

Goldberg, D. T. (ed.) (1994) *Multiculturalism: A Critical Reader*, Oxford: Blackwell.

Goldberg, D. T. and J. Solomos (eds) (2002) *A Companion to Racial and Ethnic Studies*, Oxford: Blackwell.

Goldsmith, O. (1876) *A History of the Earth and Animated Nature*, London and Edinburgh: A. Fullarton & Co.

Gonzalez, G. (2005) 'Code of conduct for TNCs reappears', Third World Network. Available online at www.twnside.org.sg/title/code-cn.htm

Gonzalez, M. (2001) 'Zapatistas After the Great March – A Postscript', *International Socialism Journal* 91(summer). Available online at http://pubs.socialistreviewindex.org.uk/isj91/gonzalez.htm

Goodhart, D. (2004) 'Too Diverse: Is Britain Becoming too Diverse to Sustain the Mutual Obligations Behind Good Society and the Welfare State?', *Prospect magazine*, February. Available online at www.prospectmagazine.co.uk/magazine/too-diverse-david-goodhart-multiculturalism-britain-immigration-globalisation/

Gorman, M. (1996) *All Different, All Equal: A Sum of Experience*, Council of Europe Publishing.

Greenslade, R. (2011) 'Islamophobia and the media – a timely book', *The Guardian*, Greenslade Blog, 12 April. Available online at www.theguardian.com/media/greenslade/2011/apr/12/dailyexpress-islam

Greenwald, G. (2013) 'Andrew Sullivan, terrorism, and the art of distortion', *The Guardian*, 25 May. Available online at www.guardian.co.uk/commentisfree/2013/may/25/andrew-sullivan-distortion-terrorism-woolwich

Griffin, J. H. (1961) *Black Like Me*, New York: New American Library.

Grillo, R. (1998) *Pluralism and the Politics of Difference: State, Culture and Ethnicity in Comparative Perspective*, Oxford: Clarendon Press.

Grossberg, L. (1996) 'Identity and Cultural Studies: Is That All There Is?', in S. Hall and P. du Gay (eds), *Questions of Cultural Identity*, London and Thousand Oaks, CA: Sage, pp. 87–107.

Guan, L. H. (2000) *Ethnic Relations in Peninsular Malaysia: The Cultural and Economic Dimensions*, Social and Cultural Issues 1, Singapore: Institute of Southeast Asian Studies.

Guardian, The (2001) 'Oldham Independent Review, Panel report', 11 December 2001. Available online at http://image.guardian.co.uk/sysfiles/Guardian/documents/2001/12/11/Oldhamindependentreview.pdf

Guardian Datablog (2012) 'Census 2011: religion, race and qualifications – see how England & Wales have changed'. Available online at www.theguardian.com/news/datablog/2012/dec/11/census-2011-religion-race-education

Gunew, S. (2001) 'Postcolonialism and Multiculturalism: Between Race and Ethnicity'. Available online at www.english.ubc.ca/~sgunew/race.htm

Habermas, J. (1970) 'On Systematically Distorted Communication', *Inquiry: An Interdisciplinary Journal of Philosophy* 13(1–4): 205–18.

Hall, S. (1980) 'Race, Articulation and Societies Structured in Dominance', in *Sociological Theories: Race and Colonialism*, Paris: UNESCO, pp. 305–45.

Hall, S. (1981) 'The Determinations of News Photographs', in S. Cohen and J. Young (eds), *The Manufacture of News: Social Problems, Deviance and the Mass Media*, London: Constable, pp. 226–43.

Hall, S. (1991) 'The Local and the Global: Globalization and Ethnicity', in A. King (ed.), *Culture Globalization and the World System*, London: Macmillan, pp. 19–40.

Hall, S. (1992) 'The Question of Cultural Identity', in S. Hall, D. Held and T. McGrew (eds), *Modernity and its Futures*, Cambridge: Polity, pp. 274–316.

Hall, S. (1993) 'What is this "Black" in Black Popular Culture? (Rethinking Race)', *Social Justice* 20 (spring–summer). Available online at www.aasp.umd.edu/chateauvert/whatis.doc

Hall, S. (1994) 'Cultural Identity and Diaspora', in P. Williams and L. Chrisman (eds), *Colonial Discourse and Postcolonial Theory*, New York: Columbia University Press, pp. 392–401.

Hall, S. (1996a) 'New Ethnicities', in D. Morley and K. H. Chen (eds), *Stuart Hall, Critical Dialogues in Cultural Studies*, London and New York: Routledge, pp. 441–9.

Hall, S. (1996b) *Race, the Floating Signifier*, film, directed by Sut Jhally Hall, Northampton, MA: Media Education Foundation.

Hall, S. (ed.) (1997) *Representation: Cultural Representations and Signifying Practices*, London and Thousand Oaks, CA: Sage.

Hall, S. (2000) 'The Multicultural Question', lecture at Political Economy Research Centre. Available online at http://red.pucp.edu.pe/wp-content/uploads/biblioteca/Stuart_Hall_The_multicultural_question.pdf

Hall, S. and P. du Gay (eds) (1996) *Questions of Cultural Identity*, London and Thousand Oaks, CA: Sage.

Hall, S. *et al.* (eds) (1978) *Policing the Crisis: Mugging, the State and Law and Order*, London: Macmillan.

Halsey, A. H. (1997) *Education Culture Economy Society*, Oxford: Oxford University Press.

Hamilton, W. D. (1964) 'The Genetical Evolution of Social Behavior. II', in G. C. Williams (ed.), *Group Selection*, Chicago, IL: Aldine Atherton, pp. 23–43.

Hammerton, J. (1933) *Peoples of All Nations*, London: Amalgamated Press.

Hannerz, U. (1992) *Cultural Complexity*, New York and Chichester: Columbia University Press.

Harding, L. (2013) 'Woolwich killing: residents reflect on murder of Lee Rigby', *The Guardian*, 23 May. Available online at www.theguardian.com/uk/2013/may/23/woolwich-attack-multicultural-multi-faith-community

Harper, D. (2005) 'What's New Visually?' in N. Denzin and Y. Lincoln (eds), *Handbook of Qualitative Research*, 3rd edn, Beverley Hills, CA, and London: Sage, pp. 747–62.

Harris, P. (2002) 'They fled with nothing but built a new empire', *The Observer*, 11 August. Available online at www.theguardian.com/uk/2002/aug/11/race.world

Hartley, J. (1992) *The Politics of Pictures*, London: Polity.

Harvey, D. (1989) *The Condition of Postmodernity*, Oxford: Basil Blackwell.

Hechter, M. (1975) *Internal Colonialism: The Celtic Fringe in British National Development*, London: Routledge & Kegan Paul.

Hechter, M. (1995) 'Explaining Nationalist Violence', *Nations and Nationalism* 1(1): 53–68.

Henderson, M. (2000) 'Liverpool Faces the Past – and the Future', *For A Change*, 1 April. Available online at www.forachange.net/browse/article/3091.html

Herman, E. S. and N. Chomsky (1988) *Manufacturing Consent: The Political Economy of the Mass Media*, London: Vintage.

Hernández Cuevas, M. P. (2004) *African Mexicans and the Discourse on Modern Nation*, Lanham, MD: University Press of America.

Hewitt, A. (2006) 'Ex-BNP man faces explosives charge', *Burnley and Pendle Citizen*, 4 October. Available online at www.burnleycitizen.co.uk/display.var.951775.0.exbnp_man_faces_explosives_charge.php

Hill Collins, P. (2000) 'Black Feminist Thought', in L. Back and J. Solomos (eds), *Theories of Race and Racism: A Reader*, London: Routledge, pp. 404–20.

History of Race in Science (1995) 'Bring Back the Hottentot Venus', *In Media*, 15 June. Available online at http://web.mit.edu/racescience/in_media/baartman/baartman_m&g_june95.htm

Hoboken, V. (2004) 'Ethnic Communications', in G. Taylor and S. Spencer (eds), *Social Identities: Multidisciplinary Approaches*, London: Routledge, pp. 199–217.

Hobsbawm, E. J. (1996) *Age of Extremes: The Short Twentieth Century 1914–1991*, London: Abacus.

Hochschild, A. (1998) *King Leopold's Ghost: A Story of Greed, Terror, and Heroism in Colonial Africa*, New York: Houghton Mifflin.

Hofstadter, R. (1955) *Social Darwinism in American Thought*, Boston, MA: Beacon Press.

Hohman, K. (2000) 'Race Relations: Whiteness Studies: A Look at White Privilege and Whiteness Studies and How They Pertain to Race Relations'. Available online at http://taboomovie.blogspot.co.uk/2004/05/whiteness-studies.html

Home Office (2002) *Secure Borders, Safe Haven: Integration with Diversity in Modern Britain*, Home Office, CM 5387.

Home Office (2012) 'Racist Incidents, England and Wales 2011/12'. Available online at www.homeoffice.gov.uk/publications/science-research-statistics/research-statistics/crime-research/racist-incidents-1112/

hooks, b. (1989) *Talking Back*, Boston, MA: South End Press.

hooks, b. (1992) *Black Looks: Race and Representation*, Boston, MA: South End Press.

Hooper, C. (2009) *The Tall Man: Death and Life on Palm Island*, London: Jonathan Cape.

Horne, D. (1964) *The Lucky Country*, Ringwood: Penguin.

Horowitz, D. (1985) *Ethnic Groups in Conflict*, Berkeley, CA: University of California Press.

Horowitz, D. L. (2003) 'The Cracked Foundations of the Right to Secede', *Journal of Democracy* 24(2): 5–17.

Horrocks, C. and Z. Jevtic (1996) *Baudrillard For Beginners*, Cambridge: Icon Books.

Howard, J. (1996) 'Robert Menzies Lecture', Parliamentary Library Research Paper 5, 1997–98. Available online at www.menzieslecture.org/1996.html

Howe, D. (2005) 'To Refer to Muslims, Hindus and Sikhs, Rather than Asians, Undermines Secularism', *New Statesman*, 17 January. Available online at www.newstatesman.com/node/149720

Hughes, I. (1995) 'Dependent Autonomy: A New Phase of Internal Colonialism', *Australian Journal of Social Issues* 30(4): 369–88.

Hughes, R. (1987) *The Fatal Shore: A History of the Transportation of Convicts to Australia*, London: Collins Harvill.

Human Rights Foundation (2011) 'Institutional Racism and Religious Freedom in Malaysia', *US House Committee on Foreign Affairs, US State Dept, Tom Lantos Human Rights Commission*. Available online at http://hornbillunleashed.files.wordpress.com/2011/12/institutional-racism-religious-freedom-1.pdf

Human Rights Watch (1998) 'Malaysia's Internal Security Act', 21 September. Available online at www.hrw.org/reports/1998/09/21/malaysias-internal-security-act

Human Rights Watch (2001) 'Malaysia: End Political Arrests', 30 April. Available online at www.hrw.org/news/2001/04/29/malaysia-end-political-arrests

Hume, L. J. (1991) 'Another Look at the Cultural Cringe' Available online at www.the-rathouse.com/Another_look_at_the_Cultural_Cringe.htm

Hume, M. (2012) 'The real lessons for Britain from Bradford West', in *Spiked*, 3 April Available online at www.spiked-online.com/newsite/article/12305

Huntington, S. (1998) *Clash of Civilizations and the Remaking of World Order*, London and New York: Touchstone.

Hutchinson, J. and A. D. Smith (eds) (1996) *Ethnicity*, Oxford: Oxford University Press.

Ifekwunigwe, J. (2004) *'Mixed Race' Studies: A Reader*, London: Routledge.

Institute for Racial Relations (IRR) (2012) '96 murders since Stephen Lawrence's', 5 January, IRR News Team. Available online at www.irr.org.uk/news/96-murders-since-stephen-lawrences/

James, C. L. R. (1963) *The Black Jacobins: Toussaint L'Ouverture and the San Domingo Revolution*, rev. edn, New York: Vintage.

Jenkins, R. (1992) *Pierre Bourdieu*, London: Routledge.

Jenkins, R. (1996) *Social Identity*, London and New York: Routledge.

Jenkins, R. (1997) *Rethinking Ethnicity: Arguments and Explorations*, London and Thousand Oaks, CA: Sage.

Jenkins, R. (2003) 'The Limits of Identity: Ethnicity, Conflict and Politics', Sheffield University. Available online at www.sheffield.ac.uk/polopoly_fs/1.71447!/file/2jenkins.pdf

Jenkins, R. (2008) *Rethinking Ethnicity: Arguments and Explorations*, 2nd edn, London and Thousand Oaks, CA: Sage.

Jupp, J. (2002) *From White Australia to Woomera*, Cambridge: Cambridge University Press.

Kafka, F. (2000) *Metamorphosis, In the Penal Colony and Other Stories*, New York: Scriber Paperback Fictions.

Kapoor, N. (2011) The advancement of racial neoliberalism in Britain. *Ethnic and Racial Studies* 36(6): 1028–46.

Katzew, I. (2004) *Casta Painting: Images of Race in Eighteenth-century Mexico*, New Haven, CT: Yale University Press.

Kavanagh, J. (1995) *Critical Terms for Literary Study*, 2nd edn, F. Lentricchia and T. McLaughlin (eds), Chicago, IL: University of Chicago Press.

Keane, F. (1996) *Letter to Daniel: Despatches from the Heart*, London: Penguin.

Kertzer, D. I. and D. Arel (eds) (2002) *Census and Identity: The Politics of Race, Ethnicity, and Language in National Censuses*, Cambridge and New York: Cambridge University Press.

Khair, T. (1999) 'Why Post-Colonialism Hates Revolutions', in *Biblio: A Review of Books* IV(5–6): 15–16.

King, B. (2004) 'Mass Media', in G. Taylor and S. Spencer (eds), *Social Identities: Multidisciplinary Approaches*, London and New York: Routledge, pp. 182–99.

Kivisto, P. (2008) *Multiculturalism and Racial Democracy*, London: Routledge.

Knightley, P. (1975) *The First Casualty: The War Correspondent as Hero, Propagandist and Myth Maker*, New York: Harcourt.

Knowles, C. (2004) *Race and Social Analysis*, London and Thousand Oaks, CA: Sage.

Knowles, C. and S. Mercer (1992) 'Feminism and Antiracism: An Exploration of the Political Possibilities', in J. Donald and A. Rattansi (eds), *'Race', Culture and Difference*, London and Thousand Oaks, CA: Sage.

Knowles, L. L. and K. Prewitt (eds) (1969) *Institutional Racism in America*, Englewood Cliffs, NJ: Prentice-Hall, pp. 104–25.

Kohn, M. (1996) *The Race Gallery*, London: Verso.

Kolakowski, L. (1985) *Main Currents in Marxism*, Oxford: Oxford University Press.

Kress, G. (1988) *Communication and Culture*, Kensington: New South Wales University Press.

Kress, G. R. and R. Hodge (1979) *Language as Ideology*, London: Routledge and Kegan Paul.

Kuhl, S. (1994) *The Nazi Connection: Eugenics, American Racism, and German National Socialism*, Oxford: Oxford University Press.

Kuper, L. (1981) *Genocide: Its Political Use in the Twentieth Century*, New Haven, CT: Yale University Press.

Kuper, L. (1996) 'Genocide and the Plural Society', in J. Hutchinson and A. D. Smith (eds), *Ethnicity*, Oxford: Oxford University Press, pp. 262–9.

Kymlicka, W. (1995) *Multicultural Citizenship: A Liberal Theory of Minority Rights*, Oxford: Clarendon.

Kymlicka, W. (2012) 'Multiculturalism: Success, Failure, and the Future', Migration Policy Institute, Queen's University, February. Available online at www.migrationpolicy.org/pubs/multiculturalism.pdf

Lacan, J. (1977) *Ecrits. A Selection*, New York: Norton.

Laclau, E. and C. Mouffe (1985) *Hegemony and Socialist Strategy: Towards a Radical Democratic Politics*, London: Verso.

Ladson Billings, G. (2003) 'Racialised Discourses and Ethnic Epistemologies', in Denzin, Norman K. and Lincoln, Yvonna S. (eds), *The Landscape of Qualitative Research* 3rd edition. Los Angeles and London: Sage, 398–432.

Lahiri, J. (2003) *The Namesake*, Houghton Mifflin.

Lamarck, J.-B. (1809) *Philosophie zoologique*, Vol. I, Weinheim: Engelmann.

Lambe, M. (2003) 'NT Labor Continue Traditional Dry Season Racism', Part 1, 15 April (no longer available online).

Langton, M. (1993a) 'Rum, Seduction and Death: "Aboriginality" and alcohol', *Oceania* 63(3): 195–206.

Langton, M. (1993b) *Well, I Heard it on the Radio and I Saw it on the Television*, Sydney: Australian Film Commission.

Langton, M. (1997) 'The Long Grass People of Darwin', *PARITY*. Available online at http://longgrass.tripod.com/langton-lg.htm

Langton, M., L. Ah Matt, B. Moss, E. Schaber, C. Mackinolty, M. Thomas, E. Tilton and L. Spencer (1991) 'Too Much Sorry Business: The Report of the Aboriginal Issues Unit of the Northern Territory. Royal Commission into Aboriginal Deaths in Custody', National Report Volume 5. Canberra: Australian Government Publishing Service.

Lanzieri, G. (2012) 'Merging populations: A look at marriages with foreign-born persons in European countries', *Eurostat: Statistics in Focus* 29/2012. Available online at http://epp.eurostat.ec.europa.eu/portal/page/portal/product_details/publication?p_product_code=KS-SF-12-029

Lareau, A. and E. McNamara Horvat (1999) 'Moments of Social Inclusion and Exclusion: Race, Class and Cultural Capital in Family–School Relationships', *Sociology of Education* 72(1): 37–52.

Lewandowski, J. D. (2003) 'Disembedded Democracy? Globalization & the Third Way', *European Journal of Social Theory* 6(1): 115–31.

Lewis, M. B. (2010) 'Why are Mixed-race People Perceived as More Attractive?', *Perception* 39(1): 136–8.

Lewis, P. (2012) 'Police face racism scandal after black man records abuse', *Guardian*, 30 March. Available online at www.theguardian.com/uk/2012/mar/30/police-racism-black-man-abuse

Lewis, R. (1996) *Gendering Orientalism: Race, Feminity and Representation*, London and New York: Routledge.

Lim, S. P. (2000) 'The Question of Diaspora in International Relations: A Case Study of Chinese Diaspora in Malaysia and South-East Asia', MA dissertation, University of Sussex.

Linnaeus (Carl von Linne) (1806) *A General System of Nature Through the Three Grand Kingdoms of Animals, Vegetable, and Minerals*, London: Lackington, Allen and Company.

Loomba, A. (1993) 'Overworldling the "Third World"', in P. Williams and L. Chrisman (eds), *Colonial Discourse and Postcolonial Theory*, New York: Columbia University Press, pp. 305–23.

Loomba, A. (1998) *Colonialism/Postcolonialism*, London and New York: Routledge.

Luke, C. (1996) 'Reading Gender and Culture in Media Discourses and Texts', in G. Bull and M. Anstey (eds), *The Literary Lexicon*, New York/Sydney: Prentice-Hall, pp. 177–89.

Lyell, C. (1830) *Principles of Geology*, London: John Murray.

Lykke, N. (2000) 'ARE CYBORGS QUEER? Biological determinism and feminist theory in the age of new reproductive technologies and reprogenetics', Conference: Bologna Sept. 28–Oct. 1, 2000. Available online at www.women.it/quarta/workshops/epistemological4/ninalykke.htm

Mac an Ghaill, M. (1999) *Contemporary Racisms and Ethnicities*, Oxford: Oxford University Press.

Macklin, G. (2002) '"Untimely Reflections" on Terror: Review of Gore Vidal, *Perpetual War for Perpetual Peace*'. Available online at www.spokesmanbooks.com/Spokesman/PDF/reviews77.pdf

Macpherson, S. W. (1999) *The Stephen Lawrence Inquiry. CM 4262-1*, London: The Stationery Office.

Madley, B. (2004) 'Patterns of Frontier Genocide 1803–1910: the Aboriginal Tasmanians, The Yuki of California and the Herero of Namibia', *Journal of Genocide Research* 6(2): 167–92. Available online at www.yale.edu/gsp/colonial/Madley.pdf

McCaskell, T. (1994) 'A History of Race/ism', Equity Department, Toronto District School Board.

McGhee, D. (2005) 'Patriots of the Future? A Critical Examination of Community Cohesion Strategies in Contemporary Britain', *Sociological Research Online* 10(3). Available online at www.socresonline.org.uk/10/3/mcghee.html

McGreal, C. (2008) 'War in Congo kills 45,000 people each month', *Guardian*, 23 January. Available online at www.guardian.co.uk/world/2008/jan/23/congo.international

McGuigan, J. (1999) *Modernity and Postmodern Culture*, Milton Keynes: Open University Press.

McKenna, M. (1997) 'Different Perspectives on Black Armband History', Research Paper 5 1997–8, Politics and Public Administration Group, 10 November. Available online at www.aph.gov.au/About_Parliament/Parliamentary_Departments/Parliamentary_Library/pubs/rp/RP9798/98RP05

McKinnon, C. (2008) 'Duplicity and Deceit: Rudd's Apology to the Stolen Generations, an interview with Gary Foley', *Melbourne Historical Journal* 36.

McLeod, J. (2000) *Beginning Postcolonialism*, Manchester: Manchester University Press.

McQuail, D. (2010) *Mass Communication Theory*, 6th edn, London and Thousand Oaks, CA: Sage.

McSweeney, D. (2012) 'Liverpool prepares to mark Slavery Remembrance Day', *Guardian*, The Northerner Blog, 8 August. Available online at www.guardian.co.uk/uk/the-northerner/2012/aug/08/liverpool-slavery

Malesevic, S. (2004) *The Sociology of Ethnicity*, London and Thousand Oaks, CA: Sage.

Malik, K. (1996) *The Meaning of Race*, London: Macmillan.

Malik, K. (1998) 'Race, Pluralism and the Meaning of Difference', *New Formations* 33(spring). Available online at www.kenanmalik.com/papers/new_formations.html

Malik, K. (2002) 'Against Multiculturalism', *New Humanist* (summer). Available online at www.kenanmalik.com/essays/against_mc.html

Malik, K. (2003) *Disunited Kingdom*, BBC2 documentary.

Malik, K. (2004) 'Too Diverse?' (A Response to David Goodhart), *Prospect*, March. Available online at www.kenanmalik.com/debates/prospect_diversity.html

Malik, K. (2008) *Strange Fruit: Why Both Sides are Wrong in the Race Debate*, Oxford: Oneworld Books.

Malik, K. (2009) *From Fatwa to Jihad*, London: Atlantic Books.

Manley, R. (1979) *Guyana Emergent*, Cambridge, MA: Schenkman Publishing Co.

Manne, R. (ed.) (2003) *Whitewash: On Keith Windschuttle's Fabrication of Aboriginal History*, Melbourne: Black Inc. Agenda.

Manzoor, S. (2011) 'Re-reading: Black Like Me by John Howard Griffin', *Guardian*, 27 October.

Manzoor, S. (2005) 'We've Ditched Race for Religion', *The Guardian*, Tuesday 11 January. Available online at www.theguardian.com/world/2005/jan/11/race.religion

Marcus, G. E. (2012; first published 1995) 'Multi-sited Ethnography: Five or Six Things I Know About it Now', in Simon Coleman and Pauline von Hellermann, *Multi-sited Ethnography: Problems & Possibilities in the Translocation of Research Methods*, New York and Abingdon: Taylor & Francis, pp. 16–34.

Marcus, S. (1974) *Engels, Manchester and the Working Class*, London: Weidenfield & Nicolson.

Marcuse, H. (1968) *One-Dimensional Man: Studies in the Ideology of Advanced Industrial Society*, London: Sphere Books.

Martin, P. (2007) 'Farm Labor Shortage: How Real? What Response', Teleconference Transcript, Center for Immigration Studies. Available online at www.cis.org/node/637

Marx, K. (1849) *Wage Labour and Capital*, Neue Rheinische Zeitung. Available online at the Marxists Internet Archive; www.marxists.org

Marx, K. (1961) *Capital*, Vol. 1, Moscow: Foreign Languages Publishing House.

Marx, K. (1976) *Capital*, Vol. I, trans. Ben Fowkes, London: Penguin.

Marx, K. (1990) *Capital*, Vol. 1, London: Penguin Classics.

Marx, K. and F. Engels (1982) *Selected Correspondence*, London: Progress.

Mason, D. (2000) *Race and Ethnicity in Modern Britain*, Oxford: Oxford University Press.

Mauss, M. (1979) 'Body Techniques', in *Psychology and Sociology: Essays*, London: Routledge & Kegan Paul, pp. 95–123.

Mauzy, D. K. and R. S. Milne (2002) *Malaysian Politics Under Mahathir*, London: Routledge.

May, S. (ed.) (1999) *Critical Multiculturalism: Rethinking Multicultural and Antiracist Education*, London: Falmer.

May, S. (2000) 'Multiculturalism', in D. T. Goldberg and J. Solomos (eds), *A Companion to Racial and Ethnic Studies*, Oxford: Blackwell, pp. 124–43.

May, S., T. Modood and J. Squires (eds) (2004) *Ethnicity, Nationalism and Minority Rights*, Cambridge: Cambridge University Press.

Mayne, A. (1997) *Black Armband History: The Future for History in Australia*, Melbourne: University of Melbourne Press.

Mercer, K. (1994) *Welcome To The Jungle: New Positions in Black Cultural Studies*, New York: Routledge.

Mercer, K. (2000) 'Identity and diversity in Postmodern Politics', in L. Back and J. Solomos (eds), *Theories of Race and Racism: A Reader*, New York: Routledge, pp. 503–20.

Metropolitam Borough Council of Oldham (2006) 'Report of the Executive Director, Education and Culture', 20 March. Available online at http://committees.oldham.gov.uk/Data/Cabinet/20060320/Minutes/Detailed%20Report.pdf

Mickler, S. (1996) 'The Perth press and problematising Aboriginal status'. Available online at www.mcc.murdoch.edu.au/ReadingRoom/dreamtime/press.html

Mickler, S. (1997) 'Some Shifts in Anti-Land Rights Campaigns after Mabo: Including the "They" Community'. Available online at www.mcc.murdoch.edu.au/ReadingRoom/impi/articles/attending.html

Mignone, J. (2009) 'Social Capital and Aboriginal Communities: A critical assessment. Synthesis and assessment of the body of knowledge on social capital with emphasis on Aboriginal communities', *Journal de la santé autochtone* (November): 100–47.

Miles, R. (1982) *Racism and Migrant Labour*, London: George Allen and Unwin.

Miles, R. (1986) 'Labour Migration, Racism and Capital Accumulation in Western Europe', *Capital and Class* 28: 49–86.

Miles, R. (1989) *Racism*, London and New York: Routledge.

Miles, R. and A. Phizacklea (1980) *Labour and Racism*, London: Routledge & Kegan Paul.

Ministry of Justice (2011) 'Statistics on Race and the Criminal Justice System 2010'. Available online at www.gov.uk/government/uploads/system/uploads/attachment_data/file/219967/stats-race-cjs-2010.pdf

Misir, P. (2000) 'The Social Construction of Race-Ethnic Conflict in Guyana', University of Guyana. Available online at www.uog.edu.gy/files/documents/prochancellor/The_Social_Construction_of_Race-Ethnic_Confilct.pdf

Modood, T. (1994) 'Political Blackness and British Asians', *Sociology* 28(4): 859–76.

Modood, T. (2000) 'Anti-Essentialism, Multiculturalism, and the "Recognition" of Religious Groups', in W. Kymlicka and W. Norman (eds), *Citizenship in Diverse Societies*, Oxford: Oxford University Press, pp. 175–95.

Modood, T. (2007) *Multiculturalism: A Civic Idea*, Cambridge and Malden, MA: Polity Press.

Montag, W. (1997) 'The Universalisation of Whiteness: Racism and Enlightenment', in M. Hill (ed.), *Whiteness: A Critical Reader*, New York: New York University Press, pp. 281–93.

Montesquieu, C. L. de Secondat Baron de (1748) *Complete Works, vol. 1. Spirit of Laws, book xv.: in what manner the laws of civil slavery are relative to the nature of the climate*, in *The Online Library of Liberty*. Available online at http://oll.libertyfund.org/?option=com_staticxt&staticfile=show.php%3Ftitle=837&chapter=71558&layout=html&Itemid=27

Moore, J. H. (1933) *Savage Survivals*, London: Watts.

Morgan, G. (2004) 'The Urban Renewal of Prejudice', *The Australian Financial Review* 5 (March) 4.

Morley, D. and C. Kuan-Hsing (eds) (1996) *Stuart Hall*, London and New York: Routledge.

Mosse, G. L. (1978) *Towards the Final Solution, A History of European Racism*, New York: Harper Colophon Books, Harper & Row.

Muecke, S. (1982) 'Available Discourses on Aborigines', in P. D. Botsman, *Theoretical Strategies*, Sydney: Local Consumption Press, pp. 98–112.

Muecke, S. (1992) *Textual Spaces: Aboriginality and Cultural Studies*, Sydney: New South Wales University Press.

Mulvey, L. (1975) 'Visual Pleasure and Narrative Cinema', *Screen* 16: 6–18.

Murji, K. and S. Neal (2011) 'Riot: Race and Politics in the 2011 Disorders', *Sociological Research Online* 16(4): 24. Available online at www.socresonline.org.uk/16/4/24.html

Myers, R. and J. Calder (2006) 'Towards Ethnic Conflict Transformation: A Case Study of Citizen Peacebuilding Initiatives on the 2006 Guyana Elections', Occasional Paper: Peace Building Series No. 4. Available online at www.future.org/sites/future.org/files/Ethnic%20Conflict%20Transformation%20in%20Guyana.pdf

Nakamura, L. (2000) 'Race In/For Cyberspace: Identity Tourism and Racial Passing on the Internet', in D. Bell and B. Kennedy (eds), *The Cybercultures Reader*, London and New York: Routledge, pp. 712–20.

Nakayama, T. K. and J. N. Martin (1998) *Whiteness: The Communication of Social Identity*, London and Thousand Oaks, CA: Sage.

NATFHE and UNISON (2004) *Implementing the Race Relations Amendment Act*, London: NATFHE and UNISON.

NHS Employers (2009) 'Reaping the rewards: re-training refugee healthcare professionals for the NHS', Briefing 64. Available online at www.nhsemployers.org/Aboutus/Publications/Documents/Reaping_the_rewards-Briefing_64.pdf

Nietzsche, F. (1954) 'On truth and lie in an extra-moral sense,' in *The Portable Nietzsche*, ed. and trans. Walter Kaufmann, New York: Viking Press, pp. 46–7.

Nkrumah, K. (1965) 'Neo-Colonialism: The Last Stage of Capitalism'. Available online at www.marxists.org/subject/africa/nkrumah/neo-colonialism/introduction.htm

North Australian Aboriginal Legal Aid Service (1999) 'Dollars Without Sense: A Review of the Northern Territory's manadatory sentencing laws', 5 November 1999. Available online at www.makingjusticework.org.au/attachments/article/76/Dollars%20without%20Sense%20-%20A%20review%20of%20the%20NT's%20mandatory%20sentencing%20laws%201999.pdf

Northern Territory Department of Community Development (2004) 'Background Brief to the Community Harmony Project'. Available online at www.dcdsca.nt.gov.au/dcdsca/intranet.nsf/pages/harmony_strategy

Northern Territory Government (2003) '9th Assembly 16th October 2001 to 5 May 2005 papers tabled'. Available online at www.nt.gov.au/lant/parliamentary-business/9th%20Assembly%20Papers%20Tabled.pdf

Northern Territory News (1996) 'Editorial', 11 March.

Nutini, H. and B. Isaac (2009) *Social Stratification in Central Mexico 1500–2000*, Austin, TX: University of Texas Press.

Office of National Statistics (2001) 'The Classification of Ethnic Groups'. Available online at www.ons.gov.uk/ons/guide-method/census/census-2001/index.html

Office of National Statistics (2011) 'Ethnicity and National Identity in England and Wales 2011'. Available online at www.ons.gov.uk/ons/dcp171776_290558.pdf

Ortner, S. (1984) 'Theory in Anthropology since the Sixties', *Comparative Study in Society and History* 26(1): 126–66.

Orwell, G. (1945 [1971]) *Animal Farm: A Fairy Story*, London: Secker and Warburg.

Pandey, G. (2010) *Subaltern Citizens and their Histories: Investigations from India and the USA*, London: Routledge.

Pandey, G. (2012) *Subalternity and Difference: Investigations from the North and the South*, London: Routledge.

Parekh, B. (ed.) (2000) *The Future of Multi-Ethnic Britain*, London: Methuen.

Parekh, B. (2004) Segment in 'So what exactly is multiculturalism?' BBC News website. Available online at http://news.bbc.co.uk/1/hi/uk/3600791.stm

Parker, D. (2004) 'Mixed Race: The Social Identities of the Future?', in G. Taylor and S. Spencer, *Social Identities: Multidisciplinary Approaches*, London and New York: Routledge, pp. 107–29.

Patel, T. and D. Tyrer (2011) *Race, Crime and Resistance*, London and Thousand Oaks, CA: Sage.

Pathak, P. (2008) *The Future of Multicultural Britain: Confronting the Progressive Dilemma*, Edinburgh: Edinburgh University Press.

Pearson, N. (2000) 'Misguided Policies: A Toxic Cocktail: Aborigines Must Renew Family Life and Eradicate Drug Abuse', *Australian*, 24 October: p. 13.

Petkovic, J. (1983) *Frame on Dreaming* (film).

Petković, T. and M. Rakić (2010) 'Megatrend Review', *The International Review of Applied Economics* 7(2). Available online at www.megatrendreview.com/files/pdf/EN/Megatrend%20Review%20vol%2007-2-2010.pdf

Phelan, S. (1989) *Identity Politics*, Philadelphia, PA: Temple University Press.

Pickering, M. (2004) 'Racial Stereotypes', in G. Taylor and S. Spencer (eds), *Social Identities: Multidisciplinary Approaches*, London and New York: Routledge, pp. 91–107.

Pieterese, J. N. (2001) *Development Theory: Deconstructions/Reconstructions*, London and Thousand Oaks, CA: Sage.

Pieterese, J. N. (2002) 'Europe and its Others over Time', in D. T. Goldberg and J. Solomos (eds), *A Companion to Racial and Ethnic Studies*, Oxford: Blackwell, pp. 17–24.

Pieterese, J. N. and B. Parekh (1995) *The Decolonization of the Imagination: Culture, Knowledge and Power*, London: Zed Books.

Pilger, J. (1986) *Heroes*, London: Pan.

Pilger, J. (1989) *A Secret Country*, London: Vintage.

Pilger, J. (2002) 'The New Statesman Special Report – At war with refugees', *New Statesman*. Available online at www.newstatesman.com/node/142083

Pilger, J. (2011) 'How the Murdoch press keeps Australia's dirty secret', *New Statesman*, May 12. Available online at www.newstatesman.com/australasia/2011/05/pilger-australia-rights

Pinkus, J. (1996) 'Foucault'. Available online at www.massey.ac.nz/~alock/theory/foucault.htm

Pitcher, B. (2009) *The Politics of Multiculturalism: Race and Racism in Contemporary Britain*, London: Macmillan.

Popeau, J. (1998) 'Race/Ethnicity', in C. Jenks (ed.), *Core Sociological Dichotomies*, London and Thousand Oaks, CA: Sage, pp. 166–78.

Poulantzas, N. (1973) *Political Power and Social Classes*, London: New Left Books.

Powell, S. (2006) 'UN verdict on East Timor', *The Australian*, 19 January. Available online at www.yale.edu/gsp/east_timor/unverdict.html

Premdas, R. (1972) *Voluntary Associations and Political Parties in a Racially Fragmented State*, Georgetown: University of Guyana.

Premdas, R. (1981) 'Guyana: Violence and Democracy in a Communal State', *Plural Societies* 12(3/4), 41–64.

Premdas, R. (1986) 'Politics of Preference in the Caribbean: The Case of Guyana', in C. H. Kennedy and N. Nevitte (eds), *Ethnic Preference & Public Policy in Developing States*, Boulder, CO: Lynne Rainer, pp. 155–87.

Premdas, R. (1992) 'Ethnic and Racial Conflict in the Caribbean', in B. Samaroo and C. Debidin (eds), *Ethnicity and Indians in the Caribbean*, London: Macmillan.

Premdas, R. (1996) 'Race and Ethnic Relations in Burnhamite Guyana', in D. Dabydeen and B. Samaroo (eds), *Across the Dark Waters: Ethnicity and Indian Indenture in the Caribbean*, London: MacMillan, 39–65.

Premdas, R. (2002) 'Identity in an Ethnically Bifurcated State: Trinidad and Tobago', in S. Fenton and S. May, *Ethnonational Identities*, Basingstoke: Palgrave.

Prewitt, K. (2013) *What Is Your Race? The Census and our Flawed Efforts to Classify Americans*, Princeton, NJ: Princeton University Press.

Price, E. (2010) 'Reinforcing the myth: Constructing Australian identity in 'reality TV'', *Continuum* 24(3): 451–9.

Qureshi, S. (2004) 'Displaying Sara Baartman, The Hottentot Venus', *Science History Publications*, XLII. Available online at www.negri-froci-giudei.com/public/pdfs/qureshi-baartman.pdf

Rabinow, P. and N. Rose (2006) 'Biopower Today', *BioSocieties* 1: 195–217. Available online at http://imap.anthropos-lab.net/wp/publications/2007/01/rabinow-rose.pdf

Ramesh, R. (2004) 'Bhopal still suffering, 20 years on', *The Guardian*, 29 November. Available online at <www.theguardian.com/world/2004/nov/29/india.randeepramesh>

Randall, M. (2003) 'Guest Media Lens Alert: Asylum and Immigration, Comparing the *Daily Telegraph*, *Guardian* and the *Independent*', 8 December. Available online at http://medialens.org/index.php/alerts/alert-archive/2003/308-guest-media-lens-alert-asylum-and-immigration.html

Ratcliffe, P. (2004) *'Race', Ethnicity and Difference*, Milton Keynes: Open University Press.

Rawlinson, C. (2013) 'Behind Bagot's walls', ABC Darwin, 29 May. Available online at www.abc.net.au/local/photos/2013/05/29/3770267.htm

Read, P. (1998) 'Whose Citizens? Whose Country?' in Nicolas Peterson and Will Sanders (eds) *Citizenship and Indigenous Australians: Changing Conceptions and Possibilities*, Cambridge: Cambridge University Press. pp. 169–78.

Refugee Council (2008) 'The facts about asylum', BMA/Refugee Council refugee doctor database, 4 June. Available online at www.refugeecouncil.org.uk/policy_research/the_truth_about_asylum/facts_about_asylum_-_page_3

Refugee Council Online (2013) 'The facts about asylum'. Available online at www.refugeecouncil.org.uk/policy_research/the_truth_about_asylum?gclid=CIeu2ebt_LkCFWLHtAodLmwA6w

Reilly, J. (2001) 'Time to "dump" Multiculturalism', *Red Action Bulletin* 4(12). Available online at https://docs.google.com/file/d/0B7gGS6hFJeBBMTdmNDU5NTQtNjU4ZS00M2U3LTk5Y2YtOWNjYTUyY2E5ZDY2/edit?usp=drive_web&urp=http://www.redactionarchive.org/2012/03/red-action

Rex, J. (1970) *Race Relations in Sociological Theory*, London: Weidenfeld and Nicolson.

Rex, J. (1980) 'Theory of Race Relations: A Weberian Approach', in *Sociological Theories, Race and Colonialism*, Paris: Unesco, pp. 169–86.

Rex, J. (1986a) 'The Role of Class Analysis in the Study of Race Relations: A Weberian Perspective', in J. Rex and D. Mason (eds), *Theories of Race and Ethnic Relations*, Cambridge: Cambridge University Press, pp. 64–83.

Rex, J. (1986b) *Race and Ethnicity*, Milton Keynes: Open University Press.

Rex, J. and M. Guibernau (eds) (1997) *The Ethnicity Reader: Nationalism, Multiculturalism, and Migration*, Cambridge: Polity.

Rex, J. and D. Mason (eds) (1986) *Theories of Race and Ethnic Relations*, Cambridge: Cambridge University Press.

Rex, J. and S. Tomlinson (1979) *Colonial Immigrants in a British City*, London: Routledge & Kegan Paul.

Reynolds, V., V. Falger and I. Vine (1987) *The Sociobiology of Ethnocentrism*, London: Croom Helm.

Robertson, R. (1992) *Globalization: Social Theory and Global Culture*, London: Sage.

Robertson, R. (1995) 'Glocalisation: Time-Space and Homogeneity-Heterogeneity', in M. Featherstone *et al.* (eds), *Global Modernities*, London and Thousand Oaks, CA: Sage, pp. 25–44.

Robinson, H. (2004) 'You know wha' is "bedding"?', *Guyana Chronicle*, 23 May. Available online at www.landofsixpeoples.com/news402/nc4052318.htm

Rodney, W. (1972) *How Europe Underdeveloped Africa*, Harrare: Zimbabwe Publishing House.

Rodney, W. (ed.) (1979) *Guyanese Sugar Plantations in the Late Nineteenth Century*, The Argosy, Georgetown, Guyana: Release Publishers.

Rodney, W. (1981) *A History of the Guyanese Working People, 1881–1905*, Kingston and London: Heinemann.

Roediger, D. R. (1994) *Towards the Abolition of Whiteness: Essays on Race, Politics and Working Class History*, London: Verso.

Roediger, D. R. (2001) 'Critical Studies of Whiteness, USA: Origins and Arguments', *Theoria* 72(28): 72–98.

Rollock, N. (2009) 'The Stephen Lawrence Enquiry 10 years on', The Runnymede Reports. Available online at www.runnymedetrust.org/uploads/publications/pdfs/StephenLawrenceInquiryReport-2009.pdf

Rorty, R. (1990) 'Feminism and Pragmatism', The Tanner Lectures on Human Values. Available online at www.tannerlectures.utah.edu/_documents/a-to-z/r/rorty92.pdf

Rorty, R. (1995) 'Feminism and Pragmatism', in R. S. Goodman (ed.), *Pragmatism*, New York: Routledge, pp. 125–48.

Rushdie, S. (1988) *The Satanic Verses*, New York and London: Viking.

Russell, B. (1991) *History of Western Philosophy*, London and New York: Routledge.

Said, E. (1978) *Orientalism*, London: Penguin.

Said, E. (1993) *Culture and Imperialism*, New York: Vintage.

Salleh, M. (2003) 'The Lie of Benevolence: review of *Web of Deceit* by Mark Curtis', July. Available online at www.socialistreview.org.uk/article.php?articlenumber=8536

San Juan, E. (2007) *The Wake of Terror: Class, Race, Nation, Ethnicity in the Postmodern World*, Lanham, MD: Lexington Books.

Sansom, B. (1980) *The Camp at Wallaby Cross: Aboriginal Fringe Dwellers in Darwin*, Darwin: Australian Institute of Aboriginal Studies.

Santas, A. (1998) *Notes on the History of Racism*, Valdosta State. Available online at ww2.valdosta.edu/~asantas/Notes/History%20of%20Racism.htm

Sardar, Z. (1998) *Postmodernism and the Other: The New Imperialism of Western Culture*, London: Pluto.

Schoenbrun, D. L. (1993) 'A Past Whose Time Has Come: Historical Context and History in Eastern Africa's Great Lakes', in V. Y. Mudimbe and B. Jewsiewicki (eds), *History Making in Africa*, Middletown, CT: Wesleyan University.

Scott, S. (2011) 'Introduction: Indigenous Peoples, Marxism and Late Capitalism', *New Proposals: Journal of Marxism and Interdisciplinary Inquiry* 5(1): 6–9.

Seabrook, J. (1996) 'Internationalism Versus Globalisation', *Third World Network Features*, 8 August. Available online at www.hartford-hwp.com/archives/27c/432.html

Shamsul, A. B. (2002) 'Malaysia's International Role Post-September 11', Universiti Kebangsaan Malaysia, Bangi, Malaysia, published in IDSS Commentaries. Available online at http://dr.ntu.edu.sg/bitstream/handle/10220/4068/RSIS-COMMENT_230.pdf?sequence=1

Sharrad, P. (1993) 'Blackbirding: Diaspora Narratives and the Invasion of the Bodysnatchers', *Span, Journal of the South Pacific Association for Commonwealth Literature and Language Studies* 34–5. Available online at www.mcc.murdoch.edu.au/ReadingRoom/litserv/SPAN/34/Sharrad.html

Sherwood, M. (2007) 'Britain, Slavery and the Trade in Enslaved Africans', in *History in Focus: the Guide to Historical Resources: Issue 12: Slavery*. Available online at www.history.ac.uk/ihr/Focus/Slavery/articles/sherwood.html

Short, A. (1970) 'Communism, Race and Politics in Malaysia', *Asian Survey* 10(12): 1089.

Sibley, D. (1995) *Geographies of Exclusion: Society and Difference in the West*, London and New York: Routledge.

Sivanandan, A. (1986) *From Resistance to Rebellion: Asian and Afro-Caribbean Struggles in Britain*, London: Institute of Race Relations.

Smart, B. (1993) *Postmodernity*, London and New York: Routledge.

Smith, A. (2003) 'Not an Indian Tradition: The Sexual Colonization of Native Peoples', *Hypatia, Inc.* 18(2): 70–85.

Smith, M. G. (1974) *The Plural Society in the British West Indies*, London: University of California Press.

Smith, R. (1997) *Fontana History of the Human Sciences*, London: Fontana.

Smith, R. T. (1962) *British Guiana*, Oxford: Oxford University Press.

Smith, R. T. (1965) *The Negro Family in British Guiana: Family Structure and Social Status in the Villages*, London: Routledge & Kegan Paul.

Sollors, W. (2002) 'Ethnicity and Race', in D. T. Goldberg and J. Solomos (eds), *A Companion to Racial and Ethnic Studies*, Oxford: Blackwell, pp. 97–103.

Solomos, J. and L. Back (1996) *Racism and Society*, London: Macmillan.

Soong, K. K. (2008) 'Racial Conflict in Malaysia: Against the Official History New Era College', *Malaysia Race & Class* 49: 33–53.

Sotiropoulou, A. (2002) 'The Role of Ethnicity in Ethnic Conflicts: The Case of Yugoslavia', MA dissertation, University of Bath. Available online at http://unpan1.un.org/intradoc/groups/public/documents/UNTC/UNPAN019076.pdf

Soysal, Y. N. (2000) 'Citizenship and Identity: Living in Diasporas in Post-War Europe?', *Ethnic and Racial Studies* 23(1): 1–15.

Spencer, H. (1860) *System of Synthetic Philosophy: First Principles*, London: George Manwaring.

Spencer, S. (2003) 'Interview with Prof. David Miller', Strathclyde University.

Spencer, S. (2004a) 'Interview with Prof. Bob Franklin', unpublished.

Spencer, S. (2004b) 'Interview with Sonia Smallacombe', unpublished.

Spencer, S. (2004c) 'Interview with David Timber', unpublished.

Spencer, S. (2005a) *'Framing the Fringe Dwellers': Visual Methods for Research and Teaching Race and Ethnicity: A Sample Case Study*, Birmingham: University of Birmingham Press.

Spencer, S. (2005b) 'Contested Homelands: Darwin's "Itinerant Problem"', *Pacific Journalism Review* 11(1): 174–97.

Spencer, S. (2007) *A Dream Deferred: Guyanese Identity Under the Shadow of Colonialism*, London: Hansib.

Spivak, G. C. (1994; first published 1985) 'Can the Subaltern Speak', in P. Williams and L. Chrisman (eds), *Colonial Discourse and Postcolonial Theory*, New York: Columbia University Press, pp. 66–112.

Sriskandarajah, D., L. Cooley and H. Reed (2005) 'Paying their way: the fiscal contribution of immigrants in the UK', Institute for Public Policy Research. Available online at www.ippr.org/ecomm/files/Paying%20Their%20Way.pdf

Stanton, G. H. (2004) 'Genocide Emergency: Darfur, Sudan'. Available online at www.genocidewatch.org/genocide/12waystodenygenocide.html

Steele, J. and R. Norton-Taylor (2005) '25,000 Iraqi civilians killed since invasion', *The Guardian*, 20 July. Available online at www.guardian.co.uk/Iraq/Story/0,2763,1532157,00.html

Stop Unfair Campaign (2012) 'Debunking the Un-Fair Campaign Myths', blog entry. Available online at www.stopunfaircampaign.org

Sukdeo, I. D. (1982) *The Emergence of a Multiracial Society of Guyana*, New York.

Taylor, C. (1994) *Multiculturalism: Examining the Politics of Recognition*, Princeton, NJ: Princeton University Press.

Taylor, G. and S. Spencer (eds) (2004) *Social Identities: Multidisciplinary Approaches*, London and New York: Routledge.

The Malaysian Insider (2013) 'Malaysians among world's most bigoted, survey shows', *The Malaysian Insider*, 17 May. Available online at www.themalaysianinsider.com/malaysia/article/malaysians-among-worlds-most-bigoted-survey-shows

Thomas, P. (2007) 'Community Cohesion, the "Death of Multiculturalism" and Work with Young People', conference paper in Europe and its Established & Emerging Immigrant Communities conference: Assimilation, Multiculturalism or Integration? 10–11 November 2007, De Montfort University, Leicester.

Thomas, P. (2011) *Youth, Multiculturalism and Community Cohesion*, New York: Palgrave Macmillan.

Tilly, C. (1998) *Durable Inequality*, Berkeley, CA: University of California Press.

Tizzard, B. and A. Phoenix (1993) *Black, White or Mixed Race? Race and Racism in the Lives of Young People of Mixed Parentage*, London and New York: Routledge.

Tobach, E. and B. Rosoff (1994) *Challenging Racism and Sexism, Alternatives to Genetic Explanations*, New York: The Feminist Press.

Turpin, T. (1990) 'The Social Construction of Immigrant and Aboriginal Ethnic Group Boundaries in Australia', PhD thesis, La Trobe University.

Tweedie, N. (1998) 'Shock Posters Send Police on the Trail of Race Commission', *Electronic Telegraph*, 22 September. Available online at www.amren.com/ar/pdfs/1998/199811ar.pdf

UK Government (2011) David Cameron's speech at the 47th Munich Security Conference, 5 February. Available online at www.gov.uk/government/speeches/pms-speech-at-munich-security-conference

UK Government (2012) 'International Day for the Remembrance of the Slave Trade', Department for Communities and Local Government, 28 August 2012. Available online at www.gov.uk/government/news/race-equalities-minister-andrew-stunell-commemorates-the-international-day-for-the-remembrance-of-the-slave-trade

United States Census Bureau (2013) US Department of Commerce, Profile America: Facts for Features, 30 July. Available online at www.census.gov/newsroom/releases/archives/facts_for_features_special_editions/cb13-ff19.html

UN Economic and Social Council (1999) 'Social and human rights questions: implementation of the Programme of Action for the Third Decade to Combat Racism and Racial Discrimination', Geneva, 5–30 July. Available online at www.unhchr.ch/Huridocda/Huridoca.nsf/0/658a0ff32e3ef7de80256862005316b9?Opendocument

UNESCO (1995) 'Multiculturalism: A Policy Response to Diversity', Global Cultural Diversity Conference, 26–28 April, and MOST Pacific Sub-Regional Consultation, 28–29 April, Sydney, Australia. Available online at www.unesco.org/most/sydpaper.htm

US Census Bureau (2000) 'Our Diverse Population: Race and Hispanic Origin, 2000', Chapter 16. Available online at www.census.gov/population/pop-profile/2000/chap16.pdf

Valdaverde, M. (1995) 'Online Book Review of Robert Young's *Colonial Desire: Hybridity in Theory, Culture and Race*'. Available online at www.utpjournals.com/product/chr/781/desire41.html

Valier, C. (2002) 'Punishment, Border Crossings and the Powers of Horror', *Theoretical Criminology* 6(3): 319–37.

Valier, C. (2004) *Crime and Punishment in Contemporary Culture*, London: Routledge.

Van den Berghe, P. (1967) *Race and Racism: A Comparative Perspective*, New York: John Wiley.

Vargas-Silva, C. (2013) 'Fiscal Impact of Immigration in the UK', The Migration Observatory. Available online at http://migrationobservatory.ox.ac.uk/briefings/fiscal-impact-immigration-uk

Vasil, R. K. (1984) *Politics in Bi-Racial Societies: The Third World Experience*, New Delhi: Vikas.

Vaughan, A. T. (1982) 'From White Man to Redskin: Changing Anglo American Perceptions of the American Indian', *American Historical Review* 87: 917–51.

Vertinsky, P. A. (1990) *The Eternally Wounded Woman: Women, Doctors, and Exercise in the Late Nineteenth Century*, Manchester: Manchester University Press.

Vertovec, S. (2007) 'Super-Diversity and its Implications', *Ethnic and Racial Studies* 29(6): 1024–54.

Wacquant, L. (2001) 'Deadly Symbiosis: When Ghetto and Prison Meet and Mesh', *Punishment & Society* 3(1): 95–134.

Wacquant, L. (2002) 'From Slavery to Mass Incarceration: Rethinking the "race question", in the United States', *New Left Review* 2nd ser. 13: 40–61.

Wacquant, L. (2009) *Punishing the Poor: The Neoliberal Government of Social Insecurity*, Durham, NC, and London: Duke University Press.

Wacquant, L. (2010) *Urban Outcasts: A Comparative Sociology of Advanced Marginality*, Cambridge and Malden, MA: Polity.

Waddington, D. (2004) 'Music', in G. Taylor and S. Spencer, *Social Identities: Multidisciplinary Approaches*, London and New York: Routledge, pp. 218–35.

Walker, A. (1983) *In Search of our Mothers' Gardens: Womanist Prose*, San Diego, CA: Harcourt Brace Jovanovich.

Wallerstein, I. (1974) *The Modern World System: Capitalist Agriculture and the Origins of the European World Economy in the Sixteenth Century*, London and New York: Academic Press, pp. 29–36.

Wallerstein, I. (1988) 'The Ideological Tensions of Capitalism: Universalism Versus Racism and Sexism', in E. Balibar and I. Wallerstein, *Race, Nation, Class, Ambiguous Identities*, London and New York: Verso.

Walter, M. (2010) 'The Politics of the Data: How the Australian Statistical Indigene is Constructed', *International Journal of Critical Indigenous Studies* 3(2): 45–56.

Wan Husin, W. N. (2012) *Cultural Clash between the Malays and Chinese in Malaysia: An Analysis on the Formation and Implementation of National Cultural Policy*, Bangkok: IACSIT Press, vol. 34, pp. 1–6.

Wang, Lu-in (2006) *Discrimination by Default: How Racism Becomes Routine*, New York: New York University Press.

Ware, V. and L. Back (2002) *Out of Whiteness: Colour Politics and Culture*, Chicago and London: University of Chicago Press.

Warmington, P. (2009) 'Taking Race out of Scare Quotes: Race-conscious Social Analysis in an Ostensibly Post-racial World', *Race, Ethnicity and Education* 12(3): 281–96.

Waters, M. (1996) *Globalization*, London and New York: Routledge.

Watson, J. (2005) *Media Communication*, Basingstoke: Palgrave.

Weatherburn, D. (2006) 'Riots, Policing and Social Disadvantage: Learning from the Riots in Macquarie Fields and Redfern', *Current Issues in Criminal Justice* 18(1): 20–31.

Webb, J. (2009) *Understanding Representation*, Los Angeles, CA, and London: Sage.

Weber, M. (1978) *Economy and Society: An Outline of Interpretive Sociology*, Berkeley, CA: University of California Press.

Weedon, C. (1987) *Feminist Practice and Poststructuralist theory*, 2nd edn, Oxford: Blackwell.

Weedon, C. (1990) *Culture, Race and Identity: Australian Aboriginal Writing*, Working Paper No. 59. Available online at www.kcl.ac.uk/artshums/ahri/centres/menzies/research/Publications/Workingpapers/WP59ChrisWeedon.pdf

Wheeler, H. (ed.) (1935) *Peoples of the World in Pictures*, London: Odhams.

Williams, B. F. (1991) *Stains on My Name; War in My Veins*, Durham, NC: Duke University Press.

Williams, B. F. (1995) 'From Class to "Trash" to Hybrid Nation: A Conversation with Brackette Williams', Johns Hopkins University. Available online at http://sites.jhu.edu/sebin/s/y/From_Class_to.pdf

Williams, P. and L. Chrisman (1993) *Colonial Discourse and Post-Colonial Theory: A Reader*, London and New York: Harvester Wheatsheaf.

Williams, R. (1977) *Marxism and Literature*, Oxford: Oxford University Press.

Williams, R. (1983) *Keywords*, London: Fontana.

Williams, R. (2011; first published 1958) 'Culture is Ordinary', in I. Szeman and T. Kaposy (eds), *Cultural Theory: An Anthology*, Oxford: John Wiley & Sons Ltd, pp. 53–4.

Windschuttle, K. (2004a) *The Fabrication of Aboriginal History, Volume One: Van Diemen's Land 1803–1847*, Sydney: Macleay Press.

Windschuttle, K. (2004b) *The White Australia Policy: Race and Shame in the Australian History Wars*, Sydney: Macleay Press.

Woodlock, R. (2002) 'Muslim Feminists and the Veil: To Veil or Not to Veil – Is That the Question?' Islamic Research Foundation International. Available online at www.irfi.org/articles/articles_301_350/veiling_and_hijab_as_understood.htm

Woodward, K. (1997) *Identity and Difference*, London and Thousand Oaks, CA: Sage.

Yegenoglu, M. (1998) *Colonial Fantasies: Towards a Feminist Reading of Orientalism*, Cambridge: Cambridge University Press.

Young, C. (1976) *The Politics of Cultural Pluralism*, Madison, WI: University of Wisconsin Press.

Young, J. (1971) *The Drugtakers: The Social Meaning of Drug Abuse*, London: MacGibbon & Kee.

Young, J. (2003) 'To these wet and windy shores: recent immigration policy in the UK', *Punishment & Society* 5(40): 449–62.

Young, L. (1996) *Fear of the Dark: 'Race', Gender and Sexuality in the Cinema*, London: Routledge.

Young, R. (2006) 'Putting Materialism back into Race Theory: Toward a Transformative Theory of Race', *The Red Critique: Marxist Theory and Critique of the Contemporary* 11 (Winter/Spring). Available online at www.redcritique.org/WinterSpring2006/putting-materialismbackintoracetheory.htm

Young, R. J. C. (1995) *Colonial Desire: Hybridity in Theory, Culture and Race*, London and New York: Routledge.

Younge, G. and J. Henley (2003) 'Wimps, weasels and monkeys – the US media view of "perfidious France"', *The Guardian*, 11 February. Available online at www.theguardian.com/world/2003/feb/11/pressandpublishing.usa

Zickmund, S. (2000) 'Approaching the Radical Other: The Discursive Culture of Cyberhate', in D. Bell and B. M. Kennedy, *The Cybercultures Reader*, London and New York: Routledge, pp. 237–53.

Žižek, S. (1990) 'Eastern Europe's Republics of Gilead', *New Left Review* 183: 50–62.

INDEX

Page numbers in bold indicate where the most definitive and central references to the topics are made in the text.

aberrant decoding 287
Aborigines 20, 40, 43; and colonialism 76, 85–6, 165; and eugenics 3, 42, 91; as 'others' 12, 20, 40, 42–3, 51, 124, 158; and land rights 78, 100, 133, 136–7, 166–8
aboriginality (discourse of) 169, 172–90
ahwe people (Guyana) 57, 260
African Americans xvi, 31, 54, 62, 63, 64, 87, 118–9, 247
alienation xv, 24, 126, 128, 279
Althusser, Louis 4, 37, 112–14, 124–5, 194, 296, 298
American Civil War 76, 106
Animal Farm (1945 novel) 53
anthropology 48, 78, 103, 120, 146
anti-colonialist 123, 149, 163
anti-racist 32, 35, 112, 145, 250
Apanjat 207
Apocalypse Now (film) 26
Arab (s) 7, 60–1, 149, 154, 242, 269, 292
Arab Spring, the 6, 221, 269
Aristotle 71, 73
Asian xv, xviii, 25, 45, 51, 87, 91, 112, 223–4, **235–6**, 242, 279; globalisation 267–8; self-identity **61–2**; tsunami 5, 7 women xxiii, **129–31, 277**
asylum seekers 5, 6, 12, 15–16, 26, 44, 107, 110, 112–13, 226, 250–1 , 254–5, 283
Auschwitz 142–3
Australia xvii, 17, 31, 48, 64–5, 100, 208
auto-colonialism 91, 94

Baartman, Sara (Hottentot Venus) 130, 138
'bad news' stories 9, 221
'bardic function' (of media) xviii, 11, 255
Barth, Frederick xvii, 12, 120
Barthes, Roland xix, 16–20, 22–3, 29–30, 36–7, 156, 294
'basic benevolence'112
Baudrillard, Jean 141, 277
Beer Can Regatta 181–2, 195
Bhabha, Homi 3, 144, 146, 158, 234, 260, 270, 290
Bhopal 93
biopower 122, 222–3, 231, **287–8**
bipolar societies xxiv, 209, 284
'black armband view' (of history) 13, 86, 171, 190, 202
black feminism xxii, 132–3, 138
Black Like Me 38
Black Skin, White Masks 24–5
black sexualities 28, 31, 129
blackness 26–30, 32, 36, 54, 66, 132, 156–7, 281
blaxploitation 26
blood quantum 42, 174, 285
body image 122, 129, 303
'body snatching' 234
Borges, Jorge Luis 141
Boundary-making xxiv, 16, 39, 53, 98, 105, 115, 119–20, 169, 209, 211
Bourdieu, Pierre xxii, 30, **124–9**, 137, **199–201**, 211, 256, 289
Boyz n the Hood (film 1991) 26
British-Born Chinese **134–7, 237–40**

British National Party 114
Bronowski, Jacob 143–4
Bumiputeras 215–17, 221

Cantle Report 225–6
Capital, Das 116
Capitalism 19, 52, 76, 92, 104, **106–8**, 111–12, 114, 117, 144, 247; 'booty' capitalism 52, 94, 115, 117, 162
Carolina Law, the 72, 123
Carter, Martin 205–6, 265
Casta paintings 81–5
Census: US xx, 58–9, 62–4; UK xx, 59–61
'centralised states' 122, 227
Chechnya 99
Chinese-Malaysians 120–1, **214–21**
Chineweizu 76
Christianity 15, 44–6, 55, 71, 73–4, 166, 179
Circuit of Culture, The (model) 3, 28–32
citizenship **226**, 234, 272, 285
Clark Doll Experiment 271
Clash of Civilizations, The 220, 281, 285, 300
class xvi, xvii, xxi, xxii, 4 , 15, 17, 19, 23, 108–9; 'in itself' and 'for itself' xxiv, 57; and race relations 35–7, 52–4, 84–9, 104–12, 114–18; and colonialism 79–85
Cohen, Stanley 177–8, 301
colonialism xvi, 7; atrocities 85–6; internal 31, 136
Columbus, Christopher 73
Confederacy 106
Congo, the 8–9, 86
connotation (semiotic level) xix, 17–18, 20, 40–1, 48, 58, 124, 141
consumption 3, 11, 28, 30 173, 267
contrast to norm of whiteness 23–8, 33–7, 56, 58; threatening 27–9, 32, 54, 170, 189–90, 254, 265, 282–3; as not fully human 72–4, 85–6
Commission for Racial Equality 28, 31, 35, 37, 251–2
creolese 57, 66
creolisation xxv, 57, 228, 269, 288

cricket 210, 221, 254
Critcher, Chas 178, 301
Critical race theory xxiii, **160–3**, 201
crossing 258–61, 269, 273, 282
cultural capital 30, 128, 201, 210, 256, **289**
cultural imaginary xix, 2, 4, 11, 25, 81, 149, 201, **289**
'cultural turn' 55, 140, 296
Culture 44, 55, 97–101; between 235, 237, 240–2, 260, 266; change 174–5, 199; definition 43, 119, 289; high 30, 201; as context xv–xxvi; dominant 41, 58, 65, 76–7, 114, 137, 174, 223–4, 257, 275, 281; working class 118
Cuvier, Baron xx, 48–51, 130
cyberspace 276–8
cyberterror 277–8

Darfur, Sudan 9, 222, 292–3
Darwin, Charles 14–15, 47–8, 51–2, 294
deconstruction 18, 123, 172, **290**
denotation (semiotic level) 17–20, 156
Derrida, Jacques 42, 158, 162, 290
deterritorialisation 268, **290**
dialectic materialism 30, 104, 109, 148, 253, 265, 269
diaspora xv, xvi, 58, 87–8, 193 **232–4**, 249, 253, 270, 284, **290–1**
'diaspora space' 233–5, 242, 260, 268
diasporization 146, 270
differance **291**
discourse xix, xxi, xxii, xxiii, 21, **291–2**; of Aborigines 156, 169, 180, 186, 199, 224; of diversity 237, 248–50, 253, 255, 272; Foucaultian **121–4**, 146; intersecting 134–7, 150–3, 157–8; racist 78–9, 81, 100, 111–12, 130–1, 141, 145, 34, 98–101, 106–7, 122; Said 149–50, 158–9
dispersed ethnic systems 209, 227
'divide and rule' 107–8, 186, 194
'doogla' 260
double burden xxii, 132, 150
double-consciousness 87

dramaturgical theory 94, 120
drunkenness 168–70, 178, 180–2, 184, 192
Du Bois, W.E.B. xxi, 87, 94
'Dunkirk spirit' 56

East Timor 91, 222, 293
elite theory 197
Enlightenment 43–5, 73–6, 141–3, 162, 180
Equiano, Olaudah 70, 72
essentialism xvii, xx, xxii, 41, 55, 100, 132–3, 144, 146, 149, 157, 159, 174, 235–6, 249, 264–5, 273, 281; anti 161–2, 237, 248
ethnic cleansing 9, 85, 91, 191, 218, **221–2**, 227, **292–3**
ethnicity: conflict 169–86; defined xvi, xvii, xviii, xxiv, 41–2, 44, **55–64**
ethnic penalty xxv, 227
ethnocentrism 10, 20, 44, 51, 98, 115, 131, 141–2, 146, 172, 175, 195, 222, 234, 277, 282, **293**
ethnography xvi, 22–3, 147; indirect xxiii
ethnonationalism 210
ethnorace 58
eugenics 3, 52, 77, 91, 130, 133, 151, 172, **293–4**
European Union 139, 248
'eviction' (semiotic process) 20
evolution 14, 21, 44, **47–52**
exnomination xxiv
exoticism xvi, 78–9, 129, 130, 153–6

'face work' 121
false consciousness 4, 106, 115,
Fanon, Frantz xxi, 24–5, 67, 86–7, 94, 143, 148–9, 300
Fatal Shore, The 172
feminism xxi, xxii, 296, 303; and post colonialism **150–7**, 161 *see also* Black Feminism
Fiji 79, 207, 210, 227, 302
Filipinos xv–xxiv
Fiske, John 9, 11, 16, 19, 164, 169, 255, 287

'floating signifier' xx, 16, 43, 192, 266, 268, 290
'fortress Europe' 15–16
Foucault, Michel xxii, **121–4**, 137, 140, 144, 151, 162, 222–3, 283, 287–8, 291–2
Franklin, Bob 8
French, the 5, 9, 13–14, 18, 24–5, 56, 73, 76, 302; Revolution 47
Furnivall, J. S. 102–4, 193

Galton, Francis 52, 293
Geertz, Clifford 98–9, 119–20
gender xxii, xx, xxii, xxvi, 2, 10, 13, 17, 25, 30, 36, 40, 104, 108, 111, 114, 120, 124, **129–37**
genocide 13, 78, 86, 171–2, 203, 222, **292–4**
Geordies 65–6
Gilroy, Paul 86, 88–9, 130, 140, 142–3, 234–5, 237, 263–4, 281, 285
'glass ceiling' (racialised) 54
globalisation xv, xvii, xxi, xxiv, xxv, 7, 10, 15–16, 92–3, 104, 107, 115, 141, 144, 148, 162, 234–6, 244, 246–7, 256–8, **266–70**, 281–2
glocalisation 268
Gobineau, Comte Arthur de 47, 77
Goffman, Erving 120–1
Goldsmith, Oliver xx, 45–6
gothic (nature of social reality) 283
Gramsci, Antonio 111–12, 114, 137, **295**
Great Chain of Being, the 44, 46
Griffin, John Howard 25–6, 38, 283
Guantanamo Bay 282
Guyana (formerly British Guiana) xxi, xxiv, xxv, 57, **67–9**, 80, 89–91, 102–3, 105, 116, 126–8, **205–10**, 213–15, 221, 227–8, **232–3**, 256, **258–60**, 265

Habermas, Jurgen 127
habitus xxii, 84, **125–9**, 199–200, 205, 228, 240, 276, 283, **294–5**
Hall, Stuart xix, xx, 2, 12, 16, 20, 31, 38, 43, 55, 56, 58, 74, 81, 100, 108, 111–12, 120, 124, 140, 146, 162, 178,

192, 233–4, 249, 250, 269, 270, 273, 297
Hammurabi Code 71, 96
harem 155–6
Heart of Darkness (novel by Joseph Conrad) 86
Hechter, M. 40, 100, 222, 298
hegemony 55, 61, 93, **111–12**, 121, 126, 128, 137, 151, 182, 192, 194, 205, 210, 228, 245, 284, **295**
hegemonic masculinity 25, 151
Hickey, T. J. 224
hierarchies xxi, 43, 45, 46–8, 53, 64, 80–3, 85, 91, 94, 99, 103, 107, 109, 117, 131, 142, 195, 197, 201, 207, 256, 258–9, 270, 273
hijab 150
Hispanic 16, 54, 58, **62–3**
Hispanicisation 81
history wars 85–6, 172, 203
Hobsbawm, Eric 144
holocaust, the 13, 88, 91, 115, **141–4**
homophobia 157
Horowitz, Donald 209, 227
human exhibition 138
hybridity xxiii, xxv, 59, 61, 84, 85, 87, 140, 142, 147, 158, 159, 161, 163, **232–42**, 245–6, 258, 259–260, 268–71, **295**; criticisms of 236–7
hybridization 146
hyperreal 29

IBM 115, 142
ideal reader 22, **295**
idealism 115, 126, 142, 159,164, 233, 275, 297
identity xv, xvi, xvii, xviii, xix, xx, xxi, xxii, xxv, xxvi, 2–4, 10, 36, 40–1, 51, 55–7, 62–3, 84, 89, 97–8, 100–2, 104, 106–7, 111 134, 137, 140, 147–8, 268, 270; Aboriginal 175, 184, 189, 192, 203; brand 3, 141; confusion 271–2, 275; class 30, 35, 54, 57, 133; collective xxv, 2, 55, 57, 59, 100–1, 107, 120, 145, 193, 195, 224, 235, 253; cultural **28–32**; formation xxii, 11, 146, 149, 207, 237,

247, 274, 284, 289; national xix, 14, 16, 57–8, 61, 144, 172, 247–8, 250, 254, 257–8, 282; self xviii, 11, 17, 61, 114, 120–1, 123, 195–7, 274, 302; negotiated xxv, 123, 207, 209–13, 222, 240, **258–9**
identity politics xx, xxii, xxiii, 15, 142, **144**–6, 159, 199, 232, 234–7, 249, **295–6**; as defeatist 146, 162, 285
ideological state apparatus (ISA) 112, 194, **296–7**
ideology 4, 24, 35, 53, 71, 107, 112–3, 123–4, 132, 146, 275, 281, 287, **297**, 302
imaginary castration (Lacanian concept) 214
imagined community 12, 57, 59, 195, 256, **297**
International Monetary Fund (IMF) 92, 94
impression management 120
inclusive fitness 98
indentureship 74, 77, 79, 87, 89, 104, 106, 113, 116, 209, 233–4, 299
Industrial Revolution, the 52, 75–6
infra-human treatment xxi, 72, 142
'inner terrorists' 206–7, 282–3
innocent(ing) (of the denotative sign) 18–20, 156
institutional racism xxii, 132, 161–2, 264, **297–8**
instrumentalism xxii, xxiii, 56, **98–102**, 107, 111, 125, 137, 142
interest convergence 160–1, 164, **201**
internal colonialism 15, 40, 165, 221–2, **298**
Internal Security Act 218
interpellation 4, 24, 114, 124, 137, 279, 296, **298**
interracial marriage 64, 72, 80–1, 83, 270, 275
intersectionality xxii, xxiv, 35–7, 102, 108, 114, 126, **131–8**, 140, 159, 161, 164
intersubjectivity xvii, 59, 197, 199, **299**
intertextuality 26–7, 31–2, 35, **299**
Intervention Policy, the (in Aboriginal communities) 183, 189, 190–1, 202

Iraq War 9, 14, 86, 93, 107, 113, 278, 282
Ireland (and Irish) 61, 99, 106–8, 298
Islam xxiv, 6, 15, 149, 151, 215, 220–1, 235–6, 269, 278–80, 291
islamophobia xv, 301

Jenkins, R. xvi, xvii, 57, 120, 126, 128
Jew(ish) 25, 43, 51, 55, 84, 108, 141, 325
Jim Crow laws 54, 118

Kafka, Franz 142
Kali Mai 233, **299**
Kenya 108, 117
Khmer Rouge 222, 231
kin selection 98
Kipling, Rudyard 76, 148
Knightley, Philip 8
Knox, John 77
Ku Klux Klan 277
Kwame Nkrumah 92

Lacan, Jacques (Lacanian analysis) 149, 155, 159, 214, 300; *see also* mirror stage
Lamarck, Jean Baptiste 47
language xvii, xviii, xxii, 11, 17, 18, 19, 24, 36, 40, 43–4, 53, 57, 59, 64, 99, 101–2, 122, 123, 124, 126, 147, 156, 163, 222, 239, 241, 242, 243, 256, 264, 274, 292
Laplanders 46
Larrakia Nation 170, 182, 183, **184–9**
Las Casas, Bartolome de 73–4
Lawrence, Stephen 6, 161, 235, 298
Le Pen, Jean-Marie and Marine 248
Lévi-Strauss, Claude 299
Linnaeus, Carolus 45–6, 48
Liverpool 69, 70, 73
Locke, John 74
'long grass'(informal camps) 175, 183, 186, 188
look, the 86–7, 155, **303** *see* **scopophilia**
Lyell, Charles 47
Mabo High Court Ruling 78, 166, 201
Mclurg's Law 9

magic formula (race as a) 109
Malaysia xxiv, xxv, 20, 42, 79, 120–1, 207, 210, **214–21**, 227, 256, 264, 302
Malthus, Thomas 52
Man from Snowy River, The (film) 199
Manichean Divide 73, 156, 158, 281, 285, **299–300**
maps xxiv, 20, 78, 97, 141, 166
Marcos, Sub-Commandante 246
Marx, Karl 53, 104, **106–8**, 115–16, 124, 287, 288
Marxism xxi, 107, 111, 115, 117, 125, 145, 194–5
masculinity 25, 137, 195
Mason, David 115–16, 139
Matrix of Cultural Identity 28–32
Mead, George Herbert 119
media xvii, xxii, xxvi, **5–14**, 29, 32, 36, 56, 99, 107, 110, 112–14, 141, 166, 169,177–81, 194, 197, 215, 221, 225, 230, 246, 254, 255, 257, 264–5, 267, 269, 270, 276, 284, 290
Mexico 81–4, **242–7**
migrant labour model 109–10
Miles, Robert xxii, 109–11, 117
mirror stage 149, **300**; *see also* Lacan
misrecognition 41, 56, 126–8, 275, **300–1**
mixed race xxv, 3, 42, 61, 64, 82, 84, 130, 222, 235, 247, 250, 255, 258, 260, **270–6** (see also 'hybridity')
Moby Dick 25
modernity 41, 55, 87, 94, 122, 172, 253, 285, 295; to postmodernity **141–5**, 148
monogenism 43, **44–5**
Montesquieu, Baron de 74
moral panic xv, 12, 112, 171, 177–8, 183, 190, 192, 202, 255, 280, 295, **301**
Muecke, Stephen xxii, 21, 124, 169, 174, 199, 291
mugging 12, 26, 212, 301
multicultural drift 235, 249–50
multiculturalism xv, xxiv, xxv, 13, 15, 16, 35, 55, 58, 88, 146, 171–3, 223, 225–7, 234–5, 237, **248–50, 253–5, 256, 257**

Muslims xxiv, xxv, 6, 16, 114, 151, 156, 220, 222–3, 235–6, 248, 254–5, 278–80, 283

myth xix, xxiii, **17–19**, 26, 28, 31, 36, 148–9, 151, 156, 165, 181, 194, 213, 255, 265, 281, **301–2**; 'bush myth' 199; of whiteness 23–6, 299

mythology 21, 45, 46, 77–8

NAFTA 244

Native Americans 45, 48, 62, 74

Nature/culture dichotomy 73, 75, 97, 199, 264

Nazism 58, 91, 115, 222, 277; neo-Nazi 284

neo-colonialism xxi, 15, **91–3,** 94, 147, 158, 282

neo-Conservativism 269, 281

neo-liberal 244

neo-Weberian xxi, **115–19**, 196

New Economic Policy 218

New Imperialism 76

News values 8–9, 284

newsworthiness 6–7, 189

noble savage, the 73, 180

Nordic racism 77

objectification 21–2, 44, 55, 129, 160, 194

obtuse meaning, the (Barthes) 29

octoroon 42

One Mile Dam community 176, 183, 187–9, 191, 192, 197

open-world states 282

Orientalism xxiii, 15, **149–52**, 155–6

Origin of Species, The 47, 51

other, the xv, xvii–xxiii, 6–7; defining **10–17**, 31, 78, 81, 87, 100, 130, 138, 234, **266,** 291, **302;** 'the pole of xix, 11, 55–6, 258, 264–6; images of 'otherness' 2, 18–23, 264; as exotically different 78–9, 142, 155–7; misrecognition of 127–8; constructed in discourse 121–4; excluded and voiceless 145–7, 149–51, 158–9; product of colonial divisions 205–14, 227

Pale, the (beyond) 16

PARIAH (website) 167–8

Paris-Match 18–19

patriarchy 25, 129, 132–4, 150–1, 157, 288, 303

Philippines, the xviii, xxiv, 81, 86, 216

photography 16, 19–20, 22–3, 156, 284, 303

phrenology 51

Pilger, John 13, 85, 250–1

plantations 22, 70, 72, 74, 79–80, 90, 94, 105

Plato's cave xix, 97

plural societies xxi, 99, **102–4**, 125, 193, **302**

political correctness 16, 28, 34, 35, 41, 146, 188, 250, 255

polygenism 43, **45–7**

postcolonialism xiii, xvi, xxii–iv, xxvii, 24, 68, 69, 94, 102–3, 110, 111, 140, **146–60,** 163, 182, 206, 207, 209–10, **233–4,** 247, 258, 265, 269, criticisms of 158–60

post-empire melancholia 88, 94

post-Fordist xv, 108

postmodernity xxii, xxiii, 87, **141–2, 144–6**, 148, 159, 161–2, 195, **199**, 260, 265, 281, 285, 290, 295, 299

post-structuralism xvii, xxi, 124, 138, 141, 145, 158–9, 290

Powell, Enoch 235

power xvii, xxii, xxiii, xxiv, 137, 143, 146, 150, 159, 163; collective 235; colonial 76–7, 81, 89, 99, 102, 147–50; economic 68–9, 92, 102, 107, 115–17, 121, 129–30, 188, 210; Foucaultian **121–4**, 137, 141, 146, 283, **291–2;** political 40–1, 57, 68–9, 100, 103, 150, 204, 209, 212, 217, 227, 257–8, 264; relations of 7, 30, 56, 62, 102, 105, 114, 125, 133, 144, 200, 256, 264, 296; white xxiii, 2, 23, 160, 197, 277, 285

powerless people 35, 74, 150, 186, 197, 244, 268

pre-Adamic beings 45

preferred reading 18, 280, 290
Premdas, Ralph 105, 207, 213
primordialism xx, 26, 32, 54, 78, **97–101,**
116, 122, 125, 137, 142, 174, 201,
209, 222, 242, 287, 297, 300
Propaganda model 112
pseudo-sciences 43, 51, 77, 142
punctum 22–3, **303**

quadroon 42
quantum, blood 42, 174, 285

Rabbit-Proof Fence 172
Race, definitions **xvi–xviii,** xx, xxii, **1–2,**
15–16, 23, 36, **41–55, 58–9,** 62–4,
70–1, 104–5, 108–10, 115–16
race relations xxi–ii, 109, 116, 118; model
102–4
Race Relations Act (1976) 29, 31
Race Relations Amendment Act (2000)
161
race 'riots' 223–7, 254, 284
racial capital 128
racism xxi–ii, 5–6, 13, 16, 21, 24–6,
54–5, **107–11,** 117, 122, 151, 157,
263–4; as normal 160–2, 265, 271;
links to capitalism 104–13, 162, 194–5
Rastafarianism 233, 299
rational choice 100–1, 137, **198**
rationalisation 52, 75, 77, 79, 107, 109,
115, 117, 141, 143, 149, 265
reconciliation (with Australian Aborigines)
165, 173
Redfern (district of Sydney) 223–4, 225,
227
referent power xviii, 11, 175, 234
refugees 12, 91, 107, **110–13,** 173, 251,
284
regionalism 40, 59, 61, 66, 127, 199, 258
reification xvii, 18, 35, 44, 55, 57, 58,
109, 150, 249, 277
religion xxiv, 15, 44, 98–9, 102, **220–3,**
233, 235–6, 265, 282, 299
reparation 88–9
repressive state apparatus (RSA) 112, 194
repressive tolerance (Marcuse) 264

Rex, John xxi, 105, 108–9, **115–8,** 140,
195–6
Rhetoric of the Image, the (Barthes')
19–23, 28
risk theory 270, 281–2
Robinson Crusoe 75
Rodney, Walter 71, 105–6, 209
Romanticism 21, **78,** 124, 142, 148, 150,
156, 174, 180, 190, 199, 237
Rorty, Richard 159, 264
Rousseau, Jean Jacques 73, 78, 143, 180
Royal Commission into Deaths in
Custody 196
Rwanda 99, 207, 210, 221, **222**

Said, Edward 75, **149–50,** 158
Saussure, Ferdinand De 6, 36
Savage Crows, The 172
'scientific' racism 55, 58 *see* pseudo-science
scopophilia 155, **303**
Second World War xviii, 8, 20, 42, 69, 81,
91, 130, 147–8
self-contempt 31, 94, 121
selfish gene, the (Richard Dawkins) 98
semi-autonomy (of race identity) xxii,
124
semiotics xxiii, 16–20, 32, 62, 119, 159,
255, 279
Sepulveda, Juan Gines de 73
sexuality xxvi, 2, 28, 79–81, 104, 111,
120, 122, 124, 161, 162; myths of black
27–8, 31, 129–31; black feminism
131–4, 138, 140, 150–**5, 277;**
intersectional with race 157, 161–2,
265–6, 292, 297
signification (process of) xxiii, **17–19,** 28,
109, 302
Simpson, O. J. 32
simulacra 158, 265
slavery xvi–xvii, 22, 54, **69–73,** 75,
77, 79, 88–90, 91, 94, 104–6, 111,
117–19, 130, 132, 147, 209, 233–4;
'natural' 71, 73
social capital 128, 200, 256; chattel 71, 118
social construction xvi–xviii, xix, xxi–ii,
xxvii, 2, 3, 7, 14, **15–16,** 26–8, 41, 53,

58, 107–9, 123–6, 129–30, 133, 140, 169, 197, 209, 274, 292
Social Darwinism **51–2,** 76–7, 98, 122, 130–1, 195
Sojourner Truth 132
'sous rature' (under erasure) 42, **303**
Spencer, Sir Herbert **51–2,** 77
Spivak, Gayatri Chakravorty 146, 150, 157–8, 273
stereotype xxii–iii, xxv, 3, 10, **13,** 20, 27–8, 34–5, 45–6, 48, 54, 56, 78, 99, 105, 107, 118, 127, 129, 134, 137, 148, 153, 178–80, 201, 205, 207, **211–14,** 227, 240, 259, 277
sterilisation (see eugenics) 91, 293
stigma (and identity) 36, 54, 121,176, 190, 223, 236
'stolen generation' 13, **170–2,** 203, 293
strategic essentialism 66, 133, 198, 207, 273
subaltern 150, **157–9,** 162,199, 291
subjectivity(ies) xvii, xix, xxiii, 10, 12, 17, 104, 113, 115, 122–4, 125, 129, 133, 138, 140, 158, 162, 195, 199, 234, 266, 272, 277, 283, 292, 299, 302
Suharto, President 10, 218
surveillance 81, 288, 291; state **281–2**
'survival of the fittest' 52, 76–7
symbolic dominance xix, xxiv, 24, 126–8, **210–14**
symbolic interactionism **119–21,** 125, **197–8**

Tasmanian Aborigines **85–6,** 169, 172, 293
taxonomies 21, 44, 82
terra nullius 78, **166–7**
terrorism xxv, 5, 12, 15, 26, 107, 113, 226, 235–6, 251, 257, 265, 270, **277–84**
Thatcher, Margaret 12, 69, 236, 248
Theft of Enjoyment **213–4,** 255
'third cultures' 234
tourism 170–5, 178, 180, 185–7, 192–4, 196, 198–9, 201–2, 268

Toussaint l'Ouverture 73
trans-national corporations **92–3,** 267
tribal (societies) 79, 99, 104, 169, 173, 189, 194, 200–1, 222
Tribe (TV programme) 79
Twin Towers, the 93

UN Convention on Genocide 292, 294
underclass 11, 54, 88, 118
Unfair Campaign 32–7
'unpeople' 10, 86, 223
'us and them' xx, xxvi, 11, 44, **55,** 100, 199, 295 *see also* 'Wedom' and 'Theydom'

veil, the 20, 150–1, **152–6,** 255, **278–80**
verstehen 119
Victoria, Queen 67-8
voyeurism 22, 155–6, 303

Wacquant, Loic xvi–xvii, 54, 118–19, 200
'war on terror' 236, 251, 282
Weberian (and Neo-Weberian) theory xxi, 92–6, 104, 115–119, 137, 195–7
'Wedom' (and 'Theydom') **12,** 93, 190, 280, 282
Welsh Not, the 66
White Australia Policy 44, 91, 96, 248
White Power 277
whiteness xix, xxiv, **2–3,** 19, 31–2, 35–6, 61, 72, 156–7, 271, 273, 281; in dominant cinema 2, 25; as myth 23–7
Wik, High Court ruling 166
Williams, Raymond 19, 43, 55
Windschuttle, Keith (see 'history wars') 85–6, 172, 203
World Bank 94, 245
'worthy and unworthy victims' 9
Wretched of the Earth, The 148

Zapata, General Emilio 245–6
Zapatistas (Chiapas movement) 244–7
Žižek Slavoj 213–14, 255

CPSIA information can be obtained
at www.ICGtesting.com
Printed in the USA
JSHW020735150522
25933JS00002B/7